If I Forget You, Jerusalem!

Discourses in Ancient Near Eastern and Biblical Studies
Series Editor: Emanuel Pfoh, CONICET & University of Helsinki

This series presents different studies of interpretative discourses, cultural representations and historiographical ideologies about the societies of the ancient Near East, ancient Egypt and Biblical scenarios appearing during the 19th and 20th centuries. The aim is to expose, deconstruct and analyze the ways in which Oriental and Biblical societies, cultures and histories were shaped by Western scholarship (Assyriology, Egyptology, Biblical studies), but also by literature and film, while attending to the main ideologies of the historiographical contexts of the last two centuries.

Published

Back to Reason: Minimalism in Biblical Studies   Niels Peter Lemche

Representations of Antiquity in Film: From Griffith to Grindhouse   Kevin M. McGeough

If I Forget You, Jerusalem!
Studies on the Old Testament

Niels Peter Lemche

SHEFFIELD UK   BRISTOL CT

Published by Equinox Publishing Ltd.

UK   Office 415, The Workstation, 15 Paternoster Row, Sheffield,
     South Yorkshire S1 2BX
USA ISD, 70 Enterprise Drive, Bristol, CT 06010

www.equinoxpub.com

First published 2024

© Niels Peter Lemche 2024

All rights reserved. No part of this publication may be reproduced or transmitted in any form or by any means, electronic or mechanical, including photocopying, recording or any information storage or retrieval system, without prior permission in writing from the publishers.

British Library Cataloguing-in-Publication Data

A catalogue record for this book is available from the British Library.

ISBN-13 978 1 80050 435 6   (hardback)
         978 1 80050 436 3   (paperback)
         978 1 80050 437 0   (ePDF)
         978 1 80050 502 5   (ePub)

Library of Congress Cataloging-in-Publication Data

Names: Lemche, Niels Peter, author.
Title: If I forget you, Jerusalem! : studies on the Old Testament / Niels Peter Lemche.
Description: Sheffield, South Yorkshire ; Bristol, CT : Equinox Publishing Ltd, 2024. | Series: Discourses in ancient near eastern and biblical studies | Includes bibliographical references and index. | Summary: "This selection of articles - never published in English before - reflects the author's position that the basic realization of minimalism has always been evident: that the Old Testament is not - exclusively - a book about history but is dominated by interests in theology both as literature and as an expression of the community in which biblical writings originated. It is a companion volume to his 2022 book Back to Reason: Minimalism in Biblical Studies"-- Provided by publisher.
Identifiers: LCCN 2023049688 (print) | LCCN 2023049689 (ebook) | ISBN 9781800504356 (hardback) | ISBN 9781800504363 (paperback) | ISBN 9781800504370 (epdf) | ISBN 9781800505025 (epub)
Subjects: LCSH: Bible. Old Testament--Criticism, interpretation, etc. | Bible. Old Testament--Study and teaching.
Classification: LCC BS1171.3 .L44 2024 (print) | LCC BS1171.3 (ebook) | DDC 221.6--dc23/eng/20240125
LC record available at https://lccn.loc.gov/2023049688
LC ebook record available at https://lccn.loc.gov/2023049689

Typeset by Sparks – www.sparkspublishing.com

Contents

Preface	vii
Acknowledgements	ix
Abbreviations	xii
JERUSALEM	**1**
1 "If I Forget You, Jerusalem!"	2
EXEGESIS	**21**
2 Emphatic Time in the Old Testament	22
3 Justice as Pre-existing World Order	41
4 Messiah in the Book of Isaiah	52
5 Old Testament Texts as Rewritten Literature	68
6 Psalm 2: Between Past and Future	90
7 The Introduction to David's Psalms: New Reflections on Psalm 2	110
8 Sociology and Prophetical Literature	119
HISTORY	**131**
9 History and Memory in the Old Testament	132
10 On History, Sociology, and Theology: Old Testament Perspectives	145
11 On Historical Memory in the Historiography of the Old Testament	158
12 Ezra and the Pentateuch	177
13 What Have We Done and Where Are We Moving? Personal Remarks About a Change of Paradigm	189
14 Après le déluge: The Copenhagen School or Chaos?	204

THEOLOGY	**225**
15 The History of Israel's Religion and the History of Israel: Identical or Different?	226
16 Geography as Memory	247
17 Israel and its Land	257
18 Israel as an Ideological Construction	268
19 The Relevance of Social-critical Exegesis for Old Testament Theology	280
APPENDIX	**293**
20 272 BCE – A *terminus a quo*	294
Bibliography	300
Index of Scripture References	322
Index of Modern Authors	327
Index of Subjects	331

Preface

I have, for years, planned to make some of my contributions in Danish available as well as a number of contributions originally in English which were for one reason or the other never published. I began translating the Danish articles as it was my original plan to establish a home page where those interested could look for them and download them.

Then I was asked why I would not include these articles in a printed volume of their own. It made sense. After all, when reviewing my "output" a number of these articles show a different face of the Copenhagen School from the one commonly known. Until now most of my publications have concentrated on historical and sociological matters, indicating that my scholarly interests were limited to these subjects. However, teaching as a professor of theology at the University of Copenhagen for more than a quarter of a century meant that I had to cover practically any subject of relevance for Old Testament studies. In this connection it is worth mentioning the series of collections published by my department since the 1980s: *Forum for Bibelsk Eksegese* (Forum for Biblical Exegesis). As long as I was in office I contributed to most of these volumes, and a number of the articles published (in Danish) has been translated for this collection.

The collection is divided into three sectors, with an introductory article about Jerusalem in Jewish, Christian, and Muslim tradition. The other three sections are called, *Exegesis*, *History*, and *Theology* respectively. "Exegesis" includes chapters on the concept of time in the Bible, about justice, the Messiah, and two chapters on the opening of the Psalter; but also included is a piece about the subject of the "rewritten Bible" with, however, a different approach to the subject than found in other studies, as the article is about parts of the Old Testament which could be considered rewritten ancient oriental literature.

As readers might expect, the section entitled "History" includes a series of "interim" reports on the development of the Copenhagen School and in this way it, in some ways, supplements my *Back to Reason* (Lemche, 2022). In his introduction to the collection of my articles published in the series *Changing Perspectives* (Lemche, 2013d) John Van Seters sounds surprised to see that I did not start as a "minimalist", but as a rather traditionally minded historical-critical scholar. This is correct. Minimalism was something that came about as my historical-critical studies showed that nothing "fitted", or as I have sometimes argued: Historical-critical scholarship was not critical at all. It, in large measure, consisted of rationalistic paraphrases of biblical historiography. Thus very few colleagues had found my *Ancient Israel* (Lemche, 1988) minimalistic. They rather saw it in the context of studies by John Hayes and J. Maxwell Miller (Hayes and Miller, 1986) and J. Alberto Soggin (Soggin, 1984). Minimalism still belonged to the future and at this point other scholars like Thomas L. Thompson and Bern Jørg Diebner had advanced much further. Still, I believe that it is important that modern scholars do not just "jump to the conclusion", meaning that they forget that the path to present ideas may have a longish history now often forgotten. Minimalism did not spring out of the forehead of Zeus like the goddess Athena. It was the result of hard work because of a frustrating tradition of scholarship. In order to elucidate the process that led to minimalism I have included a couple of these interim-reports here.

The final session, "Theology", centres on the concept of "Israel", on the relationship between Israel and its land, and on the concept of "memory", which is, at the present, a widely discussed subject.

At the end I have placed an "appendix" which I wrote in January 2023, about the year 272 BCE as the *terminus a quo* for the composition of the historical literature in the Old Testament. I believe this year to constitute the first fixed date we have for the beginning of this composition. This appendix could, it seems to me, be a new starting point for a rewriting of the formative process behind our Old Testament, placing this process in the Hellenistic period as part of the "nationalistic" revival which took place when the people of the Middle East were confronted with a superior Greek civilization – the civilization of their new masters. I may not be the person to write this new history, but at least we now have an idea – if not more – of when it started in earnest.

Two persons have helped me in bringing this collection into light. First of all, Dr. Emanuel Pfoh, the editor of this series, should be remembered, but also Dr. Jim West, who has for many years "struggled" (in the best sense of the word) to make my Danlish readable. I owe both "former" students my sincere gratitude.

Niels Peter Lemche
Huaröd, Sweden, 8 February 2023

Acknowledgements

The articles published in this collection were either originally published in Danish or presented in English on various occasions but never published. The appendix was written for this volume.

1 "If I forget you, Jerusalem!"
   Lecture at the EABS Meeting in Tartu 2010.
2 Emphatic time in the Old Testament
   Danish original "Prægnant tid i Det Gamle Testamente", in Geert Hallbäck and Niels Peter Lemche (eds.), *"Tiden" i bibelsk belysning* (Forum for Bibelsk Eksegese, 11; Copenhagen, Museum Tusculanum, 2001), pp. 29–47.
3 Justice as Pre-existing World Order
   Danish original "Retfærdighed som præeksistent verdensorden", in Kristian Mejrup, Søren Holst and Søren Feldtfos Thomsen (eds.), *Præeksistens* (Forum for Bibelsk Eksegese, 18; København: Museum Tusculanum, 2014), pp. 319–32.
4 Messiah in the Book of Isaiah
   Danish original "Messias i Jesajabogen", in Thomas L. Thompson and Henrik Tronier (eds.), *Frelsens Biografisering* (Forum for Bibelsk Eksegese, 13; Copenhagen: Museum Tusculanum, 2004), pp. 99–114.
5 The Old Testament Texts as Rewritten Literature
   Danish original "Gammeltestamentlige tekster som genskrevet litteratur", in Jesper Høgenhaven and Mogens Müller (eds.), *Bibelske Genskrivninger* (Forum for Bibelsk Eksegese, 17; Copenhagen, Museum Tusculanum, 2012), pp. 51–73.
6 Psalm 2: Between past and Future
   Danish original "Salme 2 – midt mellem fortid og fremtid", in Mogens Müller and John Strange (eds.), *Det Gamle Testamente i Jødedom og Kristendom* (Forum for Bibelsk Eksegese, 4; København: Museum Tusculanum Forlag, 1993), pp. 57–78.

7   The Introduction to David's Psalms: New Reflections on Psalm 2
    Danish original "Indledningen til Davids Salmer. Nye Betragtninger vedrørende Salme 2", in Lone Fatum and Mogens Müller (eds.), *Tro og historie. Festskrift til Niels Hyldahl* (Forum for Bibelsk Eksegese, 7 Copenhagen, Museum Tusculanum, 1996), pp. 142–51.
8   Sociology and Prophetical Literature
    Seminar: University of Stellenbosch 25th August 1994
9   History and Memory in the Old Testament
    Lecture at the EABS meeting in Leipzig 2013
10 On History, Sociology, and Theology: Old Testament Perspectives
    Danish original "Om historie, sociologi og teologi – gammeltestamentlige perspektiver", in Theodor Jørgensen and Peter K. Westergaard (eds.), *Teologien i samfundet. Festskrift til Jens Glebe-Møller*, Frederiksberg: Anis, 1998, pp. 269–88
11 On Historical Memory in the Historiography of the Old Testament
    Danis original "Om historisk erindring i Det Gamle Testamentes historiefortællinger", in John Strange and Geert Halbäck (eds.), *Bibel og historieskrivning* (Forum for Bibelsk Eksegese, 10; Copenhagen: Museum Tusculanum, 1999), pp. 11–28.
12 Ezra and the Pentateuch
    Lecture at the University of Cape Town 23 August 1994.
13 What Have We Done and Where are We Moving? Personal Remarks about a Change of Paradigm
    Danish original "Hvad er det vi har lavet, og hvor går vi hen? Nogle personlige betragtninger omkring et paradigmeskifte", in Niels Peter Lemche and Mogens Müller (eds.), *Fra dybet. Festskrift til John Strange i anledning af 60 års fødselsdagen den 20 juli 1994* (Forum for bibelsk eksegese, 5; Copenhagen, Museum Tusculanum, 1994), pp. 130–43.
14 Après le déluge: The Copenhagen School or Chaos?
    Farewell address at the Theological Faculty in Copenhagen 7th of February 2014. Danish original "Après le déluge: Københavnerskolen eller kaos?" *Dansk Teologisk Tidsskrift* 77 (2014), pp. 98–120.
15 The History of Israel's Religion and the History of Israel: Identical or Different?
    Danish original "Israels religionshistorie og Israels historie: Sammenhænge og forskelle?" Guest lecture at the University of Odense 23 Nov 1994.

16 Geography as Memory
   Lecture at the EABS meeting in Leipzig 2013
17 Israel and Its Land
   Originally a lecture at the Society of Biblical Literature's Annual Meeting, in New Orleans, the 25th of November 1996. It was published in Danish as "Israel og dets land", in Henrik Tronier and Niels Peter Lemche (eds.), *Etnicitet i Bibelen* (Forum for Bibelsk Eksegese, 9; Copenhagen, Museum Tusculanum, 1998), pp. 11–22.
18 Israel as an Ideological Construction
   Lecture given at the University of Rostock on the 6th of May 2000
19 The Relevance of Social-critical Exegesis for Old Testament Theology
   Seminar at the University of Stellenbosch, September 1994
20 272 BCE – A *terminus a quo*
   Written for this volume

Abbreviations

ANET	Pritchard, J.B. (ed.). 1955. *Ancient Near Eastern Texts Relating to the Old Testament.* 2nd ed. Princeton, NJ: Princeton University Press
AOAT	*Alter Orient und Altes Testament*
BA	Biblical Archaeologist
BASOR	Bulletin of the American School of Oriental Research
BKAT	Biblischer Kommentar zum Altes Testament
BZAW	Beiheft Zeitschrift für die alttestamentlichen Wissenschaft
DTT	Dansk Teologisk Tidsskrift
HAT	Handbuch zum Alten Testament
IEJ	Israel Exploration Journal
JSOTSS/JSOTSup	Journal for the Study of the Old Testament Supplement Series
KAI	Donner, H. and W. Röllig, 1964. *Kanaanäische und aramäische Inschriften.* Wiesbaden: Otto Harrassowitz
LHBOTS	Library of Hebrew Bible/Old Testament Series
OA	Oriens Antiquus
SBLWAW	SBL Writings from the Ancient World Series
SJOT	Scandinavian Journal of the Old Testament
TZ	Theologische Zeitschrift
ZDPV	Zeitschrift des Deutschen Palästina-Vereins

JERUSALEM

1 "If I Forget You, Jerusalem!"

1. Introduction

Years ago, I asked my late colleague in New Testament studies, Professor Heine Simonsen: why have you never visited Israel and Jerusalem? His answer was clear: "Jerusalem is in my heart!" This attitude to the Jerusalem of this world is probably quite popular – even today. I believe that my teacher Professor Eduard Nielsen only visited Israel and Jerusalem once, in connection with one of the Jewish World Congresses. Eduard Nielsen was born into a family belonging to the centre of the Danish Inner Mission. They didn't really want their dreams squashed by the grim realities of the 20th century.

In the Old Testament, Jerusalem is the city of God. It is not so much praised for its physical greatness as for its importance because it is the place where God let his name dwell. According to the Old Testament, Jerusalem was a fairly late Israelite conquest as the main tradition has David as the conqueror of the city – although it should not be overlooked that there is a competing tradition in Judges placing the Israelite conquest of Jerusalem in connection with Judah's expansion after Joshua's death (Judg 1:8). In the Deuteronomistic History everything hinges on the fate of Jerusalem, although in the Pentateuch, it is almost totally absent. Psalms mostly relate to Jerusalem, while Wisdom literature is mainly indifferent. The Prophets basically follow the historical books and Psalms in placing Jerusalem at the centre, although Hosea, of course, does not seem interested.

The biblical narrative has Jerusalem as the centre of the Israelite worship of God from David to Zedekiah, and again from the initiation of Haggai's temple to Titus's conquest of Jerusalem. It also has Jerusalem as the capital of an originally important empire, and later the independent state of Judah until 587/6 BCE.

The historical reality may have been different: When it comes to the history of the city, there was a fortified settlement here in the Middle Bronze Age with a local ruler of its own, mentioned in the Egyptian execration texts. Although a series of letters forming part of the Amarna correspondence from the *ḫazanu* of Jerusalem, Abdi-Ḥeba, have survived (dating from the 14th century), only few if any traces of a settlement have been found here from the Late Bronze Age, mostly in the form of graves.[1] The present discussion concerning the existence of a Jerusalem in the 10th century BCE, the time of David according to traditional inspired biblical historiography, is more important. After twenty years of sometimes intense discussion, the question still remains open.[2] At best the Jerusalem of the Iron Age was a minor central Palestinian settlement, a status it kept until the destruction of Lachish in 701 BCE, the major city of southwestern Palestine. Some will argue in favour of a major expansion of Jerusalem after the fall of Samaria in 722 BCE, although the Bible says not a single word about such a migration.[3] However, Jerusalem in the 7th century would be a place to remember in a nostalgic way in later times. After the Babylonian destruction of the city in – conventionally – 587 BCE, for a couple of hundred years no city called Jerusalem existed.[4] Serious resettlement seems to have begun in the fourth and especially the third century. The great city that developed into Herod's capital hardly emerged before the 2nd century BCE in connection with the Hellenization of central Palestine. After Hadrian's new founding of Jerusalem, the name of Jerusalem was, to most people, the city of God of the glorious past. Aelia Capitolina was the new name, although the old, Jerusalem, was probably kept or was reinstated by Christian emperors, until the Arabs named it *al-Quds*, the holy place.

2. Case Studies from Psalms to Amoz Oz and Fairuz

The idea of remembering Jerusalem seems an integral part of the reception history of Jerusalem. Thus Psalm 137 (NSRV):

> By the rivers of Babylon—
> there we sat down and there we wept
> when we remembered Zion.

---

[1] EA 286-290/LA 27-41. On the archaeology of Jerusalem in the LA period, cf. Cahill, 2003, 27-33. Cf., however, the much more sceptical remarks of Margreet L. Steiner who concludes: "Evidence for the existence of a walled town in or near present-day Jerusalem in the Late Bronze Age are completely lacking" (Steiner, 2001, 39).
[2] Cf. on the low chronology, Finkelstein (1996), and more recently Finkelstein and Silberman, 2006, 267-274. Critical voices, among others Kletter, 2004.
[3] On this theory of an Israelite migration to Jerusalem following the Assyrian conquest of Samaria in 722 cf. the original version in Alt, 1953. Cf. more recently Israel Finkelstein, who also attributes the growth of Jerusalem at the end of the 8th century to the consequences of the Assyrian conquest of Samaria (Finkelstein, 2001). Criticism in Lemche, 2010.
[4] Cf. Lipschits, 2005.

²On the willows there
we hung up our harps.
³For there our captors
asked us for songs,
and our tormentors asked for mirth, saying,
"Sing us one of the songs of Zion!"
⁴How could we sing the LORD's song
in a foreign land?
⁵If I forget you, O Jerusalem,
let my right hand wither!
⁶Let my tongue cling to the roof of my mouth,
if I do not remember you,
if I do not set Jerusalem
above my highest joy.
⁷Remember, O LORD, against the Edomites
the day of Jerusalem's fall,
how they said, "Tear it down! Tear it down!
Down to its foundations!"
⁸O daughter Babylon, you devastator!⁵
Happy shall they be who pay you back
what you have done to us!
⁹Happy shall they be who take your little ones
and dash them against the rock!

The keyword of this psalm is the verb זכר "to remember". We meet it in different forms: v. 1 בְּזָכְרֵנוּ, "when we remember (Zion)", v. 6 אִם־לֹא אֶזְכְּרֵכִי "if I do not remember you", and v. 7 זְכֹר יהוה "remember Yahweh". In one instance it is substituted by שכח: אִם אֶשְׁכָּחֵךְ "if I forget you".

The psalm is about remembrance and revenge: 1) the remembrance of the exile in Babylon, 2) the remembrance of the Edomites when Jerusalem was sacked. And revenge against the Edomites and the daughter of Babel! The psalm is evidently not placed in a Mesopotamian context as indicated by the introductory perfect forms: Babylon is a thing of the past, and this adds a third motif of memory to the psalm: remember when we were in Babylon!

We hardly need to include more details. The importance of memory is evident; the psalm is completely about memory, and being a biblical text, it is also part of subsequent memories of Babylon as the forlorn place, hell on earth, when the truth (if I may say so) was that compared to Palestine Mesopotamia was, in those days, a paradise. However, the memory expressed by

---
⁵ KJV has "O daughter of Babylon, who art to be destroyed".

this psalm about the exile in Babylon survived and became the inspiration for all subsequent ideas about Babylon and its influence on human history – we almost hear – or those among us who love Verdi, his *Va pensiero sull'ali dorate*:

> Fly, thoughts, on wings of gold;
> go settle upon the slopes and the hills,
> where, soft and mild, the sweet airs
> of our native land smell fragrant!
> Greet the banks of the Jordan
> and Zion's toppled towers…
> Oh, my country so lovely and lost!
> Oh, remembrance so dear and so fraught with despair!
> Golden harp of the prophetic seers,
> why dost thou hang mute upon the willow?
> Rekindle our bosom's memories,
> and speak of times gone by!
> Mindful of the fate of Jerusalem,
> either give forth an air of sad lamentation,
> or else let the Lord imbue us
> with fortitude to bear our sufferings!
>   (translation http://www.wowzone.com/pensiero.htm)[6]

Quoting the elegy about the Hebrews in captivity from Verdi's *Nabucco* in this connection is not a waste of time because this second text better than most illustrates the enormous impact which the biblical memory of Jerusalem has had on posterity. As is well known, Babylon in Verdi's text is hardly

---

[6] Va, pensiero, sull'ali dorate;
va, ti posa sui clivi, sui colli,
ove olezzano tepide e molli
l'aure dolci del suolo natal!
Del Giordano le rive saluta,
di Sionne le torri atterrate…
Oh mia patria sì bella e perduta!
Oh membranza sì cara e fatal!
Arpa d'or dei fatidici vati,
perché muta dal salice pendi?
Le memorie nel petto raccendi,
ci favella del tempo che fu!
O simile di Sòlima ai fati
traggi un suono di crudo lamento,
o t'ispiri il Signore un concento
che ne infonda al patire virtù

Jerusalem, and the Hebrews hardly Jews – and even if that was really Verdi's original intention, the public attending the first performance of the opera at La Scala in Milano in 1842 thought differently, identifying the plight of the Hebrews oppressed by the Babylonians with their own sufferings under Austrian domination. As is well known, Verdi's name was translated as an acronym for *Vittorio Emanuele, re d'Italia*. The text of *Va pensiero* was not merely a song about the past, it was definitely understood to be directed at the present. This is worth remembering when Psalm 137 is being discussed. In spite of all talk here about remembering Jerusalem, the true intention is revenge, the theme of the final section including perhaps the most horrible line in the Old Testament about smashing children against a rock (v. 9). Babylon is a whore as we have it in the Apocalypse (ch. 17–18), there often supposed to be a cipher for the real enemy, Rome, at a time when that could not be directly expressed. In Psalm 137, Babylon is a destroyer (destroyed as the KJV has it). When we give up tracing such motifs to the time of the exile, the psalm would fit a period when the enemy came from Babylon, thus making it almost certain that the psalm is inspired by the Maccabean uprising against the Seleucid – out of Babylon – Empire. The memory of Jerusalem is here clearly used as a political means to denounce the oppressor, the Seleucid ruler, by referring to something that may (at this time, the mid-2nd century) already have developed into a kind of canonical tradition.

Cultural memory is all too often considered a fairly innocent pastime. It may be, although I don't think it is. However, as a political weapon it sides with history. To put it formulaically, *cultural memory is not history*. Cultural memory has no embedded need for studying the past. It has to do with how the present imagines the past, and here it has a lot in common with history.

History in its modern disguise – post 1800 – was promoted to bolster the ideologies of the new national states.[7] Historians had, as their job, to create national histories in order to make people of a certain region believe that they belong to the same people and nation. Cultural memory is another branch of this kind of ethnic propaganda, playing with very much the same sentiments, but without any obligation to write a "correct" version of the past. It may often only be local and represent the images which people living in a certain part of the world have created about their past and about their culture (often in conflicts with the memory of neighbouring regions). This popular form of cultural memory will be dynamic as it will always accord with the situation when it is present, and without this kind of present relevance, it can never be usurped by any elite, transforming history into a political weapon on their own behalf. It is, in many ways, much more dynamic than history.

---

[7] Cf. on this Lemche, 1998d, 8–20.

After all, history is essentially only about what happened in the past, although constructed with the present in mind. Cultural memory is about ourselves, the people who carry this memory with them. It is by manipulating cultural memory that the political reality of today – and any day – can be created.

Thus the respected historians from the Romantic Period like von Ranke, Droysen, and Niebuhr were respected because of their constructions,[8] but it was people like the poet and nationalist Ernst Moritz Arndt who formed the new nationalism in Germany and elsewhere.[9] For them history was only one means among many to create a nationalistic universe.

Returning to Jerusalem, we will see how effective a political weapon the cultural memory of the return to Jerusalem has been and still is. We could start with the common Jewish greeting: *Next year in Jerusalem!* Short and impressive, and easily adaptable to a political programme. We all have Jerusalem in our heart; it is only up to us to decide how and when to reenact this return to Jerusalem.

This is not the traditional understanding of our relation to Jerusalem in Western Christianity. However, in the east the loss of the city to the Muslims in 638 gave rise to a literature about longing for the return, such as the Patriarch Sophronios' *Anacreontica* 19–20 from the time when the city came into Muslim hands:

Holy City of God,
Jerusalem, how I long to stand
even now at your gates,
and go in, rejoicing!
Let me walk thy pavements
and go inside the Anastasis,
where the King of All rose again,
trampling down the power of death.[10]

---

[8] Leopold von Ranke (1795–1886), Johann Gustav Bernhard Droysen (1808–1884), Barthold Georg Niebuhr (1776–1831).
[9] Ernst Moritz Arndt (1769–1860).
[10]   Ἅγιον πόλισμα θεῖον
Ἱερουσαλὴμ τ' ἐς νῦν δὴ
Ἐθέλων πύλας παρεῖναι
᾽Τ ἀγαλλιῶν ἐσέλθω
Βαδιῶν ἐπὶ πλακῶν σου
Ἐς Ἀνάστασεν κατέλθω
Ὅθι παντάναξ ἀνέστη
Θανάτου κράτος πατήσας

It is interesting to note that the Muslim conquest did not lead to the Christians being barred from the city. Sophronios remained the patriarch of Jerusalem with the benign consent of the Umayyad Khalif Umar.

However, returning to the Western tradition, we have, in Ezekiel (40–48), and among the Dead Sea Scrolls, a series of visions of the future Jerusalem.[11] These texts do not talk about a return but about a new city to be built in place of the old. The classic Christian idea about Jerusalem is expressed by the Apocalypse, chapter 21, as a city that descended from heaven, of gold, diamonds, and pearls. There is no return, because there is nothing really to return to such as a temple, as God is the temple. From this there is only a very short distance to the idea of Jerusalem in our hearts, as this means that we carry God in our hearts.

Reading the different versions of Pope Urban II's famous speech held in Clermont-Ferrand in 1095,[12] urging the necessity of the first crusade, it is clear that as far as the Pope included Jerusalem in his speech, it was not so much the case of a return to Jerusalem. This perspective seems not to be there. It is about liberating Jerusalem from the Turks who had – or so it was argued – turned the sacred city into a slaughterhouse and prevented pilgrims from visiting the holy places:

> From the confines of Jerusalem and the city of Constantinople a horrible tale has gone forth and very frequently has been brought to our ears, namely, that a race from the kingdom of the Persians, an accursed race, a race utterly alienated from God, a generation forsooth which has not directed its heart and has not entrusted its spirit to God, has invaded the lands of those Christians and has depopulated them by the sword, pillage and fire; it has led away a part of the captives into its own country, and a part it has destroyed by cruel tortures; it has either entirely destroyed the churches of God or appropriated them for the rites of its own religion.

---

[11] 4QNJ^a, 4QNJ^b.

[12] The original is not preserved, only later recollections, some by people present at the occasion. The different versions of Urban's speech have been put together in an English translation on the internet on the Medieval Sourcebook: Urban II (1088–1099): Speech at Council of Clermont, 1095, Five versions of the Speech (http://www.fordham.edu/halsall/source/urban2-5vers.html#robert).

This quote from the copy of the speech preserved by Robert the Monk is rather typical.[13] It was put into writing more than twenty years after the speech was delivered probably from personal memory as Robert is supposed to have been present. Later Robert has Urban continuing in this way:

> That land which as the Scripture says "floweth with milk and honey", was given by God into the possession of the children of Israel. Jerusalem is the navel of the world; the land is fruitful above others, like another paradise of delights. The Redeemer of the human race has made it illustrious by His advent, has beautified it by residence, has consecrated it by suffering, has redeemed it by death, has glorified it by burial. This royal city, therefore, situated at the centre of the world, is now held captive by His enemies, and is in subjection to those who do not know God, to the worship of the heathens. She seeks therefore and desires to be liberated, and does not cease to implore you to come to her aid.

Although the West must come to the help of God's own city, it is not a return to Jerusalem. There is no independent cultural memory involved of this city, but the description of it and its beauty is based on biblical descriptions.

Another example of the Christian attitude can be found in the poem by Bernhard of Cluny *De contemptu mundi* from c. 1150, i.e., from the time when Jerusalem was the centre of the crusader kingdom of Jerusalem, in the section from the first book known as *Urbs Sion aurea*.[14] It is a rather lengthy poem, which I will quote in part in a heavily edited but popular English translation by John Mason Neale dating from the 19th century:

> Jerusalem the golden, with milk and honey blest,
> Beneath thy contemplation sink heart and voice oppressed.
> I know not, O I know not, what joys await us there,
> What radiancy of glory, what bliss beyond compare.
> They stand, those halls of Zion, all jubilant with song,
> And bright with many an angel, and all the martyr throng;

---

[13] Robert the Monk, c 1055–1122, claims to have been present when the speech was delivered.
[14] Bernhard of Cluny is supposed to have lived in the first half of the 12th century. Latin text: Raby, 1927. The sections about "Golden Jerusalem" can be found in the first book of Bernhard's poem.

The Prince is ever in them, the daylight is serene.
The pastures of the blessed are decked in glorious sheen.
There is the throne of David, and there, from care released,
The shout of them that triumph, the song of them that feast;
And they, who with their Leader, have conquered in the fight,
Forever and forever are clad in robes of white.[15]

There is no talk about return, rather, in its place, the expectation at the end of life to return to God, and to the Jerusalem of Revelation:

Brief life is here our portion, brief sorrow, short lived care;
The life that knows no ending, the tearless life, is there.
O happy retribution! Short toil, eternal rest;
For mortals and for sinners, a mansion with the blest.
That we should look, poor wanderers, to have our home on high!
That worms should seek for dwellings beyond the starry sky!
And now we fight the battle, but then shall wear the crown
Of full and everlasting, and passionless renown.[16]
...
Jerusalem the glorious! Glory of the elect!
O dear and future vision that eager hearts expect!
Even now by faith I see thee, even here thy walls discern;
To thee my thoughts are kindled, and strive, and pant, and yearn.

---

[15] Urbs Sion aurea, patria lactea, cive decora,
Omne cor obruis, omnibus obstruis et cor et ora.
Nescio, nescio quae iubilatio, lux tibi qualis,
Quam socialia gaudia, gloria quam specialis.
Sunt Sion atria coniubilantia, martyre plena,
Cive micantia, principe stantia, luce serena.
Sunt ibi pascua mitibus afflua praestita sanctis.
Regis ibi thronus agminis et sonus est epulantis,
Gens duce splendida, concio candida vestibus albis

[16] Hic breve vivitur, hic breve plangitur, hic breve fletur.
Non breve vivere, non breve plangere, retribuetur.
O retributio, stat brevis actio, vita perennis;
O retributio, coelica mansio stat lue plenis.
Quid datur? Et quibus? Aether egentibus et cruce dignis,
Sidera vermibus, optima sontibus, astra malignis.
Coelica gratia luminis omnia non modo donat,
Sed super aethera suscipe viscera tanta coronat.

In the Latin original this part stands before the section on Urbs Sion aurea.

Jerusalem, the only, that look'st from heaven below,
In thee is all my glory, in me is all my woe!
And though my body may not, my spirit seeks thee fain,
Till flesh and earth return me to earth and flesh again.[17]

In the Christian world the idea of Jerusalem changed when the city was lost to Saladin in 1187. Now it became a place to return to, a place in memory and Christian politics but also literature had to adjust to the fact that the city was lost, although the Christian world never gave up the hope of a reconquest. The fate – especially its conquest – of Jerusalem became a theme celebrated in literature, as well as art and music, and the idea of coming home, of fulfillment is well-represented. Let me illustrate this theme with this quote from the end of Torquato Tasso's *Gerusalemme Liberata* (1581):

Thus conquered Godfrey, and as yet the sun
Dived not in silver waves his golden wain,
But daylight served him to the fortress won
With his victorious host to turn again,
His bloody coat he put not off, but run
To the high temple with his noble train,
And there hung up his arms, and there he bows
His knees, there prayed, and there performed his vows.[18]

The poem is not so much about coming home or back to Jerusalem. It is mostly a poem in line with Ariosto's *The Raging Roland* about the virtues

---

[17] Urbs Sion inclyta, gloria debita glorificandis,
Tu bona visibus interioribus intima pandis,
Intima lumina, mentis acumina te speculantur,
Pectora flammea, spe modo, postea sorte lucrantur. 300
Urbs Sion unica, mansio mystica condita caelo,
Nunc tibi gaudeo, nunc mihi lugeo, tristor, anhelo.
Te, quia corpore non queo, pectore saepe penetro;
Sed caro terrea terraque carnea, mox cado retro.

[18] Cosí vince Goffredo, ed a lui tanto
avanza ancor de la diurna luce
ch'a la città già liberata, al santo
ostel di Cristo i vincitor condure.
Né pur deposto il sanguinoso manto,
viene al tempio con gli altri il sommo duce;
e qui l'arme sospente, e qui devoto
il gran Sepolcro adora e scioglie il voto.

and bravery of the knights, a kind of summary of medieval novels and poems celebrating knighthood. Still, Godfrey's travel is over when he kneels in front of the "high temple" – a symbolic act imitating that of Mehmed, who, on the same day as he conquered Constantinople, prayed in the Hagia Sophia.

It is clear that the obsession with Jerusalem and especially the first crusade in the 16th century was inspired by reflections on the Turkish expansion in the Balkans and through the Mediterranean which was blocked at Vienna in 1529 and at Lepanto in 1571. The enemy of Pope Urban's speech had become real, not only in *Outremer*, as the Middle East was called by the crusaders, but also directly threatening the survival of the west. This memory of the Turks as the archenemy has survived to this very day as can be seen from the objections to incorporating Turkey into the European Union – who said that cultural memory is not political? The past, or rather the constructed past as it appears in our memory is still very much alive. And the idea of return was never forgotten: taking Jerusalem from the Turks, General Allenby (1861–1936) said after his conquest of Damascus: "today the wars of the Crusaders are completed".[19] We should remember that the crusaders never succeeded in conquering Damascus. He later took his words back, but the way he entered Jerusalem in December 1917, on foot, demonstrated a respect for the holy place that was also reflected by his announcement of martial law in Jerusalem. Allenby's conquest was seen by British news media as the fulfillment of the quest of Richard the Lionheart who never got closer than to look at Jerusalem from a distance (from el Qubeibe). The sentiments of a crusade also come to the surface in the words of the commander of the French army in the Levant, General Henri Gouraud, who arrived at Damascus after the First World War, when Syria became part of the French mandate: He kicked Saladin's coffin with the words: "The Crusades have ended now! Awake Saladin, we have returned. My presence here consecrates the victory of the Cross over the Crescent!"[20]

The British took control of Palestine and Jerusalem. It was the culmination of a movement that began when travellers went to the Near East beginning in the 18th century with serious expeditions, at first without any specific interest in Jerusalem. It changed when excavations started here c. one hundred and fifty years ago, conducted by the newly established Palestine Exploration Fund (1855). When excavations began, the first Jewish immigrants to

---

[19] Antonie Wessels, (1972) *A Modern Arabic Biography of Muḥammad: A Critical Study of Muḥammad Ḥusayn Haykal's Ḥayāt Muḥammad*, p. 160. Published by Brill Archive.
[20] Admittedly, this may be no more than an anecdote, popular in English news media but not referred to in French literature about this General.

Jerusalem had already founded the first colony outside the Old City sponsored by Moses Montefiore.

The importance of Jerusalem in the memory of Zionist-oriented Jews in the second half of the 19th century is obvious when reading the text to the Israeli national hymn, *Hatikva* ("the hope"), originally written by Naphtali Herz Imber following the founding of Petah Tikvah in 1878. Let me quote from the beginning of the poem:

> As long as in the heart, within,
> A Jewish soul still yearns,
> And onward, towards the ends of the east,
> An eye still looks toward Zion,
>
> *Refrain*
> Our hope is not yet lost,
> The ancient hope,
> To return to the land of our fathers,
> The city where David encamped.[21]

And it continues in the same vein. *Next year in Jerusalem* had become a political programme playing on the cultural memory of all Jews, and it had been an important part of the argument concerning where to found the Jewish homeland, a heritage from early German *Blut und Boden* ideology with roots back to the previously mentioned Moritz Arndt. Hatikva, long regarded as the national hymn of modern Israel, was only officially recognized as such in 2004 with a shortened but very pregnant text:

> A long as in the heart, within,
> A Jewish soul still yearns,
> And onward, towards the ends of the east,
> An eye still gazes towards Zion,
> Our hope is not yet lost,
> The hope of two thousand years,

---

21 כָּל־עוֹד בַּלֵּבָב פְּנִימָה, נֶפֶשׁ יְהוּדִי הוֹמִיָּה,
וּלְפַאֲתֵי מִזְרָח קָדִימָה,
עַיִן לְצִיּוֹן צוֹפִיָּה;
פזמון
עוֹד לֹא אָבְדָה תִקְוָתֵנוּ,
הַתִּקְוָה הַנּוֹשָׁנָה,
לָשׁוּב לְאֶרֶץ אֲבוֹתֵינוּ,
לָעִיר בָּהּ דָּוִד חָנָה.

To be a free people in our land,
The land of Zion and Jerusalem.[22]

When we come to decide between the Jerusalem in our hearts with the real Jerusalem, the Zionistic movement opted for the real city, although – and that became very clear when the following song was first composed: The golden Jerusalem was in our hearts, the real Jerusalem was grey, and especially, it was empty. I am of course referring to the popular song *Yerushalaim shel zahav* written and performed by Naomi Shemer on Independence Day in May 1967, just a few weeks before the outbreak of the Six Day War:

The mountain air is clear as wine
And the scent of pines
Is carried on the breeze of twilight
With the sound of bells.
And in the slumber of tree and stone
Captured in her dream
The city that sits solitary
And in its midst is a wall.
Jerusalem of gold, and of bronze, and of light
Behold I am a violin for all your songs.
How the cisterns have dried
The market-place is empty
And no one frequents the Temple Mount
In the Old City.
And in the caves in the mountain
Winds are howling
And no one descends to the Dead Sea
By way of Jericho.
Jerusalem of gold, and of bronze, and of light
Behold I am a violin for all your songs.
But as I come to sing to you today,

---

[22] כֹּל עוֹד בַּלֵּבָב פְּנִימָה
נֶפֶשׁ יְהוּדִי הוֹמִיָּה,
וּלְפַאֲתֵי מִזְרָח, קָדִימָה,
עַיִן לְצִיּוֹן צוֹפִיָּה
עוֹד לֹא אָבְדָה תִּקְוָתֵנוּ,
הַתִּקְוָה בַּת שְׁנוֹת אַלְפַּיִם,
לִהְיוֹת עַם חָפְשִׁי בְּאַרְצֵנוּ,
אֶרֶץ צִיּוֹן וִירוּשָׁלַיִם.

And to adorn crowns to you (i.e. to tell your praise)
I am the smallest of the youngest of your children (i.e. the least worthy of doing so)
And of the last poet (i.e. of all the poets born).
For your name scorches the lips
Like the kiss of a seraph
If I forget thee, Jerusalem,
Which is all gold...
Jerusalem of gold, and of bronze, and of light
Behold I am a violin for all your songs.
We have returned to the cisterns
To the market and to the market-place
A ram's horn (shofar) calls out (i.e. is being heard) on the Temple Mount
In the Old City.
And in the caves in the mountain
Thousands of suns shine.
We will once again descend to the Dead Sea
By way of Jericho!
Jerusalem of gold, and of bronze and of light
Behold I am a violin for all your songs.[23]

---

[23]

אורנים וריח כיין צלול הרים
פעמונים קול עם בים הער ברוח אשין.
בחלומה שבויה ואבן אילן ובתרדמת
חומה ובלבה יושבת בדד אשר העיר

אור ושל נחשת ושל זהב של ירושלים
כנור אני שיריך לכל הלא

ולככר לשוק המים בורות אל חזרנו
העתיקה בעיר הבית בהר קורא שופר
זורחזת שמשות אלפי בסלע אשר ובמערות
יריחו בדרך המלח ים אל נרד ושוב
של ירושלים...

לך לשיר היום בבואי אך פת
רים לקשר ולך
בניך מצעיר קטנתי
המשורים ומאחרון
השפתים את צורב שמך כי
כנשיקת־שרף
וירשלים אשכחך אים
בזה כלה אשר
של ירושלים...

The debt of this text to psalm 137, our first witness, is amazing, right to the end to the reference in this translation to a "violin". Other translations have "lute", the original Hebrew being, כִּנּוֹר. Modern Hebrew has both meanings, Ps 137:2, however, has כִּנֹּרוֹתֵינוּ, "our lutes". Both translations are acceptable and the reenactment of the psalm is clear when we think of the role of the violin in modern Jewish popular music.

Naomi Shemer was criticized by no less than the Israeli author Amos Oz: Jerusalem and its streets were not empty. Amos Oz, however, testifies to what may happen when the programme of a cultural memory is carried out in life, when "next year in Jerusalem" became true after the Six Days War in June 1967.

Cultural memory is a dream about who we really want to be more than a memory of who we really are. As I already said: History is supposed to be able to tell us who we really are, or were two hundred years ago. Nowadays we have more experience with history and sincerely doubt that this is the case. No history exists except as a narrative, and this narrative already belongs to the realm of cultural memory. This is the way Amos Oz showed the realities of the memorized Jerusalem, of the golden Jerusalem. Let me quote a few excerpts from his prose:[24]

> …
>
> On Sunday, 11 June 1967, I went to see the Jerusalem on the other side of the lines. I visited places that years of dreaming had crystallized as symbols in my mind, and found that they were simply places where people lived. Houses, shops, stalls, street signs.
>
> I was thunderstruck. My dreams had deceived me, the nightmares were unfounded, the perpetual dread had suddenly been transformed into a cruel arabesque joke. Everything was shattered, exposed: my adored, terrifying Jerusalem was dead.
>
> …
>
> But the city is inhabited. People live there, strangers: I do not understand their language, they are living where they have always lived and I am the stranger who has come in from outside. Their eyes hate me. They wish me dead. Accursed stranger.
>
> …
>
> I saw resentment and hostility, hypocrisy, bewilderment, obsequiousness, fear, humiliation and new plots being hatched. I walked the streets

---

[24] Amos Oz, "An Alien City", in his *Under This Blazing Light: Essays*. Cambridge University Press, 1995, 179–80.

of East Jerusalem like a man who has broken into a forbidden place. City of my birth. City of my dreams. City of aspirations of my ancestors and my people. And here I was, stalking its streets clutching a sub-machine-gun, like a figure in one of my childhood nightmares: an alien man in an alien city.

However, there is another side to this: The Jerusalem in our heart as set against the real Jerusalem. The shocking discovery of seeing dreams shattered by reality: A memory that did not survive. My colleague who never intended to go there was probably right: Keep the dream – the memory – and leave reality alone: Don't go to Jerusalem. Thirty years ago, I was leading a group of theological students to the Middle East. We arrived at the Mount of Olives after having crossed the Allenby Bridge earlier the same day. There was a checkpoint. Behind a screen I saw a couple of Israeli soldiers or police officers beating up an Arab: I told the students: "Welcome to Jerusalem". Harsh realities versus dreams.

The other side: Christians and Jews are not the only ones to dream about Jerusalem. The most beloved singer of the Arab world, without a doubt Fairuz, wrote in 1967 – after the Six Day War – a song about al-Quds (which is certainly not inferior to anything produced by Christian and Jewish writers) and presented in an album with the title *Al Quds Fil Bal* (Jerusalem in my heart): *al-Quds al-ᶜAtiqa* ("The old Jerusalem").[25] The song was written almost at the same time as *Yerushalaim shel zahav* but still belongs to a totally changed world:

The Old Jerusalem

I passed by the streets, the streets of old Jerusalem
in front of the shops, that were left from Palestine,
We talked about it together and they give me a vase
they told me it's a gift from the people who are waiting.

I passed by the streets, the streets of old Jerusalem
I stopped by the doors which have become my friends

---

[25] For a full discussion of the Arabic and Hebrew songs about Jerusalem cf. Sarah Pinson, "*The Voices of Jerusalem*", MA Thesis, Polis Institute of Jerusalem 2019/20. Available at https://www.polisjerusalem.org/the-voices-of-jerusalem/. For obvious reasons the thesis was not available to me when I wrote this paper back in 2010. Arabic texts: Pinson, 2019/20: appendix 11 and 12.

and their sad eyes looking from the window of the city
took me and sent me to the exile of misery.

once upon a time,
there was a land and there were hands that built
they were building under the sun and under the wind
then there were houses and blossoming windows;
there were children with books in their hands.

Suddenly, one dark night,
hatred flooded the shadow of the houses,
the black hands stripped the doors
and the houses became without their owners
there became an obstacle
between the owners and their houses
an obstacle of thorns, fire and black hands.

I'm shouting in the streets, the streets of old Jerusalem,
let my song turn into storms and thunder
my voice keep flying,
whirlwind inside the conscience of people,
tell them what's happening,
so that maybe their conscience wakes up.

my voice keeps flying,
whirlwind inside the conscience of people,
tell them what's happening,
so that maybe their conscience wakes up
tell them what's happening,
so that maybe their conscience wakes up.[26]

3. Summing Up: Cultural Memory Versus Reality

Memory is about something you lost (i.e., no longer experience or have). When you have not experienced absence, you have no memory because there

---

[26] https://lyricstranslate.com/en/quds-al-atika-old-jerusalem.html. Here the original Arabic text is also included.

is nothing to remember. The Jews have lost Jerusalem a number of times, ending with a very vivid memory of their Jerusalem. Western Christianity lost it for the first time in 1187 to Saladin, creating a memory of the lost city which we found expressed in Tasso's epic about the liberated Jerusalem. The Arabs lost it twice, to the crusaders in 1099, and again to Israel in 1967. Their Jerusalem is now a Jerusalem of memory.

As you may guess, I see no way to escape the conflict between a cultural memory (talking about golden Jerusalem, the place to return to) and the cruel reality of a city which can rightfully claim to be the centre of the world, not in reality, but in our dreams. Next Year in Jerusalem.

And a postscript added after my latest return from Jerusalem in July 2010: Nothing illustrates the status of Jerusalem as a city embedded in our heart better than the picture I took of the wall blocking the road from Bethlehem to Jerusalem. Let Jerusalem remain in our heart: On this side of the wall you are in Bethlehem, on the other you are immediately in Jerusalem, not in our heart but in the Jerusalem of today. The direction of our travel to Jerusalem is not from the Jerusalem in our heart to the real Jerusalem but from the real Jerusalem to the Jerusalem in our heart. I lived in Jerusalem in 1974 and returned many times over a period of almost forty years. It is the Jerusalem of 1974 which is still in my heart.

EXEGESIS

2 Emphatic Time in the Old Testament[1]

Quantitative and Qualitative Time

In the modern world we consider matters in time and space. Both categories are measurable. Space is reckoned in kilometres, metres, centimetres, and millimetres. Time is similarly measured in years, months, weeks, days, hours, minutes and seconds, and within science sometimes in microseconds and nanoseconds. Time and space are, as epistemological entities, understood as quantities and we have developed instruments such as watches and scales to measure them.

In this essay we will mostly have a look on time as an idea without totally forgetting that time and space are two interrelated concepts.

As an introduction it is worth asking if it was – or is – always like that? Don't we operate with a concept of time which is not only quantitative but also has a qualitative content, meaning something which is valuable even if the value cannot be measured precisely? If we, for example, take the expression "he came at the right moment" it can be understood as a quantitative assessment: The person in question managed to catch his train and the train normally departs on a previously settled time which can be found in a timetable and marked by a sign at the station. However, the expression may also have a qualitative meaning. He, bringing help, arrived before it was too late. In this context "before it's too late" indicates that his help was needed and that it arrived "in the right moment" without regard for the precise time of the arrival of the assistance.

---

[1] There is no English word that precisely covers the meaning of Danish "prægnant", though "pregnant" is approximately equivalent. Emphatic may also be equivalent. "Pregnant time" means a reckoning of time which places stress on importance, and meaning rather than being a chronological indication.

In this case time functions as a quality because it is without interest exactly at what time the help arrived. The interesting point is that it arrived when still of use and no watch can tell us that: The one who was in need of help received it before it was too late. The person in need of help may perhaps say: "Finally you came!" not because the help arrived at 17.15 and not 17.00, but because it arrived when he could still use it.

Although we still think of time in this way, mostly in common speech, it is correct to assert that the modern world is obsessed with time understood as a quantity. We measure everything and understand ourselves as living in a certain measurable time and we look forward to time advancing. It might even happen that the whole world may act like a child who could not wait but had to celebrate the turn of the millennium one year too early, as happened at New Year 2000, when the correct date of the turning of the millennium was in fact New Year 2001. Three hundred and sixty-five days, even three hundred and sixty-six later, because 2000 was a leap year, is far too long to wait. We are lost without an indicator of time: Where is my watch? – Richard Wagner's final words – What time is it? make this clear. Trains have to arrive on time or they are delayed, and time is indicated by the watch, which just goes on measuring time. We are all in the same boat as the rabbit in Alice in Wonderland: "I am late, I am late!" we are all running around with a watch in our hand.

Is it possible that we should imagine a world where time (and space for that matter) was not primarily a quantity but rather indicates a quality? A world where time has a value in itself and where it is not decisive that things may happen at exactly one specific time, if it only happens at the "right" moment?

In C.S. Lewis' world of Narnia, time cannot be measured. In his series about Narnia it is often stressed that in this world of fairytales, time elapses according to other rules than ours. The children who tumble into Narnia through the wardrobe outlive their childhood in Narnia but when they accidentally return to our world it is at exactly the same moment they left it. It is as if time never moved. Lewis' fairytale happens within their own time that has nothing to do with time in this world. Furthermore, this is also emphasized in Narnia; that time is a giant sleeping in a gigantic cavern who only wakens when the god of Narnia, Aslan, at the end of the world of Narnia, shouts: "It is time". Then time wakens and that is the end of time, doomsday.

In the world of Narnia, the world of fairytales, time may be measured but not in the same way as our quantitative, measurable time. Time follows its own rules where things do happen at the right moment. As such the world of

Narnia is representative of the world of fairytales in general. Time stops, as in the fairytale of the Sleeping Beauty, where every person at the castle sleeps for a hundred years while the world outside moves on. When time moves on it happens within defined periods. If it is a short period, a change will happen after seven days when a journey may end at its intended goal. If we speak of a longer period, it may be forty days that separate the beginning of something and its finalization. And again, if it is about a sequence of years, it is no longer forty days but forty years. The numbers seven and forty are clearly emphatic and not precise indications of time. They are meaningful in themselves but not as indicators of something measurable and play an emphatic role in the narrative. A journey may begin at one place, perhaps at the home of the hero in the popular tale, and end seven or forty days later, when the hero arrives at the place of the mysterious princess or at the place where the hero has to prove that he is really the hero of the fairytale. The time interval isn't exact and measurable but represents a period that connects and separates the single parts of the drama and moves the story to its next stage.

Quantitative and Qualitative Time in the Old Testament

A: The Emphatic Indications of Time in the History of Israel

There can be no doubt that we have in the Old Testament both a quantitative and a qualitive use of time. Quantitative time can be found in a number of indications of time where a specific period of time is meant without any qualitative importance. We may mention the indications of regnal years in 1st and 2nd Kings and the synchronisms between Israelite and Judean kings:

Thus it is written of King Amaziah of Judah that he ascended the throne in the thirty-seventh year of King Jeroboam of Israel and that he ruled for fifty-two years in Jerusalem (2 Kings 15:1–2); or about King Jotham, that he was twenty-five years at his ascension which happened in Pekah of Israel's second year. Jotham ruled for sixteen years (2 Kings 15:32–33). None of these numbers appear in any popular narrative with an emphatic meaning. Whether or not the numbers are correct is not a qualitative problem, it is probably only a historical issue.

The word "probably" in this context is worth noting because even if the numbers seem random and might have a historical background this does not prove them to be historically correct or freed from any emphatic meaning. Similar seemingly random indications of time can be found elsewhere in places such as the list of the so-called "minor judges" in the Book of Judges (Judg 10:1–5; 12:8–15):[2]

Tola from Issachar:	Judge in Israel for twenty-three years
Jair from Gilead:	Judge in Israel for twenty-two years
Ibzan from Bethlehem:	Judge in Israel for seven years
Elon from Zebulon:	Judge in Israel for ten years
Abdon from Pir'aton:	Judge in Israel for eight years

Any of these indications of time seems reasonable, but put together these five judges ruled over Israel in total seventy years. Although seventy is not seven or forty, it is still an emphatic number, the sum of ten times seven, i.e., a "round" multiplication of the emphatic number seven and inheriting the emphatic meaning of seven. How important this number is can be deduced from the indication of the length of the Babylonian exile which, according to the Book of Jeremiah, was to last for seventy years (Jer 25:11–12; 29:10; see also 2 Chron 36:21) although most scholars agree that the exile only lasted from 587 BCE to 538 BCE, i.e., fifty years.

Put together, the number of the years the minor judges ruled is a round one. This is not a precise indication of time. The single numbers are dependent on the necessity that they will amount to seventy years all together. We have no idea why the single judge gets so different regnal numbers, from twenty-three years to seven years (which in this case may not have the usual emphatic meaning). The sum of the numbers shows – apart from saying that the two fragmented lists belong together – that the emphatic number seventy takes precedence over the individual indications of regnal years. It is therefore the basis of the calculation of the individual regnal years.

---

[2] As to form and content the notes about the "minor judges" look very much like the summaries of the reigns if the kings of Israel and Judah. Compare Judg 10:1–2: "1 And after Abimelech there arose to defend Israel Tola the son of Puah, the son of Dodo, a man of Issachar; and he dwelt in Shamir in mount Ephraim. ²And he judged Israel twenty and three years, and died, and was buried in Shamir" with the note in 2 Kings 15:17.22: "¹⁷In the nine and thirtieth year of Azariah king of Judah began Menahem the son of Gadi to reign over Israel, *and reigned* ten years in Samaria. ²²And Menahem slept with his fathers; and Pekahiah his son reigned in his stead". The term the "minor judges" indicates a difference between such judges as Ehud, Barak and Gideon who are the heroes of narratives and the minor ones who only appear in lists in Judges 10 and 12. Otherwise they are unknown. On their importance for the scholarly discussion about the twelve tribe league a generation ago cf. Lemche, 1972, 74–87.

In this way the number of years assigned to the minor judges and the so-called "great judges", the heroes in the opening chapters of the Book of Judges, are in agreement. According to the information about these judges their rule resulted in a number of years of peace for Israel:

Otniel:	Peace in Israel for forty years
Ehud:	Peace in Israel for eighty years
Barak:	Peace in Israel for forty years
Gideon:	Peace in Israel for forty years

Altogether, the period of peace is two hundred years. Although two hundred is a round number, it is not particularly "round". The system is, however, the same. Every judge is followed by a long period of peace, in three cases of forty years, and in the fourth case of eighty years. The system seems to break down as Jephthah was only a judge for six years (Judg 12:7). Now, it is likely that six years may still be a "round" number: something lasts for a period of six days or years but in the seventh year something new happens.

There is an abundance of examples of this way of calculating within the system of emphatic numbers. Thus the Israelites surround Jericho for six days but on the seventh day the walls come tumbling down at the sound of the trumpets and the Israelites are able to conquer the city (Josh 6:3–5). Another example comes from the law of the Hebrew slave who has to serve for six years but in the seventh he shall be freed (Exod 21:2). After the death of King Ahaziah of Judah his mother Athaliah seizes power and rules for six years but in the seventh year she is overthrown (2 Kings 11). Therefore when Jephthah's period in office is reckoned to be six years, the meaning might be that in the seventh year something new was going to happen. We never hear about what this might have been. As it stands, the story of Jephthah seems to be a fragment of a more comprehensive tradition about him. However, the perspective changes and it is noted that after the last of the "minor" judges the Philistines oppressed Israel for forty years.

This period is also characterized by the use of an emphatic number as the indication of the period of oppression. Forty years of unrest is substituted by a new period under a judge, Samson, who was to function for twenty years (Judg 16:31). Thus, a period of Philistine oppression lasting for forty years is substituted by a period where a judge ruled for only twenty years.

The final chapters of the Book of Judges are without indications of time. These chapters have, at times, been reckoned post-deuteronomistic additions to the Book of Judges, partly because of their pro-monarchical attitude: "In those days *there was* no king in Israel, *but* every man did *that which was* right in his own eyes" (Judg 17:6; 21:25; cf. Judg 18:1; 19:1).[3] The deuteronomists are otherwise not known to be very positive to the idea of kingship in Israel.[4]

The Book of Judges has seemingly been constructed as a collection of narratives which are kept together by a system of emphatic indications of time. This information about time seems secondary to the narratives where they appear. This does, however, not mean that there ever existed a different system of dates now substituted by the use of emphatic time indications of forty years (eventually two times forty years or twenty, half of a forty-year period). In one case, in connection with the narrative about Jephthah, the information that he died after having judged Israel for six years (Judg 12:7) indicates that the story might once have had a different conclusion, that something different happened in the seventh year.

In order to conclude this section about the years in office of the judges of Israel Eli was of course in office for forty years (1 Sam 4:18), whereas we have no information about Samuel's period in office.

When we move on to the period of the Hebrew Kings as we find it described in the Books of Samuel and Kings, we, at the beginning, have a similar system functioning. David is said to have ruled for forty years, a period divided between seven years (!) in Hebron and thirty-three years in Jerusalem.[5] In similar fashion, Solomon reigns for forty years (1 Kings 11:42) whereas his son and successor Rehoboam only sat on his throne for seventeen years (1 Kings 14:21), and Rehoboam's son and successor Abijah only for three years (1 Kings 15:2). The system still functions: In total the two successors to Solomon rule for exactly half the period of Solomon, twenty years. In this way the united Israelite kingdom lasts for eighty years and is followed by twenty years of recession.

However, the use of emphatic numbers continues as Asa, Abijam's son, rules for forty years (1 Kings 15:10).[6] After Asa we have Jehoshaphat's rule

---

[3] Cf. thus Kaiser, 1984, 151–3, who mentions Karl Budde as the one who formulated this idea (cf. Budde, 1897, 110–3).

[4] Cf. Samuel's rejection of kingship, 1 Samuel 8 and 12, or the condemnation of the monarchy and its representations found in many places in the Books of Kings.

[5] 2 Sam 5:4–5 says seven and a half years in Hebron and thirty-three years in Jerusalem; however, the two other indicators of the time of David's rule in Hebron in 1 Kings 2:11 and 1 Chron 29:27 have "corrected" the number to seven years and thirty three years.

[6] Strictly speaking, Asa ruled, according to 1 Kings 15:10, for forty-one years. The "extra" year, however, creates problems in other parts of the chronological system. Thus the period from David's ascension to the throne to the death of Jehoash lasts two hundred and twenty-one years. 2 Chronicles saw the problem and solved it by saying that Asa ruled for forty years but died in his forty first year.

lasting for twenty-five years (1 Kings 21:42), Jehoram with a reign of eight years (2 Kings 8:17), Ahaziah with only one year (2 Kings 8:26), and Athaliah with one lasting six years (2 Kings 11:3).[7]

Also here we have an example of seemingly random numbers which when put together turn out to be another emphatic use of time indications. In total, the four successors to Asa rule for forty years. After this something new happens with the ascension of Jehoash, who happened to rule for another forty years (2 Kings 12:2).

After the death of Jehoash emphatic numbers are used no more. The kings ruling have a variety of regnal years: sixteen years, twenty-nine years, also fifty-five years – and then one of only three months. If we therefore calculate the regnal years during the period from Jehoash to the fall of Jerusalem, we get the number two hundred and fifty-two years.[8]

As a consequence we may divide the time of the Kingdom of Judah into two major periods, the first put together with the use of emphatic indications of time: first eighty years (two times forty years), then forty years and again forty years. This first period is quite different from the second one where such indications of time are missing. However, we get a glimpse of an explanation for the use of the emphatic indication of a time of "forty years" in the first part of the history of the Kingdom of Judah: The four kings who are assigned a regnal period of forty years have in common that their relation to the worship of Yahweh in Jerusalem is seen in a positive light. David brings the ark of Yahweh to Jerusalem (2 Sam 6), Solomon builds the temple (1 Kings 6–8), Asa reforms the cult (1 Kings 15:12–15), and Jehoash repairs the temple (2 Kings 12). At the same time the time lapses between the positively evaluated rulers and the "villains" increases from at first twenty years to, in the second instance, forty years. In the first case, the period is split between two rulers, in the second between four. Put together the reconstruction presented in the Books of Kings of this period seems both artificial and clever.

---

[7] Cf. however also above. The coup that doomed Athaliah happened in her seventh year.
[8] In this calculation of the reigns of the kings of Jerusalem we haven't taken co-regencies into consideration. These are the simple numbers as they appear in the two books of Kings which are of interest, and not the various hypotheses of modern scholars. The two hundred and fifty-two years from Jehoash's death to the destruction of Jerusalem must not overshadow the fact that an emphatic number appears if we calculate the period as from Jehoash's death to the first fall of Jerusalem in 597, a period of two hundred and forty-one years – again we have a superfluous extra year. This extra year, however, makes sense if we compare it with the note in 2 Kings 25:1 according to which the siege of Jerusalem began in Zedekiah's ninth year, exactly two hundred and fifty years after Jehoash's death.

In the case of the Kingdom of Israel we find no similar system. All indications of regnal years from Jeroboam to Hosheah seem "random" since none of them are emphatic in the meaning used here. The closest we get to an emphatic indication of time is the note about Zimri who only ruled for seven days (1 Kings 16:15) but in this case the meaning is probably only that Zimri just ruled for a few days.

Historians and students of literature may possibly find reasons to speculate why this use of emphatic numbers turns up in the literature from Judges to 2 Kings. The hypothesis is evident that there were no historical sources, annals or chronicles covering the time from the Judges to the death of Jehoash, i.e., from the grey past to c. 800 BCE, so biblical historiographers constructed their version of the history of Israel by introducing a time table based on an emphatic indication of time. This does not mean that there we no sources at all, e.g., in the form of anecdotes, popular tales, prophetic legends and the like, but this means that the framework in which such information was placed was decided by the historiographers and did not exist before the various stories were incorporated into the description of the period as a matter of fact between the conquest and the death of Jehoash.[9]

The situation changes at the end of the history of the Kingdom of Judah where we might argue that chronological, i.e., historical information, really existed to a degree that enabled the historiographers to write about the period without having to invent a historical framework for these events, as they found their information about regnal years and more in some annalistic sources. At least the indications of regnal years of the kings of Israel and the later kings of Judah seem not to be constructed in the same way as those which concern the early history, the period of the Judges and Judah's early years. Furthermore, these "historical" numbers, random indications of time, make sense when they are compared to information about Israelite and Judean kings not found in the Old Testament but in other documents from the ancient Near East such as Assyrian and Babylonian annalistic literature. Here the biblical historiographers do not make mistakes but always place individual Israelite and Judean kings correctly vis-à-vis contemporary Assyrian and Babylonian kings.[10]

---

[9] As to Judah and Jerusalem, this is in accordance with the realization among a number of scholars within the last ten years that no state emerged in Judah before the 8th century BCE, Cf. Jamieson-Drake, 1991, and the, from a methodological point of view, absolutely different Niemann, 1993. Recently the Israeli archaeologist Israel Finkelstein has expressed the same opinion (Finkelstein, 1999).

[10] Cf. further on the possibility of annalistic sources Lemche, 1999a.

B: Emphatic Time Reckoning and Precise Indications of Time: The Flood – a Hierarchical Order?

The analysis of the use of emphatic numbers in historical literature might have continued with a survey of the narratives about Israel's early history, the stories about the Patriarchs or the wanderings in the desert where emphatic numbers appear and are used several times. We might also mention two times seven years Jacob had to serve for Leah and Rachel (Gen 29:15–39) and the meaning of the seven fat and seven lean years in the story of Joseph (Genesis 41). The miracle of the manna is used to emphasize the difference between the six days when the Israelites go collecting manna in the desert in contrast to the seventh day where there is no manna (Exodus 16). Neither should we forget the four hundred years when Israel was in Egypt or the wanderings in the desert said to have lasted for forty years. And, as if this is not enough, the embalming of Jacob takes forty days followed by a period of grief of no less than seventy days (Gen 50:1–3). Thus, emphatic numbers appear everywhere in these stories and set out the frameworks of these stories – if they are not simply a part of the plot. And finally, but not least importantly: God creates the world in six days but rests on the seventh, thereby institutionalizing the Sabbath.

But instead of a longish debate about all these single instances of the use of emphatic numbers we should now turn our attention to the hierarchical order of emphatic numbers with a qualitative meaning and simple quantitative measurements of time and space. The basis of this discussion must be the chronology of the story of the Flood building on an analysis which I presented more than twenty years ago, an analysis that still stands (as I see it).[11]

The conclusion to that study was that we, in the story of the Flood in Genesis 6–8, have not two but three chronological systems. Students of the Pentateuch have normally agreed to assign the first of these systems to the Yahwist stratum and thereby to be the oldest one. Presumably this layer is only preserved as a fragment but contains the following chronological information:[12]

---

[11] Lemche, 1980.

[12] The story of the Flood is traditionally subdivided into two sources – or documents – the Yahwistic and the priestly. This is not the place to go further into the at least two different strings of narrative in Genesis 6–8. Furthermore there are signs of redaction in this narrative.

Gen 7:4:   Seven days to the coming of the Flood.

Gen 7:4:   The Flood lasts for forty days.

Gen 8:10: There are seven days between the first emission of the dove and the second.

Gen 8:12: There are seven days between the second emission of the dove and the third

All together the flood, in this accounting, lasts for sixty-one days. Every number in this part of the narrative are emphatic: seven + forty + seven + seven days. In opposition to this way of reckoning, a totally different system of calculating time in the story of the Flood appears in the priestly source or document:

Gen 7:6:   Noah is six hundred years old.

Gen 7:11: The Flood begins on the seventh day in the second month.

Gen 7:24: The water rises for on hundred and fifty days.

Gen 8:4:   The ark is stranded on Mount Ararat on the seventeenth day of the seventh month.

Gen 8:5:   The top of the mountains appears on the first day of the tenth month.

Gen 8:13: The Flood ends and the earth is dry on the first day in the first month of year 601.

Gen 8:14: The earth is dry on the twenty seventh day of the second month.

No mention here of any emphatic numbers. Instead, we are presented with a series of precise dates within the year. The time allotted to the rising water, one hundred and fifty days,[13] is quantitative and certainly not qualitative. It leads the reader to the seventeenth day in the seventh month and is decided by the precise indication of time in Gen 7:11.

What kind of calculations helped to merge the two different systems and why does the Flood itself begin on a seemingly random date like the seventieth day in the second month? The presence of the seven days is explained by Gen 7:4: It represents the interval between the end of the building of the ark and the coming of the Flood. However, we have no information on how long of time it took Noah to build the ark, although we may be allowed to present a couple of qualified suggestions.

---

[13] Here we see a stereotypical reckoning of months of thirty days.

The priestly calculation of the time of the Flood opens with a rather non-clarified note that it happened when Noah was six hundred years old. It also calculates the duration of the Flood to exactly one year. This is confirmed by the information in Gen 8:13 that the earth was dry on the first day in the first month of Noah's 601st year. However, this information is repeated in Gen 8:14, which moves the end of the Flood to the twenty-seventh day of the second month. As a consequence the end of the flood is moved by fifty-seven days. This last date seems in some way or the other related to the information in Gen 7:11 that the Flood began on the seventeenth day of the second month the preceding year. As a consequence, an extra ten days have been added to the calculation as though it was the intention that the end of the Flood should have happened precisely one year after its beginning. Still, we have this extra ten days as the Flood began on the seventeenth day of the second month but ended on the twenty-seventh day of the second month a year later. There is a possible explanation of this difference of ten days.

The ten extra days expresses the difference between a lunar and a solar year. In this way an editor of the Flood story wants to mark that if we make the calculation that the Flood lasted for one solar year and not a lunar year, we have to prolong the time of its end by another ten days. This may explain the strange day of the ending of the Flood in Gen 8:14 but not the equally strange day of its beginning.

If we calculate that the Flood, according to the priestly source, lasted for precisely one year, the end would, as indicated by Gen 8:13, match the date of its beginning if it was on the first day of the first month in the 600th year of Noah's life. However, the lapse of time between this day and the precise day given in Gen 7:11 is forty-seven days. We have an explanation in Gen 7:4.10 of the seven days, the time from Noah finishing the ark to the coming of the Flood; but no explanation of the forty days which are missing from the calculation. Accordingly, my thesis is that the truncated version of the Flood story in the Yahwist was overwritten with the incorporation of the priestly version. In the Yahwistic version Noah spent forty days building the ark. If this thesis is correct, the original Yahwistic version may have included this chronological information:

> Forty days spent building the ark.
> Seven days to the coming of the rain.
> Forty days of rain.
> Forty days until Noah opened the hatch of the ark.
> Seven days from the time he opened the hatch to the first emission of the dove

Seven days from the first emission of the dove to the second.
Seven days from the second emission of the dove to the third whereupon the earth is dry and Noah leaves the ark.

Thus we have in the Yahwistic version of the story of the Flood only emphatic numbers. The incorporation of the priestly version into the Yahwistic one forced the editor to re-evaluate the chronological information. The priestly version, which seems to have been preserved in its entirety, worked with quantitative indications of time taking the story of the Flood to last from the first day in Noah's 600th year to the first day in his 601st year whereas the Yahwist worked with emphatic numbers. The editor of the version of the story that incorporated both the Yahwistic and the Priestly stories, evidently in contradiction as to the reckoning of time, achieved his editing by paying attention to the emphatic numbers in the Yahwistic version. Therefore he moved the beginning of the Flood by forty-seven days to the seventeenth of the second month. The calculation that the water rose for one hundred and fifty days leads the narrative to settle on the seventeenth day of the seventh month. This date relates to the revision of the date of the beginning. If the Flood began on the first day of the 600th year, the one hundred and fifty days would lead to the first day of the sixth month, which would mean that the period when the waters were receding from earth until the appearance of the mountains is four months, which again means that the date the first day of the tenth month has been preserved. Hereafter two more months are to lapse before the end of the Flood.

When the priestly version was imposed on the Yahwistic one, the editor had to pay attention to the use of emphatic numbers in the Yahwist's version. The precise dates of the priestly version had to be revised in such a fashion that they would be in accordance with the Yahwistic indications of time and this revision went so far that it introduced a third system and thus changed the date of the end of the Flood. The exact numbers had to give priority to the emphatic dates of the first version, which were considered so important that they could not be changed, at least in those parts of the Yahwistic story of the Flood that have survived.

C: Emphatic Use of Time and the Sabbath

The most emphatic use of time in the Old Testament is certainly related to the Sabbath. God created the world in six days and had his Sabbath on the seventh (Gen 2:1–3). In this way God institutionalized the seven-day week and introduced the Sabbath as belonging to creation, as something that had been in existence since the beginning of the world. The command to keep the Sabbath is also one of the Ten Commandments (Exod 20:8; cf. also Deut 5:12): "Six days shalt thou labour, and do all thy work. But the seventh day *is* the sabbath of the LORD thy God". The reason for this commandment is because of the place of the Sabbath in creation (Exod 20:11).

600th The origins of the Sabbath have often been discussed. Among the more serious theories we find the derivation from the Akkadian concept of *šapattu*, which had the same meaning as the Latin *idus*. It marks the fifteenth day in a month, which in a calendar based on the lunar year will be the day of the full moon but can also be used of a period of time lasting for half a month.[14] Some have rejected this derivation asking how one day can become four days? For some time scholars referred to the Mesopotamian concept of *ûmê lemnûti*, "evil days" to explain the Sabbath. Such days were taboo-days where people should not work. However, not even these special days follows a seven days pattern. They are placed on the 1st, the 2nd, the 14th, the 19th, and the 21st in a month and are, in Mesopotamian tradition, not called *šapattu* days. Without doubt four of the days, the 1st, the 7th, the 14th, and the 21st, have to do with the duration of a lunar month. The exception, the 19th, does not fit in with the system of seven days following the phases of the moon.[15]

However, another possible explanation would be to look for the origin of the Sabbath among Mesopotamian customs. In the Babylonian version of the story of the Flood in the epic *Atraḫasis* we have the following statement by the god Enki: "On the first, seventh and fifteenth day of the month I will make a purifying bath".[16] In the reasoning for the Sabbath in Gen 2:1–3 it is characterized as "the seventh day". We might therefore think of an approximation of the Babylonian system of taboo-days and the biblical concept of the Sabbath day which led to minor discrepancies like the taboo-day on the 19th of a month out of consideration. In this way the biblical system represented the transfer of the Babylonian system to a more rigid seven-day system which appeared as a consequence of the amalgamation with the Babylonian system, or may have existed before this amalgamation that led to the formal introduction of the Sabbath.[17]

---

[14] On *šapattu*, cf. *CAD* Š/1, 449–50.

[15] Cf. Hasel, 1992, 849–56.

[16] In Akkadian *Ina arḫi sebûti u šapatti taliltam lušaškin rimka* (Lambert and Millard, 1969, 56–7).

[17] I shall not comment here on the relations between the Sabbath and the appearance of the week as a temporal concept although it is likely that the week has as its origin the division of the phases of the moon and prepares for a month with twenty eight days. When and where this happened is impossible to decide.

Emphatic Time in the Old Testament   35

The theory that the Sabbath may derive from so-called ancient Canaanite cult praxis which is based on a reference to the use of the seven-day pattern in Ugaritic literature is unlikely. Although there a several examples of the use of the emphatic number seven in Ugaritic epics such references, when the number seven is used as an indication of time, has the same literary value as an emphatic indication of time as found in many places in the Old Testament.[18] We may refer to the following passage in the Kirta epic where Kirta receives instructions for his campaign against the city of Udum where he is to find his wife:

Go for a day and a second,
A third, a fourth day,
A fifth, a sixth day.
Lo,
At sunrise on the seventh
You will come to Udum abounding in rain.
And to well-watered Udum.[19]

Kirta fields his army, arrives at Udum and lays siege to it for six days. On the seventh day King Pabil of Udum is forced to react:

They rested a day and a second,
A third and a fourth day,
A fifth and a sixth day
...
Lo,
At sunrise on the seventh,
King Pabil could not sleep[20]

The day of the Sabbath therefore represents an implementation of seven as an emphatic indication of time to indicate a period of seven real days. We don't know if the system with weeks lasting for exactly seven days already existed when the Sabbath obtained its status in Jewish religion, but the emphatic number seven became decisive for compliance with the Sabbath: For six days life goes on as usual, but on the seventh day something new happens. There is, from a principal point of view, no difference between a commandment that

---

[18] The motif of the seventh day is especially frequent in the epic of Kirta.
[19] Kirta 1.14.iii 1–5 in the translation of N. Wyatt (Wyatt, 1998, 192-93).
[20] Kirta 1.14 v 3–8.

says that you have to work for six days and rest on the seventh or, like King Kirta, have to go with an expedition with your army in order to reach your objective on the seventh day. The difference is that in the Jewish regulation of the Sabbath the number seven is no longer first and foremost emphatic as its meaning has been transferred to the daily life of a Jew. It this way the seventh day kept some of its mystery as the important day but it can be mathematically calculated to occur every seventh day after six regular days. We may say that the number seven has been bureaucratized.

It is also possible to expand the idea of the Sabbath to include the seventh year, the year of the Sabbath. The basic legislation can be found in the Book of the Covenant (Exod 21–23) and in Deuteronomy 15:

> [10]And six years thou shalt sow thy land, and shalt gather in the fruits thereof: [11]But the seventh *year* thou shalt let it rest and lie still; that the poor of thy people may eat: and what they leave the beasts of the field shall eat. In like manner thou shalt deal with thy vineyard, *and* with thy olive grove. (Exod 23:10–11)

This law about the year of the Sabbath is followed by:

> Six days thou shalt do thy work, and on the seventh day thou shalt rest: that thine ox and thine ass may rest, and the son of thy handmaid, and the stranger, may be refreshed. (Exod 23:12)

Which sounds like a free quotation from the commentary on the Sabbath day in Exod 20:9–10 (cf. also Deut 5:13–14).

Thus the reason for the year of the Sabbath is associated with the similar reason for the day of the Sabbath in Exodus. The content of the legislation about the year of the Sabbath sounds irrational. It makes sense that a fallow year is introduced for cornfields although a fallow year coming after an interval of seven years may hardly be enough. There is, on the other hand, no reason for introducing a fallow year for olives or vines, two kinds of crops not in any way related to a fallow year. The legislation in Exod 23:10–11 is a kind of armchair theorizing that has nothing to do with practical agriculture. It is no more than speculation based on the use of the emphatic indications of time: seven days – seven years.

That we are really witnesses to a learned kind of speculation becomes clear when we move on to the extension of the rules of the year of Sabbath in the legislation to the Jubilee (Leviticus 25). This legislation is introduced by a repetition of the rules for the years of Sabbath, but the perspective hereafter expands and calculations are made for a period of seven times seven years to obtain a special year of Sabbath, the Jubilee when all slaves in that state because of debt shall be set free by combining the rules of the year of Sabbath understood as a fallow year with the rules for freeing slaves of debt every seventh years (Deuteronomy 15). The Jubilee is not placed in the forty ninth but in the fiftieth year. Thus seven times seven is, according to the legislation of the Jubilee, fifty. This confirms that we do not have here ancient legislation but learned speculations regarding a Sabbath year not every forty-ninth year but instead a "round number", a fiftieth year. In this way we see the emphatic number seven being submitted to a control and part of a bureaucratic system of amnesty.

Quantitative and Qualitative time in the Old Testament

As already argued, there can be no doubt that in the Old Testament we find quantitative as well as qualitative concepts of time. This is hardly new. It is more interesting that we find this conscious use of emphatic indications of time in the literature of the Old Testament.

In the examples here we have, in the historical literature from the Book of Judges to 2 Kings, confronted round numbers; not least periods of forty years. It was also possible to move further back to study the indications of time in literature relating to Israel's earliest history and arrive at the same conclusion. The authors of these narratives created a timeframe for their stories which is clearly artificial and builds on emphatic indications of time, especially the forty years episodes. There is absolutely no reason to believe that the numbers are realistic, random, and therefore historical. Clearly they function as a part of a narrative which becomes clear the moment we connect the time assigned to the early kings of Judah to their contribution to the worship of Yahweh in Jerusalem.

The number forty which dominates in these historical narratives symbolizes the time allotted to a single grown-up generation. This is explained in the story about the punishment of Israel because it declined to follow the order of Yahweh to move into Canaan (Num 14:27–35):

> How long *shall I bear with* this evil congregation, which murmur against me? I have heard the murmurings of the children of Israel, which they murmur against me. [28]Say unto them, *As truly as* I live, saith the Lord, as ye have spoken in mine ears, so will I do to you: [29]Your carcasses shall fall in this wilderness; and all that were numbered of you, according to

> your whole number, from twenty years old and upward, which have murmured against me, ³⁰Doubtless ye shall not come into the land, *concerning* which I sware to make you dwell therein, save Caleb the son of Jephunneh, and Joshua the son of Nun. ³¹But your little ones, which ye said should be a prey, them will I bring in, and they shall know the land which ye have despised. ³²But *as for* you, your carcasses, they shall fall in this wilderness. ³³And your children shall wander in the wilderness forty years, and bear your whoredoms, until your carcasses be wasted in the wilderness. ³⁴After the number of the days in which ye searched the land, *even* forty days, each day for a year, shall ye bear your iniquities, *even* forty years, and ye shall know my breach of promise. ³⁵I the LORD have said, I will surely do it unto all this evil congregation, that are gathered together against me: in this wilderness they shall be consumed, and there they shall die.

As an indication of time the number seven refers to a much shorter period of time. Matters are going on for six days to reach their conclusion on the seventh day. On the seventh day something new happens and a new "time" begins.

Forty has a different function because, as already mentioned, it marks out one generation. A grown-up person at the beginning of a period of forty years will not see its end. The generation that was present when David became king did not live to see his death. The grownups when Solomon's kingdom broke up after his death lived to see the consequences of the division of the kingdom and might still have been alive when Asa tried to get the cult in the temple in Jerusalem re-established. On the other hand, the generation that saw the death of Asa did not live to see the temple cult renovated. It could be said that this generation had its, chance but it did not get another one.

We, finally, have the number seventy as an emphatic indication of time. The period of seventy years is much longer than forty years and includes the same kind of limitations when it comes to the life expectancy of humans. Nobody who was a grown-up person dragged into exile when Jerusalem was destroyed will ever get the opportunity to return home again. However, because the number seventy builds on the number seven it has an additional meaning: When the seventy years have passed something new will happen. The periods of forty years include an emphatic number but does not carry any message of hope for the future. When it is said that the Babylonian exile is going to last for seventy years, it is also said that it will end because something new is going to happen.

The historiographers of the Old Testament knew perfectly well the symbolic value of these numbers and used them diligently, retaining the symbolic value of these numbers. This must be the basic conclusion of this discussion.

It is, on the other hand, rather apparent that the same historiographers had moved on and also knew that numbers may have a quantitative meaning. In the story of the Flood, it seems that the extensive revision of the Yahwistic account when it was incorporated into the priestly story led to a revision of the chronology of the Yahwistic version which consisted of a number of periods of forty days, and seven days. The priestly system worked with a number of fixed dates. The system of forty and seven was, to a large degree, preserved; but being included in a combined system with fixed dates within a year, their emphatic meaning was reduced and inserted into a random, i.e., historical period. In this connection it is less important that a modern reader will understand the story of the Flood to be a myth and not history. This differentiation has only to do with genre, a differentiation made by human readers. It is not part of biblical literature.

A bureaucratic control with the emphatic meaning of the number seven is achieved in the Sabbath legislation where a possible Mesopotamian institution of "evil days", taboo-days, is pressed into a rigid system operating with weeks of exactly seven days. The Babylonian system is already approaching such a fixed system, although it has not yet become part of a calendar in complete harmony including weeks of six days of work and one day of rest according to the preserved sources. We may look for the origins of the Mesopotamian tradition in a world dominated by emphatic indications of time, where the number seven has kept its original symbolic value to mark the change from one stage to another one, even if the single stages did not all last for seven days.

At this point we might compare the institution of the year of the Sabbath, which in itself looks like a transformation of the concept of the Sabbath from a system with special days to one of a special year. For years scholars have discussed the possibility that the year of the Sabbath (understood to be a year of liberation as described in Deuteronomy 15) had as its background the Babylonian tradition of periodical amnesties. The best-known examples of this are from the time of Hammurabi, from the first part of the 2nd millennium BCE, but the tradition survived and we have references to it as late as Seleucid times towards the end of the 1st millennium BCE. In Hammurabi's time royal edicts were regularly issued. It is never explicitly stated whether it happened every seventh year, but an edict about liberation and remission of debt normally appeared within a decade.[21]

The biblical tradition of the year of liberation knows this ancient habit, and a sign of this is the technical term used in the Akkadian edicts – *andurarum* – has been preserved in its neo-Assyrian form and with the same technical meaning in the law about the Jubilee in Num 25:10. The year of the Sabbath as we have it in biblical tradition is accordingly a quantitative expression of an Akkadian tradition which does not describe a general freeing of slaves of debt every seventh year in a quantitative sense, but about this happening regularly in such a way that it could be said that "the slave shall work for six years but in the seventh he shall be freed!"

The use of emphatic time in the Old Testament has been incorporated into a literature which is no longer folktale, where an extensive use of the emphatic meaning of such numbers is found and which can be said to take place outside of time and space. The historiographers have evidently received their education from a bureaucratic system with its regular use of quantitative indications of time. Their use of emphatic indications of time is a literary trope adapted to their own bureaucratic system, but they are still acquainted with the symbolic meaning of these numbers.

---

[21] The principal discussion is more than forty years old. Cf. Kraus, 1984.

3   Justice as Pre-existing World Order

If any single idea dominated ancient Near Eastern thinking, inclusive the world which created the Old Testament, it must be "Justice". The concept that God is just dominates every single page of the Old Testament and there is a lively discussion – not least in the Book of Job, where God's justice is called into question. The answer is: there is nothing for humans to interfere with, because it is beyond the understanding of human beings. Since God (not the gods), i.e. the God who created the world, must be just, the world he created must also be just. As a consequence it is humankind following Cain's example of being lured into evil which causes the world to become unjust. Justice, however, is not an essential quality to be found in the God of creation, it is a concept that governs the acts of this God. It is therefore correct to argue that justice comes before creation or perhaps even that justice is pre-existent and provides the conditions for the creation of the world.

In the Beginning

Theological literature abounds with dense theses informing us that God created the world *ex nihilo*, out of nothing and as his very first act. "In the beginning God created heaven and earth" (Gen 1:1) as in most modern translations of the Hebrew text, and often without any note or discussion. So too in the Danish tradition. Critical voices can be found, though. Thus as well in a preliminary translation within the project of preparing a new official Danish Bible. Here we find the following translation: "In the beginning, when God created heaven and earth" (*Da Gud skabte*, 1985), which does not alter much. However, in an unofficial test-translation two scholars, Jens-André Herbener and Philippe Provançal, presented a somewhat more radical translation: "When God began to create heaven and earth".[1] Which translation is the

---

[1] Herbener and Provançal, 2001. "Scientific" should be in quotation marks because the two editors define themselves as what they consider to be scientists, which is not necessarily the only definition of science and certainly not necessarily the correct definition. However, this test translation shall be seen in the light of a campaign which Herbener had

correct one, if there is only one "correct" translation possible when we are talking about an ancient text written in a language very different from modern ones? If we take the Hebrew text בראשית ברא אלהים את השמים ואת הארץ, the decisive word is the first one, בראשית, which normally is translated "in the beginning". The problem is only that this is not what we find in the Hebrew formulation. The form בְּרֵאשִׁית is indefinite "at a beginning" or as the Danish test-translation presented here has it, "when God began to create". Normally the official Bibles follow the tradition of the Church which was made official when the Septuagint decided to translate this Hebrew verse Ἐν ἀρχῇ ἐποίσεν ὁ θεὸς τὸν οὐρανὸν καὶ τὴν γῆν: "In the beginning God created heaven and earth", and this translation was, so to speak, confirmed when Jerome, in the Vulgate, translated the text "In principio creavit Deus coelum et terram". The reformers did not want to stir up any trouble (at least so far as translations of the Bible were concerned), so Luther followed the tradition of the Church and translated "Am Anfang Schuf Gott Himmel und Erden" and the authorized English Bible from 1611, the *King James Bible*, followed: "In the beginning God created the heavens and the earth". In the English tradition we find a rebellion against the tradition in the *New English Bible*: "In the beginning of creation, when God made heaven and earth". By the time this translation was authorized as the official Bible of the Church of England in the incarnation titled the *Revised English Bible*, everything had returned to tradition: "In the beginning God created the heavens and earth", although it is interesting that "'heaven" is now "heavens". We may ask: Which tradition governs here? It seems not to be the Protestant tradition. We would perhaps rather think of a Catholic understanding going back to the Middle Ages, operating with the idea of a series of circles in the Paradise of Heaven which the deceased has to pass through in order to reach God, a concept Dante makes the most of in his *Divina Comedia*.

The question remains: Did God create at the beginning or did God begin to create? The Hebrew text, where vocalization is secondary to the consonantal text, is supported by another important text witness from antiquity, Origen's *Hexapla*. Where it is expressly noted that the Hebrew form of the first word in the Bible in its Greek transliteration, βρησίθ, is indefinite, and not definite as the Christian tradition presupposes. One manuscript of the

---

opened a few years before in the short-lived magazine *Faklen* (the torch) against the new official translation of the Bible from 1992. Probably it would be more correct to talk about a translation based on scholarly religious studies.

Hexapla, also included in the textual apparatus in the Biblia Hebraica Stuttgartensia, has the definite form βαρησηθ.[2]

I have often used the issue of the correct interpretation of the very first sentence in the Bible to explain to theological students why it is so important to be able to read Hebrew. It is not immaterial whether or not the form of the first word of the Bible is definite or indefinite. If we follow Christian tradition, nothing existed when God began to create, absolutely nothing, only darkness, tempests, and the abyss. Not even God was able to see anything and as the first act he creates light. If we follow the Hebrew tradition with its conventional vocalization,[3] then the beginning is not *the* beginning but the beginning of creation and should perhaps be translated: "At first God created heaven and earth." Nothing is said about the possibility that something existed before creation, or we may think that the creation was only about the creation of our heaven and our earth, although such a question is probably meaningless in an ancient context.

Now what does God create, and what was the intention? All commentators inclusive of Gerhard von Rad and Claus Westermann are in agreement: The author of the first chapter of the Bible was a very systematically thinking person who presented creation as if it were a model being formed of some solid material. First, light is created, and thereafter darkness which was already there but had no name. Light is separated from darkness, the verb used to express this separation is the hiph'il form of בדל, meaning "to separate something". Thus God makes a divide between light and darkness and presents a definition of both concepts. Hereafter God creates the heavenly vault seen as a bowl of metal which separates (same Hebrew verb as before) between the waters above and under the vault. Finally, the oceans and the continents are created when God orders the water to assemble in one place after which the dry land appears: Everything is in its place.[4]

"Ordnung muss sein" and this is also the principle behind the rest of the narrative about the creation. Creation seems to be well-planned and – executed. God does not create "from scratch". Every part of creation is evaluated

---

[2] The Hexapla of Origin is available in two volumes on the internet: vol. I: https://archive.org/details/origenhexapla01unknuoft/page/n5/mode/2up, and vol. 2: https://archive.org/details/origenhexapla02unknuoft/page/n7/mode/2up.

[3] The consonantal text of the Hebrew Bible is separated from the vocalization by at least five hundred years or more. The vowels were added by Jewish scholars, the Masoretes, from the middle of the first millennium CE. There is plenty of evidence of the Hebrew text without vowels among the Dead Sea Scrolls.

[4] The place where the waters assemble, Gen 1:10: מקוה: is a religious expression, the technical word for Jewish ritual baths that shall be filled by rainwater.

following its creation. The principal elements are all present before creation. Light and darkness are there but only make their entry as what they are after they had been separated. The same applies to the ocean and the dry land. Both elements are present but mixed together in the abyss. Just as light and darkness was the result of a process of separation the ocean and the dry land first appear as they are after another process of separation. This is the end of chaos which existed before order – cosmos – was called forth. This is the main purpose of the first story of creation: The birth of cosmos. Everything at the right time and everything has a specific purpose.

Finally, when creation ends God concludes that everything is very good. Every single act of creation is followed with the declaration: Good! But when it is all over God states that it is very good, meaning that not only is God satisfied, but essentially it is complete and cannot be bettered. Now the only thing left is for God to rest after having created heaven and earth. The world that came into being in the first chapter of the Bible is complete. It cannot be improved.[5]

Two Worlds – God's and Ours

The first story of creation is followed by a second, which is only the first part of a narrative which comes to a preliminary conclusion at the end of Genesis 3. Through history theologians and exegetes have been in agreement that this second narrative is a variant contrasted with the first, i.e. another way of saying the same thing. The special point in the first story is that the creation of humans is placed at the end, whereas in the second humans – more precisely man – are the first to be created. Basically the two narratives are about the same. Is this really correct? It almost presupposes that ancient Jewish theologians who let Genesis 2 follow Genesis 1 saying the same were a kind of schizophrenic. How is it possible to have so marked a description of creation in Genesis 1 only to see it substituted with another in Genesis 2? It is almost too much to ask that readers in ancient times should not be able to understand that in these two narratives creation is widely different.

---

[5] The meaning is evident from the wording of the Hebrew text where God, following each act of creation, concludes that, e.g., the light is good. At the end it is concluded when God views everything he has done that it is as good as it can be. A note follows in the Danish bible, and reveals that the present official translation has missed this point by translating "God saw that it is as good as possible".

Perhaps we should look for a quite different answer to the question. It is not the same "stuff" which is created in the two accounts of creation. In Genesis 1, it is the world of God which is created as perfect. Everything is as it should be. Then in the following chapter it is the world of humans which is brought into being. Here everything is all but perfect. In the moment humans are forced to leave the world of God, they start killing each other. Genesis 1 is the story about how it should have been but Genesis 2 (until, in reality, 2 Kings 25) tells us how it turned out, and this story is not fun. The perfect world of God is cosmos, and therefore perfect. Our world is an imitation of God's world, created with the best of intentions but far from perfect. This is illustrated by the fate of humankind. We humans were destined to live in the world of God symbolized by Paradise, the garden God planted in the east, but we belong to the imperfect, which is not God's world, but our world. Humankind could not live up to the demands valid in God's world, even if they look quite uncomplicated. Humankind simply does not belong to God's world.

The idea that the world of God was an ideal world is not a foreign one in antiquity. The best-known realization of the fact that there are two worlds can be found in Plato's idea of a world of ideas which is the real world. The difference between his two worlds is not better explained than in his *The State*, book VII, where it is noted that humans living in this world are like people placed in a cave with their back against the entrance. The reality outside the cave they only perceive as shadows cast on the wall of the cave. They are confined to our imperfect world.

One thing cannot be disputed: First comes God's world, i.e. the principles which govern God's world, meaning that these principles precede our world. These principles cannot be changed, because God has already concluded that his world is perfect. His world is unshakeable. It is not the object of wilful acts, either by God or humans – in complete accordance with oriental thinking: Cosmos is justice, i.e. good, and justice is ruling, wherever cosmos reigns. Chaos is the opposite of cosmos. Chaos is evil and the home of injustice as we experience it everywhere in our world. The destiny of humans is, as already laid out in Genesis 1, to subject the world to our will and govern it as the vicars of God.

The Role of Humans in the World

The role of humans in the world is simple: "Be fertile and many, fill up the world and subject it to you; rule over the fish of the ocean, the birds of heaven and every animal moving on earth" (Gen 1:28). Soon after we are informed that these demands are also valid in our world and the punishment for disobeying the demands is obvious: Humanity is barred from entry into God's world.

God's world is absolutely good, with all the connotations connected to the concept of "good" in the ancient world. Humans' task in our world is to carry out the tasks delineated by God. The Old Testament expresses this symbolically by bringing in the concept of the king as the servant of God, עבד יהוה, a title used of the king in concord with Near Eastern ideas about the king who is not (or: almost never) considered a god. The king is a human being installed on his throne by the gods. He is entrusted with the task of representing the divine among the humans over whom he is set to rule.

The, perhaps, finest expression of this we find in the Prologue to Codex Hammurabi from the 18th century BCE.[6]:

> When lofty Anu, the king of the Anunnaki (gods) and Enlil, the ruler of heaven and earth who destine the fate of the country, designed for Marduk, Ea's firstborn son, rulership over all human beings, made him great among the Igigi (gods), announced the exalted name of Babylon and made it great in the whole world and founded a kingdom in the heart of it eternal like heaven and earth, then Anu and Enlil announced my name as a benefit for humanity, I Hammurabi, the devout prince who honours the gods, to establish justice in the land, to expose the evil and wicked, to prevent the strong to remove justice from the weak, to rise like the Sun (Šamaš) over the black-heads and lighten up the land.[7]

To put it briefly: the king is installed by the gods to provide for the happiness of humans. Hammurabi is not shy. The name of Hammurabi was announced when Babylon was created, the holy city of the gods. It is announced that his task was to establish justice. Hammurabi was not a god, but the institution of kingship was, as expressed in the introduction to the Sumerian kings list: "When the kingdom descended from heaven …"[8] The task of human beings is to improve their world in order that this unjust world, our world, can approach the world of God.

These are not just nice words. People were quite serious about it. We have the best information about this from the time of Hammurabi, when his

---

[6] Hammurabi of Babylon reigned 1792–1750 BCE.
[7] CH i,1–49. Here translated after the text in Roth, 1997, 76.
[8] Sumerian King-List: Cf. Jacobsen, 1939.

dynasty ruled Babylon.⁹ At that time it was the custom to issue royal decrees announcing that the people who had been forced to sell themselves as slaves because of debt were not only free again, but also got their possessions back. When such decrees were issued they were followed up in the royal propaganda according to which the king had established justice and righteousness – in Akkadian *mīšaram û kittam aškun*, "I have established justice and righteousness". The ideology behind these decrees was not that the king had established something new but that he had re-established correct conditions. Since everybody is born alike, inequality demonstrates that we are far away from the perfect world which God created. The king acts as the highest servant of the God and his assistant in the project of re-establishing the ideal, i.e. the original conditions.¹⁰

The Pre-existent World Order

The central concepts in the Babylonian context are *kittum* and *mīšarum*. *Kittum* comes from Akkadian *kânu* with the basic meaning "to be solid", "to remain solid".¹¹ This meaning is also part of the translation of Hebrew כון, which also carries the meaning of (in derivative forms) "to make secure", "to establish".¹² In other Semitic languages such as Phoenician and Ugaritic the verb has the same meaning but is also used with the meaning "to create", e.g. to create the world.¹³ In other words *kittum* means what is secure, is permanent and cannot be changed, but also carries the connotation of being something that is created. When *kittum* is established it means that it is the principle which functions at the centre of the world, something that cannot be altered. When a Babylonian king issued one of his decrees with the heading that he has established *kittum*, he intends thereby to stress that he has re-established the order which is fundamental to the world. As he writes in his preface to

---

[9] The so-called Amorite dynasty which ruled Babylon from 1894 to 1595 BCE. The term "Amorite" indicates that the dynasty traces its origins to Syria and not to Mesopotamia. The most recent survey of the Amorites and their history: Burke, 2021.
[10] The most important decree we know of was issued by king Ammiṣaduqa, and was published by Kraus, 1958. Other material has been edited by F.R. Kraus, 1984.
[11] *CAD K*, 159.
[12] *HALOT*, 464.
[13] Cf. Hoftizser and Jongeling, 1995, 493, and Olmo Lete, 2004, 447. We have to add that the Hebrew verb for God's creative acts is ברא, which is generally understood as a technical expression for creation *ex nihilo*. This may not be a good choice, as God, according to Isa 45:7 using this verb, creates darkness!

his codex, Hammurabi had received his high office in order to cooperate with the gods and Babylon's Marduk to re-establish *kittum* or, perhaps better, to see to it that *kittum* was reinstalled as the *axis mundi* in a world which is everything but perfect.

Hammurabi himself was not perfect. He was a scrupulous builder of an empire who subdued most of Mesopotamia to his rule. He made it "safe with all good intentions", because when he ruled he could ensure that his message about justice and righteousness was followed in all his domains. However, inequality still prevailed in his own land. Otherwise there would have been no need of issuing more royal decrees about the manumission of slaves and the remission from debt. Such decrees were issued at intervals; mostly of less than ten years. And because humans are humans, soon new paragraphs were added to contracts that if such a decree was issued, it had no bearing on the transaction of this document. Then ensuing decrees might include a new paragraph saying that if such a paragraph was found in a document it was thereby annulled. There is nothing new under the Sun! Furthermore, we have no evidence that the tradition of issuing these kinds of liberating decrees continued after the fall of the dynasty of Hammurabi in 1595 BCE. The ideology behind them did, however, not disappear. We may say that the idea of establishing "freedom", in Akkadian *andurārum*, is, to this very day, an indispensable ingredient in our common hope for the future.

The second concept on the agenda and which is always mentioned by these decrees but also turns up in other context is *mīšarum*. The noun is a derivative from the verb *ešērum* "to be straight", which we recognize from Hebrew ישר "to be straight". This means that to establish *mīšarum* means to establish equality. We are here, then, very close to the slogan of the French Revolution: equality-brotherhood-freedom. *Mīšarum* also appears in the Hebrew words משור and מישרים with the basic meaning of "justice" an "order".[14]

We don't find משור and מישרים in the Old Testament together with *kittum*, a word with no direct equivalent in Hebrew. Instead the two words may appear in combination with משפט "sentence", "justice". Thus in Ps 99:4:

ועז מלך משפט אהב אתה כוננת מישרום

Mighty king who loves justice, you who created righteousness

---

[14] *HALOT*, 578. *The Dictionary of Classical Hebrew*, V, 264, has "righteousness", "peace", "friendship". מישרים is most likely borrowed from Akkadian including the "false" pluralis ending "-im", a misunderstanding of the Akkadian *-um*.

However already in the next line something apparently new appears:

משפט וצדקה ביעקוב אתה עשיתה

You created law and justice in Jacob

However, צדקה and מישרים are not quite the same. This can be deduced from the juxtaposition in Ps 98:9:

ישמפט תבל בצדק ועמים במישרים

He judges the earth with justice and the nations with righteousness.

צדק and צדצה may be seen as variants with the same basic meaning. These words are clear in their meaning but their juxtaposition may change the signification between משפט and מישרים. The last two words do not have precisely the same value as the two first. Thus משפט includes a practical meaning.[15] However, to be brief: God is just and he is righteous, i.e. his judgements are righteous. Here a variant seems to be embedded between the two concepts. When מישור/מישרים may be substituted by משפט we are induced to believe that the expression does not only indicate a theoretical or philosophical interpretation of "justice". Also, the practical use of the law is involved. The verb שפט does not mean "to judge" only, but also "to rule". The judge, the שפט, is certainly also the person who decides the function of the "judge" in the Book of Judges.

Συδυκ and Μισώρ and Pre-existent Justice

It is not only in the Old Testament that we find צדק and משור / מישרים combined. Philo from Byblos has, in the best Hellenistic style, a fanciful story about a divine couple Συδυκ and Μισώρ who invented the method of producing salt.[16] He has no idea of the true essence of these divinities in spite of his correct translation of Μισώρ as εὔλυτον "smooth", and Συδυκ as δικαίον, "just". Hebrew מישר can also mean "to plan something uneven", and צדק is normally translated "just". Evidently Philo is here building on an old Phoenician

---

[15] Other relevant passages include Isa 11:4; 45:19; Ps 9:9; 58:2; Prov 1:3; 2:9.
[16] PE 1.10.13–14, Attridge and Oden, 1981, 44–7.

tradition which appears on inscriptions, particularly on the Yehimilk-inscription from the 10th century BCE,[17] which ends in this way:

כמלך צדק ומלכך ישר לפן אל גבל קדשם הא

Because he was a just king and a righteous king before the holy gods of Byblos

which is another example of the combination of משור and צדק. It is by all means an established component of the Near Eastern royal titles the king was a just king irrespective of being a מלך ישר or a מלך צדיק, two recurring epithets in the titles used for the king.

If we look for these titles referring to the justice of the king in a Babylonian or Assyrian context we don't find either צדק or צדיק. The reason is simple: צדק with derivatives does not exist in Akkadian. It is substituted by *kittum* in combination with *mīšarum*; for example in connection with Esarhaddon, king of Assyria from 680 to 669 BCE. He praises himself for having "provided judgement, justice, and righteousness for his land and people": *de-en kit-te ù mi-šá-ri a-na* KUR *u ni-še*^MEŠ *šá-ra-ku*. In this context we also find references to the gods Kitti, Mīšari, and Dâni, i.e. "Justice, righteousness, and judgement". Philo's divine couple is therefore an ancient hypostasis of the idea of justice in its different versions in Western Asia.[18]

Conclusion

No doubt the concepts of justice and righteousness were a fundamental one in the ancient Near East. If there is no justice and no righteousness to govern the acts of the king, the world will dissolve into chaos. God (the gods) and their assistants, first of all the kings, constantly have to invest everything in the maintenance of justice, and if necessary, restore it. The concept of righteousness, in Akkadian, *kittum*, meaning something stable has been established once and for all, is the fundamental core of the concept. We get one step closer to a conclusion by reading an inscription found at Karatepe in Asia Minor. In this inscription the king Azitawadda writes:

---

[17] *KAI*, 4.
[18] More of this: Liverani, 1971. ET: Liverani, 2021, 61–78.

I sat on the throne of my father and made peace with all the kings and all the kings considered me their father because of my righteousness and my wisdom and my good heart.[19]

Here we find בצדקי ובחכמתי "because of my righteousness and my wisdom". Wisdom is also a concept which finds its home in this context where the principles of justice rule. Azitawadda is righteous and wise. We have a context for wisdom in a similar role in Proverbs chapter 8, in the famous passage which describes wisdom as the God's first creation before God created heaven and earth. Here both צדק (v. 8) and מישרים (v. 6) appear together with חכמה. Justice, righteous, judgement, everything is connected with wisdom. We might even say that the wisdom which, in Proverbs, is described as pre-existent (like the "word" in the Gospel of John)[20] belongs in a context that argues that the world was created as righteous. Righteousness is simply the order of the world (as maintained by Hans Heinrich Schmid in his well-known monograph from 1968).[21] The connection to חכמה confirms what has been the point of this article: that justice which governs the world and precedes everything else in the world is created by God – it is the unchangeable world of ideas (in Plato's universe). It is normally not easy to find the idea of pre-existence in the Old Testament. Predestination is an easier concept to trace. We need only think of Jeremiah, who says that he was called to be a prophet before he was born (Jer 1:4–5). God's world is pre-existent in the sense that it is wisdom, the wisdom which, according to Proverbs, inspired God when he created the world of human beings.

---

[19] *KAI*, 26, 11–13. The passage ואף באבת פעלן כל מלך here translated as "and all the kings considered me (their) father)" is much discussed, but it is of no consequence here.

[20] John 1:1 thus has an oriental background which might be just as marked as the normally assumed influence from Greek philosophy.

[21] Schmid, 1968. I will not make more use of Schmid's well-written study, mostly because he has no interest in the importance of the Mesopotamian examples, especially the use of *kittum* in contexts close to his examples from the Old Testament.

4   Messiah in the Book of Isaiah

The oratorio of Handel, *Messiah*, is heavily dependent on a series of quotes from the Book of Isaiah. The first part of the oratorio opens with the tenor reciting chapter 40:

> Comfort ye me people saith your God,
> Speak ye comfortably to Jerusalem, and
> Cry unto her that her warfare is accomplished,
> That her iniquity is pardon'd.
> The voice of him that crieth in the wilderness,
> Prepare ye the way of the Lord,
> Make straight in the desert
> A highway for our God.[1]

This is followed by an aria:

> Ev'ry valley shall be exalted,
> And ev'ry mountain and hill made low:
> The crooked straight,
> And the rough places plain.[2]

Which again is followed by a hymn sung by the chorus:

> And the glory of the Lord shall be revealed,
> and the flesh shall see it together,
> for the mouth of the Lord has spoken it.[3]

After a bass passage with quotes from Haggai and Malachi the oratorio returns to Isaiah, now quoting the famous verse Isa 7:14:

---

[1] Isa 40:1–2a.3. Handel uses, of course the KJV.
[2] Isa 40:4.
[3] Es 40:5.

> Behold, a virgin shall conceive,
> And bear a son,
> And shall call his name Immanuel,
> GOD WITH US[4].

The prophecy about the birth of Immanuel is followed by a longish sequence including a combination of quotes from Isaiah 9 that ends with the description of the birth of the Messiah (Isa 9:6):

> For unto us a child is born,
> Unto us a son is given:
> And the government shall be upon his shoulder:
> And his name shall be called
> Wonderful, Counsellor, The mighty God,
> The everlasting Father, the Prince of Peace.

The oratorio goes on with a passage using quotes from the story of the birth of Jesus in the Gospel according to St. Luke (Luk 2), only soon after to return to the Book of Isaiah to tell the story of the acts of the Messiah. The first quote is from Isa 35:5–6 be describing how the eyes of the blind shall be open and the ears of the deaf cleansed. The paralysed shall jump around and the dumb shall speak. Hereafter Isa 40:11 is quoted, where the Messiah is called the good Shepherd.

After this, the oratorio changes style and in its second part the suffering and death of the Messiah form the main subject. Here too the Book of Isaiah provides the material with several quotations from Isaiah 53:

> He was despised and rejected of men;
> A man of sorrow,
> And acquainted with grief
> Surely he hath borne our griefs,
> And carried our sorrows:
> He was wounded for our transgressions,
> He was bruised for our iniquities:
> The chastisement of our peace
> Was upon him.
> And with his stripes we are healed.

---

[4] The last line in Handel's version is not taken from Isaiah but is a translation of the name Immanuel.

> All we like sheep have gone astray;
> We have turned ev'ry one to his own way;
> And the Lord hath laid on him
> The iniquity of us all.[5]

In the remaining section of the second part of the oratorio we find no further quotes from the Book of Isaiah (except Isa 53:8). Thus we don't hear from the end of Isaiah 53 about the resurrection of the broken and lifeless servant. The description of the fate of the Messiah the oratorio quotes freely from sundry Old Testament Psalms and from the Book of Common Prayer. In the third and final part of the oratorio the Old Testament plays no role any longer – apart from a quotation from the Book of Job at the beginning (Job 19:25–26). Here it is about the future life in the kingdom of God when the trumpet sounds and the dead are restored to life. Not even the description of the kingdom of the Messiah in Isaiah 11 is found worthy to be included in this section.

It is obvious that the oratorio is following the theological fashion of its time including an exclusively Christological reading of the Old Testament. A few critical voices had arisen at this time against this way of interpreting the Old Testament. Since Spinoza, in the 17th century, occasionally critical objections had been raised not least against the idea of Moses as the author of the biblical books which are named after him. At the end of the 18th century such critical voices had prepared the breakthrough for a historical-critical reading of the Old Testament. However, in Handel's time such a breakthrough still belonged to the future.

Just like the rest of the Old Testament, the Book of Isaiah was read as a piece of writing that concentrated on the Messiah. There had hardly been any objections to the postulate that a prophet from ancient Israel who lived centuries before the birth of Christ should have predicted how Jesus was born, and how he lived and died. It is obvious that although allegorical exegesis, for the most part, had been given up, the literal reading of biblical texts, which in Protestant circles governed the day, had not (yet) led to historical analyses. Such readings only related sayings of the Old Testament to things repeated by the New Testament and in the Christian confessions.

Handel's oratorio thus follows the framework set up by the confession which refers to the birth of Jesus, his suffering and resurrection. His life, as described by the Gospels, is of little or no interest.

---

[5] Isa 53:3–6.

Taking Leave of Christology: Historical-Critical Interpretation

Towards the end of the 18th century a new view on the Old Testament appeared placing historical interpretation at the forefront. The development was prepared by, on the one hand, the insistence of Luther and the theologians following him of a literal reading of the Bible, and on the other the intellectual development during the Enlightenment and the appearance at the end of the 18th century of a critical method for the study of history which led to a rejection of the way of writing chronicles belonging to the past.[6]

A literal but still Christological interpretation of the Old Testament would understand Isa 7:14 as relating to the birth of the child Jesus. No allegorical reading wound be necessary meaning that the individual elements in the prophecy were understood to be about something else than what was plainly written: a prophecy about the birth of a child. We may say that the text was immediately intelligible, although the interpretation had to be, within certain limits, settled by the Church. These limits did not leave place for historical or critical interpretations. However, around 1800 this was exactly what happened, when the *stories of* the Old Testament became the *history* contained within the Old Testament.[7]

Or, to say it in a different way: The Old Testament was no longer understood as a book which told about the future, i.e. a book telling readers about what was going to happen in New Testament times and narrated by the New Testament. The new perspective changed this into seeing the Old Testament as referring to past events. The book lost its Christological meaning and only survived in the form of fragments in this capacity, e.g. by presenting the text to be read in churches on Good Friday (Isaiah 53). In present times we have seen endeavours to change the status of the Old Testament by incorporating more texts from the Old Testament in the liturgies of the Church. The Danish theologian Nicolai Frederik Severin Grundtvig (1783–1875) probably realized quite early the consequences of what was happening, when he declared that the Old Testament was the Book of Life, whereas he called the New Testament the Book of the Church.

The consequences for the passages from the Book of Isaiah which were formerly simply understood as prophecies about the Messiah, about his birth,

---

[6] More information about this development can be found in Lemche, 2008c, Part 1, chapter 1: "The Historical-Critical Paradigm in Its Historical Context."
[7] The story goes that young Goethe would remark, concerning the narratives of the Old Testament: "Die Geschichte sind", whereas old Goethe would say: "Die Geschichte ist".

life, and death, were considerable to put it mildly. Historical-critical analyses of the Book of Isaiah divided it into three parts, the first Isaiah – or Proto-Isaiah – whose central parts could be referred to a prophet of the name of Isaiah who lived around 700 BCE. The second part of Isaiah – also called Deutero-Isaiah – came from an anonymous prophet who lived and worked in Babylon shortly before the end of the exile in 539/539 BCE. A Norwegian "special tradition" going back to Sigmund Mowinckel will place this prophet in Judah under the exile.[8] Finally, there was also place for a third division of Isaiah called Trito-Isaiah, who was likewise an anonymous prophet who, however, was active in Jerusalem in the 5th or 4th century BCE.

The appearance of historical-critical scholarship produced a series of "doubting Thomases" who would no longer accept that a prophet living around 700 BCE should have predicted events that happened seven hundred years later than his own time – in the case of Deutero-Isaiah the lapse of time was reduced to c. five hundred and fifty years, which is not much of an improvement. As the Danish humourist Robert Storm Petersen (1882–1949) argued: "It is difficult to predict the future". It is much easier to predict what happened in the past or may happen shortly. We find a classic example of this in the text of Num 24:24 where we hear about ships from the Kittim which shall afflict Assyria. Luther saw this as a prophecy about the Roman conquest of Western Asia and thus placed the prophecy within a Christological context. Early historical-critical scholars had corrected this and saw the prophecy delivered by Balaam to be about Alexander the Great and the Macedonian conquest of the east. Num 24:24 was accordingly dated to, not before, the Macedonian conquest; i.e. before 331 BCE.[9] In this way Num 24:24 represent the genre of a *vaticinium ex eventu*, a prophecy that follows the events predicted and for that reason is much more easy to grasp.

Immanuel – Isaiah 7:14

Now it is time to have a look at the consequences the new orientation in biblical studies has had for those passages from the Book of Isaiah which Handel makes use of in his *Messiah*. And of course the obvious point of departure

---

[8] This theory goes back to Sigmund Mowinckel and was handed down by his student Arvid S. Kapelrud (Kapelrud, 1961) to Kapelrud's student Hans Barstad (cf. Barstad, 1997).
[9] More details about Num 24:24 can be found in Lemche, 2008d, 38.

has to be the famous passage in Isa 7:14 about the virgin who shall give birth to the child called Immanuel – God is with us.

It is common in translations of the Old Testament originating within the last fifty years to see the virgin transformed into a young girl. This happened in the *New English Bible*, first published in 1970, and the translation was retained in an otherwise more conservative version of it, the *Revised English Bible* from 1989. The translation "young girl" is evidently correct from a philological point of view. Hebrew עלמה does not mean "virgin" in the technical sense of the word but an unmarried young woman. The virgin was introduced into the Book of Isaiah by the Greek translators behind the Septuagint, who translated it as παρθένος, which has the technical meaning of עלמה as "virgin" – Latin *virgina* (*intacta*). The new translation created much indignation. It would be accurate to argue that a new translation such as the *New English Bible* rested not on an old tradition but on modern historical-critical scholarship.

Explanations for the change can be found in biblical commentaries; thus in the now classic German commentary published between 1965 and 1972 by the Swiss theologian Hans Wildberger.[10] In company with other modern German commentaries, Wildberger considers the prophetical saying in Isa 7:14 as a prophecy of doom directed by the historical Isaiah against King Ahaz of Judah. In Wildberger's opinion any other interpretation represents a "Verblendete exegesis".[11] In his exegetical treatment of the passage, Wildberger comments on most of the historical-critical aspects of this passage, including the way it relates to similar promises of childbirth in the Bible and the Ancient Near East. The closest is Gen 16:11, where Yahweh's angel promises to Sarah: "Behold, thou art with child, and shalt bear a son, and shalt call his name Ishmael."[12]

---

[10] Wildberger, 1965–72, 288: "Aber niemand wird doch wohl im vorliegenden *Zusammenhang* auf etwas anderes als ein Gerichtswort gefasst sein. Nur eine ganz verblendete Exegese kann in den folgende Worten etwas anderes als Drohung für Achaz sehen". This does not prevent another German commentator, Otto Kaiser, in keeping with his interpretation, to see the prophecy as having a collective meaning (Kaiser, 1963, 79–82).

[11] Wildberger 1965–72, 288: "Aber niemand wird doch wohl im vorliegenden Zusammenhang auf etwas anderes als ein Gerichtswort gefasst sein. Nur eine ganz verblendete Exegese kann in den folgende Worten etwas anderes als Drohung für Achaz sehen." This does not prevent another German commentator, Otto Kaiser, from keeping with his interpretation seeing the prophecy as having a collective meaning (Kaiser, 1963, 79–82).

[12] The second parallel mentioned by Wildberger is from Ugarit, from the Poem of Nikkal (KTU 1.24), where the following expression can be found (l. 7): *hl . ġlmt tld bn*, "See, the young girl shall bear a son"; Ugaritic *ġlmt* is linguistically the same word as Hebrew עלמה (*'almâ*).

According to Wildberger, it is impossible that Isaiah's prophecy should be directed towards anyone except a well-known woman. Many have been proposed, including that the woman must be the wife of King Ahaz. Wildberger is not totally convinced of this interpretation, which has also led to the verdict that as a prophet Isaiah was wrong in this case since the son of Ahaz was not named Immanuel but Hezekiah. However, this is explained away: Immanuel is not a name but a exclamation which interprets what the prophecy means: The woman will bear a son and see it as a sign that God is with us. Thus the prophecy may not contradict history.

Wildberger finally states – perhaps a little hesitantly – that the sign is a promise for the future. The kingdom of David will survive but Ahaz will see his kingdom sacked by the enemy.

Well, historical-critical interpretation has reduced whatever messianic content of Isa 7:14 there might have been, and has cemented it to specific historical circumstances around 734 BCE, when King Ahaz might foresee an immediate invasion by armies from Samaria and Damascus. In this situation Isaiah – according to Wildberger – delivers a prophecy which implies destruction for unbelieving Ahaz who, according to the Books of Kings, did trust that Yahweh would intervene but looked for help among the Assyrians (2 Kings 16:7), but also that against all odds Ahaz's land would survive both the threat from Samaria and Damascus and the "help" from Assur.

The prophecy about the birth of the wonder child in Isa 9:5–6, among whose attributes we find the title of Lord of Peace, miraculous advisor, and more is reinterpreted in a similar mode. According to Wildberger there can be no doubt that this prophecy is about the birth of the heir to the throne, meaning that it brings hope for the future, and this is not postponed to a late future but something that will occur very soon.[13] The content of this prophecy is permeated by royal ideology from Jerusalem and other Near Eastern royal courts. Parallels have been indicated, from Ugarit, Mesopotamia, and finally Egypt where the title "eternal father" is a royal one.[14]

In this connection we have to add that kings in western Asia did not carry the title "eternal father". This title was more probably reserved for the king's divine employer, possibly the high god El. Therefore the question is highly relevant: could the king in Jerusalem assume this title of being "eternal kings" when they, in spite of their high position, were only human and accordingly mortal servants of Yahweh? In the middle of the 20th century, the heyday of historical-critical scholarship, such questions were cleared away with the

---

[13] Wildberger, 1965–72, 376–86.
[14] Wildberger, 1965–72, 383.

postulate that such borrowings from Egypt belonged to the early part of the Hebrew monarchy when Egyptian influence at the royal court was at its strongest.[15] Since it is now more and more evident that the image of the time of David and Solomon in the Old Testament has little to do with historical realities – meaning that there hardly was a Davidic Empire in the 10th century BCE with kings ruling in mighty Jerusalem – when excavations have disclosed that Jerusalem at this time was no more than a village with perhaps up to 2000 inhabitants, if it even existed.[16] It is hardly likely that Judean "royal" language and concepts were of an Egyptian origin in those days. We will definitely have to look for another time and different circumstances to explain the presence of Egyptian court language in Isaiah 9.

In an earlier article about Psalm 2, I proposed seeing the Egyptian elements in this psalm as an indication that the psalm might be dated to the Hellenistic period where influences from Egypt might be feasible in Palestine when the Ptolemies ruled it.[17] We could possibly use the same argument in connection with Isa 9:5 prophesying the coming of the eternal father. This is, however, not a decisive argument as the title is found elsewhere in the ancient Neat East, although as part of the titles of the divine. Instead, it is probably more rewarding to discuss the dating of the passages in Isaiah to the 8th century BCE.

The Book of Isaiah as a Patchwork

In his thesis on the prophet Micah from 1987, Knud Jeppesen includes a thought-provoking chapter on the relationship between Proto-Isaiah and Deutero-Isaiah.[18] The chapter which belongs to the most important parts of the thesis is a settlement with much traditional scholarship on the Book of Isaiah and prepares for the principal thesis of the book: that the Book of Micah is made up as a "patchwork" of traditions of various origins and

---

[15] More about this in Lemche, 1993b, 63–6.
[16] Thus Mario Liverani, the author of an acclaimed history of Israel, compares David to a robber chieftain who, in the Amarna Age, roamed the mountains of Judah (Liverani, 2003, 104–9) – if there really was a historical David (cf. Liverani, 2003, 108). On Jerusalem in the 10th century cf. also Steiner, 2001, 42–53. She concludes that at the most Jerusalem in the 10th century BCE can be described as a "small fortified townlet town" (Steiner, 2001, 52). She calculates that only about 2,000 persons lived in that place at that time and adds that the number was probably much lower.
[17] Lemche, 1993b.
[18] Jeppesen, 1987, 63–84.

coming from various periods which was put together by a redactor from the time of the exile. Therefore, it is impossible to say precisely which part of the book goes back to a prophet of the name of Micah and which parts have a different origin. It is possible to present a similar working hypothesis when it comes to the two first parts of the Book of Isaiah. We cannot just presume in advance that much – not even in the first part – goes back to a historical prophet of the name of Isaiah who is supposed to have lived in Jerusalem in the 8th century BCE. We are tempted to say that the idea of a prophetic book that goes back to the 8th century BCE is no more than wishful thinking on the part of Old Testament scholars.

It has, for a long time, been accepted that the first part of the Book of Isaiah includes passages which are not only younger than the prophet himself but also younger than both Deutero-Isaiah and Trito-Isaiah. First of all, very few believe the so-called "little apocalypse" in Isaiah 24–27 is from before the late Persian period, or maybe even the Hellenistic period. It has also been the norm among Old Testament scholars to assume that the so-called "Gedenkschrift" of Isaiah, Isaiah 6–10, seemingly an autobiography, can be dated to the time of the prophet himself. However, when we return to Isa 7:14 this verse is placed in a context made up of deuteronomistic literature. The introduction to Isaiah 7 is, for the main part, identical with 2 King 16:5, where we can read about Aram's and Ephraim's (Samaria's) attack on Jerusalem in the time of King Ahaz. Deuteronomistic literature is traditionally seen as not earlier than the late period of the Kingdom of Judah. If this is the case, the verse mentioning Immanuel (from a literary point of view) is embedded in a framework which was at least a hundred years younger than the period of the prophet Isaiah. We cannot automatically assume that Isaiah himself wrote (or declamated) this message of the birth of Immanuel. It may be from him ... or just as well from somebody else.

Traditional historical-critical scholarship saw the Book of Isaiah as the result of a process of accumulation. First was Proto-Isaiah. Then the anonymous collection of prophetic writings called Deutero-Isaiah was added to First Isaiah, and finally – in the post-exilic period – Trito-Isaiah joined the two first parts. A different view on the redaction process no longer allows for a Proto-Isaiah that is much older than the second part. In reality, it is easy to imagine quite a different kind of redaction which takes Isaiah 40–55 to form a kernel which then grew both before it and after it in a series of stages where chapters 1–39 and 56–66 successively were added to the central part.

If this new model for the composition of the Book of Isaiah is correct, Deutero-Isaiah is the oldest part of the book. Most scholars even believe that it is possible to date Deutero-Isaiah quite precisely – using accepted historical-critical criteria – because King Cyrus of Persia is mentioned a couple of times as the coming saviour who shall liberate Israel from captivity (Isa 44:28; 45:1 – perhaps Isaiah 42 where Cyrus is not mentioned by name but seems to be presupposed as the one Yahweh has called from the east). Deutero-Isaiah, however, does mention Cyrus' conquest of Babylon in 539 BCE. If we accept the references to Cyrus in Deutero-Isaiah, the central part of the book may date from between 549 and 540 BCE. In 549 Cyrus freed Persia of its Median overlords and in 539 he conquered Babylon.[19]

As indicated above, most historical-critical scholars of the old school will be satisfied with this dating. We may, however, mention an alternative which would be closer to the methods of the so-called "Copenhagen School", and see the mentioning of Cyrus in Deutero-Isaiah as the result of literary considerations: Cyrus was, after his death, remembered as the king who conquered Babylon. The idea of the Babylonian exile in the Old Testament is a basic tradition. In history, but also in legend, Cyrus was the person who issued a decree of liberation and allowed the Jews to return to their homeland.[20] Seen in this light the references to Cyrus in Deutero-Isaiah may be part of this liberation legend. If this is the case, we no longer have a fixed dating for Deutero-Isaiah placing him at the end of the Babylonian exile. However, for the argumentation in this article, this problem is of little importance.

The Kingdom of God in Isaiah

Returning to Isa 7:14 and taking these elaborations into consideration, it would be proper first to analyse the prophecy about Immanuel within the framework of Proto-Isaiah, and second within the framework of the first two parts of the book.

Proto-Isaiah may broadly be divided into five sections: Isaiah 1–12 which has as its main subject the punishment of Israel and the coming of the kingdom of God; Isaiah 13–23 which for the most part is taken up by cries of woe directed against foreign nations, from Babylon to Egypt; Isaiah 24–27 which describes the end of the world and the coming of the kingdom of God; Isaiah 28–35 including cries of woe over the leaders of Samaria and Jerusalem and predicts that the kingdom to come will see the desert blossom, and finally Isaiah 36–39 which, for the most part, is identical to 2 Kings 18–20 and has

---

[19] Cf. further e.g. Lemche, 1994 and 1997.
[20] Cf. Carroll, 1998 and 2001. See also Lipschits and Blenkinsopp, 2003.

the story of Sennacherib's attack on Jerusalem in 701 BCE and the miraculous rescue of Jerusalem.

We will proceed to the content of the first section, Isaiah 1–12, which constitutes a remarkably conclusive unity. A very short paraphrase:

> Chapter 1: Headline, introductory statement: Israel is summoned to the divine court because of its disobedience: "The ox knows its owner ..." Israel is devastated. The faithful city has turned into a harlot.
>
> Chapter 2: New headline: the coming of the kingdom of God (first part): The nations are summoned to Zion from where teaching the *Torah* of Yahweh pours forth. Humans will be humiliated because of their idolatry and arrogance.
>
> Chapter 3: Yahweh will punish Jerusalem by having "children" rule it, i.e. men without wisdom. The haughty women of Zion and the men in the city shall be punished.
>
> Chapter 4: The second part about the kingdom of God: Zion shall be the place of refuge for the survivors of Israel under the protection of Yahweh.
>
> Chapter 5: The introduction is the song of the vineyard (vv. 1–7) followed by cries against those who do not listen to the teaching (*Torah*) of Yahweh. Yahweh will ask the enemies to attack Israel.
>
> Chapter 6: In a vision in the temple Isaiah is called to be a prophet. His task is described: Those who can see shall not see, and those who can hear shall not hear. Then the third part about the kingdom of God: Only a small remnant shall survive: a holy seed.
>
> Chapter 7: Foreign kings make plots against Jerusalem and Yahweh gives his answer through his prophet: Fourth passage about the kingdom of God: The birth of Immanuel, followed by another motif of punishment (the King of Assyria).
>
> Chapter 8: The son of the prophet Mahar-Shalal-Hash-Bas: "speedy plunder, hasty prey". You shall not follow the ways of this people. Isaiah seals his teaching – *Torah* – with his disciples. Those who walk in the darkness shall see light = the fifth passage about the kingdom of God.
>
> Chapter 9: Mostly a continuation of the fifth passage about the kingdom of God: The description of the Messiah – king. Samaria's punishment is announced.
>
> Chapter 10: Cries of woe over the wicked leaders. Cries of woe over the arrogant King of Assyria. The punishment over Assyria is announced. The sixth part about the kingdom of God: A remnant will

repent. The impending attack of the Assyrian army (vv. 28–32), but the majesty of Yahweh will prevail.
Chapter 11: The seventh passage about the kingdom of God: A new David shall arise and the kingdom of God become true. The people living in exile shall return.
Chapter 12: A hymn to God as saviour.

If we search for the "Leitmotif" for this first part of the Book of Isaiah we find at the forefront the nation comprising the coming kingdom of God, a kingdom which contrasts with the present evil time. The theme recurs seven times.

In desperate terms the first chapter decries the apostates who are worse than animals. An animal knows its owner! The scenario of Isaiah 1 has been compared to a trial in court where God acts both as accuser and judge.[21] Witnesses are summoned; the heavens and the earth, and the accusations against the unjust and sinful people are presented. Even God's own city has become a harlot filled with injustice. The leaders do not protect the widow and the fatherless. Therefore judgement is proclaimed over the unjust and godless, but Jerusalem and its inhabitants shall be freed.

The last-mentioned theme leads forward to the description of Yahweh's temple mount in the beginning of chapter 2. The temple mount is the unshakeable place of pilgrimage for all nations. Zion shall be the place from whence Yahweh's *Torah* emanates, when peace returns and the sword is forged into a ploughshare. The remaining part of chapter 2 has as its subject the unjust people that gloat because of their conceited greatness and richness. As a consequence it is described in chapter 3 how the leaders shall be removed and children shall take over in a process that will turn everything up and down – in the ancient Near East a sign that nothing is as it should be any more.

Chapter 4 returns to the theme of chapter 2. A remnant will live on Zion, the "holy ones, everyone in Jerusalem, written in the book of life" (Isa 4:3). The temple of Yahweh will serve as the place of refuge where the cloud during the day and the fire during the night shall be witnesses to the presence of Yahweh.

Chapter 5 returns to the previous themes of judgement. The song of the vineyard (vv. 1–7) tells the tale of the noble grapes that turned into sour grapes, another metaphor for the unnatural people we confronted in chapter one who did not know their master. This is followed by a cry of woe against

---
[21] K. Nielsen, 1978.

the greedy, the drunkards, those who curse God, those who turn from the law and think too much of themselves; in short everybody who puts themselves ahead of the *Torah* of Yahweh. By now the threats against the unbelieving people become concrete: Yahweh will send a mighty foe against his people; darkness and tribulations are waiting.

In Isaiah 6 the judgement of the many and the salvation of the few is combined when Isaiah, in connection with his call as a prophet, for his mission is told not to care about the majority of the people of God, persuading them to convert. He shall insure that the opposite will happen, that the sinful people shall not pay attention to the word of Yahweh. It is too late to convert. A major purging awaits. The land will be barren, its people led into exile, and only a fraction will remain in the land. However, in spite of the hopeless situation a promise is still there: The remnant of the people will become the holy people who, when the time comes, will assemble at Zion (cf. chapter 4) for celebration.

In Isaiah 7 it is related that Yahweh did not have to call in Ahaz's almighty foe, the king of Assyria. Ahaz, the king of Judah, can do the job himself by inviting the king of Assyria to march on God's own country. It is not that Ahaz was not warned, but as indicated in the previous chapter, Isaiah's prophecies were to be met by lack of belief. Now the people's lack of belief is illustrated by Ahaz's dismissal of support from God. When this happens and Yahweh is rejected by his own anointed king in Jerusalem, Yahweh will raise his Messiah, his anointed one, in the shape of the child Immanuel, "God is with us". Ahaz and his people will be punished by the executioner appointed by Yahweh, the king of Assyria (Isa 7:20), and his kingdom laid waste.

The mention of the king of Assyria in Isa 7:17 at the end of the passage about Immanuel (Isa 7:11–17) has often been seen as a misunderstanding. Sometimes the verse is considered an interpolation and a marginal gloss. However, the king of Assyria makes perfect sense in the context. In Isaiah 7 there are two parties or two connections. On one side we find Yahweh's prophet Isaiah, Yahweh himself, and his chosen one, Immanuel. On the other we find Ahaz, his soon to be wasted land, and Ahaz's "god" – idol –, the king of Assyria. There is a pattern in this text of Isaiah: The land and its leaders confront the looming catastrophe, and then the punishment for their rashness and injustice. This is met by the punishment understood to be a necessary cleansing preparing Yahweh's holy land to be ready to become a home for the elect few, the holy people of Israel, the people of God on Zion. The king of Assyria in Isa 7:17 has nothing to do in connection with this people of God; he is connected with Ahaz and the destruction of the land. Immanuel is fed with milk and honey. This has nothing with the destruction of the land to do although it presupposes that the destruction has taken place. Milk and honey are products of the land, so to speak, directly produced by God.

The confrontation between Immanuel and the king of Assyria is even more clear in Isaiah 8. As a contrast to Immanuel – God with us – Isaiah begets a son who gets the name Mahar-Shalal Hash-Bas, "speedy plunder, hasty prey" (Isa 8:1–4). The catastrophe was to come before Immanuel would be old enough to distinguish between good and evil; note too that it happens before Mahal-Shalal Hash-Bas can say "father" or "mother". In this passage the king of Assyria acts as Yahweh's executioner. The people rejected Yahweh; therefore they will get another god, the king of Assyria, who will flood the land like the great river. After this another prophecy follows about the salvation of the god-fearing people, while the difference between those who believe in Yahweh and the godless is explained: Those who fear God shall keep to Yahweh while the godless shall wander in darkness and curse his king and god (Isa 8:21).

For those who fear God salvation is close, and from darkness their world turns into light because the wonderful child has been born, their future ruler, the wonderful advisor, the LORD of peace (Isa 9:1–6). The new David shall govern a kingdom with eternal peace building on justice and righteousness. In this kingdom there is no space for the godless: foreign enemies had annihilated them long before the new king of David's house will rule the land.

Now the showdown with the anti-god, the king of Assyria, is waiting: "O Assyrian, the rod of my anger!" (Isa 9:5). In his arrogance the king of Assyria did not understand that he was only Yahweh's tool. He sees himself as the person who conquered the world and does not understand that he is no more than the tool of a God mightier than him. The king of Assyria shall perish devoured by Israel's holy fire. Undoubtedly the Israel ruled by the new king of the House of David is intended. There is no space for a king of Assyria who does not know his rightful place. It is so that there is no reason to fear Assyria even when its forces march on Jerusalem: Yahweh will destroy Assyria.

This section of Proto-Isaiah ends with the famous hymn to the arising of the branch from the roots of Jesse, the new David and the kingdom of peace where nobody kills (Isaiah 11). Paradise has returned, a place where animals live together peacefully and humans are thriving because the land is full of the knowledge of Yahweh, דעת את־יהוה (Isa 11:9). Everybody in exile shall return purified to Zion. Finally a *Te Deum* ends the section (Isaiah 11).

It is clear in this perspective that the prophecies in Proto-Isaiah about the birth and reign of the future king are not about the kings of Judah since early times. Judah was a society condemned and given to destruction. It is about the king of God's kingdom on earth, or more precisely it is about God's anointed, about his Messiah.

It has long been noted that the description of the society which will arise after the birth of Immanuel is not desolate and without people. Maybe a modern person will think that a diet consisting of only milk and honey being Immanuel's only food (Isa 7:15) doesn't sound like much, but that is from the perspective of a modern "cultivated" person. The saying about Immanuel's food must be compared to the following sentence which tell us how life will be in the kingdom of Immanuel: On that day a man will own a heifer and a couple of sheep, and from the milk they produce he will eat butter (Isa 7:21–22). Everybody who remains in the land shall eat butter and honey. This does not mean that the land is empty but that its inhabitants have returned to the original stage when Yahweh promised the people of Israel that he would bring them to a land full of milk and honey (Exod 3:8), full of gifts from Yahweh or the unspoiled products of nature.

This is absolutely in accordance with similar expressions in other prophetic books and in fact in the rest of the Old Testament. Here it is explained that the sojourn of the Israelites in Canaan corrupted the people. It is almost like reading Livy's talk about how the tough "sons of the desert", Hannibal's experienced veterans, became "womanized" when after the Battle of Cannae they rested for the winter in luxurious Capua. With romanticized phrases we may say that the kingdom of God represents a kind of "back to nature" understood as a cleansing process for the faithful in order for everything to return to its original state. The movement is, in the Old Testament, represented by the Rechabites, whose apical ancestor, Jehonadab Ben Rechab, assisted Jehu in his final accounting with the corrupt royal house in Samaria (2 Kings 10:15–16), and who, according to Jeremiah, renounced all the benefits of civilization and lived in tents like their forefathers (Jeremiah 35). Totally in accordance is the message in the Book of Hosea that Israel in the desert lived in the correct relationship to its God (Hos 9:10) and has to return to its original state in order to re-establish its relationship with Yahweh (Hos 12:10).

The following parts of Isaiah 1–39 do not add much to this theme, although the motifs of human ruin and the salvation of the chosen ones appear a number of times. Mostly it is about the future kingdom of the Messiah. Common for all passages in the first part of the Book of Isaiah is the statement that this kingdom is not here yet. The punishment still has to be exerted, and only when it is meted out are the survivors allowed to return to the tent of Yahweh on Zion to live there by the grace of God and benefitting from Messiah's blessed reign.

The situation is different in the second part of the Book of Isaiah. The starting point is the fulfillment of punishment, that justice has been handed out and it is time to go home. Yahweh liberates his people and guides it with

Cyrus as his herdsman. Yahweh has levelled a road through the desert and will turn his people into "a light to the nations" (Isa 49:6). Now it is time to realize the kingdom of God on earth when Yahweh concludes an eternal covenant with Israel and fulfills his promises to David (Isa 55:3). In contrast, there is not much in the third part of the Book of Isaiah that directly addresses the theme of the coming kingdom of God. We hear here a very different voice speaking. There are of course prophesies of doom directed against the infidel but already in the first passage we find an admonition to keep the Sabbath. This shows that the interests are quite different from what we found in the two first parts of the book, and that in spite of occasional allusions to themes found in Proto- and Deutero-Isaiah such as the motif of the wolf and the lamb grazing together while the lion eats straw together with the oxen (Isa 65:25), quoting from the description of the kingdom of God in Isaiah 11.

The Book of Isaiah Seen As a Narrative About the Messiah

We may, to conclude, argue that the Book of Isaiah – at least in its first two parts – can be read as one long narrative about the kingdom of God and the coming of Messiah's reign. The argumentation is perhaps neither linear nor logical in our sense. It is rather circular and repetitive, but still the logic is present: The kingdom of God is not here and now – at least not in the first part of the book: It is something that will come when the unbelievers have been punished. The future kingdom of God is mentioned seven times in Isaiah 1–12, not as something that is already here, or about to arrive tomorrow, but it will come in the fullness of time. The Messiah is not a named king from Israel's past – the only concrete thing we know is that he is a descendant of David.

It is therefore easy to understand that since the beginning of Christianity the reading of the Book of Isaiah has been Christological. The early Christians have scooped from messianic ideology the ideas about the future kingdom of God. This interpretation is obvious. However, in contrast to modern exegetes, it may be the case that it represents the correct reading of the book. Maybe these early Christians only followed the intentions of the book. The main difference was that the Messiah of Isaiah now had a name. Probably other sectors in ancient Judaism had done the same, although this does not make the Christian interpretation irrelevant or misleading, and to conclude neither is Handel's interpretation of Messiah in his oratorio.

5   Old Testament Texts as Rewritten Literature

When the discussion about the reception of biblical stories turns to the rewriting of the Bible, ancient as well as modern ideas, play a central part. Thus, most contributions to the Danish collection where also this article was first printed – in Danish – have as their subject the way biblical stories have been handled in writings from antiquity, in the Dead Sea Scrolls, especially in the Genesis Apocryphon, and in Josephus' rewriting of biblical history *in extenso*.[1] The Bible – here the very first part, the *Torah*, the Pentateuch – achieves an authoritative status and this status is transferred to its rewriting.

Rewritten biblical texts are not only how they have been rewritten in, say, Josephus' *Antiquitates* or in para-biblical literature such as the Genesis Apocryphon.[2] We are talking about an old genre belonging to the ancient Near Eastern tradition.[3] Thus the standard edition of the Babylonian Gilgamesh epic has predecessors which take us from the Sumerians in the third millennium BCE to Neo-Babylonian scribal traditions in the middle of the first millennium BCE (and beyond[4]).

One reason for this mania of rewriting stories is linked to the praxis of copying texts for pedagogical purposes. The scribal schools invested much time and energy in the copying of the canonical literature from the past.[5] In

---

[1] Cf. Høgenhaven and Müller, 2012.
[2] Text and translation: Martínez and Tigchelaar, 1997, 28–48.
[3] But certainly also to the classical tradition. We only have to think of the very free rewriting of myths in Greek plays.
[4] We have, from the Hellenistic Period, the Greek version in Berossus' Babyloniaca. The Greek original can be found here: https://www.dfhg-project.org/DFHG/digger.php?what%5B%5D=author%7CBEROSUS+CHALDAEUS&onoffswitch=on. The fragments of the text of Berossus are translated in Burstein, 1978. On the relationship between Gilgamesh and the biblical story of the Flood, cf. Gmirkin, 2006. Recent discussion of Berossus in Haubold, Lanfranchi, Rollinger, Steele, 2013, and especially about Berossus and Gilgamesh, Dalley, 2013.
[5] It is correct to talk about "canonical" in this connection, not in the biblical sense but in the meaning the word has obtained in recent times in the concept of national "canons", including literary productions seemed especially important. Making full use of the concept: Hallo, 1997.

theory every new generation of students attending these schools were handed this literature to copy it as had their predecessors. In practice this meant that every generation left its mark on the tradition. Something was added and something removed, not forgetting the language which was constantly "updated". The ancients did not pay any special attention to what was "original". It was, in a traditional society like the ancient Near East, being extremely conservative, not especially meritorious to create new narratives never heard before. So much more praise to those who were able to embellish classical narratives with new motifs and add a personal impression to the tablets. Such a practice has been described by scholars who have been working with orally transmitted poetry.[6] The same attitude to previously existing literature can also be traced in written literature: Present a well-known story belonging to tradition, but in case you feel that you have something additional to add to the story – without changing its basic meaning – add it! Naturally, as time went by, considerable changes appeared, not least when we have to do with an epic like Gilgamesh with a 2,000-year-long history of transmission.

Rewriting in the Old Testament

a) Rewritten Old Testament Texts

We may here talk about both major and minor rewritings and different techniques applied. We have, on one hand, examples of texts which have been rewritten more than once. The best-known example is the story of the wife of the patriarch in danger of being included in a foreign harem (Gen 12, 20, and 26). The first version explains how Abraham calls Sarah his sister and afterwards sells her to Pharaoh who includes her in his harem. However, Pharaoh gets a hint from God which he cannot ignore – to put it mildly – that this is very wrong. The reader may ask: What really happened while Sarah was in Pharaoh's harem? The rewriting of this story in Genesis 20 tries to explain that nothing happened. During the night God explained to the king of Gerar, the substitute for Pharaoh in the new version of the story, that Sarah was Abraham's wife and not his sister. After that Abraham explains that Sarah is actually his half-sister. He did not lie to the king of Gerar, though it seems that the narrator has just forgotten the rules in Leviticus 19 about prohibited sexual relations. It is an old example of how somebody tries to gloss over a lie by telling something that is even worse, thus making the problem even more acute. Last in the row of the rewriting of this narrative, Genesis 26, is

---

[6] Cf. e.g. Lord, 1960.

also placed in Gerar but the persons involved are Isaac and his wife Rebecca. The author behind this third version seems to have realized that something drastic had to be done in order to save the story. Therefore, he creates a scene where the king of Gerar, before anything happened, discovers how things really are between Abraham and Sarah. The result is that an originally rather offensive narrative turns into something absolutely harmless, but also into a quite uninteresting story.

We may mention other examples of such doublets in the Old Testament. A well-known example is the story of the confrontation between David and Saul in the desert when David was a refugee from Saul's court (1 Samuel 24 and 26). In both cases David has the opportunity to kill Saul but abstains in spite of the demand to do so by his followers. The first version of this episode is placed in a cavern where Saul is alone without recognizing the presence of David who was hiding in this cavern, and in the second version David enters the camp of Saul during the night. In both versions the moral is that nobody shall touch Yahweh's anointed king. Although the staging is different the main plot is the same. In this case it is not so much about "improving" the story as underscoring the importance of the moral by presenting it in two different versions.

These first two examples are about single incidents, but rewriting may be much more extensive. In Deuteronomy 1–3 we find a rewriting of the story of Israel's sojourn in the desert; a short version of the narrative which begins in the Book of Exodus and only reaches its conclusion in the book of Numbers. New elements are added to the storyline where we find the narrator informing us about his ideas about and attitudes to the previous narrative.

The most comprehensive piece of rewriting in the Old Testament includes whole books, as is the case when the Books of Chronicles represent as rewriting of the Books of Samuel and Kings.[7]

---

[7] In this connection I will pay no attention to the idea that there should be a second independent source for the Books of Chronicles, or that it is possible to see such a source as containing the primary narrative. This is, in my view, an impossible idea but relates to the "Q"-fever in New Testament studies, where the unknown "X" has been used as a kind of magic tool to explain the differences between the Gospel of Mark, considered to be the original gospel (or at least as original as possible) and the Gospels of Matthew and Luke, both adding material to Mark from this unknown source. A study of the technique of retelling stories in antiquity demonstrates that the Q-hypothesis is an unnecessary complication. There can be no doubt that Matthew and Luke have known Mark, but both evangelists also knew the other. They simply add their own ideas; but this is absolutely in accordance with procedures found in ancient literary works. As long as it is considered the same narrative the audience will have no problem when an author adds his "touch" to an existing story.

History before David is presented as genealogies. Otherwise the narrative begins when Saul dies (1 Chron 10). Hereafter the Books of Chronicles follow the chronology of Israel's history already presented by the author of Kings but takes his story a little further beyond the end of Kings, where we learn that, after the death of Nebuchadnezzar, King Jehoiachin was released from captivity to live at the royal court (2 Kings 25:27–30). Chronicles stops with the remark that Cyrus published a decree that the temple in Jerusalem should be rebuilt (2 Chron 36:22–23). In this way Chronicles directly prepares for the following narratives of Ezra and Nehemiah.

Putting aside minor discrepancies, we may argue that there are two major changes in Chronicles compared to its source in the Books of Kings. The first difference is a fundamental one: The kingdom of Israel is mostly excluded from the narrative and only appears occasionally such as when King Basha of Israel attacks Judah (2 Chronicles 16) or when we are informed about Ahab's and Jehosaphat's war against the Arameans (2 Chronicles 18). Apart from that, we never see an independent role for the kingdom of Israel in Chronicles. Without doubt we may argue that this fundamental change in Chronicles compared to the synchronistic history presented by its source is ideological in character and really represents a different view of the past. In the Books of Kings' synchronistic version, Israel and Judah move in parallel lines towards the catastrophe which, in Israel's case, occurs when the Assyrians conquer Samaria in 722 BCE. and in Judah's when Nebuchadnezzar twice conquers Jerusalem in 597 and 587 BCE. This synchronistic history is reflected by Ezekiel's prophecy of doom about the two infidel sisters Ohola and Oholiba (Ezekiel 23). But not in Chronicles, where the omission of almost every reference to the Kingdom of Israel in the Books of Kings clearly advocates a programme where there is no space for this Israel.

The second major change in Chronicles in comparison to its source includes the evaluation of individual kings of Judah such as David and Solomon and Hezekiah and Josiah. In 1 Kings it is Solomon who decides to build the temple and follows the project to its end (1 Kings 7). We already know from 2 Samuel that David was not allowed to carry the project of the new temple through to the end since we, in the prophecy of Nathan, are informed that it will only be the son of David who shall erect the house of God (2 Samuel 7).

Chronicles is absolutely in disagreement with this "arrangement". In Chronicles David makes the decision to build the temple (1 Chronicles 28). The author of Chronicles will, however, not go so far as to say – which would have been contrary to what was found in his source – that it was David who built the temple but David had, so to speak, been to "Ikea", where he "bought" all the necessary parts to build the temple. He only has to present Solomon with the plans and instructions for the temple and its paraphernalia. Solomon is no more that the "bricklayer" who put the parts together (2 Chronicles 3).

When we move on to the eulogy for Josiah in 2 Kings, which tells us that Josiah was as good as his (fore)father David because he repaired the temple and renewed its cult, bringing it back to what it used to be (2 Kings 23), Chronicles doesn't have much to say about this king Josiah, who died pathetically in a confrontation with Pharaoh after having been warned by Yahweh. Josiah had himself asked for this pitiful end by disobeying the order from Yahweh not to oppose the Egyptians (2 Chron 35:20–27). It is accepted by Chronicles that Josiah reformed the cult but Chronicles does not waste much space on it (2 Chron 34:29–33). Chronicles also mentions that Josiah celebrated Passover but the passage where this information is found mostly concerns the duties of the priests and the Levites in celebrating Passover (2 Chronicles 35).

Chronicles' description of Hezekiah is quite different. Chronicles gives him the main role as the reformer of the cult in Jerusalem (2 Chronicles 31), and says that he was the one who reintroduced the celebration of the Passover following all instructions in such a way that nobody had seen anything similar since the days of Solomon (2 Chron 35:26). In the description, Josiah's celebration of the Passover in 2 Kings it is noted "that a Passover" like this had not been celebrated as long as there were kings in Jerusalem, not since the days when the Judges ruled over Israel" (2 Kings 23:22).

The Books of Chronicles present their own programme for how to write a Jewish history, a history which in many ways can be seen as a corrective to the version found in the Books of Kings. As a rewritten version of Kings, Chronicles are in principle not different from the later rewriting represented by Josephus in his *Antiquitates* from the end of the 1st century CE. Thus, this rewriting demonstrates that the idea of rewriting the narratives present in the literary sources was not limited to the period of the canonization of biblical literature.

b) Rewriting Texts from Other Contexts than the Old Testament Itself

Rewriting in the Old Testament is not confined to the rewriting of literature which is already known from other places in the Old Testament – though we have to admit that when it happened there was no such thing as an Old Testament, only texts which would later make it into the Old Testament. We are talking about the beginning of the canonical tradition concentrating on the books of Moses, and soon also prophetic books like the Book of Isaiah. Biblical rewriting of biblical texts can therefore be compared to the rewriting of the future biblical books which we know from other ancient writings. To put it briefly: When "biblical" rewriting began, there was no Bible. When we are talking about biblical rewriting the dividing line thus goes between those examples of rewriting which found a place in the later biblical canon and those which did not make the "cut", but was excluded by, especially, the rabbis in connection with their editing of the Hebrew Bible. If anything, this process tells us that the Protestant dogma of *sola scriptura* has little historical foundation. The fixing of a tradition in writing happens within a very short time. Hereafter the tradition continues as if nothing had happened. Texts were written and rewritten through all of antiquity, and never stopped even if, as time went by, some texts received a privileged status.

The story about rewritten literature in the Old Testament does not end here. It is just as interesting that we find a series of rewritten literature in the Old Testament where we have to look for its origin not in the Old Testament but elsewhere in the ancient Near East. Some of these examples are more obvious than others but sometimes the similarity between a biblical and a Near Eastern text is striking. Here three examples, of a quite different character, with be used to illustrate how biblical authors rewrote foreign texts. The first example will be the story of Joseph and the wife of Potiphar, the second the case of Sennacherib's attack on Jerusalem, and the third involves the story of the Flood as rewritten Gilgamesh.

Excursus: Do We Have Rewritten Greek literature and Greek Mythological Narratives in the Old Testament?

It has become common among scholars to argue that it is a mistake to reduce the selection of rewritten texts to Near Eastern stories and traditions. They argue that it is just as likely that themes borrowed from classical antiquity appear in biblical rewritings. This has to do with the modern late dating of large parts of biblical literature to the late Persian or the Hellenistic periods. This author has to admit that he carries a lot of guilt here because of a lecture given at the University of Copenhagen in 1991, later published both in Danish and English.[8] A hundred years ago people were talking about a "Pan-Babylonism" in biblical studies; today this seems to be changing into a "Pan-Hellenism". An upcoming study by the Belgian scholar Philippe Wajdenbaum shows how extensive the

---

[8] Cf. Lemche, 1993a. The Danish original was published as Lemche, 1992a.

> dependence in the Old Testament on the Greco-Hellenistic tradition is.[9] We find a primary example of the embedding of a Greek tradition in the Old Testament in the note about the giants in Gen 6:1–4. Giants, a translation of Hebrew נפלים, really means "the fallen ones", from the well-known root נפל, but it has been the custom since antiquity to translate it as "giants", in the Septuagint γίγαντες. In Greek traditions the fallen gods are the titans who were thrown down into Tartarus. The rewriting of Genesis in the Book of Jubilees tells us that this was already, in antiquity, the understanding of Gen 6:1–4. Here the giants are called "angels". In Ezekiel 28 we find an echo of the Greek myth of the titans in the description of the fate of the king of Tyre.

It has, for many years, been a well-known fact that the story of Joseph is full of reminiscences of Egypt and that is no reason for surprise. After all, the story of Joseph is mainly situated in Egypt and as the Canadian Egyptologist Donald B. Redford pointed out years ago that this also includes elements which belong to the Saite Period in the middle of the 1st millennium BCE.[10] It should therefore not be surprising if the story of Joseph displays a series of traits belonging to Egyptian tradition. The best-known example of this is the Egyptian story of the two brothers Anubis and Bata.[11] Bata, the youngest brother, lives in the house belonging to his brother and his wife. Everything is sheer happiness until the day when Anubis asks his brother to go back to the house to fetch some seed and Anubis' wife asks Bata to sleep with her. Bata refuses but promises not to say anything but Anubis' wife accuses him of an attempted rape with the result that Bata has to flee from his brother's house. Anubis then sets out to persecute him. Many things happen but the most important is that Bata somehow succeeds in persuading his brother to believe that the accusation is false and that Anubis wife is the real scoundrel. Consequently, Anubis kills his wife.

Without saying that the story of Joseph and the wife of Potiphar slavishly follows the Egyptian narrative, the plot is very similar in the two stories.[12] The Egyptian version is preserved in a text dating from the 19th dynasty, i.e. c. 1200 BCE. In the shape we know it, the Egyptian narrative cannot be the direct source for the biblical story of Joseph and the wife of Potiphar. However,

---

[9] Philippe Wajdenbaum's thesis has since this article was first published materialized: Wajdenbaum, 2011.
[10] Redford, 1970.
[11] Translations in *ANET* 1950, 23–5, and in Hallo, 1997, 85–9.
[12] Hans Jørgen Lundager Jensen mentions that versions of this story are also known from Greece and India and more places (Jensen, 1998). This is undoubtedly correct but does not take away the Egyptian "touch" from the Joseph story.

the actions of both stories, the biblical and the Egyptian are so similar that the author of the Joseph story in Genesis 39 presents his version of a narrative which existed in Egypt in his time.[13] But because of the lapse of time between the two versions as we know them it is difficult to describe how far the biblical author reformulated his Egyptian source. There are too many unknown factors.

The second example of biblical rewritings of foreign texts is easier to handle. It is about the rewriting of 2 Kings 18–19 of the Assyrian record of Sennacherib's campaign to the west in 701 BCE. I have previously discussed differences and similarities between the Assyrian annals and their version of Sennacherib's siege of Jerusalem and the narrative in the Old Testament, which represents a very "extensive" rewriting of the Assyrian primary source (dating from shortly after the event itself). For that reason, there is no need for an extensive discussion here.[14]

The text of the Assyrian annals reports rather prosaically that Sennacherib led his army to the land of Ḫatti, i.e. Syria, and when he reached Hezekiah's kingdom, he made short process of it, saying that he destroyed it from one end to the other. He closed Hezekiah up like "a bird in a cage". Hezekiah surrendered and had to pay a heavy tribute. After the conclusion of this deal, Sennacherib returned to Nineveh. We find a short version of these events in 2 Kings 18:13–16, but there are some exceptions which make the tribute placed on Hezekiah less severe. Thus, Hezekiah's daughters are not handed over to the Assyrian king as written in the Assyrian report. By and large we may consider the version in 2 Kings 18:13–16 to be a shortened rewriting of the Assyrian text which shows that the biblical writer must have had personal knowledge of the Assyrian annals in some form or the other. However, hereafter the biblical writer is on his own and supplements direct rewriting with free fantasy, stating at the end that the angel of the LORD killed all of Sennacherib's army, in total 185,000 men (2 Kings 19:35). This should indicate to Sennacherib that it was time for him to return home!

The Story of the Flood as Rewritten Gilgamesh

Finally, we have the clearest example of rewriting in the Old Testament of a narrative from the ancient Near East; the story of the Flood in Genesis 6–8 which in the main follows the Babylonian version found on the 11th tablet of

---

[13] Cf. Lemche, 1999a.
[14] The Assyrian text (with translation) is easily available in Luckenbill, 1924.

the *Epic of Gilgamesh*. This epic is easily accessible in numerous translations. For the Danish original of this article, I used the Danish translation of Ulla and Aage Westenholz, but my choice here would be Stephanie Dalley's well-known translation from 1989.[15] I have, however, often told my students that if they really want to appreciate the similarities, they have to read the epic in its native language, Akkadian (as a matter of fact, several of them did). Then there will be little doubt of the basic similarity between the two versions of the story of the Flood. The events follow in the same order and even the basic details and the mood of the story are the same. We might say that the biblical and the Mesopotamian versions both belong to the same mental universe.

The Stories of the Flood

In his very comprehensive commentary on Genesis, Claus Westermann presents a scheme which presents the content of these stories, which have been found in many places around the world.[16] He breaks the narrative down into a series of elements and argues that versions coming from a high culture always include all elements while those from more primitive civilizations generally have a simpler structure.

According to his analysis a Flood story from a high culture includes the following elements:

a God or the gods decides to annihilate humanity.
b A contra-decision is made to preserve humanity.
c This contra-decision is effectuated: The coming of the Flood is revealed to a chosen one who is ordered to build a ship for rescue.
d The decision to annihilate humanity is put into effect: The Flood comes over the earth.
e The consequences of the Flood.
f The contra-decision is put to work: The Flood comes to an end when the chosen one discovers by sending out (birds) and discovering that the land is dry.
g The ship is abandoned and its inmates move out onto the dry land.
h The surviving offers a thanksgiving to God/the gods.
i God or the gods decide to spare humanity.
j The chosen one obtains a special status and is moved away to live among the gods.

---

[15] Cf. Westenholz and Westenholz, 1997. Here I use the translation in Dalley, 1989.
[16] Westermann, 1974, pp. 536–46.

Following his evolutionistic view on the development of the narrative, Westermann reckons three elements as the central ones; the coming of the Flood, the rescue from the flood, and the end of the Flood. He, at the same time, admits that some other themes can be found in more primitive versions.

When we compare the two version in Gilgamesh and in Genesis, we first have to make a decision as to the context in which they came into being, which is that they both originated in high cultures. Neither of them comes from a primitive society – to use the now obsolete terminology applied by Westermann.[17]

The Mesopotamian Tradition of the Flood

Before we make a direct comparison of the biblical and the Babylonian versions, we have to take a number of conditions into consideration which makes a comparison more complicated. I already mentioned the long tradition history of the *Epic of Gilgamesh*. The origins are unknown but we may suppose that there was more than one Sumerian source for it, thus a direct Sumerian master for the story of the Flood which was presented and translated by the legendary Samuel Noah Kramer in a popular work on the Sumerians which was translated into several languages including Danish.[18] According to Miguel Civil the Sumerian version is preserved in a copy from the Old Babylonian Period, i.e. from the first half of the 2nd millennium BCE, but the presumed original can be dated to c. 2000 BCE. It is, however, not totally clear if the tradition of Gilgamesh was already then combined with the tradition of the Flood. Civil is rather reluctant to accept this possibility and it is confirmed by the oldest Babylonian tradition where the "authoritative" version of the story of Flood is presented independently of the *Epic of Gilgamesh* in the form of the epic *Atraḫasis*.[19] The official version of this poem

---

[17] Nowadays the term "primitive society" and " primitive culture" have been substituted by "traditional society" and "traditional culture" realizing what we have learned from social anthropologists that so-called primitive societies may be very complicated and their traditions far from primitive. The real difference is between societies living according to tradition and societies impelled by change (like western societies in modern times). All societies in ancient times can be classified as traditional. Even in Rome it was definitely not a virtue to propose changes which were not based on tradition.

[18] Kramer, 1956. Here I use the Danish edition Kramer, 1958, 141–6. With Kramer's usual sense for the sensational, the chapter has the title "A Deluge: The First 'Noah'". An updated edition can be found in Civil, 1969).

[19] A first-class edition of this poem: Lambert and Millard, 1969. The hero of the flood has, in Babylonian tradition, more names than one. In the Sumerian version his name is

is from the time of King Ammiṣaduqa (Beginning of the 17th century BCE). We even know the name of the scribe (if not the author) who made the copy, Ku-Aya, but after him the epic was copied many times. Thus, we have a number of Assyrian copies of the text.

That the story of the Flood is a secondary intruder into the Gilgamesh tradition becomes clear when we look at the way it appears in the main preserved version of the epic, the one from Neo-Babylonian times. The story has no part in the plot of the epic but appears as a main ingredient of the story told to Gilgamesh by Utnapishtim the Babylonian "Noah". This happens at the island of the blessed where Utnapishtim was placed by the gods after the end of the Flood, when he tells Gilgamesh stories from the past. Utnapishtim plays no active role in the epic but the story of his experiences during the Flood is simply intended to fill out the empty space of Gilgamesh's visit to the world of the blessed. The author simply quotes from his tradition and incorporates the story of the Flood in his comprehensive epic.

When we return below to the comparison between the biblical and Babylonian versions of the story of the Flood it is important to see which Babylonian version is closest to the biblical version.

Atraḫasis

When we start with the Mesopotamian versions, large parts of Atraḫasis have been preserved. Sadly, several lacunas cause gaps which prevent us from deciding with certainty if all the parts supposed to be present in a version from a high culture are present in this version, although it seems that most of them are there.

Atraḫasis is much more than a narrative which has the Flood as its main subject. The epic opens with a long passage about the dawn of time when the gods were humans – *inuma ilum awilum* – a metaphor which indicates that the gods were forced to act like humans, till the earth and dig canals and everything else which is normally the task of humankind to perform. When finally the gods had enough of this they summoned Enlil, the head of the gods, to a meeting and threatened him in his palace.[20] The confrontation lead to a

---

Ziusudra, in the Epic of Atraḫasis, Atraḫasis, and in the *Epic of Gilgamesh*, Utnapishtim. In the Hellenistic version as preserved (in fragments) in Berossus, his name is still Xisustros or Sisithros depending on the manuscript. The fragments have been translated in Lambert and Millard, 1969, 235–6.

[20] The translation from Gilgamesh used here is from Dalley, 1989.

negotiation that ended with an agreement: One god was slaughtered and his blood mixed with clay, and in this way humans were created, who could carry out the hard work instead of the gods.

The epic continues with the information that after two hundred years humans have become so numerous that they are disturbing the gods. The gods first try to solve the problem together with Enlil by sending hunger against them, but when this is not enough, they decide to destroy humanity in a flood. The wise Atraḫasis who "speaks with his god and whose god speaks with him", obtains information in a dream sent from his god Enki about what was going to happen. He is also instructed to build a vessel and bring his family into safety. The flood comes like a howling storm and humanity perishes in the water but Atraḫasis sets sail and sails away.

Here, alas, the text breaks off and a lacuna prevents us from following the way in which the flood recedes from earth. When we have text again we are present when Atraḫasis prepares an offering to the gods who assemble around the offering like flies. The narrative ends with a brawl between the gods about what had happened, and about who was responsible for the catastrophe. The gods also discuss what to do in the future with humans when they become too many, and the epic ends with a postscriptum: *abuba ana kulla niši uzammer simea*, "I have song about the flood for all people: Listen".

Gilgamesh

The second of the two best-known major Mesopotamian stories of the Flood, the one preserved on the eleventh tablet of the *Epic of Gilgamesh*, is much shorter than the preserved parts of Atraḫasis, in accordance with the secondary role of this story in the comprehensive *Epic of Gilgamesh* where the focus has been placed on many other things, especially because the story of the Flood has little to contribute to the storyline of Gilgamesh. In spite of its brevity this version of the story of the Flood includes all the elements presented by Westermann as belonging to the story as told in high cultures. Especially the introduction has been shortened in comparison to the Atraḫasis epic, and the reference to the anger of the gods because of their hard labours and their rebellion against Enlil have been excluded. Utnapishtim goes directly to the essential part and tells us about the decision made by Enlil and the other gods to wipe the human race from earth. The contra-decision, to spare humans, is here entrusted to the wise Ea – in Atraḫasis the god's name was Enki – who bypasses Enlil's order and gives information of the coming flood to a reed hut where Unapishtim happens to stay:

kikkiš kikkiš igar igar
kikkišu šimema igaru ḫissaš
šuruppaku mar Ubara-Tutu
uqur bīt bini eleppu (ll. 11–24)

Reed hut, reed hut, brick wall, brick wall,
Listen, reed hut, and pay attention, brick-wall:
Man of Shuruppak, son of Ugara-Tutu,
Dismantle your house, build a boat.

After this comes a section describing the building of the boat and explaining how he persuades the inhabitants of his city into believing that he must leave on the boat because Enlil has become his friend. The boat is enormous:

On the fifth day I laid down her form
One acre was her circumference, ten poles each,
The height of her walls.
Her top edge was likewise ten poles all round.
I laid down her structure, drew it out,
Gave her six decks,
Divided her into seven.
Her middle I divided into nine (ll. 57–62).[21]

After having built the boat, Utnapishtim let it be filled with passengers and provisions, and sails away while the gods bring the flood over the earth. The storm rages for seven days, and when Utnapishtim looks out from his boat after the storm has subsided all human beings have turned into clay, meaning that they are dead and the "countryside is flat like the roof on the house" (l. 135). The ship is stranded on Mount Nimush[22] and remains there for six days. On the seventh day Utnapishtim sends the first bird out, a dove, but it comes back, then a second, a swallow, but also this bird returns, and finally the third bird, a raven.

---

[21] The interpretation of the passage is not unchallenged and variants are found from one translation to the next. It has also been suggested that there may be some minor lacunas in the text.

[22] Or Nisir, as was common in earlier translations. The cuneiform sign for *muš* also carries the value of *sir*. Traditionally, the mountain is supposed to be part of the Zagros range.

Now everyone leaves the boat and brings an offering to the gods who assemble around it like flies – a line which is directly lifted from the more complete version in the Atraḫasis epic. The story ends with a quarrel between the gods who attack Enlil: In the future every person must suffer for his own crimes. Humanity shall never be annihilated again. The store ends with Utnapishtim's deification. He is removed from this world in order to live forever at the fringe of the world.

There are a series of divergences between the version of the Flood found in Gilgamesh and that of the Epic of Atraḫasis. The most obvious difference is that the person speaking in Gilgamesh is in the first person. After all it is the hero of the Flood who himself tells the story. Seemingly it was not important in Mesopotamian tradition that the main character appears in the first or in the third person. Thus, we have found a fragment of Atraḫasis at Ugarit where it is Atraḫasis who tells the story in the first person.[23] When the biblical version of the story is kept in the third person it is not an important deviation from the narrative as we have it in Gilgamesh. The reason may be only a choice which the author of the Genesis version made just as older Mesopotamian colleagues had made their own choices.

The Biblical Story of the Flood

When we come to compare the biblical and the Mesopotamian stories of the Flood we have to realize that there is more than one version of the Mesopotamian narrative, but also that Atraḫasis' version is much longer – or at least was when the tablets existed in their totality – than the one included in the *Epic of Gilgamesh*. However, in spite of being much shorter there can be no doubt that it is the same narrative with the same structural elements as Atraḫasis. Still, we have two Babylonian versions to include in the comparison

However, also to be taken into consideration is the fact that we have not only one but at least two versions of the Flood story present in the Book of Genesis. The two different versions have been joined by an editor in a perhaps harsh manner, not in the form of a rewritten story where one version substitutes the other, but where one version has been, so to speak, pressed down on the other. Furthermore, the chronology presented in the present version of the flood in the Bible reveals that this kind of blending of two previous stories represents an intended combination of two originally independent stories; such that the people responsible for this narrative mixture simply added a

---

[23] The text to be found in Lambert and Millard, 1969, 131–3.

third chronological system which tries to unite the very different systems of the previous two narratives.

Traditionally, biblical scholarship worked with the presence of two written sources or documents in the story of the Flood in Genesis 6–8, respectively the Yahwistic and the Priestly documents. When the two documents were joined it happened in such a way that the Priestly version was preserved in its entirety while some parts belonging to the Yahwistic source went missing, most notably the description of how Noah constructed the ark.[24] Apart from that, the individual parts from both sources have been joined in such a fashion that we find a series of doublets as the narrative proceeds. One such doublet has to do with the number of animals brought into the ark. The Yahwist allows for seven pairs of clean animals but only one pair of the unclean ones. The Priestly version only allows for one pair of both clean and unclean animals. The obvious explanation for this discrepancy is that since the Priestly narrative does not reckon with bloody offerings before the theophany at Sinai, there is no need for more than one pair of the clean animals. The Yahwist evidently had another view on this point.

The differences between the two versions become clear when we move on to the chronological information in Genesis 6–8. The Yahwist uses a chronological system consisting of intervals of seven or forty days, two numbers with a specific narrative value,[25] while the Priestly version structures the narrative according to precise dates and time intervals. Thus, Noah is six hundred years old when the flood begins (Gen 6:7), and it reaches its climax after a rain that lasted for one hundred and fifty days on the seventeenth day of the seventh month. Hereafter the water recedes and on the first day of the tenth month the top of the mountains became visible. The first day of the year when Noah turns six hundred and one years old the earth is dry (Gen 8:13). The priestly version thus operates with fixed dates and obviously has a very different interest from the purely narrative one of the Yahwist.

Evidently there are also a series of dates which an editor has tried to reconcile obviously contradicting information in the two principal versions. These are the so-called skewed dates such as the seventeenth of the second month (Gen 7:11) when the flood begins, and the twenty-seventh of the second month in the year 601 (Gen 8:14). The first one, the seventeenth of the second month, may have to do with the time it took Noah to build his ark. Nothing is preserved about this in the Yahwistic version. The whole episode begins in the year 600, most likely understood to be the very beginning of

---

[24] A synoptic table of the two versions can be found in Lemche, 2008c, 48–52.
[25] See more about this in Lemche, 2001b.

that fateful year. The narrative comes to an end precisely one year later, on the first day of the first month, 601. So how long did it take Noah to build his ark? Most likely forty days. Then he used an additional seven days to prepare for his travels. Accordingly, the whole affair begins on the 17th day in the second month and not on the first day in the first month. We may thus assume that when the Yahwist version was overwritten by the editor, the Yahwist's story of the building of the ark was still present as a part of the narrative. This was, at a later stage, removed as redundant.

The flood ends on the twenty-seventh of the second month in Noah's 601st year (Gen 8:14). However, this information is meaningless as we already have this information from before; i.e., that it ended with the dry earth on the 1st day of the first month in year 601. Why do we have this oblique date? If we calculate one year from the date of the arrival of the flood on the seventeenth of the second month we reach the seventeenth day of the second month 601. Why then the additional ten days? Now the question is: Do we here reckon in solar or lunar years? A solar year is ten days longer than a lunar year. We can only guess what kind of speculations may lie behind the movement of the end of the flood from the seventieth day of the second month to the twenty-seventh day of the second month, but it may be that the person who was responsible for the third chronological system believed that the information in the priestly version followed the solar year, and therefore he moved the end date of the flood ten days to accommodate the additional ten days of the solar year. But why not just leave it as it is? As long as the difference is only on paper, it is immaterial. But if some religious (most likely ritual) concerns are involved, this might have been important. But basically, we don't know.[26]

There is one more element to discuss, especially because scholars have generally not been aware of its existence. Apart from the chronological differences the Yahwist and the Priestly versions of the story of the flood are basically identical. The only feasible explanation is that the Priestly version represents a rewriting of the Yahwistic one. Somehow it must have come into being as an alternative to the Yahwistic story. However, then some unknown editor choose to mould the two stories into one, probably as part of some deliberations relating to the composition of the Primeval History, Genesis 1–11. From a narrative point of view it would have been a catastrophe to let the two versions of the flood story follow each other. The mixed character of the biblical narrative complicates the comparison between the biblical story of the flood and the Babylonian ones, since we have to reckon with the Yahwist rewriting a Babylonian version. At the next stage the Yahwist version was

---

[26] More in Lemche, 2001b, pp. 39–9.

rewritten by the priestly narrator. It is now pertinent to open the comparison with a confrontation of the priestly version with a Babylonian one, since we cannot exclude but should rather expect that the priestly writer in his rewriting of the Yahwistic version had an eye on some Babylonian version.

Babylonian and Biblical Stories of the Flood

When we compare the two traditions of the flood, the biblical and the Mesopotamian, we have as our point of departure the fact that both versions of the flood in the epics of Atraḫasis and Gilgamesh belong to a common tradition which seems to have been relatively stable. The divergence between them is that one is in the first person (Gilgamesh) while the other (Atraḫasis) is in the third. This has been explained above. Evidently the narrator was not bound by a fixed tradition. Besides, it is interesting that the rewritten story of the flood in the Genesis Apocryphon from Qumran uses the first person. Not much is left of the story of the flood in the fragments preserved from Qumran but there is enough to show that it is Noah who tells the story.

Just like the Babylonian versions of the story of the flood, the biblical narrative closely follows the scheme presented by Westermann. The first point was the decision to annihilate humanity. The biblical version accordingly opens with Yahweh's decision to destroy humanity because of its wickedness (Gen 6:5–7). The priestly writer follows this in a rather elegant way by letting God announce his contra-decision that he will not destroy humanity, a decision which is announced to Noah who is ordered to build the ark (Gen 6:11–14).

If we move to the Mesopotamian versions we find in Utnapishtim's narrative no reason given for the decision to destroy humankind. In contrast, this part takes up a lot of space in the Epic of Atraḫasis. Here the cause is not the wickedness of humanity as in Genesis but simply that there are too many humans on earth, which irritates the gods because of all the noise. It seems like a rather superficial excuse for destruction; maybe there is an implicit reason behind it? When we look at the aftermath, the debacle among the gods during which they try to place the responsibility for the catastrophe on humanity, it seems that the poems are more about righteousness and punishment. Maybe the talk about the annoying and talkative humans is hinting at a motif present among the humans: They intend to be gods to replace the gods, a theme not far away from the one behind the story of the tower of Babel (Genesis 11).

The contra-decision to spare humanity by choosing one person is present in the Mesopotamian as well as in the biblical versions of the story. The priestly story in Genesis is the closest to the Mesopotamian narratives, which stress the connection between the hero of the flood and the deity who informs him of the coming flood. Noah was righteous and walked with God (Gen 6:9). The Yahwist only mentions Yahweh's graciousness (Gen 8:8).

The next part, which is about how the divine decision to destroy humankind is revealed to the hero, both in the Mesopotamian versions and the priestly narrative in the Bible in connection with an instruction to build a ship that can save the hero and his family together with the animals. It is therefore doubtful if Westermann is right when he separates the two parts, one about the contra-decision and the second about the building the ship. The connection between the revelation of the coming flood and the building of the ship is self-evident. While the biblical version seemingly accepts that one and the same god can decide both to destroy mankind and to save it – bringing an ironical touch to the narrative and certainly a logical one – is easier for the Mesopotamian writers. They have a luxury-problem: All these gods are clamouring around. This clearly shows that the story has its origin in a polytheistic environment, and it is in such a context easy to play one god against another. By contrast, the biblical God seems rather indecisive; causing a flood without really understanding the implications. Somehow the biblical writers may have been forced to include the story because of tradition: Writing the history of the early world simply meant that a story of the flood that almost annihilated humankind had to be included.

In the *Epic of Gilgamesh*, the ark or ship is formed like a cube; it is the same length on all sides and height. In some aspects Noah's ark resembles the Gilgamesh one but is longer and broader, but it is not as high. However, the interest in the details is the same in both versions. The Mesopotamian versions invest more in describing what should be brought into the ship. They thus describe how supplies are brought to the ship and stowed. Utnapishtim also mentions the carpenters whom he very wisely includes in his crew. The content of this part seems to have been rather stable in the various traditions.

A special aspect of the Mesopotamian tradition is the story of how the hero of the flood cheats his fellow humans in order that they would let him sail away before the flood. In the biblical version the ark only gets afloat when the rising waters are lifting it up (Gen 7:18). This is in accordance with the attitude of the biblical writers: After God has ascertained that the human race is wicked all people are without interest except the just Noah. We only read that everybody else died in the waters of the flood (Gen 7:21–22). The launching of the ship is common to all versions but we have to say in very different ways.

I have already discussed the span of time in the narrative which plays no role in Westermann's commentary, and have discussed the different forms of time used in the Yahwistic version and in the Priestly. In Gilgamesh, we find a use of time indicators which resemble the ones in the Yahwistic version. Like the Yahwist, the author of the *Epic of Gilgamesh* prefers time intervals of seven days. Thus, in Gilgamesh the storm and rain last for seven days and seven nights, and the ship is stranded on Mount Nimush for seven days before Utnapishtim sends the first bird away. This is absolutely logical: It rains for seven days and the waters rise, and the waters recede for another seven days before the earth is dry. The Yahwist operates with a period of forty days for the waters to rise (Gen 7:12–17). The agreement between the period of the rising waters and the period of the receding waters are kept in the Yahwistic version, although somewhat blurred because of the priestly rewriting. In the Yahwistic version, the time interval from the flood at its peak, when the waters begin to recede, and the moment when Noah sends out the dove for the first time is another forty days (Gen 8:6). The Yahwist and Utnapishtim mention different numbers, Utnapishtim seven, the Yahwist forty, but both numbers are numbers with a narrative meaning. They are not normal indications of time.

The consequences of the flood which Westermann includes on his list as the next point are described in a few words. All humans die, turned into clay (Gilgamesh). After this the next point is of vital importance: the end of the flood and the way it is realized that the waters have receded from the surface of the earth. Utnapishtim successively releases three birds. First he sends out a dove which does return, and as the second bird a swallow, which also returns. Finally he sends out a raven, which does not return. Noah also releases a raven that does not come back to him. Then he three times releases a dove. The biblical story is very precise in relating that the birds were sent out in intervals of seven days. This part is missing in Utnapishtim's story where it could just as well be that everything happened in one and the same day, although it is a fair assumption that also the Mesopotamian story operates with intervals of some length. These intervals are not mentioned because it was found unnecessary to include the information.

Perhaps the most interesting similarity and at the same time dissimilarity between Utnapishtim's story and the biblical version has to do with the releases of the birds. The Babylonian tradition seems rather persistent here, although it is not present in the Epic of Atraḫasis. As was already mentioned, this section is missing in Atraḫasis because of a major lacuna. The poem only returns when the hero is preparing his offer of thanks. However, when we read Berossus' rewriting of the Babylonian tradition of the flood, we again find the three birds mentioned. Berossus is not very specific but only mentions that three birds are released. Three birds should be enough and follows the conventions of traditional literature. However, in Genesis we find four releases of birds. This is definitely one too many, and it is not difficult to point out which bird is superfluous. This is of course the raven, which Noah releases first. It does not come back but flies around seemingly for weeks until everything is over. What role does the raven play in the biblical narrative?

Well, "and he sent forth a raven which went forth to and fro, until the waters were dried up from off the earth" (Gen 8:7). This is not far off from what we read in Gilgamesh: "The raven went out and saw the waters receding. It ate and preened, lifted its tail and did not turn round" (Gilgamesh XI:154–55). However, back to the question: What did the raven have to do with the biblical story? According to the Bible the raven is a dirty bird, unclean, and should not be the bird which is allowed to find the earth dry again. It is, on the other hand, included, even if it is a surplus number in relation to the three birds (or the three sending), which are normally a part of the story. The mention of the raven in the Yahwistic version of the story – the priestly version doesn't mention it – is to be considered an intertextual reference to the role of the raven in Babylonian tradition, most likely as we find it in the *Epic of Gilgamesh*, or a version which is close to it. When we consider the popularity of the *Epic of Gilgamesh* in the ancient Near East we are perhaps entitled to say that the Yahwist is referring to Gilgamesh: "See", he tells us, "I know the *Epic of Gilgamesh* but have a better story to tell. It is not up to the raven to discover the new world after the flood!"

The final sections in the narrative are about the ark and how it is emptied of people and animals, and the sacrifice and the elevation of the hero of the flood. Exegetes have, for a long time, found a reminiscence from the Mesopotamian hint at the gods who assembled around the sacrifice as flies, substituted with the more tasteful: "And the LORD smelled a sweet flavor…" The biblical narrator is, on the other hand, very particular about the fate of the hero and makes it clear that Noah died like everyone else, although nine hundred and fifty years old. But the biblical hero of the flood is not elevated to live among the gods (Gen 9:29), although we may speculate about the meaning of the note that Noah, before the flood, "walked with God" (Gen 6:9). The same phrase was used previously about Enoch who didn't die but was taken by God himself (Gen 5:24).

Summing up, we may say that the story of the flood in Genesis 6–8 is not a slavish rewriting of a Mesopotamian source. The narrative is quite free in comparison and only makes it clear once where to look for its source, when the absolutely superfluous raven is mentioned breaking the usual symmetry of the sending out of three birds. Rewriting in the Old Testament didn't mean that source material was just copied and presented with a new "coating". This is important to stress because much production of literature in the ancient

Near East involved a lot of copying. This is important to stress because copying was the only means to reproduce written literature. Copies were not always just a slavish repetition of what was found in the written text which was copied, but included such changes as were made necessary because of the language employed and changing geographical circumstances. This happened, for example, when Babylonian texts were copied in an Assyrian environment and the high god for that reason had to change his name from Marduk to Assur. This is, however, not relevant here since neither Marduk nor Assur play any role in the story of the flood.

Apart from copies, there existed a literature where freedom in comparison to the original was the rule of the day. We may recognize this from copies which were quite free in their relation to their sources. In relation to the biblical story of the flood such changes were made absolutely necessary because of a changing idea of the divine. Now a single deity has to carry the burden of the plot while in Mesopotamia it could be divided between various gods. As a consequence we may argue that the biblical story of the flood became quite meaningless. God wipes out his creatures because they have become wicked but when it is all over God only has to ascertain that the flood was of no help. The flood, accordingly, may seem meaningless. So, what is God doing? Maybe he is just learning what it would mean to be a god? The second time we hear about a flood, he seems better prepared. This time it is not a flood of water but a flood of sulphur and fire raining from heaven (Gen 19:24). Before it happens God had been negotiating with Abraham as Abraham asked God whether he would destroy righteous people together with the unjust which God denies but there are not even ten righteous persons in Sodom which is destroyed as it deserves, but the single righteous person there, Lot, is saved from destruction.

The flood is about collective punishment but was a fiasco not to be repeated. This is exactly the point in Utnapishtim's version of the flood story. After it ended. the gods meet to discuss what happened, and the gods are most unhappy with the decision to destroy humankind. Ea simply asks Enlil: "How could you be so rash since your thoughtlessness brought upon the earth a flood?" And he continues:

> Punish the sinner for his sin, punish the criminal for his crime,
> But ease off, let work not cease, be patient, let not …

Collective punishment never leads to something positive. Every human being is responsible for his or her own acts. It is meaningless to wipe out everyone.

This was a maxim which, in a culture so fixated on the principle of justice, really earned its own narrative: Every person is responsible for his own acts. The biblical story has this as its main theme, which is only indirectly clear from the story of the flood in Genesis 6–8 but it is absolutely clear from the second flood story which follows in Genesis 18–19.

6 Psalm 2: Between Past and Future

Prolegomenon

> Then cometh Jesus from Galilee to Jordan unto John, to be baptized by him. But John forbad him, saying, I have need to be baptized by you. And comest thou to me? And Jesus answered said unto him, Suffer it to be so now: for thus it becometh us to fulfil all righteousness. Then he suffered him. And Jesus, when he was baptized, went up straightway out of the water: and, lo, the heavens were opened unto him, and he saw the Spirit of God descending like a dove, and lighting upon him: And lo a voice from heaven, saying, This is my beloved son, in whom I am well pleased.
>
> Matt 3:13–17: KJV

At the end of the story of the baptism of Jesus we find a quotation from the Old Testament. It is not verbally identical with the text of the Old Testament, but rather a "free" rendition, as it is usually assumed that the sentence "this is my beloved son" – in Greek οὗτός ἐστιν ὁ υἱός μου ὁ ἀγαπητός, ἐν ᾧ εὐδόκησα – is from the Psalter, Psalms 2:7b where we find the following announcement about the king of Yahweh residing in Zion: "Thou art my son; this day I have begotten you." (KJV)

Also the parallels to Matthew's story of the baptism of Jesus in Mark 1:9–11, and Luke 3:21–22 know of the quotation from the Psalter and their version is closer to the Hebrew text, as we here instead of "this" have "you" as in the Hebrew psalm.[1]

Now we might argue that it is perhaps a bit easy to describe this as a quotation from the Old Testament as any person living in Palestine in the time of Jesus was of course permitted to say to his son, "You are my son", without at the same time referring to the text of the Old Testament. However, the

---

[1] Although we should not forget that some textual witnesses to the text in Matthew have σύ εἶ as the other two Gospels.

popularity of Psalm 2 in the New Testament speaks against it, and because Psalms 2:7b is actually quoted in more than one place *in extenso*, thus by Paul according to the Acts of the Apostles 13:33 referring to the resurrection from the death.[2]

The use of the text from Psalm 2 in this context is in complete agreement with the tradition of the New Testament that Jesus was a descendant of the family of King David, and for that reason the bearer of the expectations for a new David – the Messiah – about to come. The extensive genealogy in Matthew 1 but also Luke's story about the birth of Jesus in Bethlehem, in the city of David, belong to the most important and best-known testimonies of this tradition. Neither do we need to discuss how the Christian idea of the Messiah was borrowed from Judaism with roots going back to the Israelite monarchy at the beginning of the 1st millennium BCE.[3]

I have no intention of discussing the adoption of Jewish expectations to the Messiah in the New Testament. It is, however, my intention in what follows and based on Psalm 2 to present some alternatives to the traditional interpretation of the concepts of the Messiah-king understood to be the son of God in an Israelite-Jewish context. Thus it is not my plan here to engage in polemic against, say Sigmund Mowinckel's well-known thesis – at least not directly – but to show how the preconditions have changed that will certainly lead to a revision of our ideas about how early Judaism used traditions from the past, while it at the same time worked on creating a tradition which did not come from a remote past and for nostalgic reasons were taken up again. These traditions were formulated with an eye to the future which was not there when it came into being.[4]

---

[2] The complete quotation also appears in Hebrews 1:5 and 5:5 (an exact quotation from the LXX). On the other hand it seems likely that 2 Peter 1:17 quotes Matthew. LXX Ps 2:7b has the following text: Κύρος εἶπεν πρός με Υἱός μου εἶ σύ, ἐγὼ σήμερον γεγέννηκά σε, almost exactly the same as the text of the Hebrew Bible ילדתיך היום אני אתה בני אלי אמר. The difference in the word order in the complete quotations in Acts and Hebrews and the abbreviated quotations in the Gospels is hardly dependent on different versions in the LXX, but the order has been reversed in the Gospels to put more stress on "you" than on "son".

[3] There is no reason to bring in a more extensive argumentation for this which has old roots in biblical studies. I will only refer to the classical study by Sigmund Mowinckel, *Han som kommer. Messiasforventningen i Det gamle Testamente og på Jesus tid* (Mowinckel, 1951). ET: *He that Cometh: The Messiah Concept in the Old Testament and Later Judaism* (Mowinckel, 1956).

[4] I will as an introduction have to make it clear that I have recently pleaded in favour of seeing the Old Testament in its present form as the product of Hellenistic Judaism. Cf. Lemche, 1992a; ET: Lemche, 1993a). The criticism of Eduard Nielsen (Nielsen, 1992) has no new arguments to contribute to the discussion. Thus there is reason to wonder why

The Royal Ideology and the Psalms of David

While the conception in the New Testament of the Davidic origins of Jesus is clear and dominant, we find little concrete information about David in the Psalter named after him. In reality very little – if anything at all – about David and his empire turns up in this part of the Old Testament. The idea of the glorious Davidic past of the Jewish people forms the background of a series of Psalms without being expressly mentioned. Thus Psalm 72 may be taken as evidence of the idea of a great Israelite empire. An empire like David's as described in the Old Testament would have been in need of an elaborate political ideology, which, however, is seldom found in the Psalter, although a religious ideology supporting the Davidic Empire shimmers through various psalms like Psalms 2 and 110. Psalms 89 and 132 likewise formulate the belief in the importance of the kingdom of David, combining this belief with the idea of a royal covenant between Yahweh and David and about the royal temple at Zion.

Thus it is evident that the Psalter built on the idea of a glorious Davidic past for the Jewish people, and it is therefore reasonable to argue that not only theologians in general but also Old Testament scholars were entitled to connect this ideology to a real Davidic kingdom belonging to the early period of Israel's history.

It is correct that several psalms of the Old Testament express their concept of royalty. We should, on the other hand, not overlook the fact that there is not just one idea about royalty but three distinct ones, each having its historical and cultural background.

1. The king is regarded as having a divine status which may even be understood in a physical sense.
2. The king is pronounced to be the righteous ruler whose duty is to care for the interest of his people.
3. The king is connected to the national god by a personal covenant.

Eduard Nielsen, discussing the history of textual transmission, refers to the – in its own time respected – study of Frants Buhl, *Den gammeltestamentlige Skriftoverlevering* (Buhl, 1885 [ET 1892]), but simply ignores the very exciting contribution to this history found in the manuscripts from Qumran, especially the evidence from here that shows that the Hebrew manuscript tradition was simply not settled in the period 1st century BCE – 2nd century CE. A more up-to-date introduction to the history of the Canon of the Old Testament might be Sandars, 1992.

Thus the previously mentioned psalms may be distributed within each of these three types of royal ideology. Psalms 2 and 110 clearly belong to the first category, Psalm 72 to the second, while Psalms 89 and 132 obviously belong to the third category.[5] The interesting part is not that we have these three different ways of interpreting royalty within the psalms of the Old Testament. The interesting part has to do with the respective origins of each of these three notions about the kingdom. Thus Psalm 2 undoubtedly reflects the Egyptian concept of the king as a god while the related Psalm 110 on the one hand describes the king as divine but on the other hand uses religious metaphors with a past in Western Asia. The second idea about kingship is, however, in no way Egyptian but decidedly from Western Asia and is especially well known from Mesopotamian royal ideas.[6] The third variety also comes from Western Asia, but there are at the same time no direct parallels with this definition of the relationship between king and god in Near Eastern literature, although the terminology is well-known from vassal treaties both from the 2nd and the 1st millennium BCE where the relations between the great king and his vassals were regulated by written treaties.[7] A very vivid impression of the character of such relationships can be found in the Amarna letters, in the correspondence between the Egyptian court and the Syrian and Palestinian vassals of Pharaoh.[8]

The presence of three different ideologies – moreover with different origins – would in a traditional diachronically organized study be described as a development of royal ideology in Psalms. Thus one would argue that the basis of this ideology was laid down in the time of the united monarchy in

---

[5] Of course there are more "royal psalms" in the Psalter than those mentioned here. More about them in Mowinckel's works, especially his *Konge-salmerne i Det gamle Testamente* (Mowinckel, 1916), or in his *Offersang og sangoffer* (Mowinckel, 1951a, 50–91. ET Mowinckel, 1962). I will also in this case refrain from polemical attacks on the well-known Scandinavian studies of the Psalms although the results of this study will have impacts on the Scandinavian idea of a dominating cultic and mythological orientation of the royal psalms.

[6] Henry Frankfort has described the basic difference between Egyptian and Mesopotamian royal ideology in his well-known *Kingship and the Gods* (Frankfort, 1948). Its conclusions have never in a serious way been questioned.

[7] Dating from the 2nd millennium the Hittite treaties are best known from the publications of Johannes Friedrichs and Ernst F. Weidner. See Friedrich, 1926–1930 and Weidner, 1923. The Assyrian treaties of the 1st millennium has recently been collected by Parpola, 1988.

[8] The Italian Assyriologist Mario Liverani has dealt extensively with the ideological content of the Amarna correspondence, especially in Liverani, 1967, and in a abbreviated form in Liverani, 1983.

the 10th century BCE, and was later "democratized" when the experience of the Israelite empire became a remote memory from the past. This author has previously published a study trying to reconstruct the history of royal ideologies in ancient Israel (Lemche, 1991b). Here it was argued that the early Davidic kings in Jerusalem assumed a royal ideology with Egyptian roots, probably because they considered themselves the heirs of the Egyptian Pharaohs, the previous rulers of Palestine. The thesis was supported by the fact that in David's time (c. 1000 BCE) it was not that long ago since the Egyptians had withdrawn from Palestine (c. 1075 BCE), probably only a couple of generations before the introduction of the Hebrew monarchy.[9] This assumption rested on a very literal interpretation of Psalms 2:7b claiming that this verse described the king at Zion as the son of God, an assumption that was at odds with the more traditional opinion of Old Testament scholars (more about this below). Of course it was also possible to point to other "Egyptian" elements in Jerusalem in the time of David.[10]

After the dissolution of the Davidic Empire after the death of Solomon at the end of the 10th century BCE this royal ideology of the divine king hardly survived which led to a re-evaluation of the role of the king in Jerusalem. The Egyptian ideology was substituted by a more traditional concept originating in Western Asia of the king as installed by the gods as their supreme civil servant with the obligation to care for the needs of the people of these divinities. Thus Psalm 72 might be a testimony to this changing opinion of the role of the king. Here the psalm expresses very clearly the obligations of the king to rule righteously and provide for the happiness of his people although the notion of World Empire is still present in this psalm.

Finally a third variety of the royal ideology was introduced under the impression of the status of the Judean king as the vassal of Assyrian and Babylonian great kings in the 8th to the 6th centuries BCE. According to this revised impression of the position of the king, he was not the vassal of foreign kings but of the national God Yahweh, and this form of vassalage was regulated by a formalized covenant between the deity and his king in Jerusalem. At a later date after the fall of the kingdom in 587 BCE this concept was transformed by deuteronomistic theologians who substituted the king with the people of Israel as one – the inferior – part of the treaty. Simultaneously with this development other elements belonging to the previously royal ideology lived

---

[9] Cf. Redford, 1992: 290.
[10] Thus the name of David's scribe which is really an Egyptian word for "scribe", or parts of the iconography of Solomon's temple. On the first point cf. de Vaux, 1939, reprinted in de Vaux, 1967, 189–201.

on and developed into Jewish Messianic conceptions centring on the hope for a new David. So much for the said study of royal ideology in the Psalms.

The Empire of David and History

Reconstructions of this type were, until a few years ago, absolutely feasible, based on the belief that in the Old Testament we have an authentic description of the political developments in Israel and Judah in the 1st millennium BCE. However, without a Davidic Empire the foundations for such theorizing would fall apart.

Until recently no serious scholar questioned the historicity of the Davidic Empire, although it was often regretted that we did not have any evidence of its existence apart from the biblical narratives. Nobody suspected that it might have been the biblical authors who "invented" the traditions about David and Solomon in all their glory.[11]

This is still the opinion of the majority of Old Testament scholars and it is especially valid for those who has never in a serious way confronted the many problems related to the biblical tradition of this kingdom. In this connection it is a well-known fact that no Near Eastern source dating from the 10th century BCE has any information about this mighty Israelite kingdom and no extra-biblical source from the following centuries mentions it by just one word. This fact may be brushed aside by a reference to the general international political situation in the 10th century BCE where the amount of information is very limited because of the absence of the great kingdoms of the Bronze Age and their archives. Therefore little of relevance for the historians is likely to appear.[12] Whenever relations between the dynasty of David and foreign royal families are mentioned, as in the case of Solomon's marriage to an Egyptian princess (1 Kings 3:1), it is pointed out that the Egyptian

---

[11] Compare the various "histories of Israel" dating from the 1980s, such as Miller and Hayes, 1986, Soggin, 1984 and Lemche, 1984, ET: Lemche, 1988]). Among these scholars Soggin has had the opportunity to express a greater reticence as far as the historicity of the Davidic Empire goes in Soggin, 1991.

[12] The argument based on the non-existence of great empires at this time is repeated in several histories of Israel. Here only a selection: Noth, 1950, 181; and still on this line Donner, 1984, 202. In Danish Eduard Nielsen, 1960, 82, Holm-Nielsen, 1975, 125, and Otzen, 1982, 175. The issue of the missing sources has been taken up by Abraham Malamat (Malamat 1982, 189–90, and more recently Redford, 1992, 299. The absence of great powers should, however, not shadow for the fact that several local political centres continued to exist in Middle and Northern Syria with roots back to the Hittite Empire in the Late Bronze Age.

princess came from a dynasty of little importance such as the 21st dynasty which of necessity broke with the Egyptian royal tradition of never marrying real princesses to foreign potentates. This, however, does not explain the absolute Egyptian silence about this marriage.[13] The silence of the Mesopotamian sources is downgraded in a similar fashion by arguing that although the empire of David and Solomon was extensive – maybe the greatest kingdom of its time – it was hardly of the size described by the Old Testament reaching from the Brook of Egypt, the present Wadi el-Arish, to the Euphrates.[14] There is thus no reason to speculate over the fact that no Mesopotamian scribe of the 10th century ever discovered the existence of this kingdom and that no memory of it survived into later Mesopotamian tradition.

As such, the argument based on the absence in extra-biblical documents of the Davidic-Solomonic Empire is not very important. Logically it is an *argumentum ex silentio* and therefore a false argument to be rejected for formal reasons. In order to demonstrate the importance of stating that an argument from silence is a false one, we can say that without other Near Eastern sources about David and Solomon proving these figures to be historical ones, the biblical information assumes a special weight as they represent the only surviving *written* sources to the history of Palestine in the 10th century BCE.[15] If we intend to contest the information we obtain from the biblical sources, other kinds of information will have to be provided which may contradict the historical traditions of the Old Testament but also must be in accord with

---

[13] Compare Noth, 1950, 198, and still Soggin, 1984, 80–1. Sceptical as far as the historicity of this marriage goes: Miller and Hayes, 1986, 216, Soggin, 1991, 71. See also on all of this Redford, 1992, 311. A lot of speculation about the identity of this Egyptian Pharaoh has of course been around for years, especially connected to the note in 1 Kings 9:16 and the Egyptian surrendering of the city of Gezer as a dowry.

[14] Cf. the speculations of this kind in Soggin, 1991, 42–61, and in Miller and Hayes 1986, 179–80 (including a map of the "reduced' kingdom of David on p. 181). See also – outside of the circle of biblical scholars – the relevant paragraphs in Liverani, 1988, 669–72.

[15] From a historian's point of view, the Old Testament is a primary source, simply because it is a written source and also the only one. We have no better written source than the Old Testament itself, and until its evidence is contradicted by other facts its information must be considered valid. However, two points have to be made in this connection: Pro primo the Old Testament is so-to-speak the primary source to most of Israel's history before the introduction of the monarchy. It has not prevented this source to be evaluated as without historical relevance by modern scholarship. As we proceed to the early monarchy we cannot not be sure that the situation had changed. Pro secundo, we have to question the relevance of the argument of the importance of primary written documents when information from sources normally considered secondary evidence (mute information from the period itself coming from excavations in Palestine) have convinced scholars that the primary *written* sources are without historical value.

other written sources – in this case the missing written documents – which is the same as to say that a rejection of the biblical tradition about David and Solomon will have to be measured against archaeological evidence from the 10th century. And if there is nothing in the archaeological material that supports the existence of the Israelite Empire, then we have no reason to expect references to this empire in the written documents of the period. In this case the former argument from silence changes status and becomes a positive fact in accordance with another positive fact, that there is no evidence of this empire in material sources from that time.[16]

The most important contribution to such a criticism of the biblical traditions about David and Solomon from an archaeological point of view has recently been provided by the American archaeologist David Jamieson-Drake in a thesis that presents a statistical study of the material from Jerusalem and Judah in the period of the Hebrew kings (Jamieson-Drake, 1991). This is not the place to discuss the thesis in details. We only have to mention that according to the evidence from the Judean period there was never a centralized state or a political centre of an empire here in the 10th century. As a matter of fact Jamieson-Drake has to conclude that there is no evidence of a centralized kingdom in Judah before in middle of the 8th century BCE.[17] If we compare the archaeological material with the missing written evidence of the Davidic Empire (apart, of course, from the Old Testament) it is obvious that the two groups of evidence are in mutual agreement, meaning that the Davidic kingdom never existed in the way it is presented by biblical writers. In this connection it is not very important – although not without interest – that it is possible to cast doubt on certain events of the Davidic-Solomonic era, such

---

[16] Based on the rather commonplace observation that data cannot be in mutual contradiction; only interpretations of the data can be conflicting. If a conflict exists between the narratives of the Old Testament and other kinds of information, such a conflict is impossible – as both sources represent data. It is only the modern interpreter who has not found the correct explanation that unites the two sets of information.

[17] Jamieson-Drake, 1991, 138–9. We have to stress the fact that this conclusion builds exclusively on the material from Judah which could have been more extensive (although already much more extensive than from most other places in the Near East) but also is a testimony very different from the archaeological situation outside of the Judean area where we perhaps find evidence of a centralization of political life already at the end of the 10th century or in the beginning of the 9th century. If this interpretation is correct, it is difficult not to link the appearance of such a state to the Omride Dynasty's assumption of power shortly after 900 BCE, a state formation well documented by written documents from the ancient near east, such as the Assyrian inscription referring to the battle at Qarqar in 853 (*ANET* 279) and the Mesha Inscription from Moab from the middle of the 9th century (*ANET* 320).

as Solomon's relationship to the Phoenician King Hiram or the campaign of Pharaoh Shishak in Palestine in King Rehoboam's 5th regnal year (1 Kings 14:25–26).[18] Such inaccuracy supports the assumption that the biblical historical narrative lacks historical foundation but it does not prove that the narrative in the Old Testament is totally unhistorical.

Psalm 2 and Egyptian Royal Ideology

If the Davidic Empire never was, we have no reason to assume that the tradition of royal greatness expressed in Psalm 2 and other places go back to the time of David – or rather, it would be absurd to claim it. In what follows the task is to present an alternative time for the appearance of the kind of royal ideology found in Psalm 2 which developed into Jewish Messianic expectations. There are two reasons why this is important. First of all, within the context of the Old Testament Psalm 2 presents the clearest expressions of this, and secondly, Psalm 2 may present some indications of the background for these expectations to the Messiah which lie behind the actual formulations of the psalm.

In the following part it is my intention to present an argument in favour of an Egyptian origin of the idea of kingship presented by Psalm 2. Thereafter we will turn to the question of the date and origin of the psalm itself.

The decisive part of this discussion has to do with v. 7b: "You are my son; I have borne you today." I have already presented this expression as evidence of the status of the king at Zion as the son of God. It would be hard to say that this is the common interpretation. Three recent Scandinavian Psalm commentaries are testimonies to this. Thus Eduard Nielsen laconically states: "You are my son" is only an adoption formula which in this case moves the human being – the king – into a sacral sphere." (Nielsen, 1990, 72). Eduard Nielsen does, however, not inform us about the origin of this adoption formula. This information is presented by Erling Hammershaimb who refers to Codex Hammurabi §170. In this paragraph we find the Akkadian expression *marua iqtabi*, "He says: 'My sons'", in connection with the acceptance of the sons of a female slave as heirs in line with legitimate sons of a free citizen

---

[18] Cf. on this especially Garbini, 1987, 21–32, and Redford, 1992, 312–5. In both cases the chronological information creates problems but also the route of the campaign as Jerusalem seems to be the only place in Palestine not visited by Shishak – according to his own report and contradiction the information in 1 Kings 14:25–26. A list of the Palestinian place names in Shishak's inscription can be found in *ANET* 242–3.

(Hammershaimb, 1984, 59). Neither Nielsen nor Hammershaimb make it clear that this adoption formula does not appear in any Old Testament text. On the other hand, the Uppsala professor Helmer Ringgren makes this point very clear, although he still subscribes to the "adoption idea".[19]

The adoption idea also dominates outside of Scandinavia. We only have to consult the well-known commentary on the Psalms by Hans-Joachim Kraus, who refers to the difference between the idea of kingship in Mesopotamia and in Egypt but nevertheless postulates that Psalms 2:7b is about adoption.[20]

Kraus's more brilliant compatriot Erhard Gerstenberger has, in his recent Psalms commentary, demonstrated how insecure the traditional interpretation of Psalms 2:7b really is.[21] His commentary is worth a detailed discussion because of his introductory remark concerning v. 7a:

> There is no need to alter v. 7a (against Gunkel) although the Hebrew is uniquely awkward (*sippar 'el*, "announce toward") and seemingly redundant. But there is a likely connection of this phraseology to Egyptian royal ritual. Whether within a coronation ceremony (von Rad, "Royal") or within a setting of general appearance before his nobles (a kind of ancient "presidential interview"), the pharaoh used to introduce himself in a similar fashion to demonstrate his extraordinary powers…

Now Gerstenberger asks why Egyptian influence has not been acknowledged and argues in favour of the idea that we here have an Israelite adaption of ancient Near Eastern royal ideology. Thereafter he is in doubt and refers to the fact that the formula "you are my son" goes all the way back to the Sumerians

---

[19] Ringgren, 1987, 28. Ringgren's commentary is in this connection both honest and at the same time revealing. He notices that the king outside of Israel is sometimes regarded as divine but adds: "As far as Israel is concerned scholars tend to consider the formula as one of adoption. This is really the only logical conclusion because 'I have borne you today' can hardly be true on the enthronement day". And here Ringgren is absolutely correct. On the other hand, it is not necessarily a correct assumption that Psalm 2 is an enthronement psalm as is current in much Scandinavian scholarship. The idea of an adoption formula is of course not supported by the fact that the only place where we have this formula is Mesopotamia. As Ringgren admits: "In the case of Israel we have to accept the formula as it stands". This is revealing. As the German scholar Bernd Jörg Diebner puts it: "We cannot prove it – but it is a fact…"

[20] Kraus, 1977, 18–9. We have to mention that although in this place Kraus agrees with Scandinavian scholarship, he cannot abstain from an attack on this scholarship here. In this place (as elsewhere) his commentary represents a step backwards in comparison to the brilliant commentary of his predecessor, Hermann Gunkel (Gunkel, 1929, 6–7).

[21] Gerstenberger, 1988: 46–47.

and adds that the fact that it is not found in the Old Testament (apart from Ps 2:7b) may be a coincidence. In this way he identifies with the usual idea of adoption. His commentary, however, ends with the following sigh:

> Yet, the formulation of v. 7c [7b] points more to Egyptian than to Mesopotamian concepts of royal descent. Thiel quotes an Egyptian source that bears close resemblance to the words of v. 7b–c. In an inscription of Ramses II, the god Ptah says, "I am your father who begot you as a deity"…

We can safely add that Gerstenberger is riding on two horses at the same time. On the other hand, his commentary is a clear example of what happens when a scholar has already embraced a certain idea and gets into problems because his interpretation cannot be supported by the available source material.

Stating that Ps 2:7b can safely be placed within Egyptian royal ideology, we can continue our path through this psalm in order to look for further support for the thesis. The introduction to the psalm: "Why do the heathen rage and the people imagine a vain thing?" includes the first testimony. This introductory motif in Psalm 2 presenting the rebellion of the people against the legitimate prince on Zion follows an Egyptian literary trope according to which there will before the ascension to the throne of a new Pharaoh always be turmoil and chaos. J.B. Pritchard's selection of Near Eastern texts presents two examples – one relating to the ascension of Merenptah and the second to that of Ramesses IV,[22] although none of them is directly related to a real ascension ritual but represents accolades which include a presentation of the enthronement of the king as the end of a chaotic period. The translator of the two texts, John A. Wilson, simply states: "In the dogma of Egyptian Religion each pharaoh was a god who repeated the creation miracle of establishing order out of chaos",[23] or as formulated by Mario Liverani it was, according to the Egyptian *Königsnovelle*, the standard reason for wars against foreign nations that they were rebellious and a threat to Egypt, which was again the reason why Pharaoh was forced to crush the skulls of his enemies,[24] another well-known motif from Egyptian inscriptions as well as iconographic

---

[22] *ANET*, 378.
[23] Same place.
[24] Liverani, 1990, 135. *Königsnovelle* (royal novel) is the name for a written legitimation of Pharaoh which in Egypt followed a fixed pattern and had a stereotypic content. See on this phenomenon A. Herrmann, 1938, and with regard to the evidence from the Old Testament S. Herrmann, 1953–54.

representations. Psalm 2 returns to exactly this theme a few verses later: "Thou shalt break them with a rod of iron; thou shalt dash them in pieces like a potter's vessel" (v. 9).

It is possible to introduce more themes relating to Egypt and especially to the Egyptian royal novel, not least the meaning of the royal oracle in v. 7, with its parallels among divine proclamations in Egyptian texts. We will set that fact to the side momentarily and will shortly turn to the question of the title *Messiah* which appears in v. 2 in order to see whether or not this title can be related to Egyptian models.

Here we must admit that although the Egyptian origin of this title may be possible it is far from an established fact: The Egyptian kings were not anointed. Several scholars have engaged in this discussion including Ernst Kutsch (Kutsch, 1963) and Tryggve N.D. Mettinger (Mettinger, 1976), but it would be wrong to say that they have reached a clear and unanimous conclusion when it comes to the origins of the title. The closest thing to an Egyptian origin is the Egyptian practice of anointing royal civil servants, including the vassals of Pharaoh in Asia. Because of this it cannot be excluded that the custom may have survived but was locally understood differently. All of this is extremely uncertain and it is hardly possible to consider the appearance of the title in Psalm 2 as evidence of the Egyptian background of the royal ideology in this psalm.

This would have been the place to discuss whether or not the psalm was inspired by other concepts of royalty than the Egyptian ones. Here there is only space for drawing up the preliminary conclusion that Egyptian elements are certainly present in Psalm 2, and that the idea of kingship in this psalm is definitely not part of the notion of royalty in Western Asia – although quite a few scholars have tried to prove it. The idea that the king is the son of God or even God himself was not one that was well received among the peoples of Western Asia in ancient times.[25]

---

[25] We should, however, mention that we have a few a dispersed references from Mesopotamia of the idea of the divine king, but it was hardly a dominating feature of royal ideology. Ivan Engnell in his study of the phenomenon in his *Studies in Divine Kingship in the Ancient Near East* (Engnell 1943, 16–51), has not won many supporters among Assyriologists, and the same can be said about his discussion of the "divine kingship" of Ancient Syria (Engnell 1943, 71–173). He found most of the support for his thesis in Ugaritic texts, especially in the epic about King Kirta (formerly Keret) (cf. Engnell 1943, 143–173). Against this we have to add that there is outside of the epic literature no evidence of the divine status of the Ugaritic kings. Rather the epic of Kirta represents a polemic against the notion of the divine king. I refer to the passage II K (= KTU 16): "Like dogs shall we howl at your tomb / like whelps at the entrance of your burial chamber? / Yet, father / how can you possibly

Is Psalm 2 "Messianic"?

New Testament authors definitely believed the psalm to be "messianic". They had no problem accepting the literary interpretation of especially v. 7b, arguing that the king, i.e., the Messiah, is the son of God, or the God who became flesh.[26]

We should, on the other hand, not dismiss the long and important article by Marinus de Jonge about Messiah in the *Anchor Bible Dictionary* with its very poignant idea about messianic expectations in the Old Testament: "In the OT the term 'anointed' is never used of a future saviour/redeemer, and … in later Jewish writings of the period between 200 B.C. and A.D. 100 the term is used only infrequently in connection with agents of divine deliverance expected in the future."[27]

If de Jonge is right, Psalm 2 could not be "messianic" in the Christian sense of the idea, which means that it could not include a reference to a future saviour or redeemer. This evaluation of the psalm seems dubious if we are looking at the case from the perspective of the likely Egyptian background of the psalm. I already referred to the new Pharaoh who was definitely regarded as the coming saviour who should save the world from the forces of chaos and darkness and reinstate cosmos and the kingdom of God on earth. When these ideas are transferred to Psalm 2 with its expectations of the king on Zion, i.e., the Messiah, it is certainly not just a vague reference to salvation from enemies and evil. We are rather entitled to argue that such expectations make up the main subject of this psalm. Since this Messiah/king is also the son of God we have to state that de Jonge's announcement has no foundation. In order to save de Jonge's interpretation it would be necessary to argue that the weak point is the relationship in Psalm 2 between the expectations to the

---

die / or will your burial chamber be given over to howling / on the part of women, O my wretched father? / … / Is Keret then the son of El / the offspring of the compassionate and Holy One? / … / In your life, our father, we rejoiced: / In your immortality we took delight. / Like dogs shall we howl at your tomb / like curs at the entrance of your burial chamber? / Yet, father, / how can you possibly die? / or will your burial chamber (be given over to) weeping / to howling on the part of women, / O my wretched father? / How can it be said / that Keret is the son of El, / the offspring of the compassionate and Holy One? / Or do the gods die, / the offspring of the compassionate not live? (Wyatt 1998, 219–22). Although compare also the totally different and Engnell-like interpretation in Gottlieb, 1969, 88–105.

[26] The importance of this psalm in the New Testament is made clear not only by the earlier mentioned literal or free quotations from v. 7, but also in several other places that cite vv. 1, 2, 5, 8, 9, and 12.

[27] De Jonge, 1992, 777.

coming divine king and the title Messiah. This title might have an independent early history and only secondarily combined with the idea of the divine king. Hereafter Psalm 2 could be an example of a special interpretation of the concept of the Messiah or in a broader sense of the position of the king which at the same time plays with the expectations for the future king amply testified by other passages in the Old Testament – not least in some famous passages in First Isaiah.[28]

Another argument – though not very important – in favour of a secondary linking of more traditional ideas about royalty in the Old Testament and the succinct proclamation of the divine king in Psalm 2 inspired by Egyptian notions might be the enigmatic אז in v. 5. The Hebrew word אז would normally refer to the past even when followed by a verb in the imperfect.[29] In spite of this, modern translators prefer to render the passage in the present mode or even as future. Thus *King James Version*: "Then shall he speak unto them in his wrath", but the *New English Bible* from 1989: "Then angrily he rebukes them …"[30] The German tradition normally follows Luther's translation of this אז as "einest", i.e., "then" (in the past).[31]

If we prefer the usual translation of אז as "then" (past sense) we might argue that – contrary to the Scandinavian/Anglo-Saxon tradition of regarding this psalm as an enthronement psalm – this אז shows that the oracle which follows represents something that was said in the past about something which is supposed to happen in the future, and not as something relating to the present, as if it is something that is said here and now. אז might have been chosen deliberately by the author of this psalm in order to establish a relationship between an older concept of the Messiah – the king – and his own idea of the Messiah as the coming saviour – king (whoever this king might be). Thus it would be possible to maintain that Psalm 2 has a double intention: On the one

---

[28] Isa 8:23–9:6; 11:1–10 (16).

[29] Compare Gesenius 1910, § 107b and c. But the imperfect form that follows makes the argument uncertain because אז+ the imperfect may also express the future. Cf. Gesenius, 1910, § 107c. On the other hand it seems more uncertain whether it can also be used as presence. The Septuagint render אז as τότε which is reasonable as *tote* includes the same double meaning as אז.

[30] "Then angrily he rebukes them."

[31] Compare Luther's translation of v. 5: "Er wird einest mit jnen reden in seinem zorn / Vnd mit seinem grim wird er sie schrecken" (*Die gantze Heilige Schrifft Deudsch* 1545). See also Gunkel 1929, 5: "Einst aber redet er zu ihnen im Zorn, wird im Grimme sie Schrecken". The ambiguousness remains – especially in Gunkel's commentary – because although German *einst* normally refers to the past it can also be used as a reference to a (remote) future. Luther's translation reveals that he takes the psalm to be both messianic and eschatological.

hand, the author of the psalm (living in the present) relegates the expectations to the Messiah to the past, someone they prophesized about a long time ago. But on the other hand, the author reckons this Messiah to be the saviour from the evil which shall come – tomorrow, or in a more distant future.

How Old Is Psalm 2?

One problem remains which is certainly not unimportant: How old is this psalm and what has motivated its author to link the ideas of the Messiah, probably originally of a limited scale, with Egyptian royal ideology, claiming the king to be God and the redeemer of the world?

Several possibilities for dating the psalm exist:

1. The psalm comes from the time of David;
2. The psalm belongs to the time of King Josiah;
3. The psalm was written during the Babylonian exile;
4. The Psalm is the product of the Persian period;
5. The psalm is Hellenistic, and to be more precise it comes from the time when the Ptolemies governed Palestine.

Other periods might also be candidates such as the time of Hezekiah or the period of the Maccabees. However, the five options mentioned here should suffice.

When we turn to the time of David it is clear that in light of the issues of historicity of this period raised here we should stop speculating about such an early date. If there was no Judean state before the middle of the 8th century as claimed by Jamieson-Drake – it is hardly likely that a royal ideology claiming the king at Zion to be the ruler of the world should arise in one of the nooks and corners of ancient Judah.

Skipping the time of Hezekiah (the end of the 8th century) because there is not much "Egyptian" about this period which might have forwarded the import of Egyptian ideas and concepts, the next serious candidate must be the time of King Josiah (the end of the 7th century). This period is quite popular among scholars who want to focus on this period as the only remaining pre-exilic period as an alternative to the exilic and post-exilic dates for biblical literature which have become more and more popular these days. Here it is a problem that the relations between Josiah and Egypt – at least according to the Old Testament – were mainly hostile and did not last for long.[32] Even if it cannot be left out that relations existed between Egypt and Palestine – to imagine that there were no relations is absurd in light of how close the two areas are in a geographical sense – we have no information in the Old Testament or elsewhere about such relations. Josiah was, according to the Old Testament – or to be more precise the Deuteronomistic History – a real great king, and according to modern historians he was the king in Jerusalem who tried to re-establish the kingdom of David to include all of Palestine.[33] If this view of Josiah is correct we might assume that a royal ideology like the one in Psalm 2 could originate in Josiah's time.

The questions relating to the historicity of the description in the Old Testament of Josiah's time are still rather imprecise and indirect. Are we at all in possession of information which proves that Josiah was the saviour/king who might have been the prototype for the lord of the world and the divine king which is the subject of Psalm 2? There are very many reasons to doubt this. It is not to be denied that the Josiah who appears in 2 Kings is the invention of the deuteronomistic authors. This does not mean that there never was a historical King Josiah. More than likely it simply means that King Josiah ruled over the petty state of Judah at the end of the 7th century, but he probably was far from as important as described by the deuteronomistic authors. In this connection we should not overlook how the authors of Chronicles, who otherwise follow the deuteronomistic *Vorlage* slavishly, present a very different image of Josiah. According to Chronicles it was Hezekiah and not Josiah who reformed the cult in Jerusalem, including the Passover celebrations. In this way Josiah's celebrations was no more than a repetition of Hezekiah's. Moreover, the deuteronomistic hero was in the end disobedient to God like so many other Judean kings, and therefore brought his unglamorous end upon himself.[34]

---

[32] If 2 Kings 23:28-30 is to be believed, the relations began and ended in the moment when Josiah tried to block the advance of Pharaoh Necho's army at Megiddo and was instantly killed by Egyptian archers.

[33] We need not to bring in references since there has been very little disagreement between scholars as far as Josiah goes. Danish readers may consult Otzen 1977, 294-5, and Lemche, 1984, 144-6, both written *in majoram gloriam Josiae*.

[34] Compare on one hand 2 Chronicles 34-35 with 2 Chronicles 29-31, and on the other 2 Chronicles 29-31 with 2 Kings 18:1-8 and 2 Chronicles 34-35 with 2 Kings 22-23. It is normally assumed that the deuteronomistic history from a historical point of view is more reliable than Chronicles with its tendentious history writing, probably best described by Peter Welten (Welten, 1973). We may discuss whether this is a correct observation or the deuteronomistic history writers were only more subtle than their chronistic colleagues.

Finally we have to ask – in case the deuteronomists presented a correct picture of the time of Josiah after all – if this Yahweh-believing king could really be the divine king of Psalm 2. If Josiah was the divine king and still nursed expectations of recreating a Judean empire – although we do not know who his role model was – he probably was very different from the pious king of the Books of Kings. We might say that the humble (and humiliated) king of the Davidic dynasty who appears in Psalm 89 would be much closer to the ideal image of Josiah.

Although none of the arguments put forward here are decisive, we should maintain that we probably have to be more careful when we attribute to Josiah all those elements that cannot be dated to earlier periods of Judah's history. Here I especially think of the Davidic era. In reality our normal image of the time of Josiah represents a hermeneutical circle simply because scholars try to prove the correctness of their own interpretation of Old Testament history writing on the basis of their own assertions.

Preliminarily, it still has to be maintained that the period of Josiah formed the background for many traditions in the Old Testament – even if it cannot be proven – but Psalm 2 definitely does not fit in with the ideology of that time. It is probably time to turn to the time of the Babylonian exile and the Persian era.

As far as the Babylonian exile is concerned it seems to present the worst thinkable background of the *Egyptian* royal ideology of Psalm 2. If scholars really want to date the psalm to the time of the exile, it must owe its presence to refugees from Judah living in Egypt. The problem is only that although we know of such refugees from Judah in Egypt and about Judean colonies in Egypt in the following centuries, we have no clue to what kind of literature was produced under such circumstances. We may rather say that the presence

---

However, we cannot discuss the fact that the author of Chronicles generally repeated what was written in Kings in a slavish way. Against the argument here one may maintain that the death of Josiah would make him suspicious in the eyes of the Chronicler, because Chronicles rather heavy-handedly distinguishes between good and bad kings dependent on their respective fate (the famous penance of Manasseh in Chronicles is an example of this). This might have been the reason why Chronicles chose to raise the status of Hezekiah at the expense of Josiah. It is, on the other hand, just as feasible that the deuteronomists needed Josiah and his reform because it *had* to be their reform and an argument in favour of the future exclusive cult politics of the Jerusalem priesthood in the Persian and Greek periods. Whatever the correct interpretation is: Josiah was at the time when the authors of Chronicles mainly copied the deuteronomistic history not yet the heroic figure of the past but still liable to reinterpretations.

of a Judean/Jewish temple on the island of Elephantine in the 5th century definitely contradicts the ideology of Zion which also appears in Psalm 2.[35]

The Persian period presents a serious possibility, although the Egyptian impression of Psalm 2 does not exactly support a date of this Psalm in the Persian period. However, the hope for a new king of the old Judean dynasty lived on at the beginning of this period,[36] and it is likely that messianic ideas, which were hardly anything but a hope for the resurrection of the Judean monarchy, were rather popular during the 5th to 4th centuries. But even though Psalm 2 mentions the Messiah this does not mean – as already argued – that the psalm concentrated on the figure of the Messiah. It rather meant that the Messiah in Psalm 2 was combined with a new, and for the Jews of the time a totally foreign, royal ideology.

The final option is the Hellenistic period and here most likely the Ptolemaic part of it when the Egyptians – or rather their Greek overlords – ruled over Palestine,[37] and not the following period when the sovereignty over Palestine was transferred to the Seleucids residing in Mesopotamia. Even though we know very little about the period as far as the history of Palestine is concerned,[38] it is not totally unreasonable to assume that this period could form the background of the mixture of Egyptian and genuine Jewish concepts such as is the situation in Psalm 2. We may discuss whether the psalm was written in Egypt or in Jerusalem but its content speaks in favour of it being a product of Palestinian Jewry in the early part of the Hellenistic period.

The fact that the content of the psalm is rather unique,[39] does not speak against a late date of this psalm. As already mentioned, the concept of the divine king was never very popular in Western Asia. Therefore, there was little reason to assume and develop a view on royalty of this kind, and especially not in the Seleucid period when the relationship between the Seleucids and their Jewish subjects became seriously endangered because of the Seleucids' demand that they should be worshipped as a divine being. It is more feasible that the early Jewish concepts of the Messiah were generally not influenced

---

[35] Cf. also the description of this in Otzen 1977, 322–4. Otzen put stress on the fact that this colony was different from the Judaism that was the home of the deuteronomistic writers entertaining their ideas of the exclusivity of Jerusalem and its temple.

[36] On Zerubbabel and the expectations to him cf. Otzen 1977, 318. It is a pity that we know so very little about this figure, something also Otzen admits.

[37] During most of the 3rd century until Ptolemaic rule was cut short after the battle at Paneion near the sources of the Jordan in precisely 200 BCE.

[38] Cf. Otzen, 1984, 14–5.

[39] Psalm 110 is probably the only one with a comparable content, although it should not be forgotten that the details of Psalm 110 are totally different from the ones of Psalm 2.

by theories about divine kingship and accordingly should be regarded as one more example of the "humanistic" interpretation of the figure of the king common in all of Western Asia until the Hellenistic period.

We don't know how the "different" interpretation of the figure of the Messiah in Psalm 2 (the future redeemer/king) survived and was transmitted to the authors of New Testament scripture. We only know that it happened. In this way the authors of the Gospels and other New Testament books came closer to the meaning of Psalm 2 than later orthodox Jewish tradition – or modern exegetes. Perhaps it was Hellenistic influence – conscious or unconscious – on parts of Jewish society that made it possible for this foreign royal ideology to survive at least as an undercurrent under the prevailing ideas about the Messiah, and we must, in this connection, not forget that popular messianic expectations for a future redeemer at least in the 1st century CE played a considerable role in Palestinian society. This is, however, a totally different story.

Postscript

During the last twenty years quite a few things have changed within Old Testament scholarship. Just a few years ago a discussion like the one found here would have been unthinkable, when most of the psalms were dated to pre-exilic times and bound to the cult of the temple in Jerusalem (with the exception of a few psalms reckoned to come from the north). This is not the place to discuss these changes – they mainly have to do with historical issues or matters of interest for the history of early Jewish religion, or they concentrate on the date of the historical literature in the Old Testament.

On the other hand, we have to stress the fact that quite a few elements belonging to the so-called *communis opinionis* among scholars are in danger of losing their historical foundation, such as the Davidic background for parts of the Psalter. This means that although a late dating of Psalm 2 as proposed in this article will still be rejected by most colleagues, we should not forget that only a century ago scholars had no problems dating psalms to the Maccabean period, to the 2nd century BCE.[40] Perhaps somebody should take on the task of retrieving the argumentation of that time for such a late date. It might be

---

[40] A study like the one of Marco Treves, *The Dates of the Psalms. History and Poetry in Ancient Israel* (Treves, 1988) shows that not everything of past scholarship has been forgotten. Treves dates every psalm in the Psalter to between 170 and 103 BCE. There are, in Treves' study, several interesting observations but his methodology is too arbitrary to

that the argumentation for dating the psalms to an early period – so common among Scandinavians since Mowinckel but also among Anglo-Saxon scholars – in reality rest on a very weak foundation. We should not reject the possibility that a renewed discussion of the date of the Psalms and their *Sitz im Leben* might liberate scholarship from its present *nirvana*.

---

inspire confidence. Thus Psalm 2 is dated to 103 BCE and linked to the enthronement of Alexander Jannæus, but without any justification.

7 The Introduction to David's Psalms: New Reflections on Psalm 2

A couple of years ago I published a study of Psalm 2[1] in which I argued in favour of a Hellenistic date for this psalm. Psalm 2 is not an old royal psalm originating in the Judean enthronement ritual from the time of the Davidic kings in Jerusalem but probably dates from the Hasmonean Period having borrowing its idea of kingship from Egyptian conceptions of the king as the son of God. For that reason I rejected the traditional understanding of the famous v. 7.

בני אתה אני היום ילדתיך

"You are my son; I have sired you today"

This is not an adoption formula. My argument was that it should be understood literally. In this connection I referred to the use of the verse in the New Testament in combination with the baptism of Jesus (Matt 3:13–17). A Messianic interpretation of the Psalm was also proposed close to if not identical with Jewish perceptions of the Messiah in Hellenistic and Roman times.

This aspect of Psalm 2 was not my main subject in the aforementioned article. There I concentrated on dating the psalm. Here I will go further into the theme of the Messiah, and will propose it as a way to understand how the Psalter was thought to be read.

The collection of the Psalms of David in the Old Testament – in the Hebrew Bible as well as in most Western translations – consists of one hundred and fifty individual poems. This is a well-known fact. Less well-known is another fact, that the number of Psalms has not always been the same. We only need to point to the Septuagint where one more psalm appears, the 151 Psalm, which in a Danish context is quite popular thanks to Grundtvig's revised version of it ("Mellem brødre kaldt den lille" [Among brothers called the youngest]). It has been normal to exclude this psalm from Western translations because it was not part of the Jewish, i.e. Hebrew, canon, where texts

---

[1] Lemche, 1993b. English translation published in this collection.

are not normally accepted if there was no Hebrew text. This criterion is probably wrong. The texts from Qumran have brought new light to the status of Psalm 151 because the psalm scroll from cave 11 includes a Hebrew version of Psalm 151.[2] The scroll has Psalm 151 at the end of the scroll just like its position in the Septuagint, but also includes a series of differences such as the inclusion of more psalms at the end of the collection which are not found in the Hebrew Bible. Thus the Qumran evidence suggests that the collection in the Psalter had not reached its final form at the time of the birth of the Christ.[3] The most likely reason for the omission of Psalm 151 is not that it did not exist in Hebrew[4] but that the number 150 had achieved a canonical status – something also reflected by the Septuagint where the inclusion of Psalm 151 has led to a rearrangement of the numbering in such a way that there still are only 150 psalms.

It is then a question whether the number 150 already had such a status in the Dead Sea Scrolls. This cannot be answered because a complete Psalm manuscript has not been found there. It might have been, and if it were the case the inclusion of one more psalm might have led to the exclusion of the previously last psalm, Psalm 151.

There are more indications of problems with how to count the psalms if we turn to the connection between Psalms 1 and 2. According to the Acts of the Apostles 13:33 Paul quotes Psalms 2:7 in his sermon in Antioch of Pisidia as "thus it is written in the second psalm".[5] The major manuscripts have this reading. They are at the same time also the major Septuagint manuscripts and may be dependent on the way of counting the Psalms in the Septuagint. Their testimony might accordingly not be decisive. Some manuscripts read in Acts 13:33 "in the first psalm" instead of "in the second".[6] Although the evidence

---

[2] 11QPsa.

[3] James C. Vanderkam has a fine review of the importance of the DSS for the Psalter in his *Dødehavsrullerne – teorier og kendsgerninger* (Vanderkam, 1995, 145–9).

[4] The same can be said about other Jewish books from the Hellenistic Period such as Jubilees.

[5] ὡς καὶ ἐν τῷ ψαλμῷ γέγραπται τῷ δευτέρῳ. The Paul of Acts uses the place as a proof text in connection with his preaching the resurrection of Christ from the dead. This means that Paul, just like Matthew (and parallels), regards the baptism of Jesus as a "new birth". Both quotations support the idea that "Ps 2:7" does not talk about adoption. Traditional Psalm scholarship should have accepted this. If it had been part of an ancient enthronement ritual in Judah it would have meant that the king at his anointing was considered as "born", meaning as having entered a new life. The old discussion about how this could be possible as the king would (normally) be a grown-up male, is totally immaterial.

[6] τῷ πρώτῳ ψαλμῷ γέγραπται. I will not comment on the structure of the sentence in this edition of Acts 13:33, although it seems more natural.

for this reading is weaker than the normal one it is still interesting and could be older than the testimony of the major manuscripts.

However, there is more to the issue of textual criticism. The Hebrew manuscript which has, for the last one hundred years, been the main source for the Biblia Hebraica – being de facto a reprint of the manuscript – is Codex Leningradensis and it does not include a number for Psalm 1 and has therefore Psalm 2 as the first psalm. There are different explanations. The usual one is that Psalm 1 in the Hebrew tradition was not understood to be a regular psalm but rather functioned as a general introduction to the collection of David's Psalms, which properly opens with Psalm 2.[7] A few scholars disagree. J. Alberto Soggin (Soggin, 1967) has, like W.H. Brownlee (Brownlee, 1971) opted for Psalm 1 as part of some ritual of enthronement, perhaps as integrated with Psalm 2. Against this we have to object among other things that Psalms 1 and 2 belong to two very different genres. Psalm 1 is a wisdom poem, whereas Psalm 2 belongs among the royal psalms if it is not simply an enthronement psalm.[8] It is, however, also admitted that because of the missing caption to the psalms, Psalm 2 must, just like Psalm 1, be a secondary part of the collection of psalms supposed to have been written by David according to tradition.[9]

In my opinion several scholars have too easily embraced that conclusion. There is no doubt that Psalm 1, in a very conscious way, was placed at the beginning of the collection of psalms. In a way it is a kind of colophon page with information about those who put the collection of psalms together. It is therefore too easy to say that certain readers of the collection of psalms simply placed Psalm 1 at the beginning as their personal addition. In many ways we should assume that Psalm 1 reveals who edited the whole collection, while Psalm 2 might contain instructions for how the collections should be read and understood.

Perhaps it is time to have a look at the text of Psalm 1.

The psalm has three sections. The first (vv. 1–2) opens with praise of the righteous who spend all their lives studying the Law – "day and night". It is not so much about the righteous as compared to the unjust, although the last group is mentioned (חטאם), as about the study of the Law and those who practise it over against those who deride it – the "scorners" (לצים). This section opens with the declamatory אשרי etc., "blessed" or "happy". It may have

---

[7] Thus Gunkel, 1929, 3; Schmidt, 1934, 3, and in the same tradition Kraus, 1977, 3. All refer to the obviously late date of composition.
[8] See the criticism in Gerstenberger, 1988, 42 f., 45.
[9] Thus Gerstenberger, 1988, 45.

consequences for the understanding of the importance of this psalm for the collection of David's Psalms that the study of the Torah is praised in this way because it is possible to argue that it is not just an ordinary "wisdom" psalm (while most psalms otherwise belong to other genres), while it, at the same time, includes a model for the interpretation of injustice and the relationship between the righteous and the unjust in Psalms. "Righteous" may in this connection not so much be a forensic term as it may in this psalm mean "someone learned in the Law". To be unjust will be the same as to confess oneself as somebody "who does not understand the law" or "has no interest in the Law" or simply "somebody who has a different interpretation of the Law than the author of Psalm 1". As already mentioned, we may consider this psalm the trademark of the editor of Psalms and this editor is, as far as the impression we get of his self-understanding, not far away from the person who enjoys the well-provided table in Psalm 23 while his enemies will have only hunger to enjoy.

The second section (v. 3) deepens our understanding of the status of the person learned in the Law as the happy man who will have success in his life. This text can also be used as a model for how we should interpret the fate of the unjust in later psalms (cf. e.g. Psalm 36). Happiness is to know that we belong among the chosen ones and that everybody who is not engaged in the same behaviour as us, in the study of the Law, is doomed and will perish and his hopes will never be fulfilled.

The third section (vv. 4–6) sharpens the confrontation: The unjust or simply godless (now רשעזם/חטאים) will perish at the judgement (במשפט). If it is about a case for the court: The godless will never win here because Yahweh will support those who believe in him (now directly צדקים). It may be that the perspective here is already eschatological: The godless will never stand when God divides between righteousness and injustice. However, the final verse does not give a clue to a decision here – although we may find such a clue when Psalm 2 becomes part of the discussion. However, the opposition between the righteous and the godless is pointed out.

In case Psalm 1 is a wisdom poem it is definitely written with its context in mind. This conclusion is valid notwithstanding how we understand the relationship to the collections of the Psalms of David. The circle of authors have presented their idea of the opposition between the righteous and the godless: The righteous are those who devote their life to the (correct) interpretation of the Law. Everybody else belongs among the godless.

Like Psalm 1, Psalm 2 has no heading. This might mean one of two things: It may indicate that Psalm 2, like Psalm 1, is a addition to the rest of the collection of psalms, but it may also be that Psalm 2 is a direct continuation of

Psalm 1.[10] The usual view has been to see Psalm 2 as old, much older than Psalm 1 and accordingly totally different from Psalm 1.[11] If my previous proposal that Psalm 2 is from the Hellenistic period can be sustained, the lack of coherence between Psalms 1 and 2 is no longer quite as evident. Let us have a look at the end of Psalm 2 (v. 12c):

אשרי כל־חוסי בו

Happy all who believe in him.

This line is often considered an appendix to Psalm 2, among many others by Eduard Nielsen, who stresses that the pious Judeans are here compared to the rebellious foreign kings who have just been instructed to submit to Yahweh and his king (Nielsen, 1990, 73). Only Erhard Gerstenberger thinks that this line may be an integral part of the psalm with a reference to duplicate admonitions – on the one hand a warning to the rebels against Yahweh, and on the other hand an invitation to those who believe in Yahweh to trust their God – (Gerstenberger, 1988, 48).

There can, in my opinion, be no doubt that Psalms 2:12c must be considered the conclusion of the introduction to the collection of David's Psalms. The expression אשרי can only be seen as an answer to the introduction to Psalm 1: "Blessed be he who does not follow after the council of the godless"/ "blessed is he who trusts in him". The verse may of course have been added to an older psalm by the editor of the collection of psalms to mark out the unity of Psalms 1 and 2 or it may be a regular part of Psalm 2, which in that case is either composed to stand here or adapted to its function as introduction for special reasons. Those who "trust in Yahweh" are the same persons who studied the Law in Psalm 1 and are not to be found in the assembly of the mocking ones, the godless.

Maybe we can get closer to a conclusion. In the final part of Psalm 2 (if we ignore v. 12c), vv. 10–12b, we find an admonition to the "kings" that they should be wise and accept council. "Be wise", v. 10a, Heb. השכילו, is a standard expression within wisdom literature. The same may be valid for the expression "accept advice" in v. 10b, Heb. הוסרו, from the root יסר, which, however,

---

[10] The two possibilities are not mutually exclusive. Psalm 2 may be an independent poem and at the same time connected to Psalm 1, meaning that its function in its context may have been dictated by Psalm 1 and the circle of collectors of the Psalter.

[11] This is even true for Gerstenberger, 1988, 49, who reckons Psalm 2 to be rather late and "synagogical".

is rare in the specific wisdom literature, although מוסר, from the same root, meaning "instruction" or even "chastisement" is quite common.[12] The verbal roots שכל and יסר appear together in wisdom literature.[13] The whole passage vv 10–12 could be understood as a wisdom poem, or a fragment of such a one, including a warning to the godless, the kings and "judges" of the world, that they should turn to Yahweh, meaning reach the true fear of God just like the pious ones, the students of the Law of Psalm 1. The enigmatic vv. 11–12a might be understood as a call to a true relationship with God: "Serve the Lord in fear". עבדו את־יהוה ביראה. The following metaphor "Kiss his feet with fear!" is borrowed from court rituals and thus combines with other metaphors in Psalm 2 with an origin in this sphere.

The scene at the beginning of Psalm 2, the rebellion of the foreign kings when there is no king enthroned on Zion, just like the imagery of the king crushing the enemies' heads, is explained in my previous article on Psalm 2. I will not repeat the argument here. It is possible that the enemies in this Psalm are not to be literally understood as foreign kings and princes, but these titles are used as metaphors about the enemies of Yahweh, which in this connection are identical with the enemies of the psalmist.

We may go further in this direction. To begin with, we must ask why this Psalm has no heading. It would have been most appropriate to dedicate it to David since very few psalms talk so much about kings and rulers. However, only beginning with Psalm 3 do the headings to the psalms begin to appear: "Psalm of David. When he fled from Absalom, his son", etc. etc. If we read the individual psalms in isolation, this lack of a heading is strange, although there are of course other examples of psalms without headings. If we, however, read the collection of psalms not as a casual collection of poems of various origins and usages but as a collection brought together by a redaction process (the principles used may not at once be obvious), the missing heading to Psalm 2 makes sense; it might even be a kind of clue to understanding the purpose of creating this collection.

It is thus obvious that Psalm 2 cannot be לדוד, as the perspective of the Psalm is that there is not yet a king on the throne and this king may, within a Hellenistic-Jewish perspective, be no other than a "David", a sibling of the

---

[12] The translation in the Danish Bible of 1992 is not a well-chosen one. BHS presents an alternative to הוסרו, הוסדה, which here might be understood as a Nif'al of יסד 2, "to plan", cf. v. 2 "take council together", here in the meaning of "accepting advice". The verb יסר does not only mean "to accept advice", cf. Luther's translation: "lasst euch züchtigen". Kraus has "laßt euch warnen" (Kraus, 1977, 11).

[13] Prov 1:3: לקחת מוסר השכל: "accept proper admonition".

House of David. If we see the connection between Psalms 1, 2, and 3 as dynamic and the narrative Psalm one the opening an "idyllic" one: The pious are engaged in the study of the Law and will have nothing to do with the godless and the sinners. The godless for their part are free to act as they please – or so they believe – because there is no king, and therefore Yahweh does not care for his faithful. But the Messiah of Yahweh will, with his help, call the godless, the foreign kings to order in the moment he is installed on his throne on Zion. The poem therefore relates the enthronement of the Messiah – he is the son of God – and the godless are advised to submit. The introduction, Psalms 1 and 2, ends with a confession which brings the reader back to the beginning. Hereafter we have a king, a David, on the throne in Zion and the following poems are directed towards this new situation. They are accordingly provided with the heading "to David", i.e., to the Messiah.

It is difficult to believe that when the king is mentioned for the first time in the Psalms it is as the Messiah and not as David or in general as a king. The concepts of the Messiah were so widespread and so generally known in Judaism in the Hellenistic-Roman Period that mentioning "Yahweh and his Messiah" in Psalms 2:2 as the beginning of the punishment of godless enemies of that time must have been understood as a confession of messianic ideas. It is not just a neutral relic from the past to be understood as part of old and unknown Judean royal rituals. However, when the Messiah is already introduced in the introduction to Psalms, it is an instruction to the reader about how to understand the following psalms in the light of a messianic interpretation of the figure of "David", as being of the dynasty of David with the task of saving Israel and restoring the empire of King David.

The title "Messiah" is not uncommon in Psalms.[14] The only biblical books that compare in this respect are the Books of Samuel. It would be wrong to argue that the title Messiah dominates Psalms, but it is used a number of times in psalms with direct references to David and his fate.[15]

It is therefore a reasonable point of departure for an interpretation of the royal metaphors in Psalms that they shall be understood to be "messianic" and not "historical", as references to old ideas about kingship. This does not mean that the title is invented for the occasion. Not much has been said here which was not already to be found in Sigmund Mowinckel's *Han som kommer* (Mowinckel, 1951b). The difference from Mowinckel is the change of historical perspective, which is partly eliminated because it is far from certain that there was a direct line from the concept of the Messiah in Psalms to

---

[14] Ps 2:2; 18:51; 10:7; 28:8; 84:10; 89:39.52; 105:15; 132:10.17.
[15] Especially Pss 89 and 132.

religious ideas of pre-exilic Judah. This indicates that the title "Messiah" in Psalms should first and foremost be seen as an expression of ideas current in the time when the collection of the Psalms was finalized.[16] It is far more uncertain whether the concept had a past in ancient Israel.

It is not the case that we should think of the Messiah-concept as exclusively the key to the interpretation of the Psalms of the Old Testament but the argument here can be used as part of this interpretation, especially if we forego the traditional abuse of the presumed ancient cultic content of the concept among the historians of religion. The collection of Psalms seems to originate in wisdom circles as a series of commentaries to the hopes and conditions current at the time when the circle of editors was active. Among such hopes we evidently find messianic expectations. At the same time the editors used a series of metaphors seemingly coming from a different sphere; the royal and cultic. However, by their introduction to the collection of Psalms, they have indicated that such a cultic interpretation of Psalms may lead one astray. A king of Jerusalem need not be an actual king in Jerusalem, but can instead be the Messiah. The evil and godless, even foreign kings and judges, are not evil or godless in an absolute sense. Neither are they real kings: Rather they are the enemies who lived around those "who have their joy in the Law of the Lord and study his Law day and night".[17]

I have, in another context, discussed the clearly sectarian content of the idea of society in the Old Testament (Lemche, 1996a, 1998e). One of the characteristics of a sect is that it itself draws the boundaries between itself and its environment. The world outside of the sect need not consider the sect as a "sect"; it is enough that the members of the sect describe themselves as outcasts surrounded by hostile neighbours. Accordingly, the enemies in Psalms need not be real enemies in the physical sense; it was enough that those who put the collection of Psalms together reckoned them as their enemies. If this interpretation has anything to it, the language in Psalms represents a subtle

---

[16] This is also valid for the use of the title in the Books of Samuel and in other places in the Old Testament. We cannot just assume any longer that we, in such cases, are in possession of old historical narratives where we can find information about Palestine in the Iron Age. The narratives in the Books of Samuel may, from a principal point of view, be contemporary with Psalms and display the same ideas about, in this case messianism as Samuel. Cf. preliminary to this issue which is not the subject here Lemche, 1992a (ET Lemche, 1993a).

[17] Philip R. Davies has, as a joke, proposed that the Psalms came into being in the Persian Period in the Academy for Psalm composition in Jerusalem. See Davies, 1992, 121. This is of course only a joke, but, as is true of most jokes, not without a hint of reality. The usual idea that most psalms originated as cultic poetry in the pre-exilic temple of Jerusalem is probably not better founded than Davies' joke. It only has the lead because it came first.

introduction to the process of interpretation that had begun as part of Hellenistic Jewry and was to have definite consequences for the understanding of texts as found in the Dead Sea Scrolls, especially in the commentaries on the Prophets, where utterances by the prophets are without question related to conditions in the time when these commentaries were written. It is the same understanding of scripture we find in the New Testament where texts from the Old Testament were, without question, regarded as omens relevant to what was going to happen.

We may, in this light, consider the "Davidic" metaphor in Psalms including the references to the Messiah. The metaphor relates to a narrative which is known, *in casu* the narrative of the Books of Samuel and Kings. The metaphor refers to this story not as history, something that happened, but a story which is going to happen. This means that the references to historical narratives of the Old Testament are not references to the past but instead refer to things that were important for the psalmists.

When we have come this far, we may begin to look for continuity in the Psalms, involving the principles behind the compilation of the individual psalms which might have produced a kind of drama: Maybe something "happened" and hence Psalms is not a casual assembly of single poems put together without any recognizable plan. Such an analysis will of course be difficult because we cannot say with certainty that the present order of psalms is the original one (what may that mean in this connection?). The previously mentioned psalm scroll from Qumran cave 11 displays, in the case of the c. 33% of Psalms which have survived, a series of differences in relation to the version in the Hebrew Bible and it seems certain that there were several differences as to the number and place of the individual psalms. The continuity need not consist in narrative coherency – such a coherence was already present in the historical literature – but was expressed in the kind of mosaic dealing with a number of themes which together make up a unity, an extensive commentary on the fate of the people of Israel as a religious community as seen by a group of persons who considered themselves (like perhaps several competing groups in their time) the "true Israel". There are many alternatives, and this suggestion is only to open an interpretation of the Psalms of the Old Testament which differs from the traditional cultic and historical one which has dominated Psalm scholarship for most of the 20th century.

8 Sociology and Prophetical Literature

Sociology is and can be something of a bore to many people, because the relevance of sociology is far from always clear. Now, take the prophets for example: why should we need sociology to intrude on the study of the prophets – are they not, after all, providers of the message of God, and will it at all be appropriate to try to sort out what the intention of God is by applying such a worldly methodology as sociology? I mean, would preachers and pastors of our own time accept being the victims of a stray sociologist armed with a microphone and a tape recorder; would we not think that our relationship with God is very much our own and that of our congregation?

So why should we deal with sociology and the prophets today? Well, the answer is clear enough: Because I was asked to do so, and as a good soldier I just do what I am told (almost). (So I am not the only one blamed for talking about prophets and sociology, somebody around here is more guilty than I. I am, on the other hand, sure that he believes that he will be pardoned in the end. So it is my responsibility to help him be exonerated! You are the judges.)

1 Prophets: Who Are the Prophets? How Can We Imagine a Prophet to Behave?

The first sociological question is to ask about the identity of the group of figures in the Old Testament normally understood to be prophets. What kind of people were the Hebrew prophets? Are we talking about a well-defined group in ancient Israelite society, or are they rather the invention of some scribal tradition?

The classical studies on prophecy in ancient Israel are the two volumes by Gustav Hölscher (Hölscher, 1914) and Johannes Lindblom (Lindblom, 1934) respectively, both belonging to the first half of that century (although Lindblom's volume was only published in English translation after the Second World War (Lindblom, 1962)). To a large extent, both studies present a splendid overview of what could then possibly be said about prophets in Israel, in the Ancient Near East and elsewhere. Hölscher concentrated on the Arab tradition of prophecy, while Lindblom also included social-anthropological material on shamanism. Both scholars have, so to speak, prepared the way for a better sociological appraisal of prophecy than the one we should have expected from such old books, and in many ways their studies are far superior to most later books on prophecy which have really distorted our view of the prophets by moulding them into something they were never intended to be.

As indicated, it would, however, be wrong to say that these two authors have been as influential as they should have been. I shall return to them a little later. First we have to make a comparison between the Old Testament prophetical literature and some examples of prophecy as presented in ancient Near Eastern sources.

Presumably prophecy existed in all corners of the Ancient Near East. We do not know much about this, as little or nothing was written down. We know, however, of a special group of Mesopotamian temple functionaries with prophetic gifts, the *maḫḫu* priest. But the prophecies of the *maḫḫu* have almost never been recorded in writing.

The *maḫḫu* was seemingly an ecstatic of some sort, typologically related to the famous prophet whom Wenamun, the Egyptian, met in Byblus in his well-known story, and who is described in the hieroglyphical exemplar of this story as an intoxicated person, rambling mad.

Now this is important for a sociological appraisal of the position of prophets, that their sayings were almost never written down. In Western Asia this is not a surprise as the busy merchants of the Palestinian and Phoenician world – almost the only persons who at that time were acquainted with writing – would have had no time for leisure productions such as the memoirs of the mad men of God, the prophets. In Mesopotamia it is more interesting that so little has survived, and this points to the fact that prophets were at that time not very respected, and for good reasons.

The problem with prophets is, first and foremost, that they are so difficult to control: Perhaps not the prophets themselves, but their messages. It is part of the prophetic game that they are considered to be inspired persons who will simply say whatever has been put into their mind by a God or a daemon, a good spirit or a bad spirit – and how can you in advance know who is the spokesman of God and who of the devil? Recall the story of Michaiah ben Imla (1 Kings 22). The king was not satisfied with only one prophet, he needed four hundred– he must have thought of a kind of statistical proof of God's intentions: if 55% voted no, then he would have followed their advice against the 45%. Now all 100% said the same, and that showed that they could – like newspapers in totalitarian states – not be trusted, so he needed one more, the poor prophet in jail, to tell him the truth, only to have him put back into jail again.

This goes together well with the information about prophetical activities which have been provided by the correspondence of the Mari letters, the only source of importance about prophets deriving from Mesopotamia in the second millennium.[1] Here the officials of the king of Mari report home to their master that this or that prophet has done and said this or that. Their reports are shorthand, and the content of the messages is seldom very long, just a few utterances – that's all – and especially no sermons, at least not long ones. The content of the short prophetical messages is, on the other hand, not without interest, as some of the attitudes of the god in question can be compared to Old Testament prophetic typology, e.g., the complaint that the king of Mari does not address a certain god (we may guess that the king had instead visited the colleague of this god, that is the temple next door).

The crucial point in these reports is, however, hardly the message itself but the assurance that the person who was responsible for the prophecy has been contained in prison, just as happened to Michiaha ben Imla and later Jeremiah, whose "favourite" lodging seems to have been the well in the guard's court in the palace of Jerusalem. Hardly a pleasant place to stay. But here the prophet could be supervised until it was proven that he was really a prophet and not a trickster or a spokesman of a false or evil god – in which case he would probably have been put to death.

Why were the prophets not acknowledged as great heroes of the religious life of the Ancient Near East? Simply because they were "outgunned" by other specialists who were supposed to be expressing the will of God. There existed in fact innumerable categories of specialists who were much better able to predict the future in a way that was scientifically easier to control than prophets. I will only mention various kinds of soothsayers working on the basis of empirical phenomena, such as auspices, haruspices, astrology etc. These groups represented long accepted knowledge: if a liver had a certain form it meant something special and it always meant the same thing. So omens were based on sound observations of the relationship between a certain appearance and a conclusion based on this observation, and it could be repeated, should the same formation of a liver appear again.

It is of no importance that we would probably not accept this as science; it is enough to indicate that the people in ancient times thought so. It is, however, important to understand that Ancient Near Eastern culture was not primitive, but highly sophisticated. And just as we normally do not like

---

[1] Akkadian texts and translations easily accessible in Nissinen, 2003, 13–92.

the exceptional, the uncontrollable and primitive, ancient man disliked such nonsense. And prophets working "off the record" were really considered very primitive spokesmen of God.

This can be compared to the Catholic Church's attitude vis-à-vis miracles. Like us, the Catholic Church doesn't like miracles and is happy to know that Jesus performed most of them. After Jesus rose from his grave, we really don't need more miracles to prove the existence of God. However, we cannot control God. Like Aslan in C.S. Lewis' Narnia novels, God is a wild God who does as he wishes, so if he wishes to create a miracle, we cannot stop him (although he should be warned!). If therefore a miracle happens, the church will put together a commission (I believe that there is a standing commission in Rome for such matters) and it is the task of this commission to evaluate whether the miracle that happened was really a miracle – and things like this are complicated and take time. So, the Lourdes miracle from around the middle of the last century was not acknowledged as a proper miracle before the end of the century or at the beginning of the present one. No, we certainly don't like miracles!

Although I may be wrong after all, at least as far as Catholics and Lutherans are concerned, we adore miracles, if they only follow the rules that have been set by the clergy and the church. I mean miracles happen every Sunday at communion, at least in our congregations, and are acknowledged as such although they are called sacraments. Because there is nothing as good as knowing how to control the acts of God!

Prophets will always, in a sophisticated society, be regarded as a nuisance, as relics from a more primitive age, and certainly not to be believed – if they are not vindicated by history. So, I am sure that a real prophet like Jesus ben Hananiah, who, according to Josephus, showed up in Jerusalem during the Roman siege of the city, was more of a nuisance – a "just nuisance" to most of the people around the city.[2] His message was very simple "Oh Jerusalem! Oh Jerusalem! Oh Jerusalem!" and that message he repeated without interruption until the day a stone from a Roman catapult hit him and silenced him, surely to the relief of the inhabitants of the city.[3]

---

[2] Probably only understandable to people living in the Cape Province of South Africa, this is an allusion to the wonderful sculpture (there are actually two) of "Just Nuisance", a dog that lived at the naval base in Simonstown during the Second World War and was enlisted in the Royal Navy as an able seaman, and when he died in 1944 was given a full military funeral.

[3] Josephus, *Bellum Judaicum*, 6.5.3.

So prophets were neither loved nor highly respected, except perhaps at one time and place, in Assyria at the very end of her history. This is a strange phenomenon which until now has been only partially explored by Old Testament scholars, but a whole corpus of prophetical sayings have been preserved from the days of Asarhaddon and Ashurbanipal, showing an interest in prophecy that was without precedence in ancient times.[4]

The reason for this renewed interest in prophecy at that time and place is hard to say. However, my guess is that it can be linked to a general distrust at the end of the independent Assyrian and Mesopotamian history in the ancient sciences and religions. This is not my idea but has been studied by Assyriologists and biblical scholars such as, for example, my colleague at the University of Hamburg, Hermann Spieckermann, in his dissertation (Spieckermann, 1982). Such distrust is not unknown, not even today where we see a reaction against modern science and a return to more primitive beliefs and methods, not only in religion but also in medicine. Astrology is also a topic that occupies quite a number of people today – and who among us can say they have never taken a look at their horoscope (not that we believe in them – but…)?

So a sociological study of Ancient Near Eastern prophecy will probably show the prophets to have been seen to be rather unimportant except in times of general distrust in the classic methods of divination. The prophets of the Old Testament are, however, so far as they represent the God of Israel, persons whose authority should not be questioned, or you may end up like the children who were torn to pieces by a bear because they mocked Elisha (2 Kings 2:23–4). The prophets are described as the intimates and advisors of kings and princes; upon their shoulders rests the burden of knowing what is going to happen to unfaithful Israel when Yahweh deserts his chosen people.

This picture of prophecy runs counter to the Ancient Near Eastern one, and the image of prophecy we get from the Old Testament – not to speak of the Old Testament prophetic books – seems diametrically opposed to the impression we get from the study of Ancient Near Eastern systems of divination. How did that happen? Was it really the case that the Hebrew prophets were so different from their colleagues in other parts of the Ancient Near East that they alone were respected and listened to, whereas other categories of soothsayers were rejected and hunted down, killed and executed on the spot when caught and banished from official religious life – or is this only something somebody wants us to believe?

---

[4] This material has since been collected by Simo Parpola (Parpola, 1997), and studied by Martti Nissinen (Nissinen, 1998).

The notion of prophecy in the Ancient Near East and in the Old Testament seems incompatible to such a degree that it would be correct to speak about two different religious worlds. How did that happen? Who invented the Hebrew prophets? Yahweh – or was it later tradition in need of persons who could act as the spokesmen of an ideology of a much later time?

Two parties contributed to this notion of prophecy which is the prevailing one to this day, one of them ancient, the other modern. The ancient party consisted of the deuteronomistic authors of what some (e.g., John Van Seters) believe to be the oldest version of Israel's history, and who, as I see it, "invented" the Old Testament prophet as a prophetic type. The modern party consisted of mostly German Protestant scholars who believed the prophets to belong among the ministers of their own churches, or they considered them to be lay preachers who have, since the Reformation, been a well-established part of our religious universe (the last point can safely be said to contain a sociological element of its own – however, it's an element not normally recognized by our colleagues, in that it directs its attention towards the modern scholars rather that towards their subject of research – and the value of this direction of sociological analysis cannot be questioned irrespective of the relevance of sociology for the theme under discussion).

I would therefore maintain that the deuteronomists created the Hebrew prophet as a type, and the "proof" (in quotation marks – of course) is simply that almost all, if not simply all of the Hebrew prophets, belonged to ancient times; they, so to speak, died out before the time of the deuteronomists.

This is a most convenient idea, the notion that prophecy was a thing of the past. As I said, we don't need miracles, but it is nice to know that miracles happened – once upon a time. So contemporary prophets – miserable beings like Jesus ben Hananiah – were neither respected nor the model for the deuteronomistic invention of prophets as the spokesmen of God, who predicted the destruction of Israel and its temple and the exile which was understood to be the purgatory through which the nation of God had to pass to be cleansed from its significant sins.

And as I said, the modern scholar joined the deuteronomists in elaborating on the fictitious role of the Hebrew prophets, almost presenting them to be commentators like the ones we meet in the newspapers, and on television and broadcast news, who may not predict the course of history to come – although they sometimes try – but who are rather condemning or recommending what is going on. The prophets act as if they were contemporary spokesmen of the history which the deuteronomists themselves created, and were therefore placed in the deuteronomistic history but also in the so-called prophetic books at convenient places where they could make authoritative speeches condemning the unjust people of Yahweh to a destruction which really happened – as everybody in the time of the deuteronomists already knew.

I have already dealt with this theme in the Blenkinsopp Festschrift from 1992 (Lemche, 1992b), and shall not repeat myself. However, to quote "my friend" Tuco: If you want to shoot, then shoot, don't speak! (Sergio Leone: "The Good, The Bad and the Ugly"): If you want to prophecy, prophecy, don't preach. People want to know about the future, not to listen to sermons. Sermons are something that comes after the catastrophe, when we seek an explanation for what happened; it is not something that comes before. So the whole genre of biblical prophecy is wrong from a religio-sociological point – which, by the way, is also a sociological point of view.

2 A Digression Before an Answer Can Be Reached: What Kind of Literature Can We Expect to Find in the Old Testament?

Before I continue this line of argument, just a few remarks concerning my general view of the kind of literature we can expect to find in the Old Testament. Just to explain how I may imagine the deuteronomists to have created the biblical notion of prophecy.

Here it should not be forgotten that my personal point of departure is the conviction that the Old Testament is a Jewish book or a collection of Jewish writings mostly belonging to the Hellenistic Age. To some books this only applies to the present form, other books may owe their existence in total to the Hellenistic period and are dependent on Hellenistic notions of history. This certainly also apply to the deuteronomists, who wrote a history that is much closer to the Greek historical tradition than to the ancient oriental "antiquarian mode" about which John Van Seters has so often spoken, and the Pentateuch seems even more likely to be a book dependent on Greek patterns of history writing, as some of the central themes of the Pentateuch are without precedence in the Ancient Near East, whereas they are common in Greek literature: I especially think of the motif of migrating nations who conquer countries and cities. This was a new concept: if you had told old Cato that he was the descendant of a refugee from Troy, he would have said "nonsense" and have had you arrested on the spot. Nevertheless the Hellenized Vergil wrote a famous epic explaining exactly that: namely that the Romans came from Troy – and some poor historians of the modern age have safely assumed that Vergil, not Cato (whom I trust) was correct.

As Hellenistic literature we can only expect the biblical historical books to be *constructions* of history, not *real history* (if we will accept the idea that such a thing may indeed exist). We should not expect the historical books to retell the history of Israel as it happened – nobody is able to retell this history, not even N.P. Lemche! Instead, the biblical historians created their own historical universe according to the rules of history writing which were current in their own times. And here, according to the rules of that time, they were free to say whatever they wanted to say, as long as their audience accepted their constructed history, but this audience would not have been able to distinguish between what was true and what was pure invention.

We should therefore not be surprised if the image of prophecy in the deuteronomistic literature is only a matter of literature and not of the real Palestinian world of pre-exilic times, and nobody would have blamed the deuteronomists for inventing the prophets as their spokespersons; it was totally in accordance with the rules of that time that figures from the past were drawn into the light to pronounce the will of God, or the sentence over other human beings. We need merely think of the position of Solon in the history of Herodotus.

At this point some may wish to assault me with my own weapons by maintaining that as early as Wellhausen, one of my spiritual fathers, the prophetic books were understood to be older than the Law, i.e. the Pentateuch. Normally the modern followers of Wellhausen would stress his point that the prophets simply came before the law and that their notion of the Torah has little to do with the idea of the all-important law of God/Moses to be found in the Pentateuch. To a certain extent this is true, but only to a certain extent – as just a glance at Isaiah 1 will show, where we see a reference to the law of God (v. 10) which is not so far away from the understanding of the law present in the Pentateuch. I know that many colleagues maintain that here Law means "teaching", but I question this interpretation as another example of the fictitious image of prophets created by modern scholars: under no circumstances may it be permitted to say that the prophets were prophets, and so they must be preachers and teachers!

Contrary to Wellhausen and many modern scholars, I would maintain that the prophetic literature is hardly older than the historical books of the Old Testament. So, if we walk our way through chapter one of the Book of Isaiah, we encounter not an independent prophetic statement of history, but a deuteronomistic or deuteronomistic-like exposure of the fate of Israel.

It is true that in Isaiah we encounter poetic literature of a very high quality, whereas in the deuteronomistic literature and in the Pentateuch prose narrative dominates. It is also true that, from a historical point of view, poetic literature is as a genre older than the prose literature, but that does not prove a certain piece of poetry to be older than a certain piece of prose. Both pieces can just as well be contemporary or the prose older than the poetry. To maintain the opposite would be to argue that the Russian novelist Turgenjev (1818–1883) was by necessity younger than the Russian poet Pushkin (1799–1837) (they were in fact almost contemporaries), or, to remain in the Anglo-Saxon world, that Shakespeare should be seen as older than the chronicle of Holinshed (which he used as a source to create his historical plays), simply because Holinshed was written in prose and Shakespeare's dramas in poetry.[5]

Another example from Isaiah 1 that very much says the same thing consists of the verses which deal with the worship of Yahweh and where the sacrificial cult is disclaimed (vv. 10–17). Well, it is normal for Protestant scholars to doubt that the prophets were really against the cult. They were only preaching for a better cult, the participants of which were supposed to be blameless Israelites (in case such Israelites were around). Sometimes you should, however, give the prophet a chance to say what he says, and Isaiah very much says that his God does not like the bloody offerings of the Israelites; he will have repentance and righteousness, so never mind sacrifices!

Of course, I cannot prove in this short space that the prophetic literature was not older than the historical literature of the Old Testament, although I may have pointed at some evidence which indicates that this need not be the case. In the case of Jeremiah, it is obvious that it is pure nonsense to speak of the primacy of poetry over the prose parts, as it is hardly feasible that the poetic parts of Jeremiah ever existed (at least not as a collection of sayings) before they were embraced by the deuteronomistic prose narrative which holds the book together and creates a framework for the poetic parts.

Following this line of argumentation, it seems pretty obvious that the prophetic books cannot be traced back to prophetic figures of the past. Rather, they are the invention of authors roughly belonging to the same age as the history writers who composed – that is constructed – the deuteronomistic history, and perhaps also the Pentateuch (although the Pentateuch may be younger than both the deuteronomistic history and especially the prophetical literature, which shows very little interest in the Pentateuch). It is accordingly my thesis that the prophetic books were conceived as witnesses of the correctness of the deuteronomistic claim that Israel's history was a history of self-destruction. The prophets were the witnesses called upon by the deuteronomists to prove their case and to free Yahweh of any accusation of being

---

[5] If anyone wishes to compare: See A. Nicoll and J. Nicoll, 1965.

a wilful and tyrannical Lord who destroyed his chosen ones just because it pleased him to do so.

3 And Sociology

Now, can sociology be of any help here? Would it not be enough to follow the path of older scholarship to reach the same result? Yes, I believe that it would be possible, on the basis of earlier studies, to reach the same results, although I doubt that the results could be reached in such a short span of time.

As long as we work exclusively as historians we are bound to the presence of evidence: written or pictorial or both – and thereafter comes the so-called "common sense" conclusion. What is different here is that before I start such an analysis I will try to establish the identity of an Israelite prophet, and that identification is very much dependent on sociological study. As I indicated above, the works of Hölscher and Lindblom displayed more sociological sense than the more traditionally minded and theologically oriented studies of, say, Hans Walter Wolff or for that matter Gerhard von Rad. Both scholars made extensive use of material which can only be considered if not sociological in the strict sense of the word then at least social-anthropological. Here I should also mention the study of prophecy by Alfred Guillaume, another fine piece of research belonging to the first half of the twentieth century (Guillaume, 1938). All of these studies as well as specific social-anthropological ones – for example the rightfully praised study by the British social anthropologist Ian Lewis on Shamanism (Ecstatic Religion) (Lewis, 1971) – help us when we try to establish what I earlier termed the typology of a prophet in ancient Israel.

The second step was not to apply this evidence from social anthropology to the biblical material but to see whether the impression of prophecy which can be obtained on the basis of social anthropology could be confirmed by a study of Ancient Near Eastern prophecy – and here the evidence from Mari is especially interesting – and I have no trouble in maintaining that, apart from the Old Testament, oriental prophecy seems to suit the anthropological picture perfectly. It is the Old Testament that is problematic, not the extra-biblical evidence, and the Old Testament is only problematic insofar as we believe it to be something which it is not, that is, a description of Israel's past, including the prophets of ancient Israel, which can be used for historical purposes. Then we end up with a totally artificial impression of ancient Israelite society which is far removed from the realities of the Palestinian world of the Iron Age.

So my advice is to give sociology – social anthropology if you wish – a chance. If not, then we are simply duplicating the mistakes of archaeology, which was turned into biblical archaeology by theologians. We could just as well speak about biblical sociology! Both biblical archaeology and biblical sociology are conducted at the mercy of the biblical writers, and both disciplines can only be considered alternative ways of paraphrasing the Old Testament.

HISTORY

9   History and Memory in the Old Testament

When presenting the phenomenon of cultural memory/collective memory to the "uninitiated" we are often met with a certain disbelief because our audience cannot escape the impression that the discussion is somewhat diffuse. Is collective memory the same as cultural memory? And when we move on to the definitions of these concepts what is then the difference between cultural memory and history? Memory has something to do with the past but history certainly also has. Do history and cultural memory overlap, or are we speaking about two very different things?

History and Memory

In our time the last issue is particularly important because the modern world operates with a concept of history which was established during the Romantic Period and still sees it as the purpose of historical research to tell "what really happened".[1] The same can be said about memory but there are no scholarly demands that memory be methodological and embracing procedures that must be followed. Memory is simply what the person who has this memory remembers from the past, normally the past which the person in question has a personal relationship to. A person who, like this author, was part of the students' revolt in 1968 will have a personal recollection of what happened and the persons who were involved, and may be a bit confused if not dismayed by the "official" present-day historical reconstructions of what "really" happened at that time.[2]

---

[1] This definition goes back to the German historian Leopold von Ranke (1795–1886) and can be found in his early opus *Geschichten der romanischen und germanischen Völker von 1494 bis 1535* (von Ranke, 1824). See also Brunius, 1963 (www.scandia.hist.lu.se).

[2] I chaired the theological student council at the University of Copenhagen in 1968 and was in this capacity quite close to the events of that year. See also my article in Danish "Da studenterrådet blev voksen", *Hvad er imod Studentens Kaar* (Lemche, 2012b).

Those who participated in the resistance movement during the war were not always comfortable with later historical reconstructions; not so much by historians of the first post-war generation but later generations, and they certainly made their dissatisfaction public and were, as long as the veterans were still alive, certainly able to censure historical research. Now most are no more and we will, for that reason, see historians working much more freely and unimpeded with the history of the resistance and its importance during the German occupation. The relationship between history and memory can, on this level, best be compared to the function of a witness at court: A witness may throw some light on a case but the testimony of one witness is normally not reckoned enough to decide the outcome of the case. The court decides on the basis of a mosaic of testimonies. The historian will, in the same manner, apply a series of testimonies – including a variety of types, oral, written, material – and put an image of his subject of study together in order to present a historical reconstruction of his subject. The historian is in possession of a series of rules – in our language methods – which he is obliged to follow if he wants to be taken seriously.[3]

The person who remembers will not have a similar set of rules regulating the stream of remembrance. This is the reason why in a modern context we have little trouble separating memory from history. If we understand it as collective memory, cultural memory is what a society remembers. Cultural memory thus becomes the subject of historical analyses but is in itself not history.[4]

However, an important matter is how we understand memory vis-à-vis history in our time. Something else is what happens when we move back in time to a period when the modern concept of history had not yet been formulated – in reality this includes all specimens of history writing from Antiquity to the beginning of modernity. Thus, if we turn to the "father of history" Herodotus of Halicarnassus (5th century BCE), he writes at the beginning of his *Histories*:

> Here the research of Herodotus of Halicarnassus is published in order that the acts of humans through times shall not be forgotten, in order that the great and marvelous deeds of the Greeks and the Barbarians

---

[3] We should really not speak of a "series of methods". Of course there are several ways today to do historical studies each including its set of methods. It is, however, not my task to develop this theme here.
[4] In general on the subject of cultural memory and history, Cubitt, 2007.

shall not remain unknown, but also to explain why they fought against each other.

The Greek word *history* is here in the plural and translated as "research" and it does not relate to scientific studies but exactly to what journalists consider to be "research". Herodotus was not a scholar in the modern sense; he was a journalist and wrote about famous men and their acts. That is the reason why he connects Solon from Athens with Croesus the king of Lydia – it is hardly likely that they ever met – and has a lot to tell us about their meeting, and from here he continues with other tall tales such as the story about the ring of Polycrates found in the belly of a fish. Before he gets to his real subject, the encounter between the Greeks and the Persians, he makes a series of detours which, among other things, brings him to Egypt which he definitely visited himself. His digressions also include a survey of habits among inhabitants of Babylon where he may never have been. Only then does he arrive at the Persian wars fought shortly before he was born. Now we have probably reached truly historical matters but this does not prevent Herodotus from including several anecdotes in the course of his narrative.

It is obvious that the principal difference between Herodotus's "research" and other ancient history writing from modern historical studies consists of the lack of critical sense. When Herodotus occasionally shows a critical understanding of what he is narrating it is mainly in the same manner as modern journalists. His criticism is mostly formulated in this way: "This I don't believe" or "This is goose hunting". Such an example of his critical sense occurs in connection with the explanation of his Egyptian guides of the yearly inundation of the Nile as the result of melting snow in Ethiopia. Herodotus "knows" very well that so far to the south we are too close to the sun to allow for the presence of snow![5]

Herodotus' informants are local people and he includes their explanations and traditions in his "research". Thus we may say that he transmits to posterity and elaborates on the explanations of Egyptian priests. The same may be said about his famous description of the auctions of women in Babylon where girls to be married are put on auction to the highest bidders. The auction begins with the most attractive girls and the money earned from the sale of these girls is used as dowries for the not so attractive girls. In this way every girl on the market is provided for.[6] Even if Herodotus probably never visited

---

[5] Herodotus: II 19–31. In the same place Herodotus adds that this explanation is better than most other but still the most unlikely of all.
[6] Herodotus I 196.

Babylon and built his story on what he had been told by other people,[7] his story is entertaining. We are in possession of thousands of marriage contracts from Mesopotamia but none of them can be taken as evidence of the habit described by Herodotus.

Enlightened people of ancient times knew very well that Herodotus was not always to be trusted. In spite of this he was admired for his elegance and for the moral content of his stories. The last subject, morality, actually played a much more important role than historical accuracy, which has to do with the purpose of ancient retelling of the past – that it must be didactically valuable as part of the education of the next generations.[8] In contrast to Herodotus, his younger colleague Thucydides was reckoned to be more trustworthy but Thucydides also wrote about subjects and events in which he had played a part as a high-ranking naval officer in the Athenian navy during the Peloponnesian War. Military reports do not allow space for artful elaborations. Thucydides' description of the Peloponnese War is accordingly contemporary history. We may call it memory, but Thucydides had no intention of dealing with a period earlier than his own time.

Narratives of the past in ancient Near Eastern documents – including the historiography in the Old Testament – have little in common with scientific history writing. Basically it is of the same sort as Greek history writing and this commonness has become more and more relevant to recent students of ancient historiography.[9] It is obvious that the primary aim of the historiographers – biblical as well as other – was not to tell what really happened but to present a story about the past which was meant to enjoy the author's readership.

Thus this also applies to Hittite historiography, formerly often included in the discussion of biblical history writing. The many treaties concluded between Hittite kings and their vassals but also between the great king in Hattušaš and his colleague the Egyptian Pharaoh normally include a section surveying former relations between the two parts who are now involved in the conclusion of the treaty. These surveys of the past were often believed to be quite precise renderings of past events, but modern research has shown that this was not the case but the events are arranged with an eye to present

---

[7] On the question of Herodotus and Mesopotamia cf. O.E. Ravn, *Herodots Beskrivelse af Babylon* (Ravn, 1939. ET: Ravn, 1942). On the market for women, see Ravn, 1939, 92. It is interesting that Ravn reckons Herodotus' description of Babylon as "memory" (Ravn, 1939, 98–101).
[8] Cf. on this aspect of ancient education Ørsted, 1978.
[9] More on this below.

political relations. It is more or less about presenting the past in the darkest possible terms in order to stress the dawn of new times caused by the conclusion of the treaty in question.[10]

When we turn to Mesopotamia we find no such endeavours of presenting the events of the past as a coherent narrative. Here we mainly speak about Babylonian and Assyrian chronicles, listings of years including the most important events of the year or about royal annals which in a more elaborate form describes the campaigns of various kings, but we should not forget that these annals also present a kind of chronicles only embroidered with a few more details.[11] If we finally move on to Egypt, we encounter annalistic literature of almost the same kind as the Mesopotamian. In Mesopotamia as well as in Egypt efforts are made to present the present with references to the past. This past is, however, not the past as it really was but as imagined by posterity. We have narratives that transgress the scope of annalistic reports such as the famous inscription of Ramses II dealing with the battle at Qadesh in 1274 BCE followed by a series of pictorial representations of the events in the usual Egyptian style, with the dominant figure of Pharaoh at the centre surrounded by ordinary Egyptians as well as Hittite enemies all presented as pygmies.[12] We never find a critical attitude to the events as presented, although the description of Ramses II's campaign is so detailed that modern historians find material for modern reconstructions of the course of events.[13]

Historical Narrative in the Old Testament

My view of the historiography of the Old Testament may easily be perceived from my introduction to Old Testament studies, *The Old Testament between Theology and History* (Lemche, 2008c). There is therefore no reason to repeat what I already wrote in this work. To put it briefly, the book represents a showdown with two hundred years of historical research based on the stories of the Old Testament which have all too easily been abused as sources of historical information. In this way it is possible to classify the many histories

---

[10] The treaties are translated in Beckman, 1996.
[11] Most of this literature has been translated in Grayson, 2000.
[12] The Egyptian description of this battle has been edited by Alan Gardiner, *The Kadesh Inscriptions of Ramesses II* (Gardiner, 1960).
[13] And they are so plentiful and diverse that modern historians have had the opportunity for more than a hundred years to be in severe disagreement as to who won the battle, the Egyptians or the Hittites.

of Israel which have appeared as more or less critical paraphrases of the narratives of the Old Testament.

It is, however, remarkable how far the biblical narrative is in disaccord with what we de facto know about the history of Palestine in ancient times. It is somehow possible to speak about a systemic lack of compliance and, moreover, it doesn't matter much whether we deal with the story of Israel's earliest history or the description of the post-exilic period found in the Old Testament. We should, of course, not overlook the casual information about events that really took place such as the attacks of Sennacherib on Jerusalem in 701 BCE or of Nebuchadnezzar in 597 BCE. In such cases there is a fair amount of agreement between the information found in the Old Testament and in the annals of the Assyrian and Babylonian kings.[14] Such examples of agreement do not, however, change the general impression that the authors who wrote the biblical narratives were in no way interested in telling us *wie es eigentlich gewesen*. They evidently told stories with a different purpose, making use of a number of traditional narrative strategies and topics from the Ancient Near East in general. In the Old Testament such matters are put together in order to provide a certain impression of the fate of biblical Israel of old.[15]

At the centre of the biblical narrative of Israel's history we find Jerusalem and in the middle of Jerusalem we find Solomon's temple. The drama is about Jerusalem surrounded with motives of immigration and conquest of the land on one side and the exile from the country on the other. The immigration and conquest of Cana'an come after a prolonged sojourn in Egypt – in this context it appears in the Old Testament purely as fiction. This theme comes to an end when David conquers Jerusalem, which apparently did not exist at the time when most historians have dated this event, c. 1000 BCE.[16] The conclusion to this part of Jerusalem's history came with the two conquests of Nebuchadnezzar in 597 BCE and 587 BCE, the first also known from Babylonian sources. At least we know for sure that the city was totally laid waste by the Babylonians,

---

[14] Sennacherib: Cf. Luckenbill, 1924: col. III:18–33 (pp. 30–1). Nebukadnezar: Grayson, 2000: Chron 5:11–13, 102.

[15] On the history as a "memory compote" cf. Thompson, 1999.

[16] The issue of the status of Jerusalem in the 10th century BCE has mainly been discussed among Israeli archaeologists at home at Tel Aviv University and their colleagues of the Hebrew University in Jerusalem. The archaeologists from Tel Aviv are generally of the opinion that there was no city here when David and Solomon, according to the traditional dating, ruled, or it was at the most an unimportant hamlet with a population incorporating less than a hundred grown-up men. This point of view has been explained in a clear fashion in Finkelstein and Silberman, 2001, and slightly modified in Finkelstein and Silberman, 2006, 267–74.

who also destroyed practically all of Judah outside of Jerusalem.[17] After another seventy years (biblical time!) the exiled people of Israel returned from captivity and took over their old country.

However, again this is not history. Jerusalem was not rebuilt either at the end of the 6th century BCE or in the course of the 5th or 4th centuries. There are several indications that reconstruction of the city only began in a serious way in the 2nd century BCE, at a time when it was definitely not the natural centre of the country.[18] During this period the centres of the land were Samaria and Shechem to the north of Jerusalem, in an area that might previously been the real Israel.[19] The substantial pro-Jerusalemite narrative about the faith of Israel in the Old Testament is perhaps nothing but propaganda from the time when Jerusalem aimed at becoming the political and religious centre of the land at the expense of other centres to the north of Jerusalem.

Thus the narrative in the Old Testament about the fate of ancient Israel is propagandistic, written with a political purpose and with a political goal in mind in order to place Jerusalem and its temple as the centre of the land of Israel. In order to put this narrative together, the authors have used a palette of already existing but mostly different motifs. The theme of immigration and conquest is well known from classical literature which also led to the magnificent use of the theme in the story of the Trojan hero Aeneas' travel to Italy after the fall of Troy.[20] The period of the Judges represents the "heroic age", a part of many cultures' – also the Scandinavian – memories of their past.[21] The story of David connects two traditional narratives, first the epos-like narrative about the young hero who has to experience so much before he wins the princess and half the kingdom, a story well known also from the Ancient Near East,[22] then second a tale of a drama within the family which only finds its parallels in Greek dramas about the dissolution of families.[23]

---

[17] The Israeli scholar now reckoned perhaps the most important as far as this issue is concerned is Oded Lipschits. See Lipschits, 2005.

[18] As in the previous case this discussion goes on between archaeologists from Tel Aviv and Jerusalem. So far, no archaeologist has found remains of importance from the early Persian Period such as Nehemiah's wall. See recently Finkelstein, 2012, and Lipschits, 2011.

[19] See further: Magen, 2007.

[20] Cf. Vergil, *Aeneid*, composed between 29 and 19 BCE.

[21] Chadwick, 1912 is still of fundamental importance.

[22] The commonness of themes was first demonstrated by Giovanni Buccellati (Buccellati, 1962), and then analysed by Mario Liverani (Liverani, 1972; ET: Liverani, 2004).

[23] This involves both prose literature and plays such as Euripides' *Medea* and Sophocles' *Oedipus*. We may say that this topic is central to all Greek tragedy since Aeschylus' *Oresteia*.

However, to make a long story short: There is no historiography in the Old Testament. It is a modern convention that it should be there and represents a major misunderstanding of the literary phenomenon which confronts the reader of the Old Testament. We may call Old Testament narratives memoirs because they share a privilege with memoirs that they don't need to pay much attention to what really happened a long time ago. Thus it would be correct to call the narrative of the Old Testament cultural memory.

Cultural Memory in the Old Testament

Now we have reached the essential question: If historiography in the Old Testament is really cultural memory, whose memory are we talking about? This question is really not so difficult to answer if we are not looking for names of authors and their exact whereabouts and time. Such questions are really impossible to answer. Instead of such futile discussions we may turn to what is really in our possession and through this to try to establish the authors' "profile": What did they write about? Where did they find their motifs and stories? What were their intentions? What was their position within their own society?

I have previously tried to establish such portraits of the authors (Lemche, 2001a). It was demonstrated that we are speaking about learned people knowing not just only local Palestinian ("Israelite") tradition in the narrow sense but also possessing a broad acquaintance with Near Eastern tradition at large. They elaborate on Egyptian narratives like in the story of Joseph and Potiphar's wife, which is an independent revision of the Egyptian tale of the two brothers whose relationship is ruined by the wife of one of the brothers, who tries to seduce the other brother,[24] but are also well acquainted with conditions in Egypt in general.[25] In the same manner they roam around in the primary history (Gen 1–11) within Babylonian mythology and even present a rewriting of the Babylonian story of the flood, maybe even in the form we find it in the – in those days very popular – Gilgamesh epic.[26] Themes and motifs having their home in Greek tradition are not absent. Probably the best-known example is the description of the creation of the world in Genesis 1 with the priority given to the four elements, the heat (light), the cold (darkness), the wet (water), and the dry (land), which is very similar to Greek

---

[24] The Egyptian story can be found in Hallo, 1997, 85–9.
[25] Cf. Redford, 1970.
[26] Cf. Lemche, 2012c.

natural philosophy. This "philosophy" of nature has been compared to Greek natural philosophy of the kind of Thales of Miletus.[27] We may conclude that scholars by and large have obtained a better eye for the connections between the literature of the Old Testament and Greek tradition, which is hardly surprising as more and more biblical scholars are today reckoning the Old Testament, or better the literature found in the Old Testament, to belong to the late Persian or early Hellenistic periods, from the 4th or the 3rd centuries BCE[28]

When we therefore speak about cultural memory in the Old Testament, we are talking about a most learned kind of "memory" formulated by authors with a considerable and varied education and with a wide horizon. This is not the literature which originated in the nooks and corners of ancient Palestine or for that matter in pre-Hellenistic Jerusalem, which was then hardly more than a small village on a deserted hilltop in ancient Judah. Israeli archaeologists speak in this connection about a settlement covering less than two hectares and including a population of, say, five hundred people; less than one hundred grown-up men.[29] Without doubt there was a sanctuary on this spot already in the 5th century BCE including a "high priest", but we have no information about the size of this temple,[30] although the holiness tradition of this place was so strong that the inhabitants ("Jews") of Elephantine in southern Egypt sent a letter in Aramaic to Jerusalem in connection with the possible rebuilding of the ruined temple of Yahweh at Elephantine.[31]

The rehabilitation of the Samaritans and their tradition in recent times and the discovery of a major Samaritan city at Gerizim next to the Samaritan temple will undoubtedly lead to an improvement of the understanding of the importance of the Samaritans for the formation of the Jewish tradition in the Old Testament, especially if it turns out to be a correct assumption that the very name of "Israel" can originally be linked to the Samaritans and was only

---

[27] Van Seters, 1988, reprinted in Van Seters, 2011, 335–58.

[28] We may even speak of the dawn of "pan-Hellenism" not very different from earlier "pan-Babylonism", which played a dominating role in biblical scholarship more than a hundred years ago. This writer cannot, of course, plead "not guilty" as I formulated the program for such scholarship which focused on Hellas in a lecture at the Theological Faculty in Copenhagen in 1991 (Lemche, 1992a). One of the more marked examples of this trend is certainly Philippe Wajdenbaum, *Argonauts of the Desert: Structural Analysis of the Hebrew Bible* (Wajdenbaum, 2011).

[29] Cf. Finkelstein, 2012.

[30] If we do not accept the information in Ezra 3:12–13 that the Jews were weeping when they saw their new temple and remembered the greatness of their former temple.

[31] Cowley, 1923: n. 30:18: רבא כהנא יהונתן.

secondarily transferred to the Jewish society living in Jerusalem.³² If this is correct we must say that it casts a multicoloured light on cultural memory in the Old Testament. The next step will be to decide what this memory is about and what the authors wished to accomplish by writing their narratives.

It is sometimes said by students of memory that "history is a weapon of mass instruction". History is the way a society creates its own identity, which happened in Europe after the French Revolution, with its total opposition to a tradition that was founded on the relationship between the ruler (the king) and his subjects. When the king "lost his head" literally speaking, the state lost its centre and a new centre appeared, "the people". In order to create a people or rather a nation a feeling of coherence was necessary for people who had until now only been united by being subjects of the same king. The main method to achieve this was to establish a common history which shows that the "people" had been united by a common destiny through time.³³

The narrative of the Old Testament may be called the birth history of the Israelite people. It shares a great deal of communality with later European national historiography and is evidently intended to provide the "Israelites" with an image of past unity by describing how this unity came about. Previously, say until a generation ago, it was commonly assumed that the background of this historiography should be looked for in the days of David and Solomon. The intention was definitely to create unity between the various parts of the kingdom of these two great kings.³⁴ The role of this historiography was sometimes compared to Roman history writing during the early imperial period when a series of history writers and poets arose who could tell about the national history of the Roman people and in this way create the ideological foundation of the new Roman Empire. We may first and foremost think of Livy, whose only partly preserved Roman history occupied one hundred and forty-two books, and of Vergil, whose *Aeneid* tells us about Rome's first days but ends with a union between Rome and its neighbours after a long series of wars.³⁵

Within the context of the Old Testament, when the basis of an Israelite historiography in David's and Solomon's times is made impossible because

---

³² Cf. On this Lemche, 2012a. The basis for this assumption is two votive inscriptions dating from c. 200 BCE placed at Delos by people who called themselves "Israelites" coming from Crete but ensuring that their loyalty was to the temple at Gerizim.

³³ More about this in Lemche, 2008c, 312 ff.

³⁴ Cf. On this Gerhard von Rad, "Der Anfang der Geschichtsschreibung im alten Israel" (von Rad, 1944).

³⁵ Livy's history, *Ab urbe condita libri*, c. 27–25 f.Kr. Only about 35 books have survived. On Vergil, cf. footnote 20 above (p. 138).

the idea of a united Hebrew kingdom in the 1st century BCE has become redundant, it has been necessary to think of alternative solutions. It has accordingly become more relevant to include the development towards the end of the 2nd century BCE which led to the "incorporation" (it's probably more correct to say "conquest" or "occupation") of the central parts of Palestine in the kingdom of the Hasmoneans.[36]

We do not need to date all literature in the Old Testament as late as that. It is probably just as likely to call it propaganda that was issued in order to create an "Israelite" – basically a "Judean" – state who borrowed a greater part of its traditions from the Samaritans disposing at the same time of the Samaritans by making Jerusalem the centre of the tradition about biblical Israel. We may also say that while the centre was once Shechem where the temple of the Samaritans was placed, it was now moved to Jerusalem after the destruction of the Samaritan temple, whereas the Samaritans themselves were hereafter reckoned to be a pariah.[37]

When we date the story about the Israelite people to the 2nd century we also place it in a context which opened up for different streams of culture united in this story. In spite of having their political background in the resistance against the Hellenization of the central part of Palestine which only became conspicuous after 200 BCE,[38] the Hasmoneans ended up promoting Hellenization itself – perhaps in a way which is not totally different from modern Westernization of the Middle East, which has created a lot of resistance, but at the same time being both admired and adopted.

How was, in Hasmonean times, the story of the people of Israel with its centre in Jerusalem communicated to ordinary people in the new-established Hasmonean kingdom? Actually, the Old Testament provides information about this process. The centre of the kingdom was Jerusalem, chosen by God as his abode. When you worship God, you go to his temple. It could be by help of the daily cult but especially the Jewish pilgrimage festivals played a vital role; the Passover, Pentecost, and Sukkoth (Leviticus 23). All three of these feasts had as their background the Palestinian agricultural society. Passover was linked to the barley harvest, Pentecost to the wheat harvest, and Sukkoth the fruit harvest. However, as seen long ago, these feasts had become much more than simple agrarian festivals because all of them played a role

---

[36] If we speak about the 2nd century BCE, we also speak about John Hyrcanus (134–104 BCE). Many scholars, however, still prefer to point at the time of Josiah (639–609 BCE) which is handicapped by the fact that we only know about it from the Old Testament itself.
[37] Hyrcanus was the one who destroyed the Samaritan temple at Gerizim.
[38] On the Hellenization of Palestine cf. Kuhnen, 2004).

in the historical narrative and in this way have become "places of memory" in the Jewish, i.e., the Israelite, people's understanding of its past. In his *Israel* Johannes Pedersen many years ago included an excursus devoted to the Paschal Narrative as a festival legend and a commemorative narrative.[39] He was obviously right.

In the temple and as part of the programme of the festivals the most important parts of the historical narrative was communicated to the present congregation, as in principle the whole nation. However, this was not enough. One book of the Old Testament goes further than to just recommend the participation in the central celebrations in the temple of Jerusalem. Just as much emphasis is put on the teaching of the tradition within the family in Deuteronomy where the father presents the answers to his son when he asks about the Law (Deut 6:20–5), which like a credo include summaries of all of Israel's early history. Taken together, Deuteronomy consists of an admonition urging the audience to remember the acts of Yahweh in history and not to forget what Yahweh did for Israel. The key words in Hebrew are זכר "to remember" and שכח "to forget". Without exaggerating, we may present Deuteronomy as a book of propaganda and as the clearest example transmitted from antiquity of history being used as a weapon of mass instruction.

Summary

The long narrative about the fate of Israel in the Old Testament is a piece of cultural memory which, as is true of all memory, does not primarily have the past as its subject, except as the past remembered in the present (by the public of the authors). This narrative consists of several individual remembrances. Thus the role of Shechem in this chain of traditions is remarkable in a positive as well as negative sense. In his dissertation on Shechem, Eduard Nielsen demonstrated more than sixty years ago how traditions favouring Jerusalem are struggling against traditions promoting Shechem.[40] In Shechem the people are united by its covenant with Yahweh (Joshua 24), but in Shechem the people are also broken up again into two societies: Israel and Judah (1 Kings 12). Other memories, both Israelite and Judean, are mixed into this cultural memory narrative.

---

[39] Pedersen, 1960, 549–55, ekskurs 1: "*Overgangen over Sivhavet og Paaskelegenden*".
[40] Nielsen, 1955. On the place of this work in relation to present scholarship cf. Lemche, 2013c.

One thing is certain: It is not the memory of ordinary people which forms the cultural memory as found in the Old Testament. It is memory as dictated by an intellectual elite, probably only a small percentage of the total population consisting of the few able to read and write. What ordinary people remembered is lost not least because so very little has been preserved from ancient Palestine which may have been able, eventually in the form of images and statues, to inform us about what people in general believed in. Even the pottery, which exists in abundant quantities, is practically anonymous and gives no indication of any intellectual activity to be related to living memory.[41] The iconography is so primitive in execution that I sometimes cannot resist postulating that the inability to express anything in pictures may be the reason for the prohibitions against images in the Old Testament.

---

[41] If we really want to see how art may provide such a picture of how people in those days imagined their past, Greek pottery will undoubtedly provide all the information needed with their literally thousands of representations of myths and legends.

10 On History, Sociology, and Theology: Old Testament Perspectives

Jens Glebe-Møller[1] may never have forgiven me because in my dissertation I felt it necessary to launch an attack on Norman K. Gottwald's sociologically oriented *The Tribes of Yahweh: A Sociology of Religion of Liberated Israel 1250–1050 B.C.E.*[2] In the eyes of a sociologically oriented professor of systematic theology, Gottwald's (and before him Mendenhall's) studies represent a necessary and sadly delayed reorientation within Old Testament studies – something that could be compared to the reorientation within the field of New Testament studies of the German scholar Gerd Theissen.[3]

According to Gottwald (and Glebe-Møller), exegetes have traditionally demonstrated an almost panic-inducing fear of behavioural sciences, although these may represent the most important scientific breakthroughs of the twentieth century. Rather than getting involved in such issues, exegetes

---

[1] Jens Glebe-Møller (b. 1933) is a Danish theologian who served for many years as the dean of the Theological Faculty of the University of Copenhagen. I was for several years his deputy.
[2] Gottwald, 1979. Cf. Lemche, 1985b. I published an earlier review of Gottwald's study as "Det revolutionære Israel. En præsentation af en moderne forskningsretning" ("Revolutionary Israel. A Presentation of a Direction in Modern Scholarship"): Lemche, 1982. Among other contributions published by Gottwald relating to his thesis of the revolutionary Israel, I may mention his *The Hebrew Bible – A Socio-Literary Introduction* (Gottwald, 1985), *Social Scientific Criticism of the Hebrew Bible and Its Social World: The Israelite Monarchy* (Gottwald, 1986), and the collection of minor works *The Hebrew Bible in Its Social World and in Ours* (SBL Semeia Studies; Atlanta, GA: Scholars, 1993).
[3] Cf. Gerd Theissen, *Soziologie der Jesusbewegung. Ein Beitrag zur Entstehungsgeschichte des Urchristentums* (München: Kaiser 1977). It is not my intention to comment further on Theissen's contribution to sociology. Like Gottwald's approach to sociology it is more historically oriented than accepted in the present so-called "Copenhagen School of Old Testament Studies". "Historically" says that Theissen like Gottwald are ready to take more issues to be historical matters than is normally accepted by the "Copenhageners". Although the scholars mentioned are fully aware of the importance of such concepts as "reader response" – in a German environment "Rezeptionskritik" – they are, at the end of the day, still of the conviction that the text refers to something that really happened. Old Testament scholars like Thomas L. Thompson, Philip R. Davies, and this writer are not so confident.

have sought refuge within traditional historical-critical scholarship. The traditional exegete remained mostly a historian of the old school – often with a definite positivistic touch – and philologists. They scorned disciplines like psychology and linguistics but sociology too. Sometimes biblical scholars promoted analyses of ancient societies that were supposed to represent a sociological approach. Far from being that, such studies were merely expressions of a type of "common sense" without any scientific basis. The device among biblical scholars could easily be described in this way: Because we are ourselves members of a human community, we can formulate sensible ideas about human communities![4]

The critical voices that have arisen against traditional historical-critical scholarship are generally not far off the mark. Historical-critical scholarship has – because it focused on the history and not the story in the Old and New Testaments – created a kind of "meta-world". In order to achieve this it makes extensive use of rationalistic paraphrases of the biblical narratives. It, at the same time, created an edifice called "ancient Israel" constructed on a basis that consisted of a mixture of categories – on one side written texts from Antiquity and on the other a world outside the texts, i.e. the so-called "real world". This real world can, however, only be recreated if it is possible to establish an indispensable connection between texts and events. Modern historical research has shown that this connection is – when we speak about biblical texts – in most cases impossible to find.[5]

Evidently the texts are parts of their own universe. It is a universe that consists of ideas and traditions. The connection between these traditions and the history of Palestine in the Bronze and Iron Ages is probably the least interesting part of Old Testament scholarship. The problems created by historical-critical research for the survival of the biblical disciplines within

---

[4] Jens Glebe-Møller has formulated his sharp criticism of the exegetes in his *Jesus and Tradition: Critique of a Tradition* (Glebe-Møller, 1989). Old Testament scholarship is part of Near Eastern studies as well as theology (in Denmark, the oriental disciplines were more or less created by theologians who came from Old Testament studies). The biblical scholars who created these oriental disciplines have, however, in the 20th century become so impressed by the work of their colleagues, especially in Assyriology and Egyptology that they have not seen the scientific deficiency of these disciplines. No scholar of the ancient world has described the almost endemic lack of methodological updating among orientalists as well as Mario Liverani (Liverani, 1966).

[5] I will spend little time discussing recent developments within Old Testament historical scholarship. I can refer the reader to my "What Have We Done and Where Are We Moving? Some Personal Remarks about a Change of Paradigm", published in this collection [Danish original published in 1994]. A devastating attack on traditional historical scholarship and its main edifice "ancient Israel" can be found in Davies, 1992.

theology may not have been severe within the field of New Testament studies. Somehow New Testament colleagues are never in doubt about the theological importance of their scholarship. In spite of everything, the New Testament has, with success, defended its central position in the life of the Church. The Old Testament has never been allowed a comparable position.

Because of this difference, New Testament scholars have had few problems defending the integrity of their discipline when the academy had to cut resources and other theological areas were hit by administrative reductions. Their Old Testament colleagues are placed in a less enviable position, sometimes overtly critical in spite of the fact that the heyday of historical-critical scholarship also included the publication of important theological reflections based on the Old Testament. I may only mention as probably the best examples of this direction the theologies of the Old Testament by Walther Eichrodt from the 1930s and by Gerhard von Rad from the 1950s.[6]

Such excellent works were, however, placed in a kind of no-man's-land because their authors, on one side, felt obliged to present a theology of the Old Testament to a Christian readership, while they, on the other had to incorporate the results of historical-critical scholarship within their theologies. Such scholarship cannot, however, be dictated or organized either by the Church or by another religious congregation.[7]

The time of historical-critical scholarship saw important theological issues arise such as Heilsgeschichte, "salvation history". In a North American context it became "God who Acts" a headline that says that God is the acting agent in a history that was constructed by the same theologians who promoted the idea of the acting God. I need not stress the fact that the same theologians and scholars were generally of a very conservative, not to say fundamentalist, orientation. However, this narrow combination of real history and God's plan for salvation can only be characterized as a very crude rendering of the ideas of their German colleagues. It must be said that the usual histories of Israel are no more than metahistories in case the connection breaks down between the fate of historical Israel – a petty Palestinian state of the Iron Age – and biblical Israel. This combination is also called "ancient Israel" and was created by excellent scholars like Martin Noth and Albrecht

---

[6] Eichrodt, 1933–9, and von Rad, 1957–60.
[7] This does certainly not mean that such organization is uncommon. On the contrary. Most Old Testament scholarship is absolutely directed by religious institutions or controlled by the church. Cf. further on this aspect of biblical scholarship Davies, 1995), esp. 17–55.

Alt. They have little or nothing to do with things that actually happened in Palestine in a remote past.

The following section will present one example of the dilemma created by historical-critical scholarship. According to the Old Testament, Israel's history begins with a salvific act of God. God liberates his people from serfdom in Egypt. A theology oriented towards the historical truth of such an event must maintain that it really happened in order to keep this event within the history of salvation. Seen in this light, it cannot be a very satisfying conclusion to the historical investigation of the exodus from Egypt that it never happened.[8]

Scholars have, through the ages, indulged in many speculations about how they could preserve the exodus as a historical event. Thus they often reduced the event to something minimal to make it plausible: Only very few people took part in the event, not the 600,000 men plus their families mentioned by the Old Testament. The only thing that did not worry these scholars was the fact that they destroyed the point made by the biblical narrative, that God liberated the nation of Israel from Egypt.[9] Furthermore, we have no historical source of any kind outside the Old Testament that points in the direction of the exodus involving Israel's ancestors having ever happened.[10] The historical analysis mercilessly leads to a destruction of the biblical narrative when it is understood to be a report about something that really happened. A theology that is constructed upon this foundation, which presupposes that the exodus really took place, is meaningless.

Another example involves the historicity of King David. The Jewish as well as the Christian Messiah will have – no matter how differently he is conceived in either religion – to belong to the House of David. He must belong to the male line of the historical King David as explained by the Gospel of Matthew, which traces the genealogy of Jesus back to David (Matt 1:1–17). The

---

[8] The details are, in this connection, not very interesting. A recent critical but at the same time rather conservative review of the discussion about the historicity of the exodus has been published by Frerichs and Lesko, 1997. Cf. also my analysis of the narratives in the Book of Exodus in my *Prelude to Israel's Past. Background and Beginnings of Israelite History and Identity* (Lemche, 1998b, 44–61).

[9] The reduction of the exodus group into something more plausible can be found already in Julius Wellhausen, *Israelitische und jüdische Geschichte* (Wellhausen, 1884, 13). (As a matter of fact, in German academic circles this discussion goes back to Lessing and Reimarus at the end of the 18th century.)

[10] Sometimes the exodus is linked to the Egyptian tradition about the expulsion of the Hyksos. This is said to have happened in the 16th century BCE. The first to make this link was Josephus in his *Contra Apionem* I, 41. Josephus quotes the Hellenistic Egyptian historiographer Manetho (3rd century BCE) as evidence of the exodus. However, it does not seem likely that Manetho himself makes this connection.

same notion about the family of the new David can be found in the Book of Isaiah. This prophetic book sees Israel's saviour as an offspring from the roots of Jesse (Isa 11:1). This new David is supposed to lead humanity, or at least Israel, back to paradise.

David, whose offspring is supposed, one day in the shape of a David redivivus, to re-establish his empire was, according to the Old Testament's testimony, a mighty king that ruled over a great kingdom reaching – according to some biblical traditions – from the border of Egypt to the Euphrates. Thus, David's empire stretched over a territory that covered not only Palestine and Lebanon but also included most if not all of modern Syria. He is supposed to have ruled over this mighty kingdom in the beginning of the 10th century BCE. Many historians have dated the beginning of his reign to the year 1000 BCE – probably too much of a coincidence – and pay faith to the information in the Old Testament that he ruled forty years.

Recent investigations into the history of the ancient Near East in the 10th century BCE show that there is no room for a Davidic Empire in this place and at this time. There is no reason to be particular about the details. I only need to mention the fact that the capital in the glorious empire of David consisted at most of a village of small extension (if it was even in existence at the time). The central region in David's empire, i.e. Judah, was a remote and backward mountain landscape allowing for a population of hardly more than 15,000 people, including women and children. Finally, it should not be forgotten that we know of no contemporary ancient written source from the Near East that mentions the existence of this kingdom. All of this should be enough to show that the depiction of the Israelite Empire in the Old Testament has no historical support outside the literature of the Old Testament.

This is self-evident. It is, however, not enough to convince hosts of biblical scholars. Their answer has traditionally been that although the Old Testament may exaggerate a little, nothing speaks against the assumption that David might have been a local chieftain who roamed about in the Judean mountains in the 10th century BCE.[11] As long as scholars agree on one thing – that David really lived – they believe they have served theology well. The Messiah might still be an offspring of this robber baron called David. The scholars do not

---

[11] Cf. on the discussion among Old Testament scholars about the empire of David (and Solomon) the collections published by Fritz and Davies, *The Origins of the Israelite States* (Fritz and Davies, 1996), and Lowell K. Handy, *The Age of Solomon. Scholarship at the Turn of the Millennium* (Handy, 1997).

pay much attention to the fact that this figure has only his name in common with the great king of the biblical narrative.[12]

This example demonstrates how scholars, in order to keep the historicity of a biblical figure, openly reduce the biblical text to nonsense. The aim and scope of the Books of Samuel are not to tell posterity how tradition (not history) turned a local robber chieftain into a mighty ruler and even later to the ancestor of the Messiah. The Books of Samuel intend to inform readers about the Messiah as the one supposed to re-establish the kingdom of David. Thus the narrative in the Books of Samuel has a paradigmatic importance because the coming Messiah will re-establish the kingdom that existed when the biblical David ruled the world and history for a moment stopped and peace reigned throughout the world as David reigned on his throne in Jerusalem (2 Sam 7:1). This time it is going to be an enduring kingdom (according to Jewish tradition) with a priestly Messiah accompanying the Davidic Messiah so that David's mistakes should not be repeated. The historical David – if he ever existed, and it is only the Bible that says so – is, in comparison to the biblical David, rather unimportant. The messianic ideas and beliefs of Judaism and Christianity do not begin with this putatively historical David. They spin off from the narrative found in the Old Testament about the great King David who once ruled the world.

These examples may illustrate the kind of problems created by historical-critical scholarship for the Old Testament as a source for theological inspiration. They could be multiplied many times. To be sure, the "deconstruction" of the history and religion of ancient Israel has now reached a point where it is legitimate to say that the Old Testament does not contain a history of the past. If history is involved, it is a history *that is going to take place*. Thus the Old Testament includes a theological programme that involves a group of human beings which intends to establish a society of "holy people" (cf. Isaiah 4 and 6), that is to take up residence on Zion under the LORD's protection.

When understood to be literature and as such a part of the tradition of history writing current in Antiquity,[13] the history told by the Old Testament is not a history referring to the past, it is about the present and the future. This literature makes no effort depicting the past "as it was" – nothing might

---

[12] This sounds like a repetition of the previous discussion about the historicity of the patriarchs. Cf. on this Thompson, 1974, and Van Seters, 1975. On the historicity of the biblical narrative in general cf. the recent contributions by Thompson, 1999, and Lemche, 1998d.
[13] Cf. as an introduction to the study of the relationship between Old Testament and Greek historiography the recent monograph by F.A.J. Nielsen, *The Tragedy in History. Herodotus and the deuteronomistic History* (Nielsen, 1997). For a now classical introduction to the theme cf. Van Seters, 1983.

have interested an ancient historiographer less than that. The past is seen as the producer of paradigms that work in the present. The acts of the heroes and villains of the past present patterns for human behaviour and in this way indicate a direction for future generations to go. Because a hero of the past acted in a certain way, we may think and expect that a contemporary hero will act in the same way. If an ancient scoundrel sinned, this tells us that a contemporary crook will follow in his footsteps. History is a moral enterprise and presents ethical instruction. If the past does not live up to the expectations of the historiographer and his implied readership and provides the examples asked for, the historiographer feels free to recreate the past in such a way that it suits his aims. The historiographer almost never presents a critical evaluation of the content of his narrative. Such evidence of a critical mind might occur in case an author intended to tell us that his colleague has done a bad job of presenting the past as a guide for the present. Antiquity simply did not know anything remotely similar to modern critical history writing not to speak of a critical appraisal of history as a science.[14]

The narrative has, as it is presented by ancient historiographers, not created the problems that prevent modern people to read and appraise the values of the biblical depiction of the past. The problems arose hand in hand with the formulation of a changing perspective among its readers. People of modern times have gradually gotten accustomed to reading biblical stories through the lenses of a modern historian, i.e., as a history that has to do with events of ancient times as they really happened.[15]

Thus it is easy to explain why many Old Testament scholars ended up in a kind of limbo. As theologians the Old Testament provided them with no inspiration. They were in serious doubts about how to make any sense of the information in the historical books of the Old Testament from Genesis to 2 Kings (not to mention Chronicles). The Old Testament does not allow its reader to reconstruct a continuous history of ancient Israel, "as it really happened".

---

[14] It is easy to find examples of the type of moralistic history writing current in Antiquity. Among the better known examples are *The Parallel Lives* by Plutarch describing the life and acts of famous Greeks and Romans (Text and translation by Bernadotte Perrin in *The Loeb Classical Library*, I–XI, 1914–26). Suetonius' imperial biographies belong in the same genre. Highly estimated ancient historiographers like Thucydides and Tacitus also intend to have their historical narrative serve a higher goal that just to tell people what happened.

[15] Cf. further on this theme in Lemche, 1998d, 1–34. The theological consequences of a reorientation of biblical reading have been outlined in Lemche, 1998b, 214–32.

The moment we approach the prophetic books we confront very similar problems because this literature is so deeply rooted in the image of ancient Israel created by the biblical historiographers. The prophetic literature understood to be the evidence of prophets that belonged to ancient Israel is silenced the moment it is made clear that this history of ancient Israel is a construct and that the Israel of the prophets is biblical Israel as told by the Old Testament historiographers. The Old Testament is only, in very few instances, a source of information about the past – it is of course an important testimony of the time when its scripture came into being and it informs extensively about the mental universe of the authors who composed this literature.

One solution has been to substitute the idea of a *salvation history* in the Old Testament with a scientifically reconstructed history of the real world. In Denmark John Strange has advocated such a solution to the problem of the incomparability of the biblical story with history (Strange, 1989a). According to Strange we must – if we will escape being caught in the dilemma of a "double truth" or end up in a *sacrificium intellectum* – accept the fact that salvation history and real history must be identical. Rainer Albertz has proposed a similar route. Albertz sees Old Testament theology and the study of Israel's religion to be synonymous (Albertz, 1994; cf. Albertz, 1995).

Such proposals must be reckoned rather desperate reactions to a problem that cannot be solved by the historian. They belong among classical statements like: Christianity has proven its ethical and religious superiority because it was the one among several antique religions and sectarian movements that survived! It might, from an historian's point of view, simply have been the case that as a religious community Christianity was better organized than comparable groups. Because of eminent theologians who were also clever politicians, it ended up as the state religion of the Roman Empire. Real history consists of a series of coincidences. We might think some laws govern history, but such laws have nothing to do with the theological determinism of a "God who acts".

We cannot deduce from history that goodness will always prevail and that evil will invariably perish as the curtain goes down. It is a false hope to expect a deity operating behind history like the God of the Old Testament that leads Israel to its fate. It is quite convenient to mention several examples that point in another direction.[16] It is, as a matter of fact, possible to argue that the God of the Old Testament does not rule supreme in history. Sometimes matters develop against the will of God. God has to forsake his Israel because

---

[16] As advocated in the acid evaluation of history in the Italian author Elsa Morante's *La Storia* (Morante, 1974).

the history of biblical Israel leads away from God. The Old Testament does not support any idea of predestination. Life is a gift from God, to be lived as one's own responsibility.[17]

The Old Testament understands this responsibility, that has been placed on every single person by God, as a covenant concluded between God and human beings. When they have entered the covenant, no person can break it and survive. God dictated the covenant conditions to Moses on Mt. Sinai, whereupon Moses brought the Law of God to Israel, or – according to the deuteronomistic version – pronounced it to Israel on the plains of Moab (Dtn 4). Only after the conclusion of the conquest of Canaan, when Joshua urged Israel at Shechem not to enter the covenant and Israel did not follow his advice, did the conditions of the covenant become impossible for Israel to break. In spite of Joshua's warnings, that the covenant is a difficult one, hard to obey and follow, and devastating to the person who breaks it, the people enter the covenant. It is written down and as a witness a stone is erected (Joshua 24).

The Old Testament sees the covenant as the absolutely dominant part of the relationship between Israel and its God. In spite of this, historical-critical scholarship ended up removing the covenant from the religious expression of ancient Israel's faith. For many years scholars entered a long and eventful discussion about the idea of covenant in ancient Israel. George Mendenhall started the discussion when he, in 1954, in order to prove the historicity of the Sinai covenant, referred to the parallels between the Sinai covenant and vassal treaties of the Late Bronze Age.[18] In the years which followed his opening essay many studies were published, some positive, others critical of Mendenhall. These contributions shared one thing. They all introduced a long series of texts – not least prophetic literature[19] – and ideas known from

---

[17] I published my criticism of Strange's proposal as "Geschichte und Heilsgeschichte. Mehrere Aspekte der biblischen Theologie" (Lemche, 1989a). See also Strange, 1989b. I formulated my opposition to Albertz" view in Lemche, 1995a, 79–92. A theology of the Old Testament belongs to a Christian intellectual milieu. Taken in isolation it is therefore nonsense. The Gospel of Christ of the New Testament has, since Antiquity, always been the point of departure for the theological appraisal of the Old Testament. From a Christian perspective there is no Old Testament taken in isolation. The Old Testament belongs to a whole, i.e. the Bible, and should, in a theological context, always be studied and understood within this context. In a Jewish environment things obviously look differently (although Jewish theologians have never published anything remotely similar to a "theology of the Old Testament". The reason may be the position of the TaNaKh in Judaism which has never been so isolated and exclusive as happened in Christianity).
[18] Cf. Mendenhall, 1954.
[19] Hans Wildberger provides an excellent illustration of the influence of the covenant in Old Testament exegesis in his commentary on Isaiah (Wildberger, 1972), although it was

the Old Testament such as "the love of God" or the "knowledge of God" as part of covenant theology.[20]

The discussion suddenly stopped when Lothar Perlitt, in 1969 in his review of the covenant tradition in the Old Testament, concluded that this was a latecomer in the history of Israel's religion.[21] Perlitt emphasized that the central Hebrew expression for the covenant, Hebrew $b^e rît$, does not appear in specific covenant contexts except in deuteronomistic literature. Pre-deuteronomistic traditions that, according to Perlitt, also include the prophetic literature do not employ $b^e rît$ in this sense. The ancient Israelites used different expressions to characterize their relationship with God.[22] Clearly the ancient Israelites did not think that a covenant regulated the ties that bound them to their God. Only deuteronomistic theologians living at the end of the time of the Hebrew monarchy or during the exilic period changed $b^e rît$ into an expression of paramount theological importance.

Working from the perspective of historical-critical research it is difficult to escape being impressed by Perlitt's argumentation. He is obviously right when he maintains that $b^e rît$ is only occasionally used outside the historical books of the Old Testament. Perlitt is truly a "student" of Julius Wellhausen,[23] who believed the prophets "to come before the Law", saying at the same time that the Law represents a secondary religious development that changed ancient Israelite religion into Judaism. The prophets belong in the pre-exilic part of Israel's history and were not bound by the admonitions of the Law of Moses.[24] Thus Perlitt's late date for covenant theology is absolutely in accordance with Wellhausen's ideas: that in early Judaism the "gospel" of the prophets, i.e. their preaching of Yahweh as Israel's God, was transformed into the unchangeable concept of the *Torah*. Thus, the covenant was placed at the beginning of the

---

probably not Mendenhall who influenced Wildberger. It was rather Walther Eichrodt. The covenant was allotted a central position in Eichrodt's *Theologie des Alten Testament* (Eichrodt, 1962–4). Contrariwise, Delbert R. Hillers, in his *Treaty-Curses and the Old Testament Prophets* (Hillers, 1964), is definitely under the spell of Mendenhall's argument.

[20] Cf. thus Huffmon, 1966), 31–7.

[21] Perlitt, 1969.

[22] Cf. Perlitt, 1969: 129–55, on the so-called "Bundes-schweigen" among the prophets of the 8th century. $B^e rît$ is sometimes used in this literature, however, such cases are – according to Perlitt – clearly secondary additions to the text.

[23] Of course, in the sense that Wellhausen is his spiritual father. Cf., however, Perlitt's dissertation on Wellhausen's relationship to Herder rather than to Hegel (Perlitt, 1965).

[24] This is the main theme of Wellhausen's famous study, *Prolegomena zur Geschichte Israels* (Wellhausen, 1878, ET: Wellhausen, 1994).

Law of Moses in order to introduce it to human beings. The *Torah* simply formulates the conditions for the covenant.

What will happen if the prophetic literature of the Old Testament cannot be considered earlier that the Law books of the Old Testament? Then we would have to think of the existence of two circles of authors, contemporary although often in open conflict while at the same time supplementing each other; on one side the redactors who collected the prophetic literature, and on the other the group that edited the historical books. The members of the first circle preached the message of imminent punishment while the second group described the crime committed by ancient Israel, always denounced by the prophets, and the punishment that was foreseen by the prophets. Traditional historical-critical scholarship has little to say here.

Perlitt's position would be meaningless to a literary student of the Old Testament, who views this collection of texts as more or less synchronous. A scholar of this orientation would pay little attention to diachronic arguments, saying, e.g. that the prophecies included in the prophetic literature are older than the historical narratives of Joshua through Kings. In this case the answer could be that the collectors of prophetic sayings were not at all interested in the covenant that dominates the historical books. This conclusion is certainly possible and can be seen as a variant of the usual historical-critical explanation.

We may, however, question the validity of such a decision. Is it at all very important that the single word $b^e r\hat{i}t$ is not used in parts of the biblical literature as indicated by Perlitt? May we surmise that the scholars who, in the 1960s, pointed to covenant theology on almost every page of the Old Testament were all totally wrong? Can we get closer to an answer that leaves out academic wrangling about the meaning of one Hebrew word?

This author has devoted a by now quite extensive series of articles and studies to the sociology of the ancient Near East, including so-called "ancient Israel".[25] I shall abstain in this place from getting entangled in this discussion again. I would only point at a special social reality that is sometimes described as "the traditional Mediterranean way to organize a society". This organization is not the same as the family structure or the tribal system that is always

---

[25] So-called because ancient Israel is only a historical construct based on the biblical narrative about Israel on one side and other sources – written documents etc. – on the other. As demonstrated so adeptly by Philip R. Davies, this ancient Israel only exists in the imagination of scholars. Ancient Israel is not identical with the Israel found in the books of the Old Testament and neither is it the same as the small state of the same name that existed in Palestine in the Iron Age. It is a mixture of these two "Israels".

in some form or the other present in almost every Middle Eastern society. Instead of a family-centric society we here speak about a system of *clientelism*, also called *patronage*, or even *feudalism*. It is basically a socio-political system that presupposes the existence of only two societal categories, the ones who "have" and the ones "who have not".[26]

Contrary to Western civilization in recent centuries, traditional Middle Eastern society does not contain social classes in the Marxist sense of the word. A class society demands that the members of the society see themselves as belonging to different classes. Such an awareness is absent among traditional Middle Eastern communities, simply because these social realities only know of the two categories already described above as the people who have and the people who have not. The traditional Middle East does not know of a "third class" that finds itself placed between the two other categories.

Clientelism is a social-economic system that organizes according to differences of wealth. The paupers refer to well-to-do people as their protectors, and the rich collect poor people as their dependents. It is a kind of patron-client relationship that binds the poor to the rich in a contractual arrangement. The wealthy person provides security for the poor, who for his part has to serve the rich. Although it sounds very simple, the system may in a real society be very complex and including many variations. People, who in one context act like patrons, are in different social or political situations clients themselves because there will always be a person in a higher position than oneself until we arrive at the peak of the society where we find the king, the ultimate patron. At this level every subject of the king is a royal servant – or client. The patronage system embraces a special set of linguistic terms. One of these will be the notion of a covenant that regulates the ties that bind a client to his master and the master to his dependents. No party – neither the client nor the patron – is supposed to break the covenant, and the consequence of such a departure from the statements made by the covenant will be most serious.

When we approach Old Testament literature from the angle of patronage, we do not have to read very much before it becomes apparent that the language of this literature is permeated with concepts borrowed from the patronage system. One such example is the speech of God in Exod 23:20–33. Here Yahweh promises to let his angel go in front of Israel in order to cut

---

[26] Social-anthropological literature pertaining to this subject: Gellner and Waterbury, 1977. Among my contributions I would like to refer to Lemche, 1995b, 1995c, 1996c, 2013b, 2023. See also the comprehensive synthesis in Pfoh, 2016, 121–67, and the comprehensive reader published by the same author (Pfoh, 2022).

down Israel's enemies without mercy and stir up terror among them. The enemies of Israel are the enemies of its God. In another context I have characterized this angel as Yahweh's "hit man" or "gorilla". Texts like this tell us that the language of covenant in the Old Testament builds on the phraseology of patronage. Israel is undoubtedly Yahweh's client. Yahweh demands only that Israel shall worship Yahweh alone. It is strictly forbidden to approach any other god. You cannot serve two masters at one and the same time.

In Exod 23:20–33, *b^{e}rît* is used only once, in 23:32. Here the demand is that Israel will not enter a covenant with any other nation and its gods. *B^{e}rît* is not used here simply to indicate the covenant relationship between Yahweh and Israel. Thus it is more than likely that the idea of covenant – basically a patronage expression – need not be spelled out verbatim in the Old Testament as a *b^{e}rît*-relationship. This also means that concepts like love of God (we must love God and God loves us) or knowledge of God are natural parts of the patronage-covenant system. The client is supposed to "love" his master. The grace of God also belongs in this context. God is our gracious Lord, very much like the squire to his peasants in a traditional European context.

This is only one, however important, illustration of how a sociological approach to biblical texts may help us to understand their meaning. Sociology is not a miraculous device that makes everything self-evident. Sociology assists the student of the biblical texts to understand the text's social context. Thus, it elucidates the ideas and sentiments nourished by the circle of authors who created these texts probably without paying much attention to the social context of the specific language which it employed. The system of patronage thus makes up a kind of mental matrix for the production of texts.

Sociology is not likely to settle the discussion between the literary student of the Bible and the old-fashioned historical-critical scholar. We cannot say that a professional historian cannot apply sociological methodology, although it might not be absolutely wrong to maintain that most traditional historians would prefer to live without it. Sociology, like other behavioural sciences, can assist the humanistic scholar. Not because it is able to provide fixed and approved models for the study of human behaviour or mental or material development, but because it delivers to the attentive humanistic scholar a catalogue of possibilities, a richness of motifs and ideas that can be fruitful for the investigation of the whereabouts of the human species in history.[27]

---

[27] Cf. on this Lemche, 1989b.

11 On Historical Memory in the Historiography of the Old Testament

Next him Ulysses took a shining sword,
A bow and quiver, with bright arrows stored:
A well-proved casque, with leather braces bound,
(Thy gift, Meriones,) his temples crown'd;
Soft wool within; without, in order spread,
A boar's white teeth grinn'd horrid o'er his head.
This from Amyntor, rich Ormenus' son,
Autolycus by fraudful rapine won,
And gave Amphidamas; from him the prize
Molus received, the pledge of social ties;
The helmet next by Merion was possess'd,
And now Ulysses' thoughtful temples press'd.

(*Iliad* X, 260–271. Translation by Alexander Pope)

Among classical scholars this passage is famous because of the item which is in the centre of the narrative, a helmet covered by the teeth of a wild boar. This helmet is given to Odysseus by Meriones and is described as an heirloom in the home of Meriones with a very long pedigree. The helmet has played a major role in the discussion about the relations of Homer to the Mycenean world. Its presence in the Iliad suggests that in the epic of Homer at least one item is remembered with a history that goes back to the Mycenaean world while at the same time it makes it clear that Homer had no clue to what the Mycenaean world really was although many scholars claim that his epic is set in the mythical past of Greece.[1] As expressed by the Danish classical scholar Per Krarup, "the only absolutely certain archaeological remains from

---

[1] Specimens of this type of helmet have been found at Mycenae and in Crete and appear on a number of monuments from that age.

Mycenaean times recoded by Homer is the *wild boar helmet*."[2] Otherwise Homeric scholarship has been dominated by the conviction that his poems reflect the period in which they were composed and include residues from many periods including the epic tradition which forms their background. Homer is not from the Mycenaean period. He should evidently be dated much later, maybe even later than the normal date of the 8th century.[3] Rather than reflecting a specific period, the epic of Homer includes memories from many eras mingled together in a narrative that in no way seeks to be historically correct but uses the tradition as a setting for the many parts of the narrative. The epic reflects a world of fiction where heroes and gods are moving around, where everything follows rules which were – in contrast to modern ones (from the perspective of the author) – transparent and clear but nonetheless valid and to be followed. In this the epic from antiquity is similar to other literature from those days including historiography which has only a slight resemblance – apart from the name – to modern historical reports.[4] The wild boar helmet includes information from the past simply by originating in the past. It has its own story to tell, on which Homer elaborates, but it is not a primary source for the past: it is a residue from the past which in a manner unknown to us ended up in a literary context which was totally different from its original *Sitz im Leben*.

Story and Residue

In Kristian Erslev's well-known methodological introduction to historical studies, which for generations has been standard knowledge among Danish historians, we find a section of the concepts of "lævning" (in English the closest translation would be "residue") and "narratives". Danish "Lævning" is a technical term coming from the German "Überreste" (Erslev, 1968, 5–6). Together these two concepts represent the central foundation of German historical research since the 19th century. According to this scholarship the narrative represents the subjective retelling of the past influenced by the intentions of its author and the time in which it was written down. The residue,

---

[2] Krarup, 1954, 212–3.
[3] On this scholarship Minna Skafte Jensen, 1968, 1980, 1997.
[4] Cf. the short characteristic of ancient history writing in Skydsgaard, 1978. According to Skydsgaard classical historiography had to be "true and didactic", and he emphasizes the fact that the selection of themes and matters was decided by literary and not historical criteria. The theoretical writings about this subject come primarily from Cicero's and Quintilian's rhetorical textbooks. Cf. also the detailed review in Ørsted, 1978.

on the other hand, is that part of the narrative "which still remains from the past" and is a better source than the narrative (Erslev, 1968, 5). This means that the residue can be seen as a primary source to the past whereas the narrative is a secondary source. Erslev, however, is not satisfied with this division because every narrative – as he sees it – is also a residue. Here Erslev presents as his example the *Gesta Danorum* by Saxo, which is a narrative about the exploits of the Danes in the past but also in itself a residue from the period of the Valdemar's in the 12th to 13th centuries. In this way a narrative is also a residue, and it is not so easy to make a distinction between primary and secondary sources. A secondary source is at the same time a primary source.

Erslev mentions J.G. Droysen as the scholar who first made the separation of the sources into the two categories already mentioned, but he adds that there were other German historians who were sceptical (Erslev, 1968, 6). However, this part of the discussion is not very interesting at this point – apart from one important point: The scholarly investigation of the history of ancient Israel which began among German university scholars was influenced by Droysen's separation of the material into primary and secondary sources in a decisive way. Everybody who has studied German histories of Israel, at least from Rudolf Kittel (Kittel, 1909-12) to Herbert Donner (Donner, 1984-6) will be familiar with the method. It is not just accepted without question that a narrative in the Old Testament presents a historically correct image of the period which is the subject of the narrative. Before it can be of any use a narrative will have to be "cleansed" in such a way that the secondary parts are removed and only the residue, the primary source remains.

Thus, when the Israelites, according to the Book of Joshua chapter 6, conquers the city of Jericho by circling it for six days until the city walls tumbled down on the seventh when the trumpets are blown, we are certainly speaking about a miracle. Miracles have no part in historical scholarship. Therefore, we have to remove these miraculous parts. The remaining part can be considered to be a residue, including a memory of the days when the Israelites really conquered Jericho. This was at least the general opinion among Old Testament scholars until the day when excavations at Jericho showed that there never was such a conquest of Jericho because there was, at that time, no city where Jericho is supposed to be when Joshua was assumed to have led the Israelites into Palestine.[5]

---

[5] The problematic issue is the theme of practically speaking every serious – scholarly – study of the settlement of the Israelites in Palestine. Cf. Lemche, 2015, 116-7).

It can, on the basis of the example of Jericho, be argued that Erslev's point that it is wrong, in the stubborn view of Droysen, to separate between the residue and the narrative, meaning that the residue makes up the historical nucleus in a narrative which is otherwise both late, secondary and miraculous. The story about the conquest of Jericho in Joshua 6 has no historical nucleus, no residue from the past which a historian may dig out of the narrative about the conquest of Jericho. The narrative may be a reflection of knowledge in existence at the time when the author wrote his story of the fall of Jericho which might have happened at a time already unknown to the author. The narrative may be a saga or a legend – even a fairy tale – which does not really refer to a special place but only secondarily has been brought into connection with Jericho when the narrative about Israel's conquest of Canaan was drafted.[6]

The study of Old Testament history has to a large degree confirmed our impression gained by this example. In total the historical narrative in the Old Testament is, in Droysen's terminology, a *narrative*. It is late, probably not composed before the Hellenistic period, and greatly impressed by Greek historical writing.[7] It is dominated by the same attitude to the past present among classical historians who believed history to provide moral education presented in an aesthetically acceptable form. Whether or not it happened precisely as written and whether or not the persons involved acted in precisely the way described and were governed by the motives said to have been the reasons for their acting is less important. We may also express it in this way: To biblical historians as well as classical historians the governing maxim could have been: Is this true or only something that actually happened?

Old Testament scholarship has mainly followed the notion that biblical history writing is providentially the "true" description of the past rather than being devoted to a present that really happened. It has also demonstrated that previous scholarship has, to a large extent, been dominated by an idea of historical research as something principally directed towards finding out

---

[6] Cf. the use of the number seven in this narrative: The Israelites circle around the city for six days but on the seventh day the walls tumble down. The role of the number seven is well-known from folk-tales. We thus have a parallel to the account of the Book of Joshua in the Ugaritic epic of Kirta (Keret), who, with his army, travels for six days to reach the city of Udum on the seventh. Kirta lays siege to this city for six days, but on the seventh day the city capitulates.

[7] Cf. on the relationship between the Old Testament and Greek history writing Van Seters, 1983 and F.A.J. Nielsen, 1997.

what "really happened" – or in the words of Leopold von Ranke, *wie es eigentlich gewesen*. By and large the historical methodology employed has largely been incommensurable with its subject, biblical historical narrative. Instead of reconstructing what "really happed", historical scholarship reconstructed a master narrative as a kind of a *rationalistic paraphrase*. At the same time, it ignored the essential meaning of this narrative, to provide moral guidance. The historians were mainly disinterested in the reasons for ancient history writers to produce their histories and concentrated on the events supposed to have formed the background of the narrative. Thus the moment a modern historian, so to speak, forgets his role and begins to moralize – an example could be the case of David's erotic escapades – he or she is immediately warned to return to the proper task of reconstructing the past, although this historian is doing little else than imitating his ancient colleagues by extracting moral education from the past.[8]

To summarize: the traditional Old Testament scholar studying the history of ancient Israel has been badly prepared for his task. The main reason was without doubt the lack of historical methodological reflection among the students of "the history of Israel", being more or less dominated by Droysen's attitude to source criticism. The criticism of Droysen by scholars like Erslev was mainly ignored, even in Scandinavia, where biblical scholars were sorely ignorant of their colleague in general history, although they were not hampered in reading Erslev because of language barriers. As a result, they mainly produced "metahistories"; the reconstructed history of ancient Israel, a history that never happened in the way it is described by biblical history writers. This metahistory not only includes the stories about Israel's oldest history, the Patriarchs, the sojourn in Egypt, the wanderings in the desert, the conquest of Canaan, and the period of the Judges, but just the period of the Hebrew kings, including the empires of David and Solomon, and the Babylonian exile and the post-exilic period.[9]

In the same way as the *Gestae Danorum*, the history of ancient Denmark by Saxo Grammaticus, includes, in Erslev's words, both residue and narrative, the narrative being the story as told at a certain time (the period of the Valdemars – Saxo was the secretary of the archbishop Absalon), the historical

---

[8] A description of the so-called "shift of paradigm" can be found in Lemche, 1994.
[9] This is one of the main issues of the "Copenhagen School", the circle of scholars within Old Testament studies who have, over the last decade, changed the understanding of Israel's history and history writing in the Old Testament which had dominated biblical scholarship for most of the 20th century. Among the main works from this "school" we may mention Thompson, 1992; Davies, 1992; Lemche, 1998a, and Thompson, 1999, and as an update Lemche, 2022.

narrative in the Old Testament includes residue as well as narrative. As it stands it is a historical document from the past. Every book in the Old Testament is – disregarding their exact date of composition – an ancient book transmitted to posterity.

First of all, the biblical historical narrative is a historical source. Primarily it provides information about the period of its origin and about the environment in which it came into being. In this respect the Old Testament is a residue. It is, however, not a primary source to the period that pre-dated its composition. Mixing residue and narrative creates a trap, because it represents an unholy mix of different historical categories against which Erslev warned and in which biblical scholars, for more than one hundred years, blindly walked into, inspired by the wish to extract knowledge of the historical event supposed to lie behind the present narrative. However, the realization that the Old Testament can be identified as a narrative has opened the eyes of the historians to the history of Palestine in ancient times, a history to a large extent very different from the version found in the Old Testament narrative (Whitelam, 1996). The same realization also leads to the Old Testament being "liberated" from the task given to it by modern historical scholarship, which has for the last two hundred years since the breakthrough of the modern idea of history demanded that the Old Testament should provide correct information about the past.[10] Irrespective of the modern view of the Old Testament, the narratives found in it are not "true" because they refer to something that really happened. They are "true" because the story they tell is "true" even if the events related have never happened. This must be the natural consequence of the recognition of the vast difference between ancient and modern history writing, and it removes the burden from the Old Testament understood as the first part of the Bible and a source for theological understanding to be dependent on more or less random historical events to have really happened as described by biblical literature.[11]

---

[10] On this Lemche, 1998a, 1998b.
[11] This is the essential issue in a discussion between J. Strange and N.P. Lemche in *Scandinavian Journal of the Old Testament* 3/2 (1989). Compare Strange, 1989a and 1989b to Lemche, 1989a. Strange does not stand alone when he argues that salvation history and normal history must be in agreement in order to escape the *sacrificium intellectus*. And the German scholar Rainer Albertz supports this opinion (Albertz, 1995). This writer's opposition is recently described in the final part, *Theologischer Ertrag*, in Lemche, 1996b: 208-24.

On the Date of the Historical Narratives in the Old Testament

When you try to explain the attitude to biblical historiography described here, the question invariably is: Does this mean that there is no historical information in the Old Testament? Or it is demagogical to state the representatives of the "Copenhagen School's" postulate that the description of the history of ancient Israel present in the Old Testament is no more than a series of lies? We regularly receive reports that, not least, North American biblical archaeologists like William G. Dever have again indulged in presenting the "Copenhagen School" as fraudulent, and we have repeatedly had the experience at conferences of having to listen to lectures explaining how we form a threat not only to biblical studies but in fact to Western civilization![12]

To summarize: The conclusion that historiography in the Old Testament is a *narrative* is, at the same time, a confession that this historiography is also a *residue* from a remote past. Understood to represent residue, the Old Testament is a most important historical source. It is, however, decisive that we are aware of the kind of historical information we find in the Old Testament. It is therefore mandatory, before we start reading this historical source, that we know what kind of legitimate questions we can ask and what kind of questions are definitely illegitimate. Seen as *residue,* the Old Testament originated under specific historical circumstances. Any question directed to the Old Testament concerning information about the time when it came into being is legitimate simply because the Old Testament is a primary source of information about this period. This holds even if nobody can tell us the exact date of the composition of the biblical narratives. It is still possible, on the basis of the Old Testament itself, to form an impression of the general culture, the idea of humanity, and religion in that period. On the other hand, we cannot reconstruct the history of this period except in the case of other sources that conform with the historical information in the Old Testament.

The presence of such sources will be exceptions, simply for the reason that the *narrative* in the Old Testament claims to relate to a period that preceded it – often by a very long time – the time when it was written down. We thus find this issue illustrated in John Strange's article about the Book of Joshua

---

[12] Dever has now published at least a dozen contributions to this "debate". There are too many and the redundancy too evident to quote them in this connection. Dever, 1996 is representative of this "genre". A simple overview of the arguments brought forward in this discussion can be found in the discussion between W.G. Dever, K. McCarter, T.L. Thompson, and N.P. Lemche, published by H. Shanks (Shanks, 1997).

as a political manifesto from the time of the Hasmoneans (Strange, 1993). In this article Strange argues that the geographical horizon found in the Book of Joshua reflects the political ambitions of the Hasmoneans. In this way the Book of Joshua may be a literary formulation of these political aspirations. If Strange is right, the Book of Joshua is a primary source to the time of the Hasmoneans. The only question is the degree of its political ideology, and its written evidence thereto, which is definitely not certain. The Book of Joshua might indeed be even considerably older than Hasmonean ideology (in case the Hasmoneans found their political programme formulated in the Book of Joshua). As long as we are not in possession of a *tertium comparationis*, another independent source that solves the issues of preference, we are not able to decide the degree of political propaganda between the historical record and the Book of Joshua.[13]

In this way the discussion here resembles previous endeavours to connect a text in the Old Testament to the time when it might have been drafted. The best-known example of this might be Gerhard von Rad's dating of the Yahwist layer – "source" in the language of the time – in the Pentateuch to the time of King David and Solomon, a dating based on the main concept of the Yahwist who represents the open-mindedness and international orientation at the court of Solomon (von Rad, 1944). However, in this case we can, with great certainty, conclude that von Rad was wrong: According to present knowledge there wasn't an internationally oriented court of either David or Solomon serving as the background for the Yahwist. Thus David and Solomon were not historical figures in the normal sense of the word. They were rather legendary figures from the remote past.[14]

This is the frustrating reality. While, on the one hand, it is possible to obtain considerable knowledge about the time of the author of the biblical narratives and about the author himself, it is on the other hand a lot more problematic when we try to place this author within historically real time, in the "real world". It is possible to produce several reasonable proposals, but in the end it remains a personal choice which other scholars might not follow. When the main characters of the "Copenhagen School" mostly opt for a very late date of Old Testament literature – it might be in the Persian period (Philip R. Davies) or in the Hellenistic-Roman period (Lemche-Thompson) – their dates mostly rely on arguments not dissimilar from those previously

---

[13] The time of the Hasmoneans and its use of history has been extensively discussed by Doron Mendels. Cf. Mendels, 1987; 1992.

[14] To cut the discussion short a reference to Fritz and Davies, 1996, and Handy, 1997, will suffice.

used by von Rad in connection with his dating of the same documents to a much older period. Principally it is not important if we believe ourselves to be in possession of better arguments than von Rad. Future scholarship might just as well turn the matter back against us too if it finds even better arguments.

Residue in Old Testament Historiography

The conclusion to these deliberations is that the text of the Old Testament is, in an overwhelming fashion, a witness about itself. The question is as simple as this: When we are unable, with any certainty, to date the stories found in the Old Testament, how are we then entitled to ascribe any historical value to these stories in the sense of being *residues* relating to specific periods and circumstances in Palestine and the Ancient Near East in Antiquity?

Strictly speaking, it is impossible to consider the biblical *narrative* a *residue* relating to the events related by biblical historiographers. The historical literature in the Old Testament cannot ever, in its entirety, be considered a primary source to historical events that might – or might not – have occurred in the ancient Near East. At most we may talk about *secondary sources* about *narratives* where reflections over the past might be found.

The question not yet answered will be about the possible presence of *residue* within the narrative which, with the help of historical textual criticism, can be separated from their context and thus be evaluated as primary sources? Historical textual criticism was, after all, the basis of traditional historical-critical studies of the Old Testament as a historical source. Although the argument presented in this article is about the relevance or rather the non-relevance of the distinction between a narrative and a residue, the question remains: is there really nothing of historical worth? This question is at the same time naïve but also immediately understandable because there is seemingly quite a lot of historical information in the Old Testament. Thus, the stories of the separate histories of the two divided kingdoms, Israel and Judah, include so many details that the argument that none of this can be considered primary sources to the history of Palestine in the Iron Age may be difficult to accept.

Well, because the question is put in this way, we should for a moment disregard the fact that it is illegitimate – which means that we put questions to the text which it is really not able to answer either in the positive or the negative. But let us continue with a passage where the biblical story seems to be quite in accordance with documents from the ancient Near East.

In 2 Kings 15:29-30 we find this version of the campaign of the Assyrian King Tiglath-Pileser III (744-727 BCE) in the west:

> ²⁹In the days of Pekah king of Israel came Tiglathpileser king of Assyria, and took Ijon, and Abelbethmaachah, and Janoah, and Kedesh, and Hazor, and Gilead, and Galilee, all the land of Naphtali, and carried them captive to Assyria. ³⁰And Hoshea the son of Elah made a conspiracy against Pekah the son of Remaliah, and smote him, and slew him, and reigned in his stead, in the twentieth year of Jotham the son of Uzziah.

In the following chapter of 2 Kings we learn that Ahaz, because of the threat from Pekah of Israel and Rezin of Damascus ask Tiglathpileser for help and paid a tribute to the Assyrians resulting in Tiglathpileser storming Damascus, killing Rezin, and deporting the inhabitants (2 Kings 16:7-10).

One of Tiglathpileser's inscriptions describes how Tiglathpileser controlled political circumstances along the Mediterranean coast. He conquered the cities in this area and installed governors: "... the cities of ... -nite, Gala'za, Abilakka, which are on the border of Bît-Ḫumriya[15] ... the wide land of Naphtali, in its entirety, I brought within the border of Assyria. My official I set over them as governor".[16] And a little further on in the same text we read that Tiglathpileser subdued Menahem of Israel, received his tribute and let him remain on his throne, while Tiglathpileser at the same time deported all the inhabitants of Omri's House to Assyria. The regulations of political conditions in the Levant ends with a note on the death of Pekah and the ascension to the throne of Hoseah: "Pakaha their king they deposed and I placed Ausi" (Hoseah) over them as king. 10 talents of gold, x talents of silver, as their tribute I received from them and to Assyria I carried them" (Luckenbill, 1926, 293).

The tribute of Menahem to Tiglathpileser, which is also mentioned in Tiglatpileser's annals, is also related in 2 Kings 15:19-20, but not in the context of the great Assyrian attack on western Syria and Palestine. There are other discrepancies between the Assyrian and biblical versions such as the reference to Ahaz's tribute, but it is essentially the same event which both sources refer to.[17] Irrespective of how you look at this matter, there is no doubt that we, in 2 Kings 15, find reference to one and the same event. 2 Kings

---

[15] The, at that time, usual way to name the Kingdom of Israel.
[16] The Annals of Tiglatpileser III, Luckenbill, 1926, 292.
[17] A recent characterization of the Assyrian way of dealing with the inhabitants in Syria and the Levant has been published by Trolle Larsen, 1997, 104-9.

15 is accordingly in some sense a historical source to the changes in the Levant caused by Tiglatpileser III; however, would we know it if we didn't have the Assyrian records, which are contemporary with these events? Furthermore, is it certain that the Assyrian attacked the kingdom of Israel because of a secret settlement with Ahaz of Judah as argued by 2 Kings 16? The Assyrians make not a single reference to Judah before after the fall of Samaria in 722 BCE. It is as if they only discover the existence of Judah after the destruction of the Kingdom of Israel and Samaria.

2 Kings also informs us that Ahaz met Tiglatpileser in Damascus and was inspired by the local altar to construct a new altar for use in Jerusalem's Temple. This has often been seen as a sign that Ahaz was subjected to the religious policy of Assyria and therefore found a place for the worship of Assyrian deities in his own country. The Assyrian documents tell us nothing about such a meeting, and as far as altars for burning are involved, the historical content of this note is highly dubious as the Assyrians did not have altars for burning of this type, neither have we any evidence that they exported their gods to other countries, which would have meant that they would have demanded that the inhabitants living in their provinces should worship Assyrian deities (Cogan, 1974, 73–77). The episode of Ahaz meeting Tiglatpileser may have been constructed by biblical historiographers in order to inform us that Ahaz not only submitted to Assyrian rule but also introduced Assyrian religious practice and Assyrian deities into Jerusalem. The same historiographers do not place Ahaz among their favourites, we might even say that they almost say the opposite: Ahaz belongs among the minor villains of the Judean royal house (2 Kings 16:2–4).

This first example shows that a historical narrative in the Old Testament need not be without any historical memory. On the contrary, there is reason to believe that there are quite a few references to the history of Palestine in the 1st millennium. It is, at the same time, obligatory to ask questions about how useful such information is without any external confirmation, as in this case Tiglathpileser's own historical records. It is easy to be tempted into believing that just because some elements in the biblical stories have a historical background, everything else found here also includes historical information. Such a conclusion is, however, premature as the following example will show.

2 Kings 18–19 tells the story of the Assyrian King Sennacherib's attack on Hezekiah and Jerusalem. Sennacherib besieges Jerusalem but is forced to give up his plan to conquer it when the angel of the LORD kills 185,000 Assyrian soldiers during the night. The story opens with these verses:

> ¹³Now in the fourteenth year of king Hezekiah did Sennacherib king of Assyria come up against all the fenced cities of Judah, and took them. ¹⁴And Hezekiah king of Judah sent to the king of Assyria to Lachish, saying, I have offended; return from me: that which thou puttest on me will I bear. And the king of Assyria appointed unto Hezekiah king of Judah three hundred talents of silver and thirty talents of gold. ¹⁵And Hezekiah gave *him* all the silver that was found in the house of the LORD, and in the treasures of the king's house. ¹⁶At that time did Hezekiah cut off *the gold from* the doors of the temple of the LORD, and *from* the pillars which Hezekiah king of Judah had overlaid, and gave it to the king of Assyria. (KJV)

In the following section it is related that a high-ranking Assyrian commander addressed the inhabitants of Jerusalem, threatening them with immanent destruction if they do not surrender (2 Kings 18:17-37) and how Hezekiah reacted and his message to the prophet Isaiah (2 Kings 19:1-7).

Sennacherib's own annals also present a report of the Assyrian attack on Hezekiah. In the Assyrian version we are told how a group of Palestinian princes – including the Judean Hezekiah – conspired against Assyria. For that reason, Sennacherib was forced to intervene in order to re-establish order. Hezekiah was, however, a stubborn opponent, and Sennacherib had to resort to especially harsh measures to bring him to order:

> As for Hezekiah, the Judean, who did not submit to my yoke, 46 of his strong walled cities, as well as the small cities in their neighbourhood which were without number, – by levelling with battering-rams and by bringing up siege-engines, by attacking and storming on foot, by mines, tunnels and breaches, I besieged and took (those cities). 200,150 people, great and small, male and female, horses, mules, asses, camels, cattle and sheep, without number, I brought away from them and counted as spoil. Himself like a caged bird I shut up in Jerusalem, his royal city. Earthwork I threw up against him, – the one coming out of the city-gate, I turned back to his misery. The cities of his, which I had despoiled, I cut off from his land and to Mitinti, king of Ashdod, Padi, king of Ekron, and Silli-Bêl, king of Gaza, I gave. And (thus) I diminished his land. I added to the former tribute, and laid upon him, the giving (up) of their land, (as well as) imposts – gifts for my majesty. As for Hezekiah, the terrifying splendor of my majesty overcame him, and the Urbi (Arabs) and his mercenary troops which he had brought in to strengthen Jerusalem, his royal city, deserted him. In addition to the

30 talents of gold and 800 talents of silver (there were) gems, antimony, jewels, large *sandu*-stones, couches of ivory, house-chairs of ivory, elephant hide, ivory, ebony, boxwood, and kinds of valuable (heavy) treasures, as well as his daughters, his harem, his male and female musicians, (which) he had (them) bring after me to Ninive, my royal city. To pay tribute and to accept servitude, he dispatched his messengers.[18]

There is no doubt that the two texts, the biblical and the Assyrian annals, record one and the same event, Sennacherib's attack on Judah, whose king Hezekiah is forced to pay tribute to Sennacherib, who as his part of the agreement spares Jerusalem, Hezekiah's residence. One part of the tribute is the same in both texts: Hezekiah has to pay thirty talents of gold. Apart from that there are certain differences. According to the Assyrian version, Hezekiah pays eight hundred talents of silver, while he, according to the Old Testament, "only" has to pay three hundred talents. Thereafter the Assyrians claim that Hezekiah had to hand over – apart from various treasures – his daughters. The Bible does not mention this part of the tribute. The Assyrian version is most likely the correct one as we speak of a standard procedure in such cases, but we cannot decide whether the biblical account forgot these details or because of ideological considerations removed that part from the report of the tribute. These discrepancies are of minor significance. More important is the confusion created by the two sources in case the historian intends to reconstruct the course of Sennacherib's campaign in 701 BCE, the usual date of this campaign.

According to Sennacherib's own version, his third campaign was directed against the states to the west of Assyria and along the Mediterranean, first and foremost Phoenicia, and thereafter the coast of Palestine, where he conquers and plunders the cities of Beth-Dagon, Joppa, Banaj-Barqa, and Azuru.[19] Then Sennacherib turns his army towards Ekron, whose king Padi has been dethroned by his own citizens and handed over to Hezekiah. At the same time the king of Melukha[20] sent an army at the request of the citizens of Ekron but it was defeated by the Assyrians at Eltekeh.[21] After that, Sennacherib conquers Ekron and executes the rebellious citizens, whereupon Padi is reinstalled in

---

[18] Luckenbill, 1924, 32–34.
[19] All four places are today situated within the city limits of modern Tel Aviv. Cf. on the geographical information Strange, 1998, 39 Map 43.
[20] Here Ethiopia but by implication also Egypt, as Egypt was at this time ruled by a dynasty of Nubian or Ethiopian origin.
[21] Situated on the coastal plain a few kilometres from Ekron.

Ekron. Then it is Hezekiah's turn. His fortified cities are conquered and plundered while their citizens to the tune of 200,150 (Hezekiah's kingdom hardly included a population of this size) are deported.[22] Finally, Sennacherib laid siege to Jerusalem (which is surrounded by earthenworks) while Hezekiah's cities are handed over to faithful vassals of Assyria in Ashdod, Gaza, and Ekron. Hezekiah is, with the pitiful remnants of his kingdom, only saved by paying the aforementioned tribute to Sennacherib in Nineveh.

According to the version of this campaign in the Old Testament, Sennacherib attacks Hezekiah in the latter's fourteenth year as king and conquers all the fortified cities. After that Hezekiah sends a message to the king of Assyria and pays the tribute demanded. Following these events three high-ranking Assyrian officials are sent to Jerusalem, meeting Hezekiah's officials outside the city itself, threatening them to subjugation. The desperate Hezekiah sends his envoys to the prophet Isaiah, whose advice is to ignore the Assyrian threats. In the meanwhile, the Assyrian officials have returned to Sennacherib, who has moved his headquarters from Lachish to Libna (which he is besieging), while he at the same time has to fight off the king of Nubia, Tirhaka, who is threatening his position from the south. From Libna a letter is sent to Hezekiah with all kinds of threats if he does not surrender. Hezekiah now seeks help, not from Isaiah but from the temple. At this point Isaiah intervenes with a prophecy that the remnant of Judah shall have a future, and during the night Yahweh's angel kills 185,000 Assyrians, whereupon Sennacherib returns to his city of Nineveh.[23]

It is remarkable that the biblical version excludes everything that may explain the reasons for Sennacherib's campaign to the west in 701 BCE, both Hezekiah's part in the rebellion against Sennacherib – Hezekiah seems to be the person behind the rebellious inhabitants of Ekron – and Ekron's role in the rebellion. As it is, Ekron is not at all mentioned in the biblical story, which, however, has a number of references to Lachish, which is absent in Sennacherib's annals, although it plays an important part in other Assyrian documentation. It is also remarkable that there is not a word of any siege of

---

[22] Sennacherib was evidently particularly proud of his conquest of the mighty Judean fortress of Lachish, and had a series of reliefs placed in room XXXVI in his palace in Nineveh. The impression gained from these reliefs is confirmed by excavations at Lachish. See Ussishkin, 1982. Cf. also Trolle Larsen, 1997, 185–8.

[23] The story about the Campaign of Sennacherib in 2 Chronicles 30 is rather different from the one in 2 Kings 18–19, although the content is more or less the same. It is not easy to decide whether the version in Chronicles is dependent on 2 Kings or we have two independent versions. It's worth noting is the fact that 2 Chronicles does not mention any tribute from Hezekiah to Sennacherib.

Jerusalem in the biblical version. The closest Sennacherib's army gets to Jerusalem is Lachish and Libna, bordering on the coastal plain to the southwest of Jerusalem. Only Sennacherib's officers pay a visit to Jerusalem. Then the Old Testament has a short note on the Egyptian rescue expedition (2 Kings 19:9) but its consequences are not mentioned at all. If we, therefore, compare the version found in the Old Testament with the Assyrian report and try to create a kind of harmony between the two documents, we have to conclude that the version in the Old Testament is highly selective in comparison to the Assyrian annals. On the other hand, we also have to admit that chronology is a problem. The course of events is not absolutely the same in the Assyrian and biblical versions. One such problem concerns the tribute paid by Hezekiah. In the Assyrian version, Hezekiah agrees to pay tribute when he is besieged by the Assyrian army in his capital and sees no other way out of the trap. In 2 Kings Hezekiah pays the tribute when the Assyrians camp at Lachish, although after having paid his tribute, he is still threatened by the Assyrian official to surrender. Besides, the tribute is sent by Hezekiah to Nineveh where it arrives after Sennacherib had returned from his campaign, which is most likely the correct version since we are speaking about a considerable tribute that would have demanded more than just stripping the temple in Jerusalem of its treasures.

It is not because the Assyrian reports need to be correct in all details, being notoriously composed as propaganda legitimizing the ruler and his acts in the eyes of his god,[24] but the internal logic of the reports are under control. In the version found in the Old Testament this inner logic breaks down and for that reason alone they have to cede control over the events to the Assyrian versions. It is obvious that the author(s) of the story in the Old Testament had his reasons for restructuring the course of events the way he did: On one hand he admits that Hezekiah submitted to Sennacherib, while he, on the other, emphasizes that the whole campaign ended in a huge defeat for the Assyrian king who was no longer fighting against the man Hezekiah but against God himself. In this way the story of the Assyrian attack on Hezekiah in 2 Kings 18–19 is ideologically in agreement with the texts relating to the Assyrian threats in Isaiah 10 ("O Assyrian, the rod of mine anger …") promising that the king of Assyria will be punished not because he attacked the people of Yahweh (as Yahweh is using the Assyrians as his mean of punishment), but because in his rashness the king of Assyria went too far.

Taken together, the text of the Old Testament is a narrative coloured by the attitudes of its own time. The Assyrian version is also a narrative – here

---

[24] Cf. the characterization of the Assyrian annals in Trolle Larsen, 1997, 59–60.

there is no reason to disagree with Erslev – because it is likewise coloured by a series of biases caused by the situation of its composition, especially with regard to its divine addressee, the god who is to approve the conduct of the king. When it comes to a historical evaluation of the documents, we have to give precedence to the Assyrian version, simply for the reason that it dates from the time of Sennacherib and therefore is almost contemporary with the events described in Sennacherib's annals.

There is, on the other hand, no doubt that the biblical writer(s) had access to the information about the events of 791 BCE, and we may also conclude that this information did not differ in any important degree from the Assyrian documents. Parts of the information found in the biblical story are so precise that they hardly derive from some oral tradition. Therefore we, in this case – and that may also be the case with Tiglatpileser's arrangements mentioned above – will have to accept the presence of some written sources, although it is impossible to speak in any precise way how this information was preserved to be used by biblical history writers.

Then we may ask if the biblical author was a contemporary of Sennacherib and Hezekiah, or if he was in possession of annalistic literature from Judah presenting their version of the events, or if he in some way knew the Assyrian annals – and if that was the case, then we have to ask: what edition of the Assyrian annals did he have access to? We have to go further with the issue of dating the story in 2 Kings. Did it go back to Hezekiah's own time, i.e., was written down around 700 BCE or was it later and inspired by the deuteronomistic ideology, which means that it, at least in its present form, goes back to the circle of history writers behind the Deuteronomistic History traditionally dated to the 6th century BCE? If the last option is followed, more problems come up having to do with the survival of Judean and Assyrian historical information making them accessible for biblical historians.

A limited part of the narrative in 2 Kings 18–19 may, however, be considered *residues* in Droysen's sense. The main part is definitely a narrative, again according to Droysen's definitions. The question is, on the other hand, whether or not it would have been possible to reach this conclusion without the presence of the Assyrian version of the events of 701 BCE? Would a historian have been able to reconstruct how matters developed in that fateful year without having access to Sennacherib's report to the god Assur? Will the presence of a limited range of residues in Droysen's meaning of the word make a reconstruction of the events in Iron Age Palestine possible?

To get closer to an answer to these questions, I will include a third example relating to the war between Israel and King Mesha of Moab, which forms the subject of 2 Kings 3 but is also mentioned in King Mesha's famous Moabite inscription which he placed in his royal city of Dibon.[25]

According to Mesha, Israel ruled for forty years over Moab, but with the help of his god Chemosh, Mesha succeeded in reconquering the kingdom of his father: "Omri had conquered the Land of Medeba, and ruled there in all of his time and half of his son's time – all together forty years". The cities and places conquered and fortified by Israel Mesha retook and killed their inhabitants as a sacrifice to Chemosh.

2 Kings 3 also relates a war between Israel and Moab in the time of Jehoram of Israel (853/2–842/1) was waged.[26] The story says that after the death of Ahab, Mesha rebelled against Israel thus provoking Jehoram of Israel to join an alliance with Jehoshaphat of Judah to make war on Moab and invade the country. Thus, the army of Israel and Judah moves through the desert of Edom against Mesha for seven days but ends up in a hopeless position because of a lack of supplies. The army is saved by the intervention of the prophet Elisha. Elisha prophecies that Yahweh will deliver Moab into the hands of the kings of Israel and Judah. They will conquer and destroy the land. A miracle leads the Moabites into a trap and Israel conquers all of Moab apart from Kirhareseth which Mesha has fortified. Here as a last desperate measure Mesha sacrifices his son on the wall in hopes that this will change the fortunes of war. And "there was such great consternation among the Israelites that they struck camp and returned to their own land".[27]

In this case we must conclude that the discrepancies between the biblical version and the text of the Moabite stone are most evident. There is really only one point where the two texts are in agreement: that in the time of Mesha a war was fought between Moab and Israel. All other information is absolutely in disagreement. This does not mean that we should accept Mesha's version as it stands. It is biased and displays a series of stereotypical literary motifs as found in popular stories, such as the use of the number forty as the time when Israel ruled Moab. Mesha is also not very well informed about his Israelite opponent. He mentions Omri a couple of times but not Omri's son and successor Ahab – far more famous than his father, even known to the Assyrians[28]

---

[25] Dearman, 1989 includes a discussion of the details of the finding of the inscription as well as a translation and commentary.

[26] Cf. the chronology in Andersen, 1989, 41.

[27] Thus the Revised English Bible. KJV has indignation against Israel: "and they departed from him, and returned to *their own* land", which doesn't make any sense and definitely is not a correct translation.

[28] The Assyrians mention Ahab as part of an anti-Assyrian coalition of kings from Syria in 853 BCE, in an Assyrian annalistic record, *ANET,* p. 279.

– and he mentions Omri in a way that makes one wonder whether Mesha is referring to the king of Israel of this name or to the "House of Omri" which was, in this period, used commonly in foreign documents as the dynastic name of the Kingdom of Israel. And then Mesha adds that "he [Omri] ruled there in all of his time and half of his sons", but how should Omri have ruled in his son's time if it was not because "Omri" in the Mesha inscription meant the Kingdom of Israel and not the person, the King Omri?

Moreover, the narrative in 2 Kings 3 is not only biased but includes a series of miraculous events which classifies it not as a historical report but as a *narrative* written to glorify the greatness of Yahweh and his care for Israel. Thus the only thing that connects the two texts is the name of Mesha the king of Moab and the fact that a war was fought between Moab and Israel in Mesha's days. On the basis of this scant information of limited historical value a narrative is constructed not dissimilar to the one about Sennacherib's settlement with Hezekiah. The narrative opens with a few historical notes whereafter it develops with the inclusion of a number of anecdotes undoubtedly without any historical background but which alone owe their presence to the biblical writer. In 2 Kings 18-19 the historical foundation seems to come from information seemingly found in some sort of annals or royal inscriptions – either Assyrian or Judean – more or less contemporary with the events, whereas the only historical element in 2 Kings 3 is the name of the king of Moab; otherwise there is no historically important information in this chapter. Thus, nothing in the reference to Mesha and his wars against Israel in 2 Kings 3 prevents this story from being mainly based on oral tradition. The memory of this war is imprecise in every respect and thus conforms very well with the view of oral tradition at present: It is totally uncontrollable and of no or very little use for historical reconstruction. The only way to extract historical information from such a memory is to compare it to historical information that has been preserved and can be shown to go back to the time in question.

The technique used by biblical history writers is obvious. The writer finds his inspiration in some information that relates to an event in the past. It is without consequence whether or not this information is historical. Using this information as the foundation, the writer produces a *narrative* suited to the sentiments and ideas of his own time, which also means that the narrative will be received by his contemporaries as true. However, the truth is not centred on what really happened in the past, because in a *narrative* this is only a minor matter. Truth really has to do with the point of the narrative, which in the case of the three examples discussed above, has to conform to the more complex narrative about the greatness and fall of ancient Israel.

The Old Testament includes historical information about the past, but it does not present a systematically arranged collection of information. No kind of source criticism can be help us find that "historical kernel". There is no distinction between information which seems, from a historian's point of view, correct and another that is squarely without any historical foundation. The information itself is secondary to the point which is the subject of the narrative. The conclusion is that the Old Testament is of little use as an independent historical source to the past, i.e., the time that anteceded the time of the biblical history writers. Only if other sources exist will it be possible, in isolated cases, to make use of the narrative in the Old Testament in a historical reconstruction, and even in such cases – as the example of Sennacherib's attack shows – only with great caution.

12 Ezra and the Pentateuch

> When the seventh month came, and the Israelites were now settled in their towns, all the people assembled with one accord in the broad space in front of the Water Gate, and requested Ezra the scribe to bring the book of the law of Moses, which the Lord had enjoined upon Israel. On the first day of the seventh month, Ezra the priest brought the law before the whole assembly, both men and women, and all who were capable of understanding what they heard. From early morning until noon he read aloud from it, facing the square in front of the Water gate, in the presence of the men and the women, and those who could understand; the people all listened attentively to the book of the law.
>
> (Neh 7:72b–8.3) (Revised English Bible)

According to the books of Ezra and Nehemiah, Cyrus' edict (in which he released the Israelites from their Babylonian prison) was followed by a massive migration of Jews from Babylonia to Palestine and Jerusalem, numbering as many as 42,360 persons & slaves and attendants, altogether about 50,000 persons. Following the settlement of the returnees in their cities, the sacrificial cult is resumed in Jerusalem. The leader of the religious community in this period is Joshua, the son of Jozadak, and Zerubbabel, the son of Shealtiel, who build the altar of sacrifice according to the Law of Moses. The beginning of the sacrificial period is described as the 1st of the seventh month. In the second year after the return the building of the new temple began, led by Joshua and Zerubbabel, making use of products contributed by the Phoenicians from Tyre and Sidon.

However, soon the building is hampered by "the enemies of Judah and Benjamin", (Ezra 4:1) because they hear that the former exiles are building a temple, and so the work stopped as far as the government of Cyrus and Darius was concerned (Ezra 4:5). Endeavours to resume the building of the temple started during the reign of Artaxerxes, who evidently followed Ahasverus on the throne (Ezra 4:6–7). However, a letter from the Persian officers of the province "Beyond-Euphrates" put an end to the rebuilding of the city. Not before the second year of King Darius was the building on the temple resumed (Ezra 4:24). This king was also approached by the officers of "Beyond-Euphrates", but after having investigated the case and found Cyrus' permission to build the temple, the work can continue so that the temple can be completed in King Darius's 6th year, as ordered "by the Persian kings of Cyrus, Darius and Artaxerxes". First, then, follows the mission of Ezra to Jerusalem (Ezra 7) in Artaxerxes' 7th year. He was devoted "to the study and the observance of the Law of the Lord and to teaching statute and ordinance in Israel" (Ezra 7:10). A list of the members of the Jewish community in Mesopotamia who followed Ezra to Jerusalem follows (Ezra 8). In Jerusalem, Ezra is aghast when he is informed of the status of the Jewish community in Jehud, that they have, in great numbers, indulged themselves in marrying foreign women: Canaanites, Hittites, Perizzites, Jebussites, Ammonites, Moabites, Egyptians, and Amorites (Ezra 9:1). The rest of the Book of Ezra is more or less devoted to the cleansing of Jewish society which forced Jewish men to divorce their foreign wives.

At this point the Book of Nehemiah starts with year 20 of Artaxerxes' reign (Neh 1:1; 2:1) as Nehemiah informs the king that Jerusalem is still in ruins, and that he must go back to rebuild the walls of the city. Eventually, and in spite of vehement opposition from a number of named persons, Nehemiah succeeds in building this wall. We have evidently now reached the 32nd year of Artaxerxes' reign (Neh 5:14). Now the problem is social injustice done by the Jews to the other citizens of the land, a problem Nehemiah has to attend, before he can finally complete the rebuilding of the wall (Neh 6:15). At this point follows a list of the Jewish immigrants who left Babylonia (Nehemiah 7), a list that is an exact copy of the one in Ezra 2. This list introduces Ezra, who is asked to bring the book of the Law of Moses, which he, as mentioned in the quotation that introduced this lecture, read aloud in front of the people. Thereafter it's time for the feast of Booths (sukkoth) (Nehemiah 8) after which follows a public day of repentance (Nehemiah 9), the declaration that people shall not break the law (Nehemiah 10), another list of the inhabitants of Jerusalem and Judah (Nehemiah 11), one concerning the priests and the Levites (Nehemiah 12), and finally some regulations of social and religious affairs (Nehemiah 13).

In Jewish tradition, Ezra's proclamation of the law meant that the completion of the writings later included in Hebrew Bible was achieved, and that nothing dating after the days of Ezra could be part of sacred scripture. As we know, this works perfectly in the Hebrew Bible, in that even very late scripture like Daniel and presumably the Song of Songs are also, by tradition, situated to a time before Ezra; Daniel by being attributed to a prophet living in the Days of Nebuchadnezzar, Belshazzar and Darius, and the Song of Songs by being ascribed to King Solomon. That the Rabbis did not automatically accept whatever piece of literature that maintained itself to have been written by Solomon is, on the other hand, evident, as some of the books of the Septuagint, the Greek Bible, such as the Odes and Psalms of Solomon were not included in the Hebrew Bible – either because no Hebrew manuscript existed or because even the most naïve Rabbi would know that apart from Psalm 72 and maybe the Song of Songs (a lot of discussion was raised in rabbinic circles concerning the status of this book) Solomon did not normally create poems but proverbs!

In modern scholarship this theory of the origin of the Hebrew Bible in the days of Ezra has only partially been accepted, as evidently much literature in the OT must be younger, among which of course stands Daniel. However, as the closing date of the collection, normally considered the oldest, is the Pentateuch, this date is generally accepted. Not that it is exclusive, as large parts of the present Pentateuch is normally considered to be much older – but apart from some Jewish scholars today, the community of OT scholars have generally accepted the Jewish tradition, at least as concerns the Pentateuch. And so it came to be accepted that the Pentateuch was formed over a period of about five hundred years, reaching back to the time of Solomon, rewritten and reshaped again and again over the next centuries, until the final priestly revision (if not the blending together of the old work with a more recent Priestly source). Scholarship seemed satisfied – even if some imperturbable colleagues had dared to question the whole edifice, among them most notably C.C. Torrey.[1]

In Jewish history the character of Ezra is, as a matter of fact, a rather problematic one. The problems not only concern the time of his mission, but also the man himself and the relationship between Ezra's and Nehemiah's books. Let us therefore start the critical part of this lecture by reviewing the evidence as I see it – not trying to remove in advance any part of it from the discussion.

First, we have to fix the chronology as presented by the books of Ezra and Nehemiah, thereby at the present disregarding claims that none of this information is historical – if this is at all possible. People who have been working

---

[1] In his *The Composition and Historical Value of Ezra-Nehemia* (Torrey, 1896), expanded in many ways in his *Ezra Studies* (Torrey, 1910). It is not my intention here to review Torrey's overlooked work – mostly dismissed as the work of an outsider, not to be read or taken seriously – but tracing Giovanni Garbini – a scholar of the same character as Torrey – to vindicate his approach. The more intricate parts of Torrey's argument need to be revised in another context.

with this topic will know that whereas Nehemiah's mission seems to be clearly indicated not only by the dates mentioned, from Artaxerxes' 20th to his 32nd year, but also by the names of officials opposing Nehemiah, who are known from other sources – especially the Elephantine Papyri[2] – it is much more difficult to access the correct date of Ezra's visit. According to this knowledge, the Artaxerxes of Nehemiah can only be Artaxerxes I Macrocheir who, after his father Xerxes' assassination in 465/4 BCE, was to reign for the next forty years. According to this estimate, Nehemiah would have arrived in Jerusalem in 445/4 BCE and have left Jerusalem, at least for a while, in 433/2 BCE. Should we follow the date of Ezra's arrival, he would have come to Jerusalem in the 7th year, that is in 458/457 BCE. The Book of Nehemiah, however, seems to reckon both Nehemiah and Ezra to be contemporaries (Neh 8:9), but that seems to be impossible. The events recorded in Ezra mostly happened in the second year after his arrival, that is 457/456, but at that time another twelve years had to pass before Nehemiah arrived. Also, do the regulations mentioned at the end of Nehemiah indicate that Ezra's reforms were not yet enacted, which is again unlikely in light of the last chapters of the Book of Ezra.

Accordingly, most scholars – or so I believe – opt for another solution, forcing Ezra and Nehemiah to separate. Artaxerxes I was not the only king of this name to rule the Persian Empire. In fact he had two colleagues with the same name as his: Artaxerxes II Mnemon, who ruled between 405/404 and 359/58, and Artaxerxes III Ochus, the king of Persia from 359/358 to 338 BCE. The reigns of both kings are long enough to allow for Ezra to travel to Jerusalem in the seventh year, that is either in 399/398 or 353/352 BCE. In general, scholars settle for the first date (however, without seriously considering the last one – which may be just as good, after all). That will place the conclusion of the Pentateuch, the law of Moses, to around 400 BCE, but no traditionally minded Old Testament scholar is worried by such a "low" date, but the possibility cannot be excluded that the last date is just as appropriate, which would lower the date to about 360 BCE, although the lower date does not normally appeal to any scholar of the aforementioned group.

However, the date of Ezra's arrival is still constructed on the basis of a rather dubious chronology. As it stands, the Book of Ezra begins where 2

---

[2] Most notably Sanballat, who is also mentioned in the Aramaic papyri from Elephantine and maybe elsewhere. It should, however, be noted that there is supposed to have lived another Sanballet (II) in the 4th century BCE – and if two, why not three or four, or an unknown number of persons of this name. See on these "Sanballats" among others, Williamson, 1977 and Williamson, 1988. Williamson reckons all of them to belong to the same family occupying, so to speak per tradition, the office as governors of Samaria.

Ezra and the Pentateuch

Chronicles comes to an end, in 539/8 BCE as Cyrus releases the Jews from bondage in Babylonia. It presents a long list of Jews who returned, and a description of the building of the temple which started in the days of Cyrus but stopped while he was still king of Persia, and was not taken up in the days of Darius and Ahasverus. This information brings us down to 465/4 before anything can be done to the temple again, as it is only Artaxerxes who allows rebuilding. It is true that Ahasverus is immediately and without any ado substituted in Ezra by his son Artaxerxes. It is also true that the Book of Ezra omits the short reign of Cambyses – so short that it is of no importance here. However, it is not a minor thing that the chronological information starts again by mentioning the completion of the temple in Darius' 6th year. So the whole chronology is mixed up should this Darius be the first one as is normally assumed, Darius I, who ruled between 522/21 and 487/6 BCE. The second Darius cannot, however, be excluded and a case for him could be made. The second king of this name ruled from 424–405 BCE, and to place the completion of the temple in his reign, that is in 419/8 BCE, would not create problems for the Ezra mission which followed shortly after that date, but certainly to other parts of the OT, especially Haggai and Zecharaiah, so perhaps it is best to conclude that the chronology of Ezra – but not that of Nehemiah – is completely mixed up, and that it can be concluded that we have no clear indication of the date of Ezra's mission, whether it be 457/456, 399/398 or 353/352 BCE.

Such chronological confusion must be a problem, as we are here speaking about an incident of the utmost importance for the establishment of the Jewish nation. The proclamation of the law of Moses and what follows can more or less be considered the foundation story of post-exilic Judaism – and we have absolutely no safe way of deciding the date of this foundation.

On top of this – but perhaps significant in itself – the identification of Ezra seems to be just as uncertain as the chronology of his stay in Jerusalem. We are informed by the Book of Ezra (8:1) that Ezra was the son of Seraiah, who, for his part, was the son of Azariah, the descendant of Hilkiah, the son of Shallum – and so eventually back to Aaron. In this way Ezra is to be reckoned a member of the family of the high priest, counting among his forefathers the Hilkiah who found the law book in Josiah's days, and thus the chain that links Ezra's lawbook to the law book of Moses proclaimed by Ezra himself seems safeguarded.

The genealogy of the father of Ezra, Seraiah, is to be found in 1 Chronicles 6:27–41, according to which Seraiah was truly the son of Azariah, the son of Hilkiah. However, Seraiah's son was not named Ezra, but Jozadak (1 Chron 6:40), who was to become the father of the high priest Joshua, as indicated by Ezra 3:8, who lived in the days of Zerubbabel. Joshua's sons and brothers are also mentioned (Ezra 10:18): Maaseiah, Eliezer, Jarib, and Gedaliah, but no Ezra, meaning there is not the slightest reference or indication of his presence. It is therefore rather obvious that Ezra's name has been grafted to Seraiah's genealogy, and that we, in Ezra 7:1, have a clear case of what is technically called genealogy manipulation, and that the person's family relations are totally fictitious.

So now we have a person of dubious origin – to say the least – and without any secure indication of the date of his mission. Can we penetrate further into the secret world of Ezra, the Scribe?

Yes, I believe we can, by an analysis of the respective books of Ezra and Nehemiah: how are they related to each other? In general it has, on one side, been discussed whether the books of Ezra and Nehemiah can be considered original parts of the Chroniclers History, and on the other whether there was originally only one book, later divided into two.

As they stand, the missions of Ezra and Nehemiah are blended together to form almost two sides of the same mission, that is the establishment of the Jerusalemite Jewish society after the exile. It is, on the other hand, just as clear that the two persons, if they were at all historical characters and not only characters in a book, had nothing in common, except that they are both supposed to have arrived from Mesopotamia in the time of the Kings of Persia (whoever these kings were). If we speak of an originally single work and simply join the two books together, then what remains? A very uneven work clumsily put together, mixing things together that should not be mixed, and presenting a most confusing chronology. This does not seem likely, even for a writer who is normally supposed to have lived in the Persian period (I very much doubt this date, but that's another question).

In a short lecture it is hardly possible to present a definite proof of this hypothesis. It is, however, an astonishing fact that we do not need Ezra to understand what's at stake in Ezra-Nehemiah. Nobody would miss him if we had a single book that passed from the completion of the temple on to the mission of Nehemiah. In fact, the structure and purpose of that book would become much clearer. The Present Ezra begins with the decree of Cyrus ordering the Jews to return in order to build the temple. On top of this outright order, Cyrus provides the returnees with the lost treasures of their old temple, so that the new temple can be properly built. No doubt we have here a kind of a "Gründungslegende" concerning the erection of the second temple. It takes some time before local opposition, led by persons who were not in Mesopotamia along with local Persian officials, is overcome so that the temple can reach its completion which happens in Darius' sixth year, probably in 518/17, as normally assumed – however, the historical dimension of the text is perhaps not the most important part of it. The temple is now built and completed, then remains the reconstruction of the city and its walls, a project already mentioned before the completion of the temple. Once more a mission out of Mesopotamia is necessary to bring this rebuilding of Jerusalem to a successful end, and again the intruder, in this case Nehemiah, is opposed by local people and governors, but in the end Nehemiah succeeds and can, after having rebuilt the walls of Jerusalem, thereby providing a shelter for his fellow countrymen, the emigrants, proceed to arranging social and religious affairs as well. This structure is so clear that it is amazing that so few have seen it. The tale of this original book is, to a large degree, schematized, and follows for both parts basically of the same pattern, i.e. the narrative is certainly very artfully arranged, and what is legend and what history can be questioned. Even the style of the Book, which is in large part an autobiography by Nehemiah, may be artificial, as is well known, perhaps belonging to the Hellenistic Age when spurious "autobiographies" was a popular literary genre. That does not concern us here, nor that the author of the Book of Nehemiah displays some knowledge of places and names belonging to the 5th century BCE. That was to be expected, and it places the book squarely in line with the Deuteronomistic History so far as the deuteronomistic description of the period of the kings goes. The historicity or non-historicity of Nehemiah does not call Ezra into life, if his existence can otherwise be doubted, which is the point here.

Poor Ezra: No family, no history and no book: No family name and reputation left for him, no date of arrival indicated that can be trusted – remember that it happened in the seventh year, surely a date not without ideological biases of its own – and no original book that was his: only spurious family relations, an unknown historical setting of his work, and a few chapters grafted upon a literary work belonging to someone else. Not much left indeed. But the tribulations of Ezra do not end here, as it can be shown that nobody knew him, at least not before the 2nd century BCE.

By this remark I should like to introduce the famous review of the history of the chosen people, presented by Jesus Sirach and which is normally supposed to come from the beginning of the 2nd century BCE, though some will say ca. 180 BCE. Without discussing the biographical and historical information about the Book's own fate, how it was translated from the Hebrew of the old Jesus Ben Sira by his grandson allegedly between 132 and 117 BCE, and the interesting story of the relations between the Greek version of the Septuagint and the Hebrew fragments from the geniza of the Cairo synagogue – now amplified by DSS fragments – I must maintain that the historical survey contained in chapters 44–50 is really extraordinary – if not for anything else then at least for leaving Ezra out of this historical overview. Let me just quote the passage of interest (Sir 49:11–13):

> "How can we tell the greatness of Zerubbabel,
> Who was like a signet-ring on the Lord's right hand?
> With him was Joshua son of Jehozadak;
> In their days they built the house,
> Raising a holy temple to the Lord,
> Destined for eternal glory.
> Great is the memory of Nehemiah,
> Who raised our fallen walls,
> Constructed gates and bars,
> And rebuilt our ruined homes". (NEB)

After that the overview in Sirach continues after a digression about Enoch, to Simon the high priest, the son of Onias, which takes us right down to the days of Sirach himself. If anybody has ever been conspicuous by his absence, this must be the great champion of the Jewish people, Ezra, but his story seems not to be acknowledged by Sirach.

Of course, it could be taken as an *argumentum ex silentio* and therefore dismissed – if it was not for the analysis of the Ezra and Nehemiah traditions presented here. The way the post-exilic period is described by Sirach, however, almost proves my hypothesis to be true; that once the present books of Ezra and Nehemiah were only one and the same book containing, exactly, as is made clear by a study of the books themselves, one single narrative divided into two parts, one dealing with the temple and attached to Jehoshua the high priest and Zerubbabel, the other to Nehemiah and dealing with Jerusalem and its walls.

The conclusion to be reached seems inevitable – however much you may dislike it: Ezra is an intruder into the history of the Jewish people, and has been introduced for only one purpose, to proclaim the Law of Moses. This may have happened before the days of Jesus Sirach, however, it was not acknowledged by him as a legitimate description of how Israel became the people of God's law. There is, on the other hand, an indication that the version of the early history of the nation known by Sirach departed from the official version preserved by the present Pentateuch (although in many aspects it is very close to it), in that the initial part of the primeval story is not mentioned. The first hero of the past is Enoch, not Adam, and after Enoch comes Noah, and then Abraham. These may seem to be small deviations from the standard version, but may point to a date where the final content of the early history of Israel had not yet been settled.

If all of this is true, then we reach the amazing conclusion that the Pentateuch was still far from finished around 200 BCE, which indicates that it took perhaps another generation before it was finalized. Instead – since there is no reason to believe that the traditions contained in the Pentateuch were not in circulation around 200 (or a lest a comprehensive part of them) – there may be reason to think that the traditions of the Pentateuch – and by this I mean the normative tales and laws of the present Pentateuch and not some first draft of them – had obtained neither their present shape nor general approval around the time of the old Sirach.

Instead, it may be so that several competing versions of Israel's past were in circulation at that date. Let's have a look at what we know about them – a full treatment of the problems involved will have to wait for another occasion. In fact, already in the Hebrew Bible, we have several versions and in addition to these of course the one in Sirach, normally taken to be the oldest of the apocryphal books of the Old Testament. The first, and now most comprehensive, is the historical survey in Genesis, Exodus, and Numbers, but this one is followed up by a competing one in Deuteronomy, chapters 1–3. However, this is not the last one. Apart from casual deuteronomistic references to the past as in the famous so/called "credo"-passage in Deuteronomy 26:5–9, the most comprehensive in the Deuteronomistic History may be in Joshua 24 – a chapter often considered to be something of an outsider in the deuteronomistic literature. Then we have the survey in Nehemiah 9 and, last but not least, the one in Psalms 104–106. All of these are related insofar as they accept the same general outline of Israelite history – as also does Jesus Sirach. I can therefore safely say that ca. 200 the basic outline was without doubt in existence, but preserved in various forms, short as well as long.

It is not possible to deal with the different version in this short space. However, one famous difference between the versions consists in the "omission" of the Sinai complex in the so-called "credo-Text" as remarked many years ago by von Rad (Von Rad, 1938). This has been taken to prove that the earliest versions of Israel's history did not contain this part. However, the evidence which I refer to may simply tell us that some versions included it while for unknown reasons it was omitted by other versions. However, to mention just a few deviations, the patriarch Jacob is called an Aramean in Deut 26:5, who went down to Egypt with a few followers (not a word about his family), whereas in Joshua 24 – a chapter that otherwise follows the train of the narrative in the Pentateuch quite closely – another "unknown" tradition may be referred to: the sending of wasps that drove away the Canaanites. The meaning is uncertain as the Hebrew צרעה may also mean "terror" or "panic" as in the REB (NEB). In the first case the reference points at an incident otherwise unknown, in the second some resemblance to the present Book of Joshua may be intended, stressing perhaps clearer than Joshua that the Israelites did not conquer their land – it was in fact Yahweh who vanquished the Canaanites. In comparison to this a historical review of the mighty hymns of Psalms 104–106 has to be mentioned as well, especially because the primeval history has been reduced to the creation (Psalm 104), whereas the real survey starts in Psalm 105 with Abraham. This Psalm follows the Pentateuch quite closely except from Sinai/Horeb where only the golden calf is mentioned. On the other hand, we find a description and especially an evaluation of the sojourn in the desert that is obviously very different from the one found in the book of Numbers. Here this review breaks off, but at almost the same point as the hymnic overview of Israel's history in Nehemiah 9 does. Nehemiah 9 starts with creation and goes immediately after that (like the three psalms) directly to the patriarchal history. Here, however, Sinai is included and has a central function, as are the following parts of the narrative of the Pentateuch, to the time of the judges. Here the author mentions the killing of prophets, a theme otherwise placed at another point in the deuteronomistic interpretation of history; however, here is added part of the theme of the Book of Judges. Another difference in Nehemiah 9 is the omission of David and Solomon. In fact, the period of the Hebrew kings is only remotely mentioned and – strangely enough – the exile is almost left unmentioned. Instead of it a new theme is provided by the end of the Nehemiah survey: that the Israelites of Nehemiah's days are the slaves of kings in their own country, kings who have been placed there by Yahweh – here we are really let down by the text: Is the narrator referring to the Hebrew kings, and the text an echo of 1 Samuel 8 (Samuel's dismissal of the kingdom as institution), or is he referring to Persian or Hellenistic kings of the post-exilic period, that is kings contemporary (Achaemedian, Seleucid, or Ptolemaic ones?) with the author?

It was formerly assumed that this kind of survey stood at the beginning of history writing in Israel. So von Rad's famous study on the small credo-text was pivotal in this respect, even if later refuted by Leonhard Rost especially (Rost, 1965). Recently the theme (not so much the Credos as historical survey's themselves) have been taken up again by Sigfried Kreutzer in a dissertation from Vienna, who in reaction to an old theory of Anton Jirku concludes that these texts are pretty recent (although Kreutzer would hardly have thought of a date as low as the one proposed here) (Kreuzer, 1989).

Here the point of interest is not the respective age and sequence of these surveys but their very existence (which is here taken to indicate that the historical tradition of the Old Testament may be much more recent and much more fluid than was formerly believed). And as I have already said, much speaks in favour of a situation where the Jews of the early 2nd century had not yet settled on the final version of their history – which reminds me of an interesting study by Doron Mendels, in which he deals with the phenomenon of nationalism in the Hellenistic world, including the interest in national histories – which is thought-provoking, to say the least (Mendels, 1992).

Still one mystery remains to be solved: how did it come about that the Pentateuch obtained the position it was to possess over the centuries to come? And why was Ezra "invented" as the spokesman of the Torah, the Pentateuch? I cannot answer these questions in any exhaustive way here. Giovanni Garbini, who has dealt extensively with the Ezra-case (Garbini, 1988, 151–69), argues that this happened during the competition for power between various factions and parties around the temple of Jerusalem in 159 BCE, in that one party, presumably the one that came out victorious, used Ezra as their protagonist and the version of Israel's past they accepted as the orthodox version of God's will. The other part had to depart, and again according to Garbini created their version of the law, better known as the Temple Scroll from Qumran. Whether this be true or[3] not has to be proven, and proof is not important here. The important thing to my mind is that the status then of the present Pentateuch definitively proves the Pentateuch, as well as the rest of the Old Testament, to belong to the Hellenistic Age.

Undoubtedly this hypothesis – in reality a very old one[4] – will be questioned and for many reasons. However, most of these will probably come from analyses of the Pentateuch itself of the usual sort that tries, because of internal evidence, to date the book. To me such studies are far behind in methodology, and not very strong evidence for anything. Any person who has studied the history of Old Testament research knows that so many different proposals for dating the Pentateuch and the various parts of it to different periods on the basis of some sort of internal evidence have appeared that it can truly be said that this approach leads nowhere – or, and that is just as bad – everywhere. In the neo-Albrightian school of studies which we have inaugurated in Copenhagen, we simply dismiss such internal evidence as a logical failure, and we maintain that to dismiss such matters as an inevitable part of the hermeneutical circle is obviously a false conclusion which cannot be defended. On the contrary, this circle is like all kinds of circular argumentation absolutely false and should be refuted – buried, never to be awakened to live

---

[3] Cf. on this Lemche, 1993a.
[4] Compare Seidel, 1993, 172–3.

again. It should simply have no place and home in scientific studies, not even in theology which itself cannot ever afford again to embrace methodologies that are otherwise banned from the universities. No, we want hard evidence, external evidence, as good as this may be. I have tried here to introduce what can be achieved by making use of external evidence instead of internal proofs. And I would like to see my theories accepted or refuted by applying external evidence – not internal evidence which I cannot accept – to the discussion.

But returning at last to Ezra, we should certainly not forget the tradition of 2 Maccabees 2:13 which states that it was Nehemiah, not Ezra, who created a library of ancient Jewish writings!

13 What Have We Done and Where Are We Moving? Personal Remarks About a Change of Paradigm

John Strange has always played the role of an ugly duckling in the company of Old Testament scholars at the University of Copenhagen. He has, on one side, always been an inspiring and innovative colleague, while on the other against almost everything. In the 1960s during my studies in Copenhagen, Strange was the young rebel among his colleagues, the inspiring teacher who prepared many of the bullets which we subsequently used for our guns. When the results of our "duck shooting" began to appear, Strange remained very sceptical – maybe because he still intended to prepare more bullets for new sharpshooters.

The Past

Allow me to illustrate this introduction by quoting an example of Strange's "subversive" strategies. Thirty years ago, Old Testament scholarship in Europe was dominated by a number of hypotheses which themselves made up a paradigm. A narrow circle of German scholars attached to Albrecht Alt (1883–1956) and his gifted student and spiritual heir, Martin Noth (1902–1968), had created the paradigm. Central to the paradigm was the idea that early Israel was organized as a sacral league – an Amphictyony – that consisted of twelve tribes ethnically different from the Canaanite population of Palestine and worshipping a god unknown to pre-Israelite Palestine. Ca. 1200 BCE this Israel – i.e. the twelve tribes – had immigrated to Palestine from neighbouring regions and had consolidated their sway over the highlands of Palestine. The biblical traditions about the patriarchs, the sojourn of Israel in Egypt, and the origin of Yahwism all belonged to the community of the Amphictyony and were nourished and kept in memory at the central shrine of the Amphictyony by its members as part of their cultic experiences. In this way the hypothesis about the Amphictyony made it possible to keep together every important aspect of the biblical tradition. It incorporated such themes as Israel being a special nation with Yahwism as its adopted monotheistic religion and the early date of the biblical narrative tradition.

At the end of the 1960s a small group of theological students at the Faculty of Theology at the University of Copenhagen began to doubt that the foundation of the Israelite Amphictyony was very solid. As a matter of fact, the opposite was the case: The hypothesis about the Amphictyony found no support at all in the historical narratives of the Old Testament. Central among this circle of students was John Strange, who in his usual flamboyant style claimed that "we have all been brainwashed by the deuteronomists", saying that all of us have, in the most uncritical fashion, adopted the description of Israel's past created by the deuteronomists. In this way Strange's students were encouraged to give up the governing paradigm and to construct a totally new one.

The rebellion against the Amphictyony found its first concise formulation in a student's thesis by Kjeld Nielsen from 1966/67. This thesis, which has never been published, included a radical score settling with the theory of the Amphictyony and everything connected to it. More importantly, however, was the formulation, by the University of Copenhagen, of the theme for a gold medal thesis for the year 1968: "The conditions in and outside of Israel for the appearance of David's empire". Three theses were handed in; the second being this author's, for which he received marks of "highly recommended".

The most advanced thesis, Heike Friis, included an important discussion of almost every aspect of contemporary biblical historical scholarship. It concluded that the theory of the Amphictyony has little support in the Old Testament and that the hypothesis about the immigration of the Israelite tribes ought to be substituted by George Mendenhall's reconstruction of "the Hebrew Conquest of Palestine" – at the time only recently published in an inadequate form (Mendenhall, 1962). It was also Heike Friis's conviction that the biblical tradition about early Israel did not have its roots in Israel's ancient past; it appeared much later as a reflection on the Judean exile in Babylonia. It is a scholarly disaster that this remarkable thesis was not immediately made generally available to the public. It only appeared in 1986 in a German translation, as a book technically less than perfect (Friis, 1986). Danish readers were, however, able to get a first impression of it when a central part was published in *Dansk Teologisk Tidsskrift* in 1975 (Friis, 1975).

Because of the vagaries of fortune this writer's more imperfect thesis was destined to become more important. The first chapter appeared as a separate monograph as early as 1972. Because of this and in spite of its modest size it opened – at least among Scandinavian scholars – the discussion about the merit or lack of merit of the classical historical paradigm for Old Testament studies (Lemche, 1972). It is, in many ways, a very traditional study. However,

What Have We Done and Where Are We Moving? 191

exactly because of this quality – because it was otherwise not considered to be very provocative[1] – it was well suited to the role of "deconstructor" of the hypothesis of the Amphictyony that was demolished step by step.

Now it would be a mistake to assume that Copenhagen was the only centre of destruction of the old paradigm of Old Testament studies. We might not even have been the first to begin this process. We were, however, the first to publish our results. Thus, my study of the Amphictyony from 1972 was subsequently joined by a series of similar studies published by scholars belonging to very different milieus and places who, without knowing the existence of my Danish monograph, more or less sided with it in demolishing the amphictyonic hypothesis.[2]

In Scandinavia a definitive change of orientation then occurred when, in 1977, Benedikt Otzen published his history of ancient Israel as a textbook for students of theology in Denmark (Otzen, 1977). In his book, Otzen simply chose to ignore the amphictyonic hypothesis, although he still kept some of its components. Among the important innovations in Otzen's approach to the history of Israel we may count his recognition of the character of the deuteronomistic redaction. The deuteronomists intended to present a picture of early Israel as a community consisting of all of the twelve tribes (Otzen, 1977, 118–21).

Reading Otzen's report on ancient Israelite history, it soon becomes evident that his study is situated right in the middle of a changing paradigm. On the one hand, Otzen decides to side with scholars with a critical attitude to a central part of the old paradigm, i.e. the amphictyonic hypothesis, while he, on the other, does not see the possible consequences of the changes caused by the removal of the Amphictyony from the Israelite scene. It is exactly at this point that Heike Friis' thesis from 1968 was exceptional. It would take another twenty years before any scholar was able, in such a direct way, to

---

[1] The importance of being harmless, or as it can be pleasantly put, "to be in accordance with your own time" has been illustrated most illuminatingly by Eduard Nielsen, who refers to the fate of the French Old Testament scholar Maurice Vernes, who was active at the end of the 19th century (Nielsen, 1992, 169–74). Because of his very "modern" ideas, Vernes was, by his contemporaries, considered to be "mad" and indifferent and was subsequently totally forgotten. Maybe Vernes should have quoted the French composer Hector Berlioz who is supposed, in a conversation in Paris with Richard Wagner, to have argued that his career would certainly change for the better in about one hundred and fifty years' time! (As a matter of fact, Berlioz was right).

[2] The early debate about the Amphictyony was reviewed by Otto Bächli in his *Amphiktyonie im Alten Testament. Forschungsgeschichtliche Studie zur Hypothese von Martin Noth* (Bächli, 1977).

liberate him- or herself from deuteronomistic brainwashing. We are forced by a changing paradigm not only to make critical notes about the deuteronomistic narrative – something that did not prevent scholars from keeping most of the deuteronomistic framework of their historical reconstruction. The obvious conclusion is that in case the central theme in the deuteronomistic history of an early united Israel is misleading, the other parts of the deuteronomistic history are likely also to be distorting the facts of history. The central issue is – something Heike Friis understood as early as 1968 – that the history of ancient Israel was not written by the biblical historiographers in order to present the past. The history was composed in order, in a paradigmatical way, to explain to its readership why a specific event – the destruction of Jerusalem and its temple and the ensuing loss of statehood – ever occurred. There is at present no reason to change this idea of Heike Friis, i.e., that the idea of history in the Old Testament must be seen as the product of the Babylonian exile. It is simply dependent on the exile and cannot be understood without an exile.

The Present

It is meaningless at this point to present an exhaustive review of the development of Old Testament scholarship since 1970. I will only mention that while we, on one side, have not moved beyond the major points made by Heike Friis, we have, on the other, provoked a series of changes to occur that affects almost every single point of the old paradigm. As a consequence a new paradigm for the study of the Old Testament has arisen that has substituted the old one from the 1960s. The main issues of the new paradigm are:

1) It is important that we, i.e. the circle of scholars to which this author belongs, no longer speak about an "Israel" ethnically distinct from its neighbours. There was no Israelite *nation* in the pre-exilic period. Several routes took us here. First and foremost, the studies in the settlement process of the Israelite tribes inaugurated by George Mendenhall, later joined by Norman Gottwald (Gottwald, 1979), made it obvious that the Israelites belonging to the pre-monarchic period did not constitute an ethnically distinct group. Most "Israelites" originated among Palestinian society at large. They were – or so we got accustomed to saying – "Canaanites".[3]

---

[3] This was still the case in my doctoral thesis *Early Israel: Anthropological and Historical Studies on the Israelite Society Before the Monarchy* (Lemche, 1985b), and in my textbook *Ancient Israel: A New History of Israelite Society* (Lemche, 1988).

The general climate of discussion became more harsh when I, at the beginning of the 1990s, published a study claiming the "Canaanites" were not an ethnic group (Lemche, 1991a). They were part of the fictional scenario created by biblical historiographers. These history writers understood the Canaanites to constitute an "anti-nation" as opposed to the true nation called "Israel".

Philip R. Davies subsequently supported this idea of mine. He, however, went further and claimed that the Canaanites were not the only biblical nation never to have existed. The "Israelites" of the Old Testament were also a fictional nation created by deuteronomist historiographers who considered the biblical Israelites to be the predecessors of the "new Israelites" – i.e. Jews – of their own time.[4] Accordingly, we should – or so Davies maintains – make a distinction between three "Israels": 1) *historical Israel*, i.e. the Israel of the real world that appears in the inscription of the Egyptian Pharaoh Merenphtah from ca. 1200 BCE,[5] or in inscriptions from the 9th or 8th centuries BCE, 2) *biblical Israel*, i.e. the Israel whose fate is described in the Old Testament and only exists here, and finally 3) *ancient Israel*, i.e. the Israel created by modern scholars who are of the conviction that they can recreate this Israel on the basis of the information in the Old Testament. This is an Israel that only exists in the minds of these scholars. The necessary connection between these three "Israels" is less than apparent. It depends on the character of rationalistic paraphrases of the biblical account employed by modern scholars in order to reconstruct their ancient Israel, thereby cleansing the biblical texts of any superstitious traits like the acts of God.

2) In combination with a changing idea about the identity of biblical Israel, the character of the exile in Babylonia is being discussed. Is it safe to assert that the Jews of the post-exilic period were ethnically related to the Judaeans of the pre-exilic period? Could it be the case that in the Persian period a newly emigrated elite that had settled in Jerusalem by claiming to be the descendants of the ancient Israelites wanted to establish a legitimate hegemony over the province, while they, at the same time, dismissed its local inhabitants as "Canaanites"? Such questions take up space, not least in Philip R. Davies' study.

Another angle to these matters would lead to other questions. Is it at all legitimate to speak about the post-exilic period – at least as far as the literature found in the Old Testament is concerned? The answer might lead to new

---

[4] Davies, 1992. According to Davies' introduction, his study could not have been published without inspiration from Thomas L. Thompson's, *The Early History of the Israelite People from the Written and Archaeological Sources* (Thompson, 1992).

[5] English translation: John A. Wilson, *ANET*³, 378.

conclusions. Although the idea of an exile is crucial to the historical narrative in the Old Testament, and is also presupposed by the prophetic books, it may not have ended in connection with the Persian conquest of Babylon in 539 BCE and Cyrus' decree. These events are supposed to have set the Jews of Babylonia free to return home in 538 BCE but may in fact not have been the end of the "exile".

While Davies thought of a Palestinian milieu for the biblical literature, the reformulation of the importance of the exile to biblical authors makes a different answer feasible. Most, if not all, of the books of the Bible came into being in "exile", whether or not this exile was real or fictional. Thus, it is possible that it was members of the Jewish Diaspora living in Mesopotamia in the Persian or Hellenistic period that created the history of biblical Israel narrated in the Old Testament and the books containing it.[6]

3) Hand in hand with the deconstruction of the biblical narrative about Israel's history goes the deconstruction of the biblical report on the origins and developments of Israel's religion. It would be wrong to maintain that this part of the project of changing the paradigm has moved as far as the changes brought about in historical studies. It is evident that it is no longer possible to keep intact the biblical image of this monotheistic creed and its roots in pre-exilic Israelite society. We only have to mention one serious blow to the biblical way of imagining Yahweh, delivered by the discovery of his "pre-exilic" wife, Asherah, not only present in small rural shrines but even in the temple of Jerusalem.[7]

4) The changes of direction of historical and religious studies also concern literary matters. We also have to reconsider the character of the historical narrative provided by the biblical authors. Historical considerations tell us that Abraham, Isaac, and Jacob never existed except in the imagination of the biblical storytellers. It also tells us that historical Israel was never in Egypt or left Egypt in order to conquer the land of Canaan, that no judge ever ruled Israel, and that David never ruled over a major empire. All of this will have consequences for future evaluations of so-called "Israelite history writing".

The historical narrative in the Old Testament can no longer be considered to be history writing in any sense remotely similar to modern historical

---

[6] The reasons for a Hellenistic date have been presented in Lemche, 1993a.

[7] Cf. on Asherah the studies by Tilde Binger, *Asherah. Goddesses in Ugarit, Israel and the Old Testament* (Binger, 1997), and Steven A. Wiggins, *A Reassessment of "Asherah"* (Wiggins, 1993). Cf. also concerning the relationship between Yahwism and the religions of Western Asia at large the collection of studies published by Walter Dietrich and Otmar Keel, *Jahwe unter den Göttern und Göttinen des alten Orients* (Dietrich and Keel, 1993).

studies. The history of the Old Testament is not the result of a historian's efforts. It does not claim to be historically correct. Its "truth" is a literary one, something narrated and not something that happened. The recognition of the character of the biblical historical narrative has probably contributed more to the establishment of a new paradigm than anything else. The revised view of Israel's history, religion, or literature has not, in itself, caused the construction of a new paradigm. It is the interest of scholars that has changed direction. Scholars no longer occupy themselves with historical-critical problems, but turn their attention to other areas.

When modern historians of the biblical world more or less cut the bindings between the historical narrative of the Old Testament and historical realities (whatever they were) in ancient Palestine, many Old Testament scholars choose the easy way out of the dilemma. They simply ignored history and historical investigations in order to concentrate on literature studies. They do not consider the biblical texts to be a corpus of historical documents from the past but read them as sources immediately available to a modern (or postmodern?) society looking for guidance. I shall return to this theme later.

Within biblical studies such developments are likely to provoke a theological reaction. John Strange's article on "Salvation History and History" from 1985 is only one example among many of this crisis in the relationship between the Bible and educated people of the Modern Age.[8] In his article, Strange sets out to explain the growing discrepancy between the history of Israel as related by Old Testament historiographers, and modern historical investigation. According to Strange, the biblical narrative constitutes a "salvation history" that leads from the creation to the last judgement as seen from the vantage point of the paradigm "promise-fulfillment". Thus, a fracture has appeared that separates historical investigation from theological reflection. This split is, from an intellectual point of view, intolerable. We are, therefore, in need of a new version of salvation history – not the one found in the pages of the Bible, but real-world history as interpreted by faith. We have to give up the idea of the biblical canon as a closed Jewish-Christian collection of scripture. The history and culture of the ancient world of Palestine and Western Asia will, in combination with their written evidence have to take up the charge as the foundation of the theological reflection on salvation history.

In my discussion with Strange himself I made the point that the history of the real world cannot substitute the salvation history related by the Bible (Lemche, 1989a). The history of the Bible is not the history of the real world.

---

[8] "Frelseshistorie og historie. Et synspunkt på bibelsk teologi" (Strange, 1985; German translation Strange, 1989b).

Ancient authors wrote it. Some of it may have happened, much more belongs to the realm of fantasy. Insofar as the biblical historiographers intended to write a history of salvation, and Christian theologians adopted it as their history of salvation, the narratives of the Old Testament about the fate of biblical Israel constitute a salvation history. The history of historical Israel cannot represent a salvation history if it is not identical with the history of biblical Israel. Such an identity is, however, impossible to establish. It is of less importance in this connection whether or not we accept the biblical history to be a salvation history about the saving acts of God in history with a promise for future greatness. We may see it as presenting a kind of *theodicé* that has to explain why God has totally rejected his chosen people.

The competing statement that the history of the real world represents a salvation history relies on a kind of *historical determinism* that is not uncommon among Christian believers. Many biblical scholars have, through the ages, interpreted history in the light of Paul's "in the fullness of time" (Gal 4:4), and seen the mission of Christ as related in the New Testament as the final goal of history. Among the better-known modern examples of this position we may mention William F. Albright, who reconstructed the history of the ancient Near East according to this paradigm (Albright, 1940). In this way Albright absolutely lives up to the expectations of Strange who claims that it is the history of the ancient Near East that has to take the place of a salvation history. Strange as well as other scholars following this lead will, however, have to admit that Albright, in order to achieve his end, had to write his doctorate on this Near Eastern history. Albright not only changed this history on minor points to make it fit the biblical version, he actually made drastic revisions to it in order to make real history conform with his preconceived theological idea of history.

I doubt that such a theological project is legitimate. It would be the same as to argue that Christianity conquered the Roman Empire not because of its values and divine message but because God wanted it regardless of its qualities.[9] It would also be the same as to deny the free will of human beings and lead to a determinism to which not all theologians will subscribe.

The conflict between the narrated history and the "real" history that has been outlined here will continue to exist. I am sorry to say that there is no way to reconcile the evidence of the two histories on a historical level of interpretation. In order to overcome the problem of a "double truth" and a *sacrificium intellectum* – something Strange warns us against – we have to base

---

[9] By this statement I do not intend to leave out of consideration other reasons for the success of Christianity.

the theological discussion between the historians of the real world and the biblical world on the literary evidence of the Bible, not on the real history of ancient Palestine and Western Asia.

The Future

According to Ecclesiastes there is a time to break down and a time to build up. Now, after having been in the business for the last many years of breaking down the old historical paradigm, it may be time for a change. The four points made above – all parts of a changing perspective in biblical studies – can hardly be considered a complete substitute for the old paradigm. We may be in a situation almost like before creation, when "there was neither shrub nor plant growing on the earth": there was no Israelite nation, no Israelite religion, no Yahwistic monotheism, no Old Testament, nothing.

A lot of work remains before a modern and operational new paradigm has been constructed for future studies in the Old Testament. I will conclude this review of the present situation with a few preliminary observations concerning the future.

1) The distinction made by Philip R. Davies between historical, biblical, and ancient Israel is a fundamental one when the subject is the history of Israel. Historical Israel was part of Syro-Palestinian society at large. Its history developed within the context of greater Syria. It is a mistake to consider historical Israel very different from any other petty state of Palestine or Syria in the Iron Age – Israel was not different before a much later biblical tradition made it into something special. We are hardly in need of more histories of Israel in the classical sense of the word. The historical analysis will have to concentrate on the history of Palestine in ancient times. This history is not "negative" and dismissive because it leaves biblical Israel out of consideration. It does not. Historical analysis does not take place in a closed room without regard to the information contained within the Old Testament. It, however, does not reckon biblical information to be more important than it can possibly be.

Historical research should not deliver itself into the hands of biblical historiographers but must fulfil the demands of modern historical analysis. When studying ancient Palestinian society, it must stress the degree of continuity. Only when emphasis is placed on societal continuity will it be possible to track even minor changes that tell us that continuity is about to be broken or has changed into something different. Previous scholarship made the mistake of assuming that the history of ancient Palestine was dominated by discontinuity. The evidence that told a different story about continuity was dismissed or overlooked as unimportant – the most obvious case being the question of continuity between Palestine in the Bronze Age and in the Iron Age.[10]

2) We should also put emphasis on the continuity between religious ideas and sentiments in the ancient Near East. This continuity appears in written sources from Palestine and Syria on one hand and in the Old Testament on the other although within a different context. As far as the study of general religion goes, a change of direction has already occurred. In spite of problems raised by more conservative circles, we have to give up the idea of an original monotheistic Yahwism, while we, at the same time, must be open to the possibility of investigating other religious phenomena within historical Israel.

Thus, it is necessary to stress the fact that historical Israel belonged among the "magic societies" (as described by Frederick H. Cryer). It was not a society with a highly developed theological system. Magical practices and rituals were common, including the worship of deceased spirits, black and white magic, etc. We have no evidence indicating that such practices were condemned or prohibited – except in biblical Israel.[11] Other subjects worth reevaluating in this context will by prophetism as well as the background of the psalms of the Old Testament. Little has changed in the last few generations. As far as the study of the psalms is concerned, we are still where Sigmund Mowinckel left it in 1922. The study of prophetism has not moved in any serious way further than described by Johannes Lindblom in 1934.[12]

3) Within literary studies a lively debate has been the rule of the day for many years. Evidently students of the literary message of the Bible believe to

---

[10] The late Gösta W. Ahlström took the first steps in the direction of such a new type of history writing, in his magnum opus published by Diana Edelman, *The History of Ancient Palestine from the Palaeolithic Period to Alexander's Conquest with a contribution by Gary O. Rollefson* (Ahlström, 1993). Ahlström only partly succeeded in presenting such a history. When the history of the Hebrew monarchy is introduced, this history changes from a history of Palestine to a history of Israel in the traditional sense of the word. In many ways Ahlström's history belongs to the same scholarly situation as my much more modest Ancient Israel from 1988. Ahlström's contribution – like my own – demonstrates how difficult it is to get rid of the old paradigm and establish a different one. J. Alberto Soggin has published another example of the same process, originally with the title *A History of Israel from the Beginnings to the Bar Kochba Revolt, AD 135* (Soggin, 1984); the second edition included a remarkable change of title: *An Introduction to the History of Israel and Judah* (Soggin, 1993).

[11] Cf. on this Cryer, 1994, and Bloch-Smith, 1992.

[12] The important and trench setting works are Mowinckel, 1922 and Lindblom, 1934 (ET Lindblom, 1962).

be vindicated by the deconstruction of the prevailing historical-critical paradigm. Many literary critics have therefore decided to leave out any historical consideration and have turned to modern systems of analysing biblical texts, methods borrowed from general literature. There are two sides to this development. I can only describe them briefly. It is a positive consequence of recent historical research that the biblical text has moved into the centre of interest, not because it is a source of information about something else – i.e. ancient Israel – but because of itself. The modern student of the text of the Bible will be interested in knowing what the present text tells us. He or she will be less interested in what the text says about a presumed past.

This might sound cryptic. It only says that the "truth" of the biblical text – if we may be allowed to say so – has to do with its character of being a text that makes an impression upon its reader because of the story it has to tell. The "truth" is not something outside of the text, for example an historical event of some sort. The historical event (if there ever was one behind the narrative of the text) narrated by a biblical text belongs to the past and must be considered of no importance, because it has no consequences for the events of today. The narrative about an event of the past (which might or might not have occurred) is brought to life whenever it is retold.

In order to illustrate the importance of this observation, we might refer to the traditions in the Old Testament about the Israelite conquest of Palestine. This conquest never took place.[13] If the narratives in Joshua about the conquest had no other aim than to inform modern readers about the past and therefore perforce had to be historically true, the problem would be apparent. The Book of Joshua presents a historical scenario that never existed and has to be dismissed as nonsense – eliminated from our biblical canon. It is, however, not the case that most people of the modern world read the Bible because it refers to the past "as it was". Modern people might choose to believe in the historical truth of the Bible in spite of every kind of evidence that points in the opposite direction. If there had been no Book of Joshua there might never have been a modern state of Israel in Palestine. No group could claim the right to return to the land of their fathers after almost 2,000 years of absence. We would not be impressed by the claim that Joshua is indeed telling

---

[13] Except among evangelical ("fundamentalist") circles, everyone is in agreement here. The agreement, however, ends here. Conservative so-called "maximalists" (as they style themselves) still claim that the Books of Joshua and Judges have a historical nucleus of some sort, whereas the so-called "nihilists" or "minimalists" have given up looking for this spectre.

us the historical truth. The real historian will have to educate such people and tell them that it, in fact, cannot be the case.

The negative side of the question has to do with the diminishing interest among literary students about the author and his or her implied readership. Modern literary students tend to work within a closed room which we could call the "canon", something placed outside the normal category of time. The text is allowed to make its impression on a modern readership without regard for the context in which it came into being and without respect for the intentions of its author. There can be no doubt that such readings may bring about many interesting, even elucidating interpretations of the biblical text, and the text may lead to conclusions never intended by its author. The danger is that modern reading may lack direction and become arbitrary; the fear of any author ancient as well as modern.[14]

Here the previous example of the Israelite conquest also works. In connection with the modern use or abuse of this text for political reasons we may certainly speak about a conscious or unconscious disregard for any historical doubt about it being historically correct or incorrect. Without concern for their original contexts, modern politicians have changed ancient writings into pieces of propaganda for their own nationalistic projects. They don't care much about the historical dimensions of the text and are totally indifferent as to its historical exactness.

When we move into theology it becomes obvious that the process of liberating the Bible from history may be looked upon by conservative and evangelical Christians (or for that matter conservative Jews) with relief. Now they are allowed to read the stories of the Old Testament and believe them to be true. Such people might even believe the texts to be *historically* true, simply because they have lost the historical dimension of the texts. They have only heard that it is not any longer necessary to pay any attention to historical studies. Historical studies are unimportant. The truth lies in the text.

The historian will have to re-enter the scene exactly at this point. The historical analysis will have to continue and be sharpened. First of all, it is important that it can be decided whether or not a text has a historical nucleus. This is important, not because the truth of a text depends on its historical correctness, but because a conclusion on this point may help us to isolate the reasons why the text in question was ever written. We may speak about a dialogue between real history and the biblical narratives. This dialogue must

---

[14] Remember the famous anecdote about the death of the Roman poet Vergil, who on his death bed demanded his main opus, the not yet finished *Aeneid*, to be burned. As is well known, his spiritual heirs did not obey his last wish.

remain open in case the biblical narratives do not refer to anything that ever happened in the real world.

The interest of the historian should concentrate on the authors of the biblical literature and try to characterize these authors within their own cultural and historical contexts. This sounds like a classical historical-critical project, and indeed it is. However, the historical analysis should be carried through to its very end without regard for the consequences. Furthermore, the historian should make full use of the available sources as they have been handed down.

I would like to refer, here, to an analysis of the patriarchal narratives which I only recently concluded – not because this analysis is more original or profound than most but because it presents a clear picture.[15] The patriarchal narratives include an extensive series of themes and motifs borrowed from folk literature, especially fairy tales.[16] This is not new. The reader of the stories in Genesis might be induced into believing that the patriarchal narratives are themselves folk literature that originated in a traditional society and was not part of an intellectually highly sophisticated milieu. In their traditional setting, the patriarchal narratives were believed to be stories about the heroes of the past "told around the camp fire". However, when we analyse the stories of Genesis it soon becomes clear that these stories are not folk literature. On the contrary, they represent a highly developed literary tradition that of course includes themes and motifs from folk literature – all good literature is likely to do so – however, transformed into sophistically and elaborately adorned narratives. Thus, the author must have been a highly educated and very well-informed literary person. The implied readership is supposed to have understood this literature (otherwise it is meaningless) and can accordingly be characterized as a demanding and highly educated group. The patriarchal narratives do not pretend to have been told by folklorists sitting around campsites.

In spite of recent claims among modern literary students I am of the conviction that some attention should be paid to the intentions of the author of any text. Seen in this light, the historian should try not to disregard the narrative by looking for a different type of information within the narrative. The historian should concentrate of helping the author make his or her message understood. The historian will need assistance from students of general literature in order to better understand the motifs embedded in a text, while

---

[15] Lemche, 1996d (ET: Lemche, 1998b).
[16] Hermann Gunkel's study, *The Folktale in the Old Testament* (Gunkel, 1987. German original *Das Märchen im Alten Testament* [Gunkel, 1921]) is still of fundamental importance. Cf. also the more recent survey by Kirkpatrick, 1986.

he, at the same time, enforces the historical dimension of the literature to the student by stressing the importance of the historical context of the text in question.

Many Old Testament texts are not affected by any changes in their historical situation. It is not very important whether or not they refer to real or imaginary historical events. The meaning and importance are universal and can be understood by everyone, without regard for their historical context. A few texts are artistically so dull that even the most sophisticated reading cannot make them very interesting to the general reader. Other biblical texts have a more subtle content and their meaning is concealed within an elaborate literary or mental framework. In such cases it is certainly important that the interpretation of such texts is as precise as possible. If the historian can help the literary student break into the universe of the text, the historian has done his job.

I shall end my review of the past, present, and future at this point with the question, where do we go from here? I've attempted to point in the direction of a future more "neutral" in its historical analysis (this should not be taken to mean "objective" analysis in the positivistic sense of the word – it is only more neutral because it is independent or at least aims at being independent from preconceived religious sentiments). This also means that future biblical studies will concentrate on biblical literature as texts. Therefore, this final admonition: Shall we allow literary students to read their texts without regard for historical issues or is it essential that the historian continuously reminds literary students about the quality of the biblical text as being a part of the past and accordingly *a historical document*?

Postscript anno 2023

Now we should not allow biblical texts to be read as if they were written today, as if they were expressions of modern sentiments and ideas! We still have to remember Johan Philipp Gabler's (1753–1826) remarks about Paul's declaration that women shall be quiet in assemblies; that this may have made sense in Paul's time, but today we are living in the 18th century, and the situation is quite different.[17] I am quite convinced that many conservative theologians, after having rejected modern analyses of biblical history among themselves, are quite happy with the removal of the Bible "from history". The *past-ness* of biblical literature is not limited to the story it tells about the past; it is just

---

[17] Gabler, 1787. Gabler spoke in Latin. ET: Gabler, 2004.

– and even more relevant to every and all aspects of life recorded in these texts.

When I, throughout my career, have talked about liberating the Bible from history, the meaning was not that the Bible stands outside of history. It is very much a historical document. But it has been liberated from our history, from our way of understanding and studying the past.

14 Après le déluge: The Copenhagen School or Chaos?

The Roman grammarian Terentius Mauro once wrote, *libelli habent suam fatam*, "books have their own destiny". In this case the title had its own destiny. I originally intended to write "après nous, le déluge", a famous quotation attributed to Madame Pompadour after France lost the seven-year-war to Prussia and Friedrich the Great. The formulation changed, by having any idea as to how it happened, to "Après le déluge", "after the flood". Perhaps here there is material for some reflections. Will the Copenhagen School be followed by the flood, or was it the Copenhagen School itself which was the flood?

When I left my position at the university, it was as the last original member of the Copenhagen School. The original four members of the school – sometimes also dubbed "the four-man gang" – were, apart from me, Thomas L. Thompson, who was professor at this university until 2009,[1] Philip R. Davies,[2] and Keith Whitelam,[3] both professors at the University of Sheffield. However, before I proceed, I have to add a note: We didn't invent the designation "the Copenhagen School". It was a term which was attached to us by scholars from the world outside of Copenhagen (and Sheffield) some twenty years ago.

---

[1] Thomas L. Thompson (b. 1939) is best known from his early work, *The Historicity of the Patriarchal Narratives: The Quest for the Historical Abraham* (Thompson, 1974), which in many ways may be considered a proto-Copenhagen-School work. There is nothing "proto-" about his *The Bible in History: How Writers Create a Past* (Thompson, 1999), and *The Messiah Myth: The Near Eastern Roots of Jesus and David* (Thompson, 2005).

[2] Philip R. Davies (1945–2018) was for many years the editor of the *Journal for the Study of the Old Testament*. He has written countless books. The best known in this connection is his *In Search of "Ancient Israel"* (Davies, 1992), which for years counted as "required" reading for the exam in the Old Testament in Copenhagen.

[3] Keith W. Whitelam (b. 1951) is well-known from his *The Invention of Ancient Israel: The Silencing of Palestinian History* (Whitelam, 1996), which represents a showdown with the Israel-centric form of history writing which leaves everything which is not directly related to the Israel of the Bible in oblivion.

What Happened? The Decline and Fall of the Old Testament

We are entitled to say that, since it is an epoch which is running out of time, it is perhaps the right moment to present an overview of what happened. It is hardly necessary to write a complete review – at least not now, but I may refer the reader to my contribution to the John Strange Festschrift from 1994 (Lemche, 1994). In this article I presented a sketch of the development within Old Testament scholarship during the last forty years or more. It was a breakthrough which led to a general settlement with the dominant "historical-critical" method. This method, with its roots in German scholarship from the 19th century, was believed to have resulted in an adequate description of ancient Israelite history, religion, and literature but it also had another consequence; that the Old Testament lost its natural position within theology as part of the Christian Bible. Instead, it turned into a collection of texts for religious-historical studies.[4]

The consequences are well known. When I studied during the late 1960s the amount of attention allotted to the Old Testament compared well to that which was allotted to the New Testament, or just as much as any of the classical theological disciplines of the study of theology. The New Testament had a special status: As in dogmatics, the student had to pass his examination in New Testament but was allowed to fail in the other subjects: Old Testament, Church History, and Religious Philosophy. The candidate exam in theology was considered one common exam. There was a famous example demonstrating this: My predecessor Professor Svend Holm-Nielsen had a test in church history. The examiner was the well-known Professor Hal Koch: Towards the end of a catastrophic exam the desperate Hal Koch simply asked the candidate: Tell me, do you know anything about Danish church history? Svend gave an absolutely correct answer: No! That was good enough; now he had said something which was correct and was allowed to pass, not the exam in church history but the general theological exam.[5]

From a scholarly point of view, it was an interesting development because it had led to the feeling within Old Testament studies that it was free from being suffocated by the control of the Church. But in the context of the study of theology it was also the same as saying to the students: Why shall we

---

[4] The historical-critical scholars of that time were considered to belong to the religious-historical school.
[5] Although – as I will make clear in a moment – the role of oral tradition in Old Testament studies is no longer what it used to be, this anecdote is absolutely in every aspect oral and transmitted from one generation of students in Copenhagen to the next.

continue to read and study the Old Testament? Nobody had a ready answer. The German church historian Adolf von Harnack had, however, expressed this in a poignant way in his book about the iconoclast Marcion from the 2nd century who might have been the first to question the presence of the Old Testament as a part of the Christian Bible (von Harnack, 1921, 127):

> It was a mistake to reject the Old Testament in the 2nd century, and the Church was in full right to dismiss the idea. To keep the Old Testament in the 16th century was a destiny which the Reformation was not able to free it from. But to preserve the Old Testament since the 19th century as a canonical document in Protestantism is the result of a religious and ecclesiastical paralysis.

As I wrote in my overview from 1994, the showdown with Old Testament scholarship did not originate in other departments of theology. My feeling is that people here mostly were shaking their heads and continued their own enterprises without paying much attention to what happened in the Old Testament. Saying that they actually just ignored what was supposed to constitute 20% of the study of theology – in this way the paralysis just continued. We saw some opposition to the hermeneutical principles employed in historical-critical scholarship because the most important argumentative form was circular argumentation and rationalistic paraphrases and biblical narrative (and in this place I hardly dare to whisper: *Argumenta ex silention* – thinking of the German scholar Bernd Jørg Diebner's insolent characterization of Old Testament scholarship: "You cannot prove it, but it is a fact!" (Diebner, 1984)) – however, in a Danish context we may rather think of the criticism from scholars such as the students of K.E. Løgstrup, Svend Bjerg, and Jan Lindhardt, although mostly in an oral form and therefore easily forgotten – in general, peace reigned.

A Scholarly Paradigm Becomes Redundant

The clash between old and new began for the simple reason that the results of the historical-critical method seemed more and more absurd. If we read Thomas Kuhn's famous book about the revolution of science which originally appeared decades ago (Kuhn, 1962), among other things we learn that dominant paradigms within science have a tendency to become too "heavy" because their adherents more and more believe that these paradigms may explain everything. Around 1970 historical-critical scholarship was of the opinion that it had solved all of the central issues related to the sub-disciplines within Old Testament scholarship: history, history of religion, and history of literature.[6] The paradigm had become too heavy mainly because its members in large part had ignored theoretical developments in fields other than the Old Testament.

The Italian Assyriologist Mario Liverani described the problem in an article from the beginning of the 1960s. The problem is shared between Old Testament scholarship and students of the ancient Near East in general. All these disciplines, technically speaking, demand a lot of time spent on learning difficult languages. Therefore, there is less time available to include taking into consideration progress within other fields.[7] An Old Testament scholar worth his salt was supposed to know Hebrew, Aramaic, and preferably other Semitic languages, especially Ugaritic and Akkadian. However, when it came to the philosophy of science he was probably ignorant. I do not remember any discussion among Old Testament scholars from my youth where, e.g. Ludwig Wittgenstein was introduced, and Karl Popper with his falsification theories was practically unknown, and for good reason. Had he been taken into consideration, it would have been necessary to make a distinction between legitimate theories and baseless assertions. Our historical-critical scholar, however, did not realize this. When I entered historical studies one of the first things I noted was that the many histories of ancient Israel which were around in 1970 never included any theoretical discussion of the subject.[8] It was the scholars'

---

[6] This does not mean that there were no differences of opinion among the scholars belonging to this direction of scholarship. But it was mainly a matter of individual preferences. In general, they agreed on most. The major controversy was between German and North-American scholarship represented by, on one side Albrecht Alt (1883–1956) and Martin Noth (1902–1968), and on the other William Foxwell Albright (1891–1971). In spite of the often badly moderated language used about the opponents, especially from the side of the Americans, it is revealing to see that Albright's student mostly moved in the direction of his German opponents and gave Albright's positions up to American conservative evangelical students. For an update of this survey of scholarship cf. Lemche, 2022.

[7] Liverani, 1966. Mario Liverani (b. 1939) is an Italian Orientalist and Assyriologist. He published his criticism in "Problemi e indirizzi degli studi storici sul Vicino Oriente" (1966). In his later years Liverani has spent more and more time on biblical studies exemplified in his *Oltre la Bibbia: Storia antica di Israele* (Liverani, 2003; ET: Liverani, 2005). He distinguishes between the "real" history, dealing with what happened – once – in the ancient world, and the invented history, the fairytale of ancient Israel present in the Old Testament. Cf. also – with a reference to Liverani – Lemche, 1998c, 270–71.

[8] In this there was little to distinguish the histories of Israel which were published by Martin Noth (representing the German school) and John Bright (representing the Albright-school). Cf. Martin Noth, 1950 and John Bright, 1960. On this phenomenon see also Lemche, 2022, 65–72.

attitude that if you were able to read a text from the Old Testament in Hebrew, you were able to understand it. Liverani is supposed once to have said that although he might not be a world champion in reading cuneiform texts he sometimes gets the feeling that he is the only one who understands what is written in them. Mogens Trolle Larsen, who, together with me, proposed an honorary doctorate for Liverani at the University of Copenhagen, added that Liverani was more than adequately qualified for reading cuneiform signs!

The future members of the Copenhagen School did not have to create their own methods. Old Testament scholarship was like all theological disciplines of that time based on philology, history, and philosophy. Systematic theologians were probably already realizing that the world was changing: Philology had turned into linguistics, history into sociology, and philosophy into psychology – and those who had chosen Jørgen Jørgensen's *Psykologi på biologisk Grundlag*[9] (a somewhat "unusual" approach to the field) as the textbook for their philosophical introduction course at the university had gotten a hint of what was going on, but for the most part these developments had bypassed theology, especially in Copenhagen.

In the years surrounding 1970, systematic theology was moving towards the future although the walls that separated the theological institutes at the university were still as impenetrable as the Berlin wall. However, the first time I presented my programme and the changes which I saw coming within Old Testament studies was, in the spring of 1978, at the Institute for Systematic Theology – just a couple of months before my move to the University of Aarhus. At that time, my conclusion was that in the future we would see the study of the Old Testament move intellectually away from church history and towards systematic theology because the set of historical methods applied by church historians and adopted by the exegetes were breaking down within the exegetical disciplines. Afterwards, Professor Theodor Jørgensen (1935–2018) who had invited me to give the lecture, always maintained that it all started at the Institute for Systematic Theology.

Sociological History

Within general history, the second half of the twentieth century was regarded as oriented towards integrating methods from sociology. This was what I intended to say by arguing that history has been supplanted by sociology. Old

---

[9] Jørgensen, 1941. It was republished several times in extensively enlarged editions, the latest from 1957.

Testament scholarship had, as I said, missed the changes. What had been published was amateurish and of little importance. It was, however, apparent that in the future the study of the Old Testament within a historical context would have to turn to sociology – or perhaps rather to social anthropology – in order to find more modern methods.

My own contribution, which appeared in 1985 in the shape of my dissertation *Early Israel* (Lemche, 1985b), represented an endeavour to place the Old Testament within a socio-cultural context. The historical narrative of the Old Testament places the society of ancient Israel in a Middle Eastern context in antiquity. It would be correct to say that few had shown any interest in investigating what that meant. All sorts of stereotypes about the Middle East had entered the discussion, most of them unconsciously, and these stereotypical concepts were used as models for nearly everything relating to ancient Israel as it appears in the Old Testament. I was not the first who introduced models from socio-anthropology to Old Testament studies. A few years before the appearance of *Early Israel,* Norman K. Gottwald published his *opus magnum* of more than 1,000 pages, *The Tribes of Israel* (Gottwald, 1979). Sadly, Gottwald's study belongs to the genre dubbed "armchair-sociology" by professional social anthropologists, meaning that it was exclusively built on theoretical models and didn't pay sufficient attention to the field-work of sociologists and social anthropologists.[10] That was the reason that several stereotypes survived in Gottwald's work, which was also the major reason for the criticism of Gottwald found in Lemche, 1985b.

The Consequences for the "History of Israel"

I presented the immediate consequences of the new study of history as far as the Old Testament and ancient Israel are concerned in the Festschrift for John Strange mentioned earlier. When I summarized what had happened, I had to conclude that almost every central idea of traditional historical-critical

---

[10] The problem that caused this is the lack of "case-studies", i.e. descriptions of actual societies, in this case in the Middle East. Lemche, 1985b includes a comprehensive series of such "case studies" (Lemche, 1985, 95–201). It was my good fortune that when I applied for a position at the University of Aarhus a first draft of *Early Israel* was reviewed by the social-anthropologist Klaus Ferdinand (1926–2005), who had conducted his field studies among traditional societies in the Middle East. Klaus Ferdinand used exactly this term: "armchair-sociology" about what I had written at that time. So everything was rewritten, and he was very satisfied with the final outcome as a reviewer of the dissertation a few years later.

scholarship relating to the history of ancient Israel had vanished, the patriarchs – mostly due to Thomas Thompson's critique – Israel's sojourn in Egypt, the Exodus and wanderings in the desert, the conquest of Canaan, the period of the Judges and of David and Solomon, etc. etc. They had no place any longer in historical studies written by scholars having or going to have any relation to the Copenhagen School. These ideas did not survive the renewed historical methodology which came to be used by the members of the school.

The difference becomes much cleaver if we compare the standard version of "Israel's history" from the 1960s, such as – in a Scandinavian context – Eduard Nielsen's *Grundrids af Israels Historie* (E. Nielsen, 1960), a book every student of theology had to learn, almost by heart, and Svend Holm-Nielsen's *Det gamle Testamente og det jødiske folks historie* (1962),[11] with my own *Det gamle Israel* (Lemche, 1984). The last one may seem pretty conservative to contemporary readers. In my book, the history before 1000 BCE is no more a history of Israel but a history of Palestine. It includes a comprehensive review of Israelite tribal society, of the kingdom of David and Solomon, the time of the Hebrew kingdoms, and the Babylonian exile, and the post-exilic period. In the preface to the 4th edition of 1991 I was able to summarize the changes since the first appearance of the book.

The view of the history of Israel in my *Ancient Israel* rested on four main theses, printed at the back of the book:

1. Israel arose as the result of a social development within Canaanite society in Palestine in the second half of the 2nd millennium BCE and not as a consequence of immigration from the desert.
2. Israelite religion was "originally" a Canaanite religion. Only at the middle of the 1st millennium BCE did it develop the special form, "Jewish" monotheism.
3. The Old Testament includes hardly any historical source which is older than the 7th–6th centuries BCE. We cannot reconstruct Israel's history before the emergence of the Israelite state c. 1000 BCE. on the basis of the Old Testament. Here we are forced to rely on archaeological evidence and sources not in the Old Testament.
4. The historical view found in the Old Testament is a consequence of the political catastrophes that hit historical Israel shortly before the middle of the 1st millennium BCE.

In the preface to the edition of 1991 these four "theses" have changed.

---

[11] Final edition Holm-Nielsen, 1975.

Now the first thesis sounds like this: The concept of "Israel" rose as the result of an ideological reflection among the population from Palestine which was deported to Mesopotamia in connection with the Babylonian conquest of Jerusalem and the state of Judah. The Canaanites, who still had a role to play in the original edition, had vanished and had turned – according to a book I published the same year – into a literary concept as a counterpart to the ancient Israelites (Lemche, 1991a). Canaanites and Israelites are thus characters in a novel but it is more than doubtful that the Canaanites even belong to history.

The second thesis also appeared in a new form: Gone was the idea of a pre-exilic Israelite (or better yet Jewish) monotheism. The Jewish religion appeared in the exilic-post-exilic period in competition with similar forms of religion which, during the 1st millennium BCE, spread to most of the Middle East.

The historical sources – the third thesis – were no longer dated to the Iron Age, i.e. to the time of the Hebrew Kingdoms. They are clearly later. This means that when I argued in the first edition that it was not possible to write a history of Israel from before 800 BCE, this was now changed in the statement that such a history cannot be written at all. In contrast – and I quote directly from the introduction: "we are able to write a history which covers the landscape Palestine in the Bronze Age as well as in the Iron Age until the coming of Hellenism."

The fourth thesis (about the reasons for my understanding of history in the Old Testament) was kept unchanged.

And because I am not necessarily a good prophet, I predicted back in 1991 that it would be possible within three years to present a totally new edition of the book. It never appeared; but seventeen years later I was able to publish a completely new introduction in the form of *The Old Testament between Theology and History* (Lemche, 2008c). Here the historical part is confined to an appendix: "Israel's history or Palestine's History". Here we have a sketch of the history of the landscape of Palestine in ancient times, including a look at the further history of Israel (until 1948 CE). The Old Testament plays a very reduced role (if any) in this sketch. So, the very last section of the appendix carries the title: "… and Israel": What happened to Israel in this history? To be honest, it has almost totally disappeared (Lemche, 2008c, 382–3). It was thus possible in the preface of this book to present one more edition of the theses from 1984.

As my first point I made it clear that the concept of "ancient Israel" is an ideological one, which does not go back to the Israelites and the Jews of ancient times. It was created by modern biblical scholars and this ancient Israel has little in common with what "happened on the ground" in Palestine in antiquity.

Second: Israelite religion as found in the Old Testament is not an ancient Palestinian religion but a product of Judaism and only describes what Jews in antiquity thought about the origins of their own religion.

The revision of the third thesis was just as important. It argues that the main part of the writings included in the Old Testament are from the Hellenistic period, and more: that the Old Testament as a collection of books hardly pre-dates early Christianity.

A Hellenistic Book: Part I

In the article in the Strange Festschrift (Lemche, 1994) I mentioned that a new trend arose in the 1960s proposing a lower date of the Old Testament literature. At the end of the 1960s Heike Friis had taken up the mantle from the Canadian Old Testament scholar Fredrik Winnett who, in a lecture from 1965, had suggested that the historical literature in the Old Testament should be dated to the time of the Babylonian exile (Winnett, 1965). In her prize-winning thesis from 1968 she presented an analysis of the Deuteronomistic History which placed it in the time of the exile.[12] The rest followed, not least thanks to the contribution from a student of Winnett, John Van Seters, who has mostly published within the field of Pentateuchal studies. Van Seters places the Yahwist, whom he considers an author and not a collector or editor, not at the court of Solomon as had been the opinion since Gerhard von Rad's study on historical writing, but in the Babylonian exile.[13]

The Book of Deuteronomy was one of the sources for the Yahwist. I had, shortly before the article in the Strange Festschrift, published the Danish original lecture on the Old Testament as a Hellenistic book.[14] Like Winnett's lecture, it has been the start of a shift of paradigm in the study of the historical books in the Old Testament. The shift of paradigm is still going on and

---

[12] Heike Friis' thesis was never published in Danish, but Bernd Jørg Diebner, whom I mentioned above, translated and published it as *Die Bedingungen für die Errichtung des davidischen Reichs in Israel und seiner Umwelt* (Friis, 1986). But see also Friis, 1975.

[13] Cf. John Van Seters (b. 1934), 1974. For the whole of his career Van Seters held this opinion, dating back to 1975. Thus, in his most recent contribution to the discussion (Van Seters, 2013). Before that he had even contested the very concept of an editor behind the Pentateuch (Van Seters, 2006a). Gerhard von Rad's view was published in von Rad, 1944.

[14] Lemche, 1992a. Translated into English as Lemche, 1993a. Reprinted more than once, the last in Lemche, 2013d.

not yet understood – at least in certain circles. However, sometimes it goes so fast that I have had to warn the "young lions" within the discipline against ending in a form of "Pan-Hellenism" where the Old Testament simply looks like a Greco-Hellenistic book. It is not. It is a Jewish collection of writings from the Hellenistic-Roman Period; a conclusion I negotiated with Jesper Høgenhaven years ago (Høgenhaven, 1993).

Old Testament scholars have traditionally seen themselves as one generation ahead of their colleagues in the New Testament, who were often seen as lost in the dark, not able to free themselves from trivial issues like: "Who was Jesus?" They often proudly mentioned that form criticism was invented by Hermann Gunkel[15] years before it was introduced into New Testament studies by scholars like Rudolf Bultmann[16] and Martin Dibelius.[17] Now it seemed as if their New Testament colleagues had indeed bypassed them. The ideas proffered by Van Seters, e.g. about the Yahwist as an author, had already for a long time been *au courant* in New Testament studies, where it had been convincingly shown that the authors behind the Gospels were not merely anonymous collectors of traditions about Jesus which they then combined into coherent narratives, looking over the shoulders of their colleagues. The individual authors wrote their individual accounts, three among them on the basis of a common model, but all of them with their own agenda.[18]

---

[15] There can be no doubt that Hermann Gunkel (1863–1933) was the leading Old Testament scholar at the beginning of the 20th century. His scholarship embraced the whole of the Old Testament. His most important contribution to the form history and its use of oral tradition can be found in his commentary on Genesis (Gunkel, 1901) and in his commentary on the Psalms (Gunkel, 1929). It was central to Gunkel that the traditions contained in the Book of Genesis originated in oral tradition, an idea which was taken up especially in Scandinavian scholarship. We may say that the attitude to oral tradition is a bit more sceptical. After all, we only know ancient "oral" tradition from written sources. Of basic importance here are the studies of Walter J. Ong (1912–2003), whose main published book, *Orality and Literacy: The Technologies of the Word*, appeared in its thirtieth edition in 2012 (Ong, 2012). On Ong and the Old Testament Ong, 2012, 168–79. In line with Ong we find the British anthropologist Jack Goody (1919–2015), who stressed that when we talk about oral societies, societies relying on oral tradition, they remember nothing. Cf. Goody, 2010. In spite of occasional references to oral tradition – like in Robert D. Miller II, 2011 – it is correct to say that its role in Old Testament studies has been severely reduced. Cf. also Lemche, 2008, 173–85.

[16] Rudolf Bultmann (1884–1976) needs no introduction. When it comes to form history his main opus is *Die Geschichte der synoptischen Tradition* (Bultmann, 1921).

[17] Martin Dibelius (1883–1947). His best-known work is *Die Formgeschichte des Evangeliums* (Dibelius, 1919). Dibelius began as an Old Testament scholar. Cf. his dissertation: *Die Lade Jahves: Eine religionsgeschichtliche Untersuchung* (Dibelius, 1906).

[18] From this period we may remember works like Conzelmann, 1954.

Within Old Testament studies the opposite attitude is today represented by scholars such as Thomas Römer and Konrad Schmid; both from Switzerland. They don't reckon with a Yahwist nor with a Deuteronomistic History.[19] Both the Yahwist and the Deuteronomistic History are no more than examples of patchworks, in which all kinds of narrative recollections have been joined into one major story, although it is not always easy to perceive what happened.

We traditionally find the same attitude when moving into studies of the prophets. Thus, in the Book of Isaiah, which has since the time of Bernhard Duhm (more than one hundred years ago) been considered a work to be divided into three sections: Proto-Isaiah from the 8th century BCE,[20] Deutero-Isaiah from the 6th century BCE, and Trito-Isaiah from the 4th century BCE.[21] We do not know why these parts were joined together in one book. Scholars at the time only forgot that we, in Proto-Isaiah, have several elements which can be dubbed "deuteronomistic", and at the end, in chapters 36–39, four chapters which the Book of Isaiah shares with 2 Kings 18–20, a part of the Deuteronomistic History and hardly pre-exilic. It is often forgotten that the youngest part of the Book of Isaiah can be found in the first part, supposedly from the 8th century BCE. Chapters 24–27 are often named "the little apocalypse" and are normally dated to the 2nd century BCE, i.e., to the time of the Book of Daniel.

Literary Studies

In 1994 in the article for the Strange Festschrift, I predicted (as is expected at such occasions) that the future of biblical studies would be literary studies, and to be more precise it would adopt modern ideas of literary studies and changes in the hermeneutical debate within literary studies. I was certainly

---

[19] Römer, 2006; K. Schmid, 2006. Both contributions appeared in Dozeman and Schmid, 2006. But see also the refutation by John Van Seters in the same volume (Van Seters, 2006b).

[20] Berhard Duhm (1847–1928), in Duhm, 1892. Duhm was also the first who isolated a special group of songs about the servant of the LORD in the Book of Isaiah 42:1–4.(7); 49:1–6; 50:4–9; 52:13 to 53:12. As to the deuteronomistic history cf. Römer, 2005.

[21] Duhm thus dated Isaiah 24–27 to 128 BCE. Among newer commentaries sharing the same opinion we may quote Wildberger, 1978, 885–1026; Kaiser, 1983, 141–86; Blenkinsopp, 2000, 346–379. Blenkinsop is a little more conservative and regards the little apocalypse to date earlier than the 2nd century BCE. He also thinks that the name "the little apocalypse" is misleading.

right, even if I have to admit that it wasn't a big deal to understand what happened. Biblical scholars were no longer able to prove that the Bible right – historically speaking – so better not to deal with history at all. It is preferable to ignore such historical questions because they were becoming too "dangerous". As a consequence, a series of variant methods of reading biblical texts came to the fore and ended up being dominated by the undoubtedly correct but at the same time pretty useless insight that texts have their origins in the interplay between those who write them and those who read them. From here there is only a short leap to the idea that a biblical text only has any importance if I – the reader – realize that it has importance for me. This means that in case I cannot figure out what it is about, it is of no importance (this is probably an attitude many theological students would endorse when having their final exams).[22]

Over the years an unending series of studies belonging to this genre have appeared. They, in large part, have in common that a text is read and analysed using a modern language edition – and because the original author is of no importance, there is no reason to read the text in the language the author used. Of course this is a kind of caricature of this trend within Old Testament studies but it seems that it is now dated and losing importance – apart from, in many places, having resulted in the loss of Hebrew in the curriculum as unnecessary historicism.

Another approach to understanding the biblical literature is related to linguistics and semiology and its most important representatives, the structuralist Algirdas Julien Greimas (1917–1992) and social anthropologist Claude Lévi-Strauss (1908–2009). Among my colleagues who did their most to present this scholarship to the Faculty of Theology in Copenhagen, I should mention Geert Hallbäck (1948–2017),[23] and in Denmark in general the Aarhus professor Hans Jørgen Lundager Jensen and his dissertation from 2000, *Den fortærende ild*. Both methods of literary analysis are vastly different from the previously mentioned reader-response criticism, simply because they are looking for meaning in a text, not in the reader of this text. They actually pose the suggestion that a text will have a meaning in itself and that it is possible to deduce it from the text by very exact means of analysis. Sometimes we see the structuralists referred to as the last positivistic readers of texts. Today they are, of course, an established part of the guild of exegetical

---

[22] An early harbinger of these new ways if reading texts in biblical studies is connected with James Muilenburg (1896–1974) and reader response criticism. In general literature, some of the early names are Stanley Fish (b. 1938) and Roland Barthes (1915–1980).
[23] Cf. Hallbäck, 2012.

analysis of biblical texts because they are related to the endeavour within Old Testament scholarship to place a text and its author in a context. Linguistic studies are, however, not common in recent debates among Old Testament scholars, and when it comes to semiological studies not much has appeared since *Den fortærende ild*.

Cui bono? Who Benefits from the Story of Israel?

To make the point, nothing written in the Old Testament ever happened. However, if this is the case, what is written? Of course, this is a caricature. Much written in the Old Testament did in fact happen, but not in the way it is described. If we look for an example of what I am hinting at, we shall look at the narrative in 2 Kings 18–20 concerning the king of Assyria's attack on Hezekiah and Jerusalem in 701 BCE. We know the precise year when it happened because this Assyrian king – Sennacherib – had the "facts" recorded in his own annals from that year. The Assyrians used a similar system as the Romans when naming a year. The Romans named a year after one of the consuls who that year was in office. The Assyrians had an official, a *limmu*, who gave his name to the year.

We read about Sennacherib's attack on Jerusalem in the short Notice in 2 Kings 18:13–16:

> In the fourteenth year of King Hezekiah, Sannacherin, the king of Assyria, came up and conquered all the fortified cities of Judah, Judah's king Hezekiah sent a message to Sennacherib: "I have sinned. Go home again! Whatever you ask for, I will pay".

The king of Assyria demanded that Hezekiah should pay a tribute of three hundred talents of silver and thirty talents of gold and Hezekiah gave him all the silver found in the temple and the royal treasuries in the palace of the king.

In Sennacherib's version the text reads:

> In my third campaign I went to Hatti Land …

Hereafter follow a series of details relating to the campaign are recorded, but it continues in this way:

> As to the Judean Hezekiah, who did not submit to my yoke: I conquered 46 of his fortified cities including the small towns around them by leveling them to the ground, using siege ramps and having foot soldiers storming them ... 200,150 people, big and small, men and women, horses, mules, donkeys, camels, cattle and sheep without number I removed from them and considered it my booty. Himself I locked up in Jerusalem, his royal city, like a bird in a cage ... As to Hezekiah the glory of my majesty overwhelmed him, and the Arabs and his mercenaries whom he had brought in to strengthen Jerusalem his royal city deserted him. In addition to the thirty talents of gold and the 800 talents of silver came juvels (...) furthermore his daughters, his harem, his male and female musicians whom he brought after me to Nineveh my royal city.[24]

Although the tribute which Hezekiah had to pay to Sennacherib is smaller in the biblical version than in the Assyrian – we notice the missing information about the Judean princesses in the version in 2 King 18 – we can safely say that both texts are referring to the same event. But this is only the beginning of what we read in 2 Kings 18–20. First, we have the story about the Assyrian emissary from the camp of Sennacherib at Lachish (a city he conquered. Both Assyrian texts and reliefs tell us this[25]) to Jerusalem. His task is to threaten Hezekiah into submission (ignoring the fact that Hezekiah had already submitted to Sennacherib's strength before the arrival of the emissary). After that follows the fable of Hezekiah's prayer to Yahweh which, as a result of it, has it that the angel of the LORD kills 185,000 soldiers in Sennacherib's camp during the night. This leads understandably to Sennacherib's withdrawal. Well, according to the Assyrian annals, Sennacherib had already returned home before Hezekiah's tribute was sent to him in Nineveh.

We may say that in the biblical narrative, facts and fantasy play together and have been united into one narrative. The most unpleasant part of Hezekiah's submission has been excluded. Neither do we hear one word about the reasons for Sennacherib's campaign to Palestine in 701, that Hezekiah had created problems in the whole territory by bullying his neighbours. He had kidnapped the king of Ekron who seems to have been Sennacherib's ally.

---

[24] Translated after the text in Luckenbill, 1924, 29–34. Many endeavours have been made through time to find a historical background for all of the tales of 2 King 18–20. For a recent and comprehensive study (among many) Evans, 2009, and the discussion in Grabbe, 2003.

[25] For the Assyrian illustrations cf. Ussishkin, 1982.

The conclusion is that there are indeed references to something that really happened in the Old Testament. It is, however, not always easy to distinguish between what is real and what is freeform fantasy.

The Modern Idea of History and Its Consequences

Thirty years ago, when I gave a lecture in Aarhus about the wife of Yahweh and similar subjects,[26] my good friend from systematic theology Mogens Stiller Kjærgaard approached me after the lecture and told me about the conversation between two elderly ministers of the Church sitting behind him: "Who is the young man up there?" His colleague: "I don't know. An absolute mad *Hypothesenmacher* who only wants to become famous!"

The attitude is probably typical for people who haven't and who will not understand what has happened in historical theology in recent years. We find this attitude both among scholars and among laypersons. The reason is that too many have never understood where modern historical studies have turned since the Enlightenment. The idea of history changed dramatically around 1800, but the terminology was still mostly the same. When people before that change talked about history, they really intended to say "narrative" ("story"). When Herodotus, in ancient times, uses the concept "history" it meant not "history" in any scientific sense but "investigation" or "research" as a journalist would say today. Since all narratives (except science fiction) are about the past, something that preceded the narrative, history was thus about the past, whether it was the remote or the recent past.[27] Although the past did not exist any more, identity was created in the present by referring to the past.

The changing perspectives changed historical writing away from producing narratives from the past to becoming a scientific reconstruction of past events. I have explained how this happened in *The Old Testament Between Theology and History: A Critical Survey.*[28] Here only a short note will have to suffice: The past – also after 1800 – defines who you are; now it depends

---

[26] This was only a few years after the discovery of a couple of inscriptions from Khirbet el-Qom south of Hebron (from the 7th to 6th centuries BCE) and Kuntillet Ajrud in the northern part of Sinai (from the end of the 9th or the beginning of the 8th century BCE). In these inscriptions Yahweh appears next to the goddess Asherah, e.g. in the formula: "I bless you by Yahweh from Samaria and by his Asherah" (Kuntillet Ajrud inscription no. 1). For more cf. Binger, 1997. My lecture was published as Lemche, 1985a.

[27] According to Liddell & Scott, (1940) Greek mythos should be translated as "inquiry" (p. 842), but history as "tale, story, narrative" (p. 1151).

[28] Lemche, 2008c, 101–109.

on real events. Terminology remained the same and was the reason why most people didn't understand what had happened and often reacted sharply against the results of the new historical methods; not because of the new methods *per se* but because the changes were seen as a threat against identity. Within a Christian environment such changes led to Christian fundamentalism (named after a series of writings that were published at the beginning of the 20th century, *The Fundamentals*).[29] Any attack on the basic Christian story and its content was automatically seen as an attack on the ideas of history – especially the biblical one – which had been taught not only in Sunday schools but in normal schools, and therefore a threat to your own identity as a believing person.

Confronted with this kind of criticism, historical-critical scholarship was falling short. When it comes to it, most people are unable to absorb a, new understanding of the Bible. After all, especially in Protestant environments, the Bible functioned as the ultimate foundation of our existence. Now the Bible was under attack, or so it seemed, and in the view of traditional Bible readers this was the same as an attack on themselves. As a result of this we have often seen the members of the Copenhagen School accused by American conservative Christians of being a threat to Western civilization, if not worse.[30]

The writings now included in the Old Testament do not have the past as their primary subject. The past is a narrative which explains how their authors and readers saw themselves. This is my best offer at an explanation of what we find in the Old Testament. Old Testament scripture came into being to inform Jewish society in antiquity about who they were and where they came from. I have previously described this literature as "diaspora-literature" more than once. It evidently considers "Israel" as the home of all Jews and proposes that every Jew should migrate to "Israel" and live there. However, if we study the reality, it is easy to see that the reading public did not live in Palestine but belonged to the Jewish Diaspora.[31] Small wonder that the original Hebrew writings were soon translated into Greek. The majority of Jews living in the Diaspora in the Hellenistic and Romans periods did not read or understand Hebrew. They were, so to speak, Jewish Greeks or Greek Jews.

---

[29] *The Fundamentals*, 1–12 (Los Angeles: Bible Institute of Los Angeles, 1910–15).

[30] For example, Anti-Semites. The most vociferous mouthpiece of this discourse turned against the members of the Copenhagen School has been the archaeologist William G. Dever, his criticism synthesized in his *What Did the Biblical Writers Know and When Did They Know it? What Archaeology Can Tell Us about the Reality of Ancient Israel* (Dever, 2001, 23–52). I analysed the phenomenon in Lemche, 2000.

[31] See especially Lemche, 2008c, 209–11, 233–4.

Cultural Memory

In recent years a centre at the Department of Biblical Studies focusing on the subject of "cultural memory" received a lot of interest.[32] I am not sure that everybody understands how central this concept is for understanding the literature in the Old Testament, and most likely also for the New Testament. The whole thing may seem somewhat confusing and I have to admit that when I joined the project, I had a lot of problems limiting the theme and defining it precisely.

The name of the subject "cultural memory" goes back to a German Egyptologist from Heidelberg, Jan Assmann, who thirty years ago began to speak and write about cultural memory.[33] He was soon supported by his wife, Aleida Assmann, herself a professor also from Heidelberg and daughter of the, in his time, famous German Professor of New Testament Günther Bornkamm.[34] They are both, they say, building on studies in "collective memory" by the French sociologist Maurice Halbwachs (1877–1945).

When I add "they say" this is because the matter is perhaps not as simple as they describe it. Jan Assmann and Aleida Assmann are both humanists (Aleida Assmann's subject is English literature). Halbwachs was not. He was a sociologist and a student of Émile Durkheim (1858–1917). His first major study in this field has the title *Les cadres sociaux de la mémoire*,[35] "the social frames of memory". We don't meet, in connection with Habwachs, the subject defined as "collective memory" before his posthumous and incomplete work (Halbwachs died in Buchenwald concentration camp in February 1945), *La mémoire collective*.[36] But, and it is a major but, Halbwachs's collective mem-

---

[32] The centre for the Bible and Cultural Memory (BICUM). The centre came into being on the initiative of Pernille Carstens and was active from 2010 to 2012. I might just refer to a thematic issue of *Dansk Teologisk Tidsskrift* 76 (2013), pp. 1–80, with articles written by the members of the centre, apart from Pernille Carstens also Niels Peter Lemche, Trine Bjørnung Hasselbalch, Bo Dahl Hermansen, and Michael Perlt. The most important publication to appear was Carstens, Hasselbalch, and Lemche, 2012.

[33] Jan Assmann's (b. 1938) main contribution to the subject is his *Das kulturelle Gedächtnis: Schrift, Erinnerung und politische Identität in frühen Hochkulturen* (1992); ET: *Cultural Memory and Early Civilization: Writing, Remembrance and Political Imagination* (2011).

[34] Aleida Assmann (b. 1947), *Cultural Memory and Western Civilization: Functions, Media, Archives* (2011).

[35] Maurice Halbwachs, *Les cadres sociaux de la mémoire* (1925), first modern edition by Gérard Namer (Halbwachs, 1994).

[36] Halbwachs, 1950. The first critical edition by Gérard Namer (Halbwachs, 1997). None of Halbwachs' opera has been translated into English in their entirety. A selection, however,

ory is not the same as when Assmann talks about cultural memory. Assmann refers to societies, such as the Jewish society in ancient times. Halbwachs might rather speak about the collective memory (and probably nobody will, in this case, talk about a "cultural memory") among, e.g. Brøndby Supporters, or any other particular group within a society. French scholars who study the subject may today define the issue as "mémoire sociale", social memory.[37]

Both terms are important. Halbwachs' "cadres sociaux" is about the circles in which a certain common memory can be found, and it can be everywhere within a given society. Jan Assmann speaks about a society's collective memory which he explains as "cultural". We may join the two concepts in one synthesis which may provide an answer to what we find in the Old Testament. We can, following this lead, ask where in ancient Jewish society this memory belongs – disregarding at the same time other Palestinian circles in the Pre-Hellenistic period. Whose memory is preserved in the Old Testament? This is easy to answer: It is the memory of people able to read and write, never more than a tiny fraction of an ancient society (in the Hellenistic world perhaps never more than 10% of the population).

A Hellenistic Book? Second Part

When we look at the Old Testament and try to scrutinize the narrative found here in order to see where they belong and what kind of Hellenistic themes are found here, then it is obvious that it is impossible to point to any one place. Last year I gave a lecture at the conference here at the Theological Faculty, *Changing Perspectives*. The subject was the Primeval Story in Genesis (Lemche, 2016). In this story we have a mixture of elements belonging to Greek tradition and elements from Near Eastern – especially Mesopotamian – tradition as well. No Greek narrative from Hesiod (8th century BCE) and onwards and no narrative about the earliest times from the ancient Near East includes all the elements found in the biblical Primeval Story. Actually, the closest version where practically all elements are present is Ovid's *Metamorphoses* from the time of the Emperor Augustus.[38] Ovid definitely builds on Hellenistic originals, an indication that the version we find in the Primeval

---

was published as Maurice Halbwachs, *On Collective Memory*, edited, translated, and with an introduction by Lewis A. Coser (Halbwachs, 1992).
[37] Thus Gérard Namer, *Halbwachs et la mémoire sociale* (2000).
[38] More precisely c. 1–9 CE.

Story belongs to the Hellenistic period, although the myths included therein are much older.

Making the Primeval Story our point of departure – other scholars have reached further and included the narratives in the Pentateuch at large, including the Belgian Old Testament scholar Philippe Waidenbaum and his book *Argonauts of the Desert* (Wajdenbaum, 2011) playing with the title of Apollonius of Rhodes's epic on the Argonauts[39] – the authors of these narratives of the Old Testament were learned intellectuals who, in the Hellenistic period, created the myth of ancient Israel as their cultural memory, a story which was soon to become a common possession for everyone. We shall, in this case, not speak about any cultural memory among the ordinary population, not in Palestine or elsewhere. The biblical narrative represents this group's – sometimes referred to as *literati*[40] – story about the past.

As I said before, the pre-modern idea of history was different from the modern one. We have many times discussed the ability among ancient historiographers to distinguish between historical facts and myths, as if this meant much to these historiographers. It is possible that memory research can give an answer. In the present the difference between memory and history is considerable.[41] A historical explanation of past events builds on sources – facts – otherwise it does not count as a real historical reconstruction. Nobody, however, demands that a memory represents a precise account of the past. Memory is something very personal. We may study memory in order to sort out elements which have survived from the past, and they are certainly there. But they have been mixed together with often very personal recollections, or with something someone has told you maybe so many times that you may believe that it is your personal memory. In this way memory is a subject of research which belongs to psychology (if not psychiatry) rather than historical studies.

The stories in the Old Testament about the Israel of the past seem not to be about something that "really happened". They represent "memory", something which is construed on the basis of many types of recollections from the past often with very different content. The example with Hezekiah's and Sennacherib's showdown representing a mixture of fiction and facts illustrated

---

[39] Apollonius wrote the Argonauts sometime in the first half of the 3rd century BCE. He worked as a librarian at the famous library in Alexandria, the most important centre of learning in his time.

[40] The use of this expression among Old Testament scholars seems to have been established by the Canadian scholar Ehud Ben Zvi, who uses it in countless publications. See also his self-presentation: http://www.ualberta.ca/~ebenzvi/ebz-researchinterests.html.

[41] On history and memory cf. Cubitt, 2007.

very well how memory functions when it is not controlled by scholarly historical methods.

Historiographers from antiquity had no access to these methods. We may accordingly state that when they wrote about history it was not about history as we understand it but about their own cultural memory, or rather about the cultural memory which they had constructed with the intention of forming a collective consciousness; a collective memory about who they were and from where they came. We may be able to date the production of this memory, we may be able to determine the origins of most of its components, and we may be able to explain the reason for its being: to create a collective identity. Without memory there is no identity, which is a phenomenon that has been discussed since the beginning of memory research.

A secondary benefit (which in a theological context is much more than a secondary benefit) has to do with the date of the literature in the Old Testament in the Hellenistic period. The important consequence of this is that the cultural memory which is the Old Testament is also the earliest Christian memory. Today we are more than ever able to repair the damage done to the understanding of the Bible for more than two hundred years when the Old and New Testaments were separated as one theological discipline. I have often discussed with Mogens Müller whether it is not time to unite both parts of the Bible into one discipline. We might, in this connection, talk about both parts of the Bible as the common cultural memory of early Christianity which is a much better way to characterize the unity than the common "cultural heritage".[42]

And what to do now after le déluge?

The question is: Was the Copenhagen School the flood or are we now waiting for it? I am still not able to answer that question. Maybe it was the flood, or a metaphor for the changes within the scholarly discipline which I and my colleagues are parts of. Not much of what was reckoned standard and accepted scholarship when I was young has survived. However, this is not universally so. Old Testament scholars are like Russian soldiers in the time of Napoleon: The French said that it was not enough to shoot them; you also had to go over and blow on them before they would fall down. During the I.O.S.O.T. meeting in Paris in 1992, Philip Davies came to me with the programme in hand:

---

[42] Cf. also Lemche, 2008b, chapter 10 "'Københavnerskolens' bidrag", pp. 190–208. ET: Lemche, 2008c, 379–92.

"Nobody would believe that this programme is post-1970 if the year 1992 was not printed on it!" I did not return to an I.O.S.O.T. meeting before 2013 when it was held in Münich, and still nothing had changed.

We may have good reason to be happy about that. It is still quite a task in front of us to convince the historical-critical scholars that they are no more.

THEOLOGY

15 The History of Israel's Religion and the History of Israel: Identical or Different?

It is an established fact at the Faculty of Theology at the University of Copenhagen that no theological discipline has changed so radically as Old Testament studies. Whenever we visit old students of ours – normally now established ministers in their parishes – their reaction is almost always the same. They can hardly recognize the discipline they studied at the university just a few years before. As one of them told me a few years ago: This was not the way we did the history of Israel in my time. No irony intended here, just a slight sense of complaint. He had just experienced my destruction of the classical Scandinavian tradition of cultic interpretations of the Psalms of the Old Testament, including the concept of the enthronement feast of the king in ancient Israel, and the belief in Yahweh as, at one time, a dying and rising god.

In Copenhagen, we consider ourselves to belong among the frontrunners as far as recent progress in our field is concerned – thereby claiming to be members of a school of studies, the "Copenhagen School". Some of the characteristics of this "school" are:

1. The importance of the Old Testament as a source for the history of Israel's religion and Israel's general history is extremely limited: if it can be considered a source of knowledge of this religion and history at all, this source is an indirect one only.
2. The methods of reading Old Testament texts no longer rely on some kind of "archaeology of the text", that digs into the text in order to excavate its oldest stratum in order to isolate a valid source for the study of Israelite religion.
3. Our methodology is under the influence – so to speak – of a certain kind of new positivism, which maintains that we would very much like to possess evidence, facts, data, or whatever you may want to call true information from the past. We cannot any longer be satisfied with guesswork, fantasy, and hypotheses without basis in extant sources.

The History of Israel's Religion and the History of Israel

In what follows I shall try, in a more precise way, to illustrate these three basic assumptions.

1 The Old Testament as a Historical Source

Traditional understandings of the Old Testament as a source of historical investigations are based on the assumption that there is a direct connection between Old Testament texts and the events narrated by these texts. The narrative about King David was either composed in the days of this king of Israel or soon after his death. A lot of ink was spilled on speculations about whether the person who wrote the so-called "Succession Narrative" (2 Samuel 8 to 2 Kings 2), the narrative about King Solomon's ascension to power, would have been his priest, Abiathar, or some other well-known person from his time.

Less confidence was invested in the preceding periods, such as the reign of King Saul, as the Israel supposed to have existed before David was hardly considered so developed as to allow for literary ambitions such as those which got people interested in preserving the life of David in writing. Therefore, tales from the time of the Patriarchs, from Israel's sojourn in Egypt, or wanderings in the desert, and from the time of the Judges, were reckoned to be tales. They could not be compared to the historical reports supposed to have been written by an eyewitness that are preserved in the Books of Samuel and in 1–2 Kings. The tales about Israel's remote past were the results of a long period of oral transmission and therefore – although not 100% accurate, at least 70 or 80% believable. It was the job of historical-critical analysis to remove the 20 or 30-odd % without historical value – however, let this rest for the moment.

I would agree that this idea of sources accepted to be historical when cleansed of non-historical material led to a de facto dismissal of historical as well as critical scholarship. What was done in those days was mostly a kind of rationalistic paraphrase disguised as historical investigation. "Rationalistic paraphrase" means that we consider the Israelite victory over the Amalekites (Exod 17:8–6) to be historical and "forget" that the Old Testament sees this victory as the result of Yahweh's direct participation in the battle. More famous is Joshua's request to Yahweh that he should stop the sun in the valley of Ayalon (Josh 10:12), in order to allow the Israelites to finish off their Amorite enemies. No serious historian can allow such a thing to pass, that the sun should be stopped, as according to any scientist worth his salt this would have brought about the destruction of the universe (or at least our solar system). No, instead of reading the biblical story as narrative, the miraculous part of the narrative is dismissed as unsuitable for historical evaluation. Hereafter only the simple historical reconstruction seems to remain a valid objective of the historian.

Both examples are of course primitive and nobody should think highly about a discipline behaving like this, although this methodology is certainly an old part of biblical scholarship (as well as much history writing dealing with the ancient Near East) – and hard to remove from the academic agenda. To emphasize my point I shall introduce two quotations. The first comes from an Italian Assyriologist, Mario Liverani, who, educated in an independent scholarly environment not sharing the North European and North American romantic idea of the objective scholar, does not believe that positivistic historical reconstruction is possible. The second quotation was formulated at the beginning of this century by a German historian of the ancient world, Eduard Meyer, perhaps the greatest historian of the ancient Near East of all times.

> The indolence of the historians is considerable. When they deal with a certain period and they are confronted by a continuous account of the course of events, which has already been included in some sort of "ancient" documentary source (which is perforce not contemporary with the events themselves), they all too happily adopt the account. They confine their work to paraphrasing it or even rationalizing it.[1]

Eduard Meyer's formulation is nowhere more kind to his colleagues. In his famous monograph on the Israelites and their neighbours from 1905 he writes:

> Besides, then and now I regard every endeavour to be futile and beyond dispute, which tries to answer these questions or even to translate the Israelite sagas into history according to the very much appreciated fashion. Generally, they deliberately skip – without considering how fantastic the enterprise is – half a millennium and deal with the narratives as suitable historical sources, irrespective of their youth and after they have brushed them up by rationalising means. They even consider these sources to be the imperturbable basis of Israel's nationality and religion.[2]

The difference between these scholars – Liverani is a contemporary scholar who published this verdict in an article on Hittite historiography dating from 1977 – seems unimportant. After having formulated his verdict on

---

[1] Quotation from Liverani, 1977, 105. Translated in Liverani, 2004, 28.
[2] Quotation from Meyer, 1905, 50 (translation N.P. Lemche). Cf. also Engel, 1979, 77–8.

contemporary scholarship, Liverani continues to destroy (in order to avoid the idea of a Derrida-like "deconstruction"[3]) the reconstruction of early Hittite history as found in the Decree of Telipinus from the 16th century BCE. Eduard Meyer – still very much a child of his own time – continues to present rationalistic paraphrases of the biblical history. What turned out to be only a slight modification of the direction of scholarship in Meyer's production, has, in Liverani's scholarship, become a demand for a radical change of course – or maybe we should say that we find here a demand to start over.

I shall have to leave this theme shortly. It is in fact not very interesting (except perhaps among biblical scholars), as it mostly tells us that scholars in our field tend to be both naïve and lazy. The important issue is that our interest has changed in a fundamental way. It no longer concerns what may be the background of a text in the world described by the text itself. We are not so much interested in a text to ascertain how much or how little an ancient author knew about the past. We are much more interested in asking questions such as: Why did he write this text in that way? Some may even say that we are really only interested in the confrontation between the reader of the present day and the text of the Bible in order that the biblical text act as a mirror that reflects our own existence. Be this as it may, it is certainly true that the connection between a text and its reader is primary in comparison to the alleged connection between a text and a past narrated by that very text.

2 How to Read a Text

In the good old days theological students used to underline the different sources in the Pentateuch with red, green, or blue ink, in order to be able, at their examination, to answer intricate questions about J (the Yahwist), E (the Elohist), and P (the Priestly document). For scholars belonging to the school of higher criticism, the differences between these three strata of the Pentateuch were considered to be both Alpha and Omega, and it was considered a deadly sin not to be capable of pointing out which passage belonged to which stratum. However, to be honest, it must be recognized that passages were moved rather freely from one stratum to the next and back again. This was not so important; important was that one acknowledged all three strata to be present.

---

[3] Actually, the "Hindersicht" of many years tells me that that was exactly what he did. It was a Derrida-like "deconstruction".

Well, our students worked very hard to find the right place for the different passages, yet what was the value of their endeavours? To give one example: at the beginning of Genesis we find two different stories about the creation of the world. Why do we need two? One should suffice! According to the so-called higher criticism, this was a very easy question to answer: the version belonging to J in Genesis 2 does not supplement the one by P in Genesis 1; it is merely some centuries older. The collector or the redactor (as this enigmatic function is usually called in scholarly literature) in a most mechanical way simply glued the two stories together: one piece of creation narrative from one source, and a second piece from another source. We could thus all leave the problems concerning narrative coherence behind us and be happy ever after.

It was considered an advantage to this kind of reading of Genesis that it not only produced a twin-headed changeling from J and P contained in Genesis 1–3. It was also believed that a basis of diachronic analysis capable of tracing the development of the minds of the ancient Israelites had been created between the J stratum, assumed to date to the 10th century BCE, and the P source, from the exilic or post-exilic period. To the historically oriented scholars of the past century, this capability was considered a great thing, as they were thereby able to trace the religious development of ancient Israel from the 10th century to the 5th century BCE The primitiveness of J was, it was thought, demonstrated by this source's extensive use of anthropomorphic images of God. Among Other things, Abraham invites God to a dinner party (Genesis 18). The more "civilized" P would never have thought of, or even have allowed such a direct encounter between God and man to take place. P, accordingly, was seen to represent a more developed religious stage than that of the cruder J – or this was at least what scholars of that time thought.

The example is a well-chosen one. It shows how the interest of the reader has been diverted from the text itself, from Genesis 1–2 where the two creation stories are printed. Instead, the interest of the scholar was directed towards an alleged religious development of an ancient Israel that is supposed to have taken place sometime between the composition of the J stratum and that of the P source. As a matter of fact, we know nothing about such a development. We only base it on a diachronic reading of Old Testament texts.

The more intelligent scholars were of course not satisfied with a simple statement like this one. They also asked questions about the motives and intentions behind the decision of the redactors to include both creation narratives. Instead of a mechanical literary-critical analysis alone, they opted for a so-called redaction-historical reading of the biblical texts. This reading paid more attention to the content of these texts than to such paraphernalia as how

J or P used the name of God. By introducing redaction-history, they paved the way for the shift of paradigms that has taken place over the last twenty odd years in Old Testament studies. As soon as one gives up the reconstruction of the alleged historical developments between the two different perspectives – in this case the individual outlook of the two creation narratives – and begins asking questions about why these narratives are placed next to each other, the historical perspective (that is, the assumed lapse of time between the composition of both narratives) is out of focus. It may completely disappear or become irrelevant to the analysis, if it is no longer considered necessary to explain why the two creation narratives appear next to each other.

Without doubt scores of such explanations may be found, and although it would be easy to quote quite a few of them, I shall abstain from doing that here. My personal opinion is that as the two creation narratives are very different and carry two different perspectives, they were not thought to be competing narratives, but they were rather believed to supplement each other. The perspective of Genesis 1 is universal: the creation of the universe and the conclusion to this creation is reached when man is created, but only as God introduces the Sabbath (Gen 2:1–4a). In contrast, the narrative in Genesis 2 may be considered to represent a totally different opinion of creation, according to which man is placed at the centre of God's attention. Gen 2, furthermore, leads forward and may be considered the introduction to the narrative about the fall of man in Genesis 3, as it is inextricably connected with this narrative and should not be read without regard to this second part.

Modern literary approaches to texts do not think highly of their diachronic dimension. The assumption that such a dimension is present is entirely based on the presumed diverse times of composition of the individual parts of a text. It also presupposes that the texts of the Old Testament can be cut into pieces that can be redistributed among different strata attributed to different and discrete periods over a time of several hundred years. The appearance of such new literary approaches is a consequence of the consolidation of the social sciences in the 20th century CE. Here the social truism that different ideas may exist at the same time and even in the same milieu and actually do so is especially important. This is indeed a very commonplace observation and it should here be unnecessary to refer to it, if only traditional Old Testament scholarship had been more ready to accept these sciences as valid to our field. With a few honourable exceptions, such as the Danish scholar Johannes Pedersen (1883–1977), no breakthrough of the social sciences was experienced in Old Testament studies before the 1970s.

Pedersen, who can hardly be called a professional social scientist, was a student of Vilhelm Grønbech (1873–1949), a (in his time) famous Danish professor of religious studies. Pedersen's remarkable *Israel I–IV*, which was published in Danish between 1920 and 1934, could hardly have been written without Grønbech's influence. Pedersen's background in religious history created a new synthesis in his study of the Semitic cultures, among which ancient Israel belonged. It was not the aim of Pedersen to present a history of these cultures in the ordinary sense of the term but rather his purpose was to understand these cultures from within. This unusual lack of interest in history (for its time) is very conspicuous in Pedersen's *Israel*, which nearly lacks a historical dimension altogether much like Grønbech's multivolume study of the culture, respectively of the Greeks and of the Teutons.[4] As a direct consequence of his approach to biblical studies, Pedersen generally denounced the literary-critical methods of his own time, especially as found in German scholarship. It is also in this light that his lack of interest in diachronic perspectives should be understood. Instead of this, Pedersen preferred to look for intellectual differences.

I shall, in this place, skip the details of the development of a new paradigm. It is enough to say that it is today possible to teach our students to read and understand the Pentateuchal narratives without resorting to the old sources, J, E, and P. We will normally, as a part of the general introduction to Old Testament studies, include a brief overview of the classic theories but we can do well without any special emphasis on these. We certainly don't invite the students to dissect their texts in the time-honoured fashion any more. We simply, in a very naïve way, ask our students to read their texts and analyse them "as they are printed". They must give up the idea that they have to do exegesis on a text which may – or may not – have existed once upon a time but does not exist any more except in the imagination of the biblical scholar.

The old business of excavating texts cannot be considered a favoured pastime in Copenhagen today. Text archaeology intends to uncover its various strata and to date these as independent narrative strings, until the "reader-archaeologist" reaches the original text, the *ipsissima verba*, e.g. of some old Israelite prophet, if not of Moses himself. It is as if they were archaeologists who, in their excavations, cut through the strata of a settlement present here for centuries. In the past scholars often assumed that, when they had reached or isolated the oldest stratum of text, they were in possession of a valuable

---

[4] Cf. V. Grønbech, *Hellas: Kultur og Religion I–V* (1942–5). When we compare this work to Pedersen's Israel it is as if we only have to change the names of the heroes and heroines from Greek to Hebrew. The difference between Homeric Greece and ancient Israel seems to vanish. The same can said about the second major work by Grønbech, *Vor Folkeæt i Oldtiden* (ET: *The Culture of the Teutons* [1932]).

old historical source, as close to the historical reality of the real world in pre-exilic Israel as we may ever come. Today we know, or should know, that this world behind the texts may be likened to the famous simile of Henrik Ibsen: his hero, Per Gynt, is searching for the core of his onion. However, an onion has no core. When Per Gynt has finished his search, the onion is no more. Although scholars might be looking for the historical reality behind a text, it may never have existed. There is certainly no compelling reason to assume that a text must have a historical kernel.

3 New Positivism

This leads us to my third point, a modern form of "positivism" in biblical studies. I recapitulate: A text should first and foremost be read and understood as a text, as it is preserved in writing, related to the time and the people who lived when it was composed. It is, at the same time, interpreted by readers of another period, who were never intended to be the interpreters of this text. We therefore have to accept and understand that we can only partly present a valid interpretation of a text from the ancient world. Any text from Antiquity may contain elements which we cannot understand and which we may never discover. We cannot see them, and we can only hope but not take for granted that renewed and refined methods may, in the future day, help us to a better understanding of the ancient text.

Progress can be achieved, as has sometimes happened for example in the French sociological school connected with Claude Levy-Strauss (1908–2009) (and his predecessors and students), e.g. in connection with his idea of another kind of "logic" – *la pensée sauvage*. "Wild thinking" is absolutely different from the logical pattern of modern thinking. We may also mention the French school of religious studies exemplified by scholars like Jean-Pierre Vernant (1914–2007) and Georges Dumezil (1898–1986), who have, among other things, demonstrated the existence of different mental worlds behind the production of ideas and texts in Antiquity. These scholars have also indicated that such a mental subconscious world related to the ancient one may exist behind our own thinking, which helps to structure our own thinking. One famous example: Dumezil's notion of the importance of the number three for Indo-European thinking. The presence of this subconscious structure is evident from the way we often structure our arguments: in triads, although we sometimes argue that *tertium non datur*, e.g., in opposition to the alleged importance of the number three. The manner we in Europe have structured pre-historical periods into triads is famous. In Antiquity, history was divided into three ages, the Golden Age, the Silver Age, and the Iron Age.[5] In modern scholarship, prehistory can be split into the Stone Age, the Bronze Age, and the Iron Age. But also these ages can be split into another three periods, such as, respectively, Palaeolithicum, Mesolithicum, and Neolithicum, or the Early Bronze Age, the Middle Bronze Age, and the Late Bronze Age. The Iron Age already belongs to the historical period, something that often makes its tripartite division less conspicuous. In Scandinavian archaeology it is thus common to speak about the Celtic Iron Age (400 BCE–0), the Roman Iron Age (0–400 CE), and the German Iron Age (400–800 CE), although the existence of the Celts may be no more than a modern myth, and the Romans never were here.

It goes without saying that such knowledge provides obstacles for the historical reconstruction of the past, as we should by now accept that such a reconstruction has more to do with the persons who produce it than with the past. My favourite quote in this connection is the famous remark by Lucien Fevre (1878–1956), a founding father of the French school of historians called Les annales, who is supposed to have argued "that we know nothing about the past; we are always reconstructing it". I have to add that I would rather prefer to change this sentence to "we know nothing about the past; we are always constructing it!"

In Old Testament studies we not only have to modify a large number of age-old commonly "accepted" opinions, we are simply forced to dismiss them. This demand is valid as far as the history of Israel and its religious history are concerned. Here, the logical distinction between three different Israel's (another triad!), historical Israel, biblical Israel, and ancient Israel, is of preeminent importance.[6]

Historical Israel is the Israel of the real world, that is, the state of Israel that existed in northern and central Palestine between, say 900 and 700 BCE. This Israel was only one (although a major one) among an extensive number of small states in Palestine in the Iron Age. This state inherited the name of Israel from the Israel present in Palestine at the time of the Egyptian Pharaoh Merenptah (c. 1200 BCE), who in a famous inscription claimed to have destroyed "Israel".[7] We have no idea about how the name was borrowed or whether any continuous history existed between the Israel of Merenptah

---

[5] The classic triad has been preserved among us to indicate cultural phenomena such as literary golden and silver ages, for example the golden period of Latin literature (Cicero among others) as compared to the silver age of literature of, among others, Tacitus.
[6] Cf. Davies, 1992.
[7] *ANET*³, p. 378.

and the Israel of the Iron Age. The dynastic name of the state of Israel was Bīt Ḫumriya, "the House of Omri". It is mentioned in a couple of inscriptions dating from the 9th and 8th centuries BCE; the Mesha inscription and the Tel Dan inscription(s) (provided the last mentioned is genuine).[8] It certainly relates in some way to biblical Israel, which is the Israel of Old Testament tradition that concerns the people of God which came from Egypt to conquer the country of their forefathers, the patriarchs Abraham, Isaac, and Jacob, the receivers of God's promises. This Israel is biblical because it can be found nowhere except in the Old Testament. It is also a mythical Israel as it foundation is itself a myth and should be interpreted as a myth: a chosen people, a Promised Land, and a covenant between Israel and Yahweh. However, this Israel was destroyed because it broke its covenant with God, and only a remnant survived after having returned from exile. This Israel cannot in any way be identified with historical Israel. It consists not only of Samaria but also of Judah – the "Israelites" who went into exile were, as a matter of fact, the inhabitants of Judah and Jerusalem – and Palestine at large. It sometimes also includes a greater part of modern Jordan. The Old Testament also says that the ideal borders of this Israel should reach from the Euphrates to the Brook of Egypt.

From a historical-political point of view this state never existed. Thus, within Old Testament studies a discussion rages that may eventually result in the removal of the united Hebrew kingdom under David and Solomon from history. The biblical idea of an early Israelite empire may be no more than a fata morgana of another age. It presumably dates from the Hellenistic period and should be considered a Jewish "copy" of the Greek empires, either the Seleucid one of Syria or the Ptolemaic one of Egypt. As heirs to Alexander the Great both the Seleucids and the Ptolemeans claimed the right to rule all of Syria and Palestine. The Old Testament concept of an Israelite empire is part of biblical Israel; it has nothing to do with historical Israel. It does not exist outside the Old Testament.

These observations suggest to us that biblical Israel should be considered a reflection of ideas current at the time of the authors who wrote the Old Testament narratives. They were either commonly accepted by the authors as well as their audience, or they were simply created by these authors in order to make a specific impression on their readers. This Israel is therefore a very "honest" one. It was certainly in existence, however, not in the real world.

---

[8] Mesha inscription, *KAI*, 181; also Dearman, 1989. The Tell Dan inscriptions, cf. Biran and Naveh, 1993 and 1995. As to the present writer's present position concerning these fragments, cf. Lemche, 1998c, 38–43 (on the Mesha inscription, Lemche, 1998c, 44–6).

Indeed, it may be far removed from any political reality present in Palestine in ancient times. Biblical Israel and historical Israel only share the name. It could of course be maintained that they share a common capital, Samaria, as far as the biblical description of the northern Hebrew kingdom goes.

How do we get to ancient Israel? Simply by combining historical Israel with biblical Israel: One dose of historical Israel thinned by a far bigger amount of biblical Israel; however, a biblical Israel which has been rationalistically cleansed of anything supernatural. In this way the biblical Israel of literature is transferred or transformed into the world of history, the world of the historical Israel. The tiny fragments of knowledge which we possess about the historical Israel are at the same time placed inside the framework of this transformed biblical Israel, and – hocus-pocus – a scientific monster has appeared: Ancient Israel. However, where are we to look for this ancient Israel? Only in one place, in the imaginations of the scholars. Ancient Israel is certainly not the same as biblical Israel, nor is it to be likened to historical Israel, but it is a new Israel, a constructed Israel which, however, in the scholarly mind, has eliminated the historical Israel. In this way it can be compared to biblical Israel – the product of the imagination of the biblical writers – being exactly that, the brainchild of modern historians.

It should never be forgotten that we know nothing about history, we only construct history. Ancient Israel is our mental construction and nothing else. As a mental construction, ancient Israel will always change form from one scholar to the next. It can never be the same. Only historical Israel will, from a logical point of view (but only from that point), always remain the same. We could also say that historical Israel is unimportant or irrelevant as it only exists on a historical level, as part of the past. It is only relevant for us when we reconstruct our own Israel(s) for our personal entertainment, a reconstruction that can be accomplished with more or less scholarly finesse. This writer is, after all, a natural-born historian. He is still likely to accept many modern constructions of ancient Israel as closer to the real world than for example the early Israel of C.B. de Mille's *The Ten Commandments* (old as well as new versions). De Mille's Israel may, on the other hand, be much closer to biblical Israel than my ancient Israel.

The next step would be the religious story of Israel. Everything so far seems equally valid when we turn our attention to this subject. We may accordingly maintain that just as we should distinguish between three Israels, we also have to distinguish between three different religions of Israel. We may refer to religion in historical Israel, or to the religion of biblical Israel, and finally to the religion of ancient Israel. History and religion seem here to be only two different sides of the same coin. Of course, some sort of religion was in existence in historical Israel – the ephemeral central Palestinian state in the Iron Age. This religion may also be labelled "the religion of Israel". This religion is a historical fact that may be studied only as far as sources have survived from between 900 and 700 either in the form of inscriptions or in the iconography of the period allow it. Religious architecture may also be of interest to the study of religion. A quite substantial number of personal names have among other things been passed down to us, often found on ostraca or in clay impressions of personal seals. Such personal names are likely to be of the theophoric variety, containing a god's name. This is absolutely commonplace, but in biblical studies it is sometimes necessary to be banal in order to be understood. Sometimes banality is not enough to make sense of the data to people. However, let us turn to a real example from historical Israel, the Samaria Ostracon no. 1 (9th cent BCE).[9] It can be translated in this way: "In the tenth year. For Šᵉmaryaw from Bᵉʾērayim a jar of old [wine]. For Rāgāʿ, the son of ʾElīšāʿ, 2. For ʿUzzā, son of Qadbeś 1. ʾElība 1. Baʿalā, son of ʾElīšāʿ, 2. Yᵉdaʿyaw 1". Two names contain the theophoric element yaw, i.e. a short version of Yahweh, one or two the divine name Baʿal[10] and one or two name the divine name El.[11]

If these names are taken to contain evidence about the kind of religion in Samaria, in the capital of historical Israel, in, say the 9th century BCE, they inform us of the fact that in those days three divine names were current, Baʿal, El, and Yahweh. This information will provide an impression of religion in historical Israel that is not the creation of the authors of the narratives of the Old Testament. According to the biblical authors, after biblical Israel broke with the Davidic dynasty its religion represented a deviation from the correct faith in Yahweh. The religion of biblical Israel is, according to the biblical authors, condemned as heresy. However, the inscriptions from historical Israel have no relation to such accusations. Only biblical historiographers tell us that religion was heretical. I do not say that these historiographers were perforce wrong. Maybe religion in historical Israel did not live up to the expectations of orthodox Yahwism. We have no contemporary information to help us. The question whether or not Yahwism in historical Israel represented a deviation from the norms of genuine Yahwism is moot. It cannot be answered. Late biblical historiographers were of the opinion that the religion of biblical Israel (not historical Israel) represented a revolt against genuine Yahwism *as they saw it*. They accordingly condemned the religion of biblical

---

[9] *KAI*, 183. For a recent commentary Renz, 1995, 89–90.
[10] Provided that אלבא is a short form of אליבעל, "My god is Baʿal."
[11] Again if אלבא is really אליבעל. Cf. the preceding note.

Israel. Whether the people of historical Israel would agree is doubtful. After all, the Yahwistic names on this ostracon represent 40% of the total amount of names preserved in the text.

We cannot say with any certainty that all the three gods mentioned on this ostracon were worshipped at Samaria around 800 BCE. Modern experience says that in the modern world names can be extremely conservative, although the specific meaning of the name has been totally lost. Thus, in Scandinavia in the 20th century CE, personal names containing the theophoric element "Tor" are extremely popular.[12] Should such names be used in a future analysis of Scandinavian religion in the 20th century, the analysis may result in a totally misleading impression of Scandinavian religion in our time, among other things because there are just as many children being christened "Torben" as "Christian". Although this may apply to the situation in Scandinavia in the 20th century CE, it is certainly not automatically true that it was also the case in ancient Palestine. Hebrew personal names of the Iron Age seem to provide more information about religion than the names of the modern Western world. If a child carries the name Yᵉdaʿyaw, "Yahweh knows him", this is not only a name but also a confession to Yahweh as the protecting god of the child. Or in case אלבא of the ostracon already discussed really means "My god is Baʿal", it must be seen as a confession that Baʿal is a god.

We must repeat that the history of historical Israel's religion must build on information coming from historical Israel; it should not be based on material contained in the Old Testament. The, in itself, rather unimportant inscription from Samaria says that at least three deities were worshipped at Samaria ca. 800 BCE, Baʿal, El, and Yahweh. More divine names appear on other parts of the collection of Samaria ostraca, such as Gad ("Happiness"). Apart from that very little can be said about the religion of historical Israel on the basis of sources of this kind. So far it is still impossible to write a history of historical Israel's religion.

The history of the religion of biblical Israel is, on the other hand, easily accessible, as it is nothing except a paraphrase of the Old Testament narrative about Israel and its God, Yahweh, from the beginning of history to the return of the Jews from Babylon. This narrative is comprehensive and includes fairytales and drama, different kinds of novels and short stories, tales about success and disaster, the exploits of heroes and heroines and of villains and witches. It is not only a narrative; it is already a history of biblical Israel's religion. Authors who constructed biblical Israel composed this "history". They

---

[12] A few examples: Torben, Torvald, Torbjørn, Torsten, Torgrim, Torleif. Further information about this can be found in Binger, 1997, 30–5.

considered their Godforsaken forefathers to be part of biblical Israel. These forefathers were sent into exile to be punished because of their transgressions against the God of Israel. After the punishment Israel – i.e., the sons of the heretical fathers – was allowed to return.

This narrative does not present any problem to the modern reader. Any interesting narrative can to be told and retold several times. It will always be transmitted to a new audience and reinterpreted. Few writers of the past have, however, been so successful as the people who wrote the Bible. It is difficult to surpass their version of the fate of biblical Israel. The best thing to do is probably – as happens in the Synagogue – to read the narratives as found in the Bible. It is, however, problematic to create a changeling dubbed "the religion of ancient Israel" by mixing the religion of biblical Israel with the scattered information about the religion of historical Israel, as if they belonged in the same category. Although such a mixture is logically a mistake, scholars have repeated it several times. Such scholars employ this mixture of fiction and fact to prove that the child of their imagination – i.e., ancient Israel – is also historical Israel. This is an impossible conclusion. The two Israels can never meet. Historical Israel is a thing of the past, something that vanished a long time ago. It can never be brought to life again. Biblical Israel is still very much alive. It is as a narrative contained in a book known and accepted by Jews as well as Christians since Antiquity. Because of its popularity the Old Testament historical narrative exists in a kind of historical "limbo" – ancient Israel – with only very few relations to the historical Israel of the past.

It would be a mistake to argue that the Old Testament narrative is just plain wrong, though, because it presents a false picture of Israel's religion. This is far from the case. The only thing requested is that the scholar and his or her audience must know which Israel is implied. In short: it is the mixture of different categories that is false. We cannot blame the historical Israelites nor the biblical writers for mistakes committed by modern readers because of false methodologies and expectations.

Three more examples will illustrate how such modern false readings of biblical texts occurs. The first example will concern the study of ancient Israelite religion. It involves the hypothesis of the enthronement festival of Yahweh. The second example has to do with the distance between biblical and historical Israel and will concentrate on early Israelite religion. The third example illustrates why the religion of biblical Israel is so distinctly different from ancient Near Eastern religions in general.

The enthronement festival belonged, until a few years ago, to the standard questions at examinations in theology. When they heard the magic words "the enthronement of Yahweh", students of theology and of general religion were expected to provide sensible answers. Where does the information about this festival come from? Do we possess ancient sources of information about Yahweh's enthronement? Let us begin with historical Israel. Do we find any indication of such a feast of Yahweh in the sources pertaining to historical Israel? The answer is negative. Not a single line or anything else of interest has survived. The ostracon from the 10th or 9th century BCE from Gezer, which includes a kind of agricultural calendar, has nothing to say about such a feast.[13] Although this cannot be disputed, it can certainly be argued that the material from historical Israel is of so limited a nature that nothing can really be said about the basis of this information. The feast of enthronement might have existed in spite of any ancient documentation. This is definitely an *argumentum ex silentio*, and totally out of place. It cannot be used as an argument in favour of an enthronement feast of Yahweh. It is a postulate, because it is impossible on the basis of extant evidence to say whether or not the festival existed. Logically any argument of this kind must be false. In traditional historical-critical scholarship the next step would be to turn to the tale about biblical Israel in the Old Testament, in order to look for traces of the festival. The answer will be inconclusive. The Old Testament contains a rather detailed festival calendar with a special emphasis on the three main feasts, Easter, Pentecost, and Sukkoth (the feast of Booths). Two other religious events appear in connection with the last mentioned, the Day of Atonement, and Rosh Hashshana – New Year's Day. Nothing indicates that an old feast of Yahweh's enthronement ever took place, not even at the New Year's festival.

Sigmund Mowinckel presented the classic theory about this enthronement feast in 1922.[14] At that time he was able to draw on external sources from many corners, not least Babylonian documents mostly from the middle of the 1st millennium BCE pertaining to the Babylonian festival of the Akitu.[15] In the texts relevant to this feast it is described how Marduk, the city god of Babylon, once every year has to leave his temple in order to pay visits to other gods living in temples not belonging to Marduk. After having fulfilled this obligation, Marduk returns to his own temple and is greeted by everybody there eagerly waiting for their god to return. It was assumed that Marduk also had to fight – at least in a ritual form – against the powers of chaos. This

---

[13] *KAI*, 182, cf. Renz, 1995, 30–7.
[14] Mowinckel, 1922. An updated version of the thesis is to be found in Mowinckel, 1951. For a recent assessment, cf. Petersen, 1998.
[15] This festival was after the appearance of Mowinckel's study, studied in more details by Pallis, 1926. Mowinckel relied mostly on Zimmern, 1905. Cf. also the appendix to the reprint of Mowinckel, 1922, 326 ff.

assumption, however, rested on a rather tendentious interpretation of the Babylonian sources which included the information that the poem of Enuma Eliš was proclaimed on the fifth day of this festival in front of the statue of Marduk. Mowinckel accepted this interpretation of the Babylonian sources. Controlled by his interest in cult and rite he declined to consider the Babylonian material to include only historical remembrances of the time when Marduk assumed royalty for himself and became the city god of Babylon.

However, on the basis of these kind of sources, Mowinckel found evidence in a number of psalms of Yahweh as a god that had to fight for his position among the gods. In Mowinckel's version of ancient Israel Yahweh had to fight against the powers of chaos in order to regain his throne. In this connection the acclamation of his victory was pronounced by the words: "Yahweh has become king!"

Although it is not difficult to find evidence of Yahweh as the god who once vanquished the powers of chaos in the Old Testament, not a single line indicates that his victory was in any way related to a yearly festival celebrated in connection with New Year's Day. Mowinckel's enthronement festival remained and still remains a postulate that cannot be vindicated on the basis of extant sources. It is, however, an excellent example of what may happen when comparisons are made between Old Testament texts and documents from the ancient Near East.

Although often quoted in this connection, the texts from Ugarit do not help. The Ugaritic poetic circle about Ba'al that only became available after Mowinckel published his hypothesis includes the scene of a battle between Ba'al and the god of the ocean, Yam.[16] It was originally believed that this text refers to an enthronement festival at Ugarit. Ugaritic religion was formerly seen as an early version of the religion found in the Old Testament. Therefore, this text proved Mowinckel to be correct, or so many scholars thought.

In this way a hypothesis was constructed on the basis of a tendentious reading of some biblical psalms. The evidence of these psalms was compared to early interpretations of Babylonian texts. When the Ugaritic texts appeared some years after the publication of Mowinckel's thesis, the hypothesis was already in existence and used to illuminate the content of the Ugaritic poems. When seen in this light, the Ugaritic texts became the final proof that Mowinckel's hypothesis about the enthronement festival was correct.

---

[16] *KTU* 1.1–1.2. Several English translations are currently available, the most recent being by Dennis Pardee in *COS* I (1997), 243–9, Mark S. Smith, in Parker, 1997, 87–105, and Wyatt, 1998, 39–69.

Sometimes biblical scholars seem to believe that, as in mathematics, two minuses make a plus, i.e., that two postulates are able to prove that a hypothesis can be verified. This certainly happened when the evidence of the Ugaritic texts was twisted in order to conform to an older theory based on textual evidence from other times and places. Things changed when it became evident in some circles that the Ugaritic poems are not cultic or ritual texts, they are epic literature in many ways comparable to the epics of Homer. It is therefore a distressing fact that ritual texts from Ugarit have no information about an enthronement festival whatsoever which was celebrated in the temples of Ugarit.

The second example has to do with the understanding of the position of Yahweh and the idea of an exile in the Old Testament. According to the evidence of the Old Testament, Yahweh only revealed his true identity to the Israelites on Mt. Sinai. Thereby Yahweh demanded to be accepted as the only God of Israel. He presented the Israelites with an offer they could not refuse. In the years to come Israel became the people of Yahweh and Yahweh the God of Israel. Israel's religion was from its very beginning a monotheistic faith, but things soon changed for the worse when the Israelites broke their covenant with God and began to worship other gods.

A recent analysis of the personal names in Israel and Judah (scholars often "forget" to make a distinction between the two) in the 8th and 7th centuries says that about 85% of the personal names at that time and place were "Yahwistic".[17] Yahwistic names means that the name of Yahweh is part of the personal name. This investigation is certainly to be criticized and for many reasons. However, if statistics are worth anything, it is obvious that Yahweh was a very important deity in Palestine in the Iron Age.

A name is only a name and it may, at different times and places, carry different meanings. If an inscription from Palestine from the 8th or the 7th century BCE mentions names including a reference to Yahweh, does it automatically prove that this Yahweh was the same god as we find in the Old Testament? We may ask as well concerning the wellbeing of his spouse, Asherah. What happened to Asherah? She appears in a couple of inscriptions together with Yahweh.[18] In the description in 2 Kings 23 of the religious changes in Jerusalem at the time of King Josiah we are told that this goddess was banished from Yahweh's temple and from Jerusalem together with a number of other gods, named as well as unnamed. Evidently the writer of this story knew

---

[17] Tigay, 1986. For a criticism of this analysis cf. Binger, 1997, 30–4.
[18] From Kuntillet ʿAğrūd and Ḥirbet el-Kōm, respectively. Cf. the discussion in Binger, 1997, 94–105, and Renz, 1995, 59–64 (Kuntillet ʿAğrūd) and 202–11 (Ḥirbet el-Kōm).

something that nobody was supposed to know: Yahweh was, in pre-exilic Judah and Jerusalem, the patriarchal head of a divine pantheon, including Asherah as his consort. Although this information is part of the image of biblical Israel created by the biblical historiographers, the evidence of 2 Kings 23 does not conform to the general picture of Yahweh in the Old Testament. Here the historiographer may have transmitted information from the past. Asherah was indeed part of the official religion in pre-exilic Judah.[19] Then somebody might ask why the ancient Israelites were condemned for paying attention to this goddess? Would it not have pleased pre-exilic Yahweh to see his wife honoured?

The answer is easy. Although historical Israel worshipped Asherah as the consort of Yahweh, the Judaism of the late 1st millennium BCE could not tolerate this worship any longer. Therefore biblical Israel sinned because it paid attention to the needs of the goddess; another example of the idolatry that condemned biblical Israel to destruction and exile.

This example throws light on some of the secret intentions behind the construction of biblical Israel. Biblical Israel never existed in the real world. Biblical Israel should, however, not to be identified with the Israel of the writers who created this mirage of the past. No Israel existed between 722 BCE and 1948 CE, except in ideology. The biblical historiographers were brought up within this ideology. Their hope was that in the future a new Israel would arise that was not biblical Israel. Biblical Israel provided the explanation for the disappearance of Israel but also legitimated the hope for a successor of the same name.

The biblical historiographers needed an exile. In order to travel into an exile, the biblical Israelites had to break their covenant with the God, not of historical Israel but of biblical Israel. This time we have to place this biblical God in his real surroundings, in the early Jewish society of the Persian and especially the Hellenistic periods, a society acknowledging only one God, the Lord. According to Jewish standards, the biblical Israelites were idol worshippers. This has nothing to do with the fact that no evidence from the pre-exilic periods indicates that idol worship was a problem for the historical Israelites. As a matter of fact, the evidence points in the opposite direction. The exile creates a line of division between the Jewish society of the late first millennium BCE and biblical Israelites. These Israelites were worshippers of foreign gods, we – the Jews – are the holy seed, the purified remnant that survived

---

[19] True, we cannot say with certainty that she was the only consort of Yahweh in historical Israel. This may have been the case, but the possibility cannot be excluded that other goddesses such as Anat may also have played this role.

the tribulations of the exile (cf. the "gospel" of the Book of Isaiah). However, the exile does more than that, as it also creates a linkage between the biblical Israelites and their supposed heirs the Persian and Hellenistic Jews. The Jews are accordingly – or considered themselves to be – the legitimate heirs to the possessions of their fathers, that is the Promised Land, Palestine – in spite of the fact that this may not be, from an historical angle, an actual fact.

The third example involves the rather particularistic characteristics of biblical Israelite religion. A short recapitulation is needed. According to the biblical narrative, the Yahwistic faith was from its very beginning a monotheistic creed. Yahweh, the only God of Israel, had revealed his identity to the Israelites on Mt. Sinai and had demanded to be the only God worshipped by this Israel. In this connection, scholars have paid special attention to Yahweh's warning that he is "jealous God", in Hebrew El qanah.

Some of the more traditional modern histories of Israel's religion scholars have been especially interested in this expression and have considered it to be an original part of Yahwism. Such histories considered the Israelite religion as it – according to the Old Testament – appeared in the days of the Hebrew kings to have resulted from a syncretism that blended genuine Yahwistic elements with Canaanite religious practices and beliefs. The religion of the Israelites in the period of the kingdom was a mixture of two different religions belonging to two separate nations; on one hand the Israelites, and on the other, the Canaanites.

This interpretation has to be questioned simply because the Old Testament image of two conflicting nations and two conflicting religions in Iron Age Palestine is hardly relevant as the basis of a historical analysis of religious developments in Palestine in the Iron Age. Thus, it is highly likely that the Canaanites of the Old Testament do not represent a historical nation. Just like their opponents, the biblical Israelites, they should be considered biblical Canaanites, a literary invention, and playing the role of the adversary of biblical Israel. The Canaanites, like their opponents, the biblical Israelites, only show up in the pages of the Old Testament. They are part of biblical Israel, and they only have a part to play in the narratives about biblical Israel. From a historical perspective, the biblical differentiation between Israelites and Canaanites is without foundation. It is preferable to argue that in the biblical narratives the Canaanites play the role of the villains, whereas the Israelites come out of the story as the heroes.[20]

This idea already formed part of my reconstruction of pre-exilic Israelite religion, as I presented it in my *Ancient Israel* (Lemche, 1988). It was based on

---

[20] Cf. further on this Lemche, 1991a.

the results obtained by extensive investigations of Palestinian civilization in the Early Iron Age that showed that there was no cultural difference between the "Canaanites" and the "Israelites". This had already been an acknowledged fact among many students of early Israelite history for some time, and had led to a reconstruction of the history of early Israel (still believed to be ancient Israel) that departed in a fundamental way from the biblical narrative. In my history of Israel, I maintained that the Israelite religion was originally a Canaanite religion, or rather that it was a West Semitic religion similar to religions elsewhere in Syria and Palestine. Only a late Jewish reformulation of the religious traditions of Palestine had changed its character and transformed it into monotheistic Yahwism. This hardly happened before the postexilic period.

In conclusion: Israelite religion as described by biblical sources is part of biblical Israel; it is not the religion of historical Israel. In this connection, the idea of a jealous God as well as other idiosyncratic parts of biblical Yahwism is very important. In the religious world of the ancient Near East in the early first millennium BCE anything like this is unknown. The only parallel to the worship of biblical Yahweh could be the short-lived worship of Aton in the days of Pharaoh Amenophis IV – also called Akhnaten – in Egypt in the 14th century BCE.[21]

It is easy to name scholars who see a direct connection between Akhnaten and Moses. They argue that Moses' monotheistic creed had its origins in the sun worship of the Egyptian Pharaoh.[22] This idea is no longer part of the discussion about early Israelite religion among biblical scholars. The idea of a direct connection between Israel and Egypt as far as monotheism goes relied on a series of hypotheses that were not based on facts. In recent times such ideas have been discredited, mostly because Akhnaten's reforms may not have been so exclusively monotheistic as previously believed.

In spite of this separation of early Israelite Yahwism from the Egyptian Aton worship of Akhnaten, early Israelite religion as described by the Old Testament displays some similarities to the Egyptian phenomenon. The German Old Testament scholar Rainer Albertz may have provided an answer to this question in his recent history of Israelite Religion (Albertz, 1992). This history can hardly be said to represent a radical departure from the common opinion of the majority of Old Testament scholars. It is fairly conservative, although important because of its author's sociological angle to the study of

---

[21] Although the precise character of this religion may be the subject of discussion among contemporary Egyptologists.
[22] A famous example is Albright, 1940.

religion. Albertz, however, reaches the conclusion that the religion of early Israel, i.e. Israel before the formation of the state, includes certain characteristics that can best be described as sectarian. Translated into normal language, this means that the religion of early Israel should be called the religion of a sectarian group. It was definitely not the religion of a normal nation or society belonging to the Near Eastern world between, say 1200 and 1000 BCE. It is therefore highly likely that members of a sectarian group created the image of biblical Israel's Yahwistic religion. These sectarians simply created a reproduction of their own religious beliefs and sentiments and retrojected it onto the time of early biblical Israel. It is, at the same time, a religious projection of ideas believed to reappear in the golden age future to come.

A sociological analysis of the society where such ideas were entertained as are found in biblical literature will, without doubt, arrive at the conclusion that the sectarian and particularistic character of biblical Israel must be understood in the light of the society that produced the biblical literature. The narrative of the Old Testament is not a part of biblical Israel or of historical Israel. They are the products of a society that saw itself as the heir of the very oldest biblical Israel. This society was the Jewish society of the Persian and Hellenistic-Roman periods.

I believe that I have presented enough examples to illustrate my point: Israelite religion and the history of Israel as found in the Old Testament are closely interconnected and not to be separated. I also believe that we are now in a better position to deal with these phenomena in a (from a methodological vantage point) more adequate manner. It should also be said in this connection that students of religion must respect the fact that different logical levels exist. They should not transgress the borderlines between these levels. Any such transgressing will surely lead to a mixture of different logical categories and logical mistakes. It should also be remembered that such mistakes cannot be repaired, but they invariably have as their consequence that serious scholars have to waste time correcting such false attempts. They are no longer part of the scholarly discussion. Traditional biblical scholarship has committed a long series of logical mistakes. We accordingly have to disregard many of its conclusions as false. Maybe that is the reason why so little of the scholarly literature belonging to the field of biblical studies is worth reading.

16 Geography as Memory

Di Provenza il mar, il suol – chi dal cor ti cancello?
Al natio fulgente sol, qual destino ti furò?
(Francesco Maria Piave: Libretto for Verdi *La Traviata*)

The quotation from Giuseppe Verdi's *La Traviata* (1853), "Di Provenza il mar, il suol – chi dal cor ti cancello?"[1] is a reflection of the meaning of home to a poet of the Romantic Period and accords as well with sentiments of the present day. The question is whether or not the "home" also carried the same notions in ancient times.

At a conference years ago a colleague of mine, although from another department, lectured on the reformation theologian Sebastian Franck's (1499–1543) view of nature, presenting Franck as almost a modern ecologist – almost a member of Greenpeace. In the discussion after the lecture a specialist from church history asked quietly: When Franck spoke about nature, didn't he mean human nature? The silence was thundering; you could really hear the needle falling on the carpet. And of course, the church historian was right. We were, in Franck's days, a couple of hundred of years from the modern – romantic – idea about nature and the way the concept is used today.

I open with this example of what happens when we confuse modern sentiments with ancient. In this case it was the concept of nature in previous, pre-romantic times, today it is geography. Does the ancient understanding of this concept concur with modern ideas of geography? It is a huge question, and one of which I will only in this place be scratching the surface. But it is quite obvious that ancient people did not understand geography as we do. As late as the Enlightenment there are obvious examples of geography and nature being stylized in the garden architecture of that time, reflecting developments within the conception of nature that had been ongoing since the Renaissance. These gardens, such as the most famous example, the garden at Versailles, but which are found all over Europe, tell a story of a geography that did not

---

[1] In English: "The sea and soil of Provence – who has erased them from your heart? From your native, fulsome sun – what destiny stole you away?" (transl. Jonathan H. Ward). The aria goes on along the same path for several more lines.

concentrate on the real world but on a constructed geography, which if anything was about controlling nature. In literature it was very much the same. A clear example can be found in a poem by the German poet Friedrich Gottlieb Klopstock (1724–1803), who, for an important part of his life, worked in Copenhagen. I haven't read this poem since my days in high school, and haven't been able to trace again – the poem was in Danish, a translation from German. It belongs, intellectually, to the period to which Klopstock belonged, the pre-romantic period, more closely to the "Sturm und Drang" period of the late pre-Romantic era.[2] In Klopstock's image of the world the centre was the inhabited land, with the city as the turning point. Around this centre there was a series of circles of cultivated landscape, and only at the fringe do we find what today has almost in the common expression of the world turned into the centre; nature untouched by humans.

Moving from organized poetry of the kind found in Klopstock's poems, and on to popular literature (the folktale), we see this image of the world confirmed. When, in such stories, a change has to happen, the hero and heroine move out into the woods, where all kind of dangerous adventures are waiting for them. In Northern Scandinavia the mountains took over the function of the "dangerous place", and as is or should be well known, in the Middle East it is the desert. Be that as it may, it is clear that we are far from modern ideas of geography, and very far from any recognition of how beautiful nature, i.e., the forest, really is. Geography is mythical, and the woodland represents the dangerous place, the home of demons, whereas the closest circles around the inhabited place – as in Klopstock's poem – is the well-known space, safe to travel and live in.

Armies travelling in those days avoided such areas, not only because of the danger of being ambushed there – which in the case of a major army would not really be a problem, but because of the demons living in the woods. And for good reasons, or so history tells us. Thus, the story goes that in Sweden shortly after he had liberated the country from Danish rule and a local rebellion had broken out in Småland in the southern central part of Sweden because of harsh taxation, Gustav Vasa sent his German mercenaries into the woods of Småland – and never saw them again. Of course, the best-known example must be the Roman defeat in the Teuteburger Forest in 9 CE. The forest as the idyllic hiding ground of outlaws like Robin Hood and his merry

---

[2] It was printed in Falkenstjerne and Jensen, 1942. However, it has been excluded since 1979 from modern editions of this schoolbook. It might have been one of these two poems by Klopstock: "Die Frühlingsfeyer" or "Der Eislauf" both written during his time in Denmark.

fellows of Sherwood Forest is the invention of English popular imagination, always very different from Central European constructions of Gothic horror attached to unholy places like the woods.[3]

When we move to ancient times and concentrate on texts, the situation is the same. In a wonderful passage in the Odyssey (XIII:236–249) Athena describes Ithaca to Odysseus just woken up from his sleep at the coast of Ithaca where he had been put by the Phaeacians:

> Then the goddess, flashing-eyed Athena, answered him: "A fool art thou, stranger, or art come from far, if indeed thou askest of this land. Surely it is no wise so nameless, but full many know it, [240] both all those who dwell toward the dawn and the sun, and all those that are behind toward the murky darkness. It is a rugged isle, not fit for driving horses, yet it is not utterly poor, though it be but narrow. Therein grows corn beyond measure, and the wine-grape as well, [245] and the rain never fails it, nor the rich dew. It is a good land for pasturing goats and kine; there are trees of every sort, and in it also pools for watering that fail not the year through. Therefore, stranger, the name of Ithaca has reached even to the land of Troy which, they say, is far from this land of Achaea."[4]

Ithaca is described to Odysseus, not as a specific beautiful land, but as renowned all over the world and then its virtues are counted, a fine place for agriculture and husbandry. Going home, which is the central idea of the Odyssey as well as other Greek *nostoi*-poems, is not about seeing the mountains and woodlands of home again, it is about returning to the place of one's origin, praised for its wealth; in the case of the Odyssey, agricultural wealth.

The mysterious experience of the world, divided into the known and the unknown, would have been ordinary people's impression, as ordinary people did not do much travelling. Mostly, people stayed where they were born, and for 90% of the population this meant staying and tilling their land. If they left home, it would be to travel to the nearest town and its market and sanctuary.

---

[3] The difference has never been better described than in Fussell, 1975, when he explains the difference between the reception of the tribulations at the Western Front among British poets like Robert Graves, Edmund Blunden, and more, and in Ernst Jünger's *Im Stahlgewitter*. It seems like the Anglo-Saxon tradition enabled the British soldiers to mentally pass over their sufferings in a totally different way from what happened to their German adversaries.

[4] Translation A.T. Murray, www.perseus.tufts.edu/hopper/text?doc=Perseus%3Atext%3A1999.01.0136%3Abook%3D13%3Acard%3D217.

For the greater part of the population, people had no interest in leaving home, and found existence in exile – forced or chosen by them – intolerable. Thus, the Middle Kingdom novel of Sinuhe presents an absolutely ideological image of Palestine where Sinuhe was forced to live for a while: A wild and barren country with a wild population.[5] That this period, the first half of the 2nd millennium BCE was the most wealthy of Palestine's history before the arrival of the Greeks is of no consequence for this Egyptian narrative.

But this does not mean that there was, in other parts of society, no interest in geography, and the will to remember geography was important, not only in later Greek and Roman tradition but certainly also in the imperial traditions of Mesopotamia and Egypt.

In Egypt the debate between two learned scribes about their respective knowledge of the geography and topography of Asia tells us that in this stratum of Egyptian society knowledge of the world was appreciated and considered to be of importance.[6] However, in the Babylonian tradition, Humbaba is the monster protecting admission to the Cedar Mountains where the gods live, a monster Gilgamesh and Enkidu set out to slay, the location of the Cedar Mountains of course being identified as in western Syria and especially Lebanon because of the tree mentioned in the legend.

One tradition seems different, and that right from the dawn of civilization: The military report and literature and art are based on such reports. The will to identify people and places can be found in Egyptian tradition with early testimonies like the Narmar plate, and multiplied by the annalistic literature and art in especially the Middle and the New Kingdom. When Ramesses II puts up his commemorative inscription of the campaign that led to the battle of Kadesh, it is followed by a pictorial illustration of the various phases of the campaign and a – for its time – quite detailed layout of the battlefield at Kadesh. For all posterity, it was the idea that learned people could read about the great deeds of the Pharaoh, and ordinary people wonder over the miracles carved into the pylons at Thebes celebrating the victory over the Hittites – well, the Hittites were not very impressed by Ramesses' propaganda. They probably believed that they were the victors, and therefore we also have the ironic letter from Hattusilis III to his friend Ramesses II: "Were you alone, really alone?" Probably a Hittite envoy to Thebes had seen the reliefs and reported home about them.[7]

---

[5] *ANET* 18–22.
[6] *ANET* 475–9.
[7] Edel, 1949, 195–212. On this Liverani, 2021, 123–134.

Most of the Assyrian war reports of the 1st millennium are known from royal annals. However, it was usual for Assyrian propaganda to be included in royal palaces as inscriptions carved into reliefs describing the king's marvellous exploits. The most famous among these is undoubtedly the reliefs from Sennacherib's palace depicting the conquest of Lachish, followed up by textual representation. Moreover, the place recorded here, Lachish, is so precisely depicted that it could almost serve as a guide for modern excavations. What is seen on the relief is what was found, especially the foundation of the siege ramp but also the layout of the city.

Other Assyrian reliefs describe the landscape through which the Assyrian army marched, not as an adventurous and dangerous landscape but rather as a landscape consisting of mountains and woodlands. To the Assyrians, as earlier the Egyptians, the will to explore the world was certainly present, and it is not a coincidence that an Assyrian king, when he reached the Mediterranean, travelled on the Mediterranean.[8]

In order to preserve geographical knowledge as *lieux de mémoire*, conquerors throughout Antiquity put up memorials in the form of inscriptions, most often accompanied by pictorial representations, or steles of various forms.[9]

In the classical tradition, among the literature preserved from ancient times, we find a number of important geographical works, or works with important geographical information, most notably the geography of Strabo (63 BCE–23 CE), the natural history of Pliny (the older) (23–79 CE), and the description of Greece by Pausanias (c. 80–110 CE). This is not the occasion to go into details. They are very different in character and ambition but this is of no importance here. The important fact is that they are preserved to this day, Pliny's *Naturalis Historia* being the largest work from Antiquity to have survived in its entirety, although Pausanias and Strabon probably only survived in a single manuscript from the Byzantine Empire. Without a readership, there would have been no chance of survival. And when these authors wrote about the world in which they travelled, they were serious about what they were doing.

Thus Pausanias opens his description of Attica in this way:

---

[8] Tiglath-Pileser I (1114–1076). Text translated in *ANET*² 274–5.

[9] Thus, the UNESCO Memory of the World Site at Nahr el-Kalb includes at least twenty inscriptions ranging from Ramses II to modern times, including also Assyrian, Babylonian, as well as Greek and Roman carvings. Cf. also for a recent review the article, "Stelae of Nahr el-Kalb", Wikipedia https://en.wikipedia.org/wiki/Stelae_of_Nahr_el-Kalb.

On the Greek mainland facing the Cyclades Islands and the Aegean Sea the Sunium promontory stands out from the Attic land. When you have rounded the promontory you see a harbor and a temple to Athena of Sunium on the peak of the promontory. Farther on is Laurium, where once the Athenians had silver mines, and a small uninhabited island called the Island of Patroclus. For a fortification was built on it and a palisade constructed by Patroclus, who was admiral in command of the Egyptian men-of-war sent by Ptolemy, son of Ptolemy, son of Lagus, to help the Athenians, when Antigonus, son of Demetrius, was ravaging their country, which he had invaded with an army, and at the same time was blockading them by sea with a fleet.[10]

Precise and meticulous if anything.
And Strabo: from the beginning of the tenth book of his *Geography*:

Since Euboea lies parallel to the whole of the coast from Sunium to Thessaly, with the exception of the ends on either side, it would be appropriate to connect my description of the island with that of the parts already described before passing on to Aetolia and Acarnania, which are the remaining parts of Europe to be described. 2. In its length, then, the island extends parallel to the coast for a distance of about one thousand two hundred stadia from Cenaeum to Geraestus, but its breadth is irregular and generally only about one hundred and fifty stadia.[11]

Common to ancient geographers is the way they use stories and tales from the past, as illustrations. They were, in intention, not very different from modern Baedekers – tourist guides.

To the educated person in Hellenistic-Roman times, the knowledge and interest in geography was evident and required. Thus, to turn to military matters, a general like Caesar does not jump into his war reports but introduces them with a description of the topography of Gaul (also worth quoting):

All Gaul is divided into three parts, one of which the Belgae inhabit, the Aquitani another, those who in their own language are called Celts, in our Gauls, the third. All these differ from each other in language, customs and laws. The river Garonne separates the Gauls from

---

[10] Pausanias, Ἑλλάδος Περιήγησις, 1.1.1. Translation by W.H.S. Jones (Loeb Classical Library). Online: www.theoi.com/Text/Pausanias1A.html.
[11] Strabo, Γεωγραφικά, X 1–2. Translation H.L. Jones (Loeb Classical Library).

the Aquitani; the Marne and the Seine separate them from the Belgae. Of all these, the Belgae are the bravest, because they are furthest from the civilization and refinement of [our] Province, and merchants least frequently resort to them, and import those things which tend to effeminate the mind; and they are the nearest to the Germans, who dwell beyond the Rhine, with whom they are continually waging war; for which reason the Helvetii also surpass the rest of the Gauls in valor, as they contend with the Germans in almost daily battles, when they either repel them from their own territories, or themselves wage war on their frontiers. One part of these, which it has been said that the Gauls occupy, takes its beginning at the river Rhone; it is bounded by the river Garonne, the ocean and the territories of the Belgae; it borders, too, on the side of the Sequani and the Helvetii, upon the river Rhine, and stretches toward the north. The Belgae rises from the extreme frontier of Gaul, extend to the lower part of the river Rhine; and look toward the north and the rising sun. Aquitania extends from the river Garonne to the Pyrenaean mountains and to that part of the ocean which is near Spain: it looks between the setting of the sun, and the north star.[12]

The Romans were definitely interested in geography and topography, and Tacitus' *Germania* is highly relevant in this connection. In this work Tacitus tries to describe the German tribes as differently from the Romans as possible. The political and military upper class would all have had a comprehensive knowledge of the world and know the geographical peculiarities of the various provinces of the Roman Empire.[13]

Now what about the Old Testament? Will we find a similar interest in geography as a provider of *loci memoriae*, as the Latin term behind Nora's *lieux de mémoire* must be rendered – although definitely not with the same meaning?[14] To be honest, we find nothing like the classical tradition of geography in the Old Testament, neither the curiosity displayed by Mesopotamian and Egyptian artists in depicting foreign languages. We have evidently little interest in ethnic peculiarities in biblical writings, nothing similar to, say the reliefs in Queen Hashepsut's mortuary temple at Dayr el-Bahri in Upper Egypt, where we have a pictorial representation of what an Egyptian

---

[12] Caesar, *Bellum Gallicum* I.1. Translation W.A. MacDevitt. Online: www.gutenberg.org/cache/epub/10657/pg10657-images.html.
[13] For a most inspiring study of Tacitus' Germania: Krebs, 2011.
[14] Classical *loci memoriae* form a kind of "to-do list", to be used by the orator during his speech whereas Nora's *lieux de memoire* are places to be remembered, memorials.

expedition was met with when they arrived at Punt, somewhere along the northeastern coast of Africa. Here we find particularities about the population, and especially the extremely fat Queen of Punt is difficult to forget, and also of the flora and fauna, specimens of which were brought back to Egypt.

It is not that biblical writers did not know about the world or were unfamiliar with arranging its population into different groups, as evidenced by Genesis 10. There are also quite a significant number of Egyptian themes in the story of Joseph, but apart from some very general knowledge of the geography, especially the presence of the Nile in Egypt and the Euphrates and Tigris in Mesopotamia, little time and space is wasted on a detailed description of the landscape and the topography of places visited by the Israelites. And definitely no systematic description of foreign people and places. Maybe the best examples of such depictions of foreigners can be found in prophetic tirades against the foreign nations, and the hatred against the Philistines is pronounced, but they were also uncircumcized.

Let's see how it works in the Pentateuch, including the story of the patriarchs and the exodus followed by the migration through the desert.

The geographical information opens in Genesis 11–12 when Abraham's family decides to go to the land of Canaan, and moves from Ur to Harran. The only special information provided is that they came from Ur in Chaldea. In Harran Abraham (still Abram) is told by Yahweh to go on to Canaan. Then we are shortly informed about Abraham's age, and the people who went with him, and the journey begins. However, the journey is over before it begins: Abraham departs from Harran, and enters Canaan. It is a journey of about 500 kilometres or more taking the party through many important stations and different landscapes. The author of Genesis 12 has no interest in all of this. In Canaan things change a little, as Abraham continues to Shechem and its sanctuary and to Bethel to pitch his tent between Bethel and Ai. The distance is a few kilometres, and it is not exactly a mountainous area as noted by Genesis 12: We are in the mountains but this spot is rather flat and easy to travel. I know, I walked the tour years ago, when the local peasants were harvesting olives. It didn't take long. Abraham, however, continues to travel all the way to the Negev.

From the Negev, Abraham travels to Egypt, and when he returns from Egypt, he returns to the place between Bethel and Ai already mentioned. Here his family splits, and Lot goes on to Sodom. It goes on like this for the rest of the Abraham story, where his residence is at Mamre near Hebron. A few other places are mentioned like Gerar and the country of Moriah but we cannot talk about geographical memory, although a place of memory is established when Abraham buries Sarah in Hebron.

In all of these stories, as in the following Isaac and Jacob stories, a few place names are mentioned again and again, especially Bethel, but nothing like a topological layout of the country of Canaan is offered. Geographical memory seems not to have interested those who wrote these stories.

We get very much the same picture moving on to the story of Israel in Egypt. Naturally there are details about living along the Nile, but no further details are related. When Moses is forced to leave Egypt, he goes to Midian, but the lack of geographical precision does not help in identifying this place. When it comes to the Israelites escaping from Egypt, they pass the *Yam Suph* without any further attempt to identify the place. Travellers have ever since tried to locate the exact place where God split the waters. And moving into the Sinai, and arriving at the mountain of God, no further details are provided. Thus, the description of the place of revelation has been debated for a very long time, at Jebel Mousa and the monastery in southern Sinai, or at Kadesh Barnea in northern Sinai. The Old Testament leaves us in the dark.

Basically, what we meet here is characteristic of the attitude to geographical information in the Old Testament. There is no outspoken interest in the real geography of the world of the Old Testament writers. They know some names, and some general characteristics of the land of Israel, but nothing detailed, and they produce nothing like an exhaustive description of the country. We might even say that people in the Old Testament are travelling in a country of literature, and not in the real world of the Middle East. I have already described the scene of Abraham leaving Harran and in the next moment to enter Canaan as on a stage in a theatre where Abraham leaves one part of the stage to walk through the door to the next stage. What happens between the two stages is immaterial and therefore of no interest to the authors of these stories. It might be correct to say that the people who wrote such narratives as those found in the Old Testament were not interested in the real world; their universe was the world of narrative.

We can also say that the landscape is not really a part of the narrative. It is always embedded in stories and with an ideological meaning not far away from the use of the landscape in folk stories and sagas. It is not that the authors were not learned people. There are many indications of well-educated people behind these narratives, but they were certainly not interested in the landscape as a series of places of memory. The stages, say in the Sinai narratives, are not presented as mere snapshots, but because they, in one way or the other, explain what is going on in the progress of the story. Thus, places like Massah and Meribah are not identified as places in their landscape. They are places in the narrative and play a role there. Even Jerusalem is not a place in the geography of Palestine; it is a place chosen by God. When revisited, for instance, by Ezekiel in a dream, it is precisely in a dream and has nothing to do with any Jerusalem of this world.

I dealt with the theme of Jerusalem as a place of memory, "Jerusalem in my heart" in a lecture at these meetings a couple of years ago, and will not repeat what I said there.[15] I will move on to my conclusion, which brings the study of the concept of geography as a study of places of memory in line with the general thrust of what I have been writing and saying about cultural memory over the last few years: In ancient times cultural memory was the memory of the few intellectuals who could write and read. It was not the memory of ordinary people, forever lost. The cultural memory was referring to a constructed world, as a matter of fact the constructed world of biblical Israel.

Years ago, I was attacked because of my seeing biblical Israel as a monstrous society, probably because of some shortcomings in American English, understanding "monstrous" as evil, whereas it in this connection it was only supposed to mean "weird", probably not of this world, a literary construction. However, just like the history of biblical Israel found in the Old Testament has only a peripheral relationship to the history of Palestine in the Late Bronze-Early Iron Age, the "geography" of the Old Testament has only a peripheral relationship to the topographical peculiarities of the ancient Near East.

---

[15] "If I forget you Jerusalem!" lecture at the EABS Meeting in Tartu 2010, included in this collection.

17 Israel and its Land

The study of the Old Testament moved from the modern into the postmodern age in a rather non-dramatic way as far as the reading and interpretation of texts is concerned. After all, it is only about different ways of reading texts, and in a postmodern environment we may say that every type of reading is acceptable as long as the method is consistent and meaningful. However, when we change from reading a text as literature to understanding it as a source for the study of the history seemingly included in the text in question, the situation is quite different. Thus, it is difficult to remember all the types of attacks launched in recent years in leading journals against the so-called new school of studies in the history of Israel. Here we often find emotional titles of the type: "Will the Real Israel Please Stand Up?"[1]

Such contributions to the discussion are often filled with pathos and are declamatory in style similar to the speeches held by lay preachers in a fundamentalistic, Christian environment, in the mission halls of the Lutheran Mission, or in tent revivals, but not in a debate between scholars. The "enemy" – because that is probably the right expression when we see polemics of this character – are the members of a group of scholars who go under different names such as "the Copenhagen School", "the revisionist school", or (in Germany) "Die Vierbande". This group includes scholars employed at the University of Copenhagen but also in Sheffield University and Stirling University in Scotland.[2] A North American archaeologist thus describes this group of revisionist scholars as misled by "false assumptions, oversimplifications, undocumented assertions and contradictions – not to forget ideological bias" (Dever, 1996, 36).

It is obvious that an overreaction like this should not be seen as a fair and scholarly evaluation of new directions within the study of the Old Testament. There is no doubt that other non-scholarly motives must lie behind them, and living in a postmodern age, it is self-evident that I personally do not believe

---

[1] Dever, 1995.
[2] I have outlined the history of this "Copenhagen School" in Lemche, 1994. ET in this collection. Cf. also the critical commentary in Høgenhaven, 1996. P.R. Davies puts forward his position in Davies, 1992 and Whitelam in Whitelam, 1996 (cf. on this Lemche, 1996b).

in "pure scholarship" – the ivory towers of the past. Accordingly, I intend in this article to look for the motives and reasons behind such unpremeditated attacks as we have seen in recent years and in this connection the question of Israel's relationship to its land is a good place to start because recent scholarship does not only present a challenge to modern historical interpretation but certainly also to our idea of nationality. This scholarship has simply challenged two of the most highly regarded parts of the self-identification of the European and North American male population.

In the summer of 1995, I gave a lecture at a conference concerning Dead Sea Scrolls Studies in Copenhagen with the title "The Understanding of Society in the Old Testament and in the Dead Sea Scrolls" (Lemche, 1998e). In this lecture my argument was that while on the one hand the idea of society in a text like the Manual of Discipline was clearly sectarian, it is on the other hand also correct to stress that the idea of society as found in the Old Testament is not far away from the one in the Dead Sea Scrolls. In my lecture I took as my point of departure the description of the future society in Isa 4:1–6:

> In that day shall the branch of the LORD be beautiful and glorious, and the fruit of the earth *shall be* excellent and comely for them that are escaped of Israel.
>
> And it shall come to pass, *that he that is* left in Zion, and *he that* remaineth in Jerusalem, shall be called holy, *even* every one that is written among the living in Jerusalem:
>
> When the LORD shall have washed away the filth of the daughters of Zion, and shall have purged the blood of Jerusalem from the midst thereof by the spirit of judgment, and by the spirit of burning. And the LORD will create upon every dwelling place of mount Zion, and upon her assemblies, a cloud and smoke by day, and the shining of a flaming fire by night: for upon all the glory *shall be* a defence. And there shall be a tabernacle for a shadow in the daytime from the heat, and for a place of refuge, and for a covert from storm and from rain.

The description of a future society of holy people in Jerusalem must of course be seen from – to use conventional language – a post-exilic perspective, from the perspective of the society that came into being in and around Jerusalem in the Persian and Hellenistic periods. At the same time the description of pre-exilic society in the historical books as well as in prophetic literature is equally infested by a long series of characteristics which we should likewise consider sectarian – or should we cut the discussion short and simply call this society a sectarian one? Therefore, it is to be argued that the distance (if any at all) between the idea of society in the Old Testament as one selected by no other than God himself and whose constitution was given to it by the same God and in possession of a series of foundational myths of the kind present in almost every sectarian organization. It must, in this connection, be stressed that the description of Israelite society in the Old Testament has little in common with any society of this age.

The description of Israelite society in the Old Testament seems to be based on the notion of what constitutes a society, according to which a society is composed of people with a common origin – common blood – which only has one god – common religion – and is in possession of a certain country which only belongs to this people. In reality it is God's own country but he has given his chosen people the right to live in his land. This people is a holy people, whereas all other peoples are unholy and can expect nothing but annihilation in case they, like the Canaanites, dare to settle in God's country.

Now few people with an understanding of the notion of society in ancient times will be in disagreement with me when I characterize this definition of a people or nation as very close to the definition of what constitutes an *ethnos* in the Greek historian Herodotus' (5th century BCE) work.[3] According to Herodotus the reason for the Greek victory over the Persians was that all Greeks shared three things; blood, language, and religion. Because of this the Persians, in spite of all the treasures of the Persian Empire, were unable to bribe some of the Greek states and thereby create discord among the Greek states, because, at the end, the feeling of belonging to the same people would prevail over greed.

If we look at the criteria for what binds a people together in the Greek historian and among biblical authors it is remarkable that two of the three criteria are the same: Common blood and a common religion. In the Old Testament the third criteria in Herodotus, a common language, has been substituted by another, the country to which a people is bound. To the Greeks belonging to a people which already in Herodotus' day had spread all over the Mediterranean and was going to extend their culture to most of the then known world the idea that to be a Greek you must live in one specific country must have seemed absurd. Here language was much more important, something that connected all Greeks and was decisive for the identification of a person as Greek. A person who did not speak Greek was classified as a barbarian – and it must be remembered that the Greek word βάρβαρος simply meant "one who does not speak Greek".

---

[3] Book VIII, 144.

We have to confess that although language is not a direct part of the identification in the Old Testament of someone as "Israelite", the idea of the role of the language to separate nations is still not far away. According to the Old Testament, all people in the world began with one and the same language and only when God dispersed the nations in connection with the construction of the tower of Babel (Genesis 11) and God confounded their languages, making persons unable to understand other persons, could they do so no longer. In the biblical narrative this led to a separation that made it possible for God to select the ancestor of the specific people chosen to be his (Gen 12:1–9).[4] Still, it is correct to argue that we, in the Old Testament, never find anything similar to the Greek notion of the Greek language as a cultural separator between what is Greek and what barbarian. In the Old Testament it is an exception that language is used to separate people of different origins. A well-known exception is the plea to the Assyrian general Rabshake to speak Aramaic and not Judahite (2 Kings 18:26) as the leaders of Jerusalem were able to understand Aramaic, which was unknown to ordinary inhabitants.

In 1964 in a well-known modern definition of ethnic coherence, the North American anthropologist Raoul Narroll presented four criteria as decisive (Narroll, 1964). According to Narroll an ethnic group

1. Is biologically able to reproduce itself
2. Shares cultural values and is able to express these culturally
3. Constitutes a unity of communication and interaction
4. Consists of a group of members who can identify themselves and are identifiable by others, i.e., forming a category that can be distinguished from other categories of the same species.

It is rather obvious that the description of an ethnic group concords very well with the classic definition of Homer. We may indeed say that the two definitions are almost one and the same. The first criterion mentioned by Narroll, the ability of biological reproduction, sounds like a modern paraphrase of the ancient idea of common blood. A modern scholar like Narroll will of course not talk about a people going back to an apical ancestor in the physical sense, as is the case in the Old Testament where Abraham plays the role as the father of all Israelites. Instead, he blurs the discussion with enigmatic

---

[4] Herodotus shared this idea of an original oldest language. Thus, he tells a story about how it was decided which was the oldest language in the world. Two newly born children were isolated in order to investigate in which language they choose to communicate, and the result was Phrygian (Book II.4).

language about biological reproduction. Thus, the idea of a common blood is definitely part of the definition of ethnicity in the classical sources as well as that expressed by a modern anthropologist. It is to be assumed that an author from the past would not have wondered over Narroll's use of words. We might thus think of Pliny the Elder's remarks about the community at the Dead Sea Scrolls which was, according to his sources, a very special society that was able to reproduce itself without breeding their own children.[5]

Narroll's second criterion deals with common cultural values. As I understand these criteria it sounds like a modern secularized paraphrase of Herodotus's talk about common religious practices, since religion in antiquity had a much broader meaning and was almost synonymous with culture, a concept that was, on the other hand, meaningless to ancient people. An ethnic group thus consists of human beings sharing common cultural values, i.e., religion, and also the consequences of this shared religion. Thus, the membership of the community of believers was, according to the Old Testament, marked out with a specific bodily phenomenon, i.e., circumcision, something every male member of the group had to go through, but members were also bound by common legislation going back to Moses, the founder of the society. In this way the definition in the Old Testament of the people of Israel is more or less the same as that of Herodotus – and of Narroll.

Narroll's third criterion, which deals with communication and interaction, is another paraphrase of Herodotus who speaks about a common language as a characteristic for a specific ethnic group. Its importance as an ethnic marker for the Israelites was, according to the Old Testament, peripheral. The fourth criterion is more important because it stresses that an ethnic group should be able to determine who is a member of the group and who is not.

It is arguable that this part of the definition is totally "biblical" because according to the Old Testament it was a decisive part of the definition of the people of Israel that it was chosen by God. We may say that the first three parts of the definition of ethnicity following these four criteria, blood, language, and religion, are subordinated to the fourth because it is the blood, language, and religion characterizing the members of the group which make it possible for the members themselves to claim their membership in the group as well as for others to realize that this is a special ethnic unit.

If it was not so, the situation might be the same as we find in the old story about the King of Akkad Naram-Sin (23rd century BCE) and his struggle against the Umannanda, the horde from the north who had invaded Naram-Sin's kingdom. According to the legend, Naram-Sin sends an envoy who shall

---

[5] Plinius, *Historia naturalis* 5, 73.

pierce one of the enemies to find out whether they are human or demon. The report from the envoy says that the enemy was bleeding which was a great relief because in that case he was human and could be fought.[6]

It is common ground for all biblical authors of historical literature in the Old Testament, from Genesis to the Books of Ezra and Nehemiah, that it is most important to be able to distinguish between Israelites and other nations. If an Israelite married a Canaanite woman or simply any foreign wife it would, as a consequence, mean that the categories of pure and impure would be mixed. Therefore, such marriages were forbidden to Israelites.[7] The theme comes up for the first time with the instruction of Abraham to his servant that he should travel to Haran to find a wife for Isaac his son in order that Isaac should not marry a Canaanite woman (Gen 24:3). The theme continues with Esau, who marries Hittite women belonging to the early inhabitants of Canaan – to the regret of Isaac and Rebecca (Gen 26:34). Isaac and Rebecca therefore send their second son, Jacob, to Haran that he should not repeat his brother's mistake (Gen 27:46).

The issue of how to deal with the Canaanites is taken up several times in the Books of Exodus and Numbers – perhaps most radically in Exodus 23 where it is said that the angel of God will travel in advance of the Israelites and annihilate the nations of Canaan, the Canaanites, the Hittites, etc. It is at the same time strictly forbidden to Israelites to mix with the Canaanites and participate in Canaanite religion. The theme can be found in the books of the Old Testament which follow Exodus and Numbers and is of course the governing theme of the Book of Joshua in the story of the Israelite conquest of Canaan (having almost as its theme that the only good Canaanite is a dead Canaanite). The score with the Canaanites is finally settled when Ezra forces those among his fellow countrymen to divorce their foreign wives (Ezra 10).

Now some may ask why we need this discussion. After all the idea of ethnicity in the Old Testament squares well with a modern definition such as that of Narroll. Wouldn't it be possible to argue that the definition of ethnicity in the Old Testament is close to being modern although the wording is of course somewhat old-fashioned and non-scientific? It would be possible to answer the question largely in the affirmative, but then we have to ask if

---

[6] Legends concerning Naram-Sin have been handed down in a number of Akkadian and one Hittite version. The Hittite version was published by Gurney, 1955, and the Akkadian by Güterbock, 1938. The various editions have been translated in Foster, 1993, 257–69. The passage referred to here can be found in its Neo-Assyrian version in Foster, 1993, 265.

[7] Although it must be admitted that in the Old Testament – as always – there are exceptions such as Ruth, a Moabite woman who is praised in the Book of Ruth as the ancestress of David's house.

Narroll's definition is still of any value. It is today quite elementary really to argue that a definition of ethnicity like Narroll's is too rigid and lacks flexibility, moreover most present sociologists would prefer to substitute such definitions with more dynamic explanations, as they see the concept of ethnicity as something that covers a phenomenon that is constantly changing as human society develops.[8]

It is important to understand that a definition of ethnicity such as that found in Narroll's study is a modern definition because it belongs to an understanding of society which originates in the modern world, a world which, to those acquainted with the development of European thinking, is hardly more than a couple of hundred years old, although it has to be admitted that it was prepared for by intellectual development since the Renaissance and especially the Enlightenment. If we look for the preconditions for the modern age and its idea of ethnicity, we have to put stress on two interconnected ideas, both with roots that carry them back to Antiquity. The first idea is about history, the second about the nation. Together these two ideas, in a most dramatic way, change the viewpoint in preceding periods on ethnicity and in such a way that it became more and more popular among sociologists to see ethnicity as something that is different from nationality, which to some degree is an incorrect opinion. Nationality and ethnicity are indeed two facets of the same complex of ideas connected to the separation of so-called discrete groups, and it is maintained among the members of a certain group.

If we open with the idea of the ownership of land, it was, before the French Revolution, principally a question of who owned the land. When saying this I have in mind the situation in Europe, where different areas belonged to different princes (which was also the case of the colonies in North America and in other parts of the world) who had divided the world between them. The Enlightenment was, at the same time, also a time of absolutism throughout Europe (although never in England) and in such forms that would remind you of gigantic patronage systems where the king decided everything.[9] The king

---

[8] Breaking new ground in the discussion of ethnicity is the definition published by Fredrik Barth (1928–2016) in his introduction to the volume he edited, *Ethnic Groups and Boundaries* (Barth, 1969), 9–37. For a modern assessment of the theses of Barth, cf. Eriksen and Jakoubek, 2019.

[9] A patronage system is a system where the members of a society are divided into two groups, "those who have" and "those who have not", making the last group dependent of the first one as clients are dependent on their patrons. This definition is more open than the normal definitions of patronage which limit the patronage system to a specific area (the "Mediterranean family system") understood to form a substructure within a larger society such as a state. The definition does not pay attention to the oft maintained assertion that

had absolute power and could do with his country as it seemed fit to him. He could give it away as a gift or lose it in futile wars against his colleagues. Thus in 1468 King Christian I of Denmark pledged the Orkney Islands in order to get money for the dowry for his daughter who married into the Scottish royal house. It remained in the possession of the Scottish royal family at first as a pledge but a hundred years later it was definitely a Scottish possession and remained so until England took over Scotland.

This attitude to the possession of land changed around 1800 when the "people" – which people we are speaking of does not matter – assumed power after the French Revolution. Now it is well known that the "people" consisted of the well-educated and wealthy citizens of the European cities and it was members of this social group which first formulated the idea of the nation based on its knowledge of the classical definitions of ethnicity. Later they forced their ideas on the general populace, creating national unities and especially ethnic homogeneity even where such had never existed before. Among the most important means to teach European peasants that they belonged to national states was *history*, which aimed at creating a sense of unity based on the notion of a common destiny for all members of the nation: We all belong together because we always belonged together – we are, so to speak, one family. Another notion related to the first and just as important was the idea of a common land that exclusively belonged to one nation and no other for historical reasons. By propagating such ideas, the spiritual leaders of Germany succeeded, in the Romantic Period, to meld together the often quite isolated populations of the many German minor states to become one unified nation, which reached its final objective with the establishment of the German Empire in Versailles in 1871, although such an empire had never existed before. The notion of the land and its inhabitants as the two constitutive elements in one and the same nation became so common among the different peoples of Europe that we instinctively reacted against any infringement of our national territories not only in the present but also in the past. In its worst form the idea of the nation linked to its land developed into the "Blut und Boden" ideology which became one of the main pillars of the ideology of the Third Reich of a Germany that embraced every German-speaking person in Europe. Of course, this ideology led to both racism and ethnic cleansing. These ideas are today so well established that the once so splendid and idealistic plans for a united Europe may soon be a matter of the past.

---

patronage systems are fundamentally different from feudal systems such as those known from the European Middle Ages.

Now it is hardly a coincidence that the discipline "the history of Israel" originated in Germany in the 19th century, in the centre of fast-growing European nationalism. In this way it was German scholars who created the idea of a historical Israel, not as much as a reflection over the past as a projection of their own national aspirations. In this way the wanderings of the tribes of Israel through the desert to the cultivated land could be compared to the wanderings of German tribes when Antiquity developed into the dark ages of Europe, and the conquest of Palestine by Israelite tribes could be compared to Germanic tribes assuming power in central and northern Europe. Continuing along this line, it would be possible to argue that Martin Noth's famous thesis about the Israelite amphictyony as a union of twelve tribes supposed to have been in existence in the period of the Judges but dissolved as Israel changed from a tribal society into a kingdom[10] – soon to become an empire – constitutes a remarkable parallel to the way the union of German petty states was dissolved by Otto von Bismarck and incorporated into his German Empire. In this way the establishment of ancient Israel followed closely the development of German nationalism.

A further illustration of this development is how history evolved as a discipline in Central European universities in the course of the 19th century, which was in many respects a particularly German experience. Thus, it is hardly a coincidence that the greatest historian of his time was the German Leopold von Ranke (1795–1886) who also happened to be Bismarck's favourite author. The influence of von Ranke was enormous and he and his colleagues succeeded in solidifying the myth that history is principally about "the past as it really was" – *wie es eigentlich gewesen* – which became the slogan of positivistic historical research. This notion of history attracted almost every historian of the modern age (at least in Europe and North America) and is without doubt still a central idea in most recent historical research in spite of the challenge to positivistic history writing from other ideas of history. To put it briefly, the historians following the lead of von Ranke succeeded in turning the interest from a text telling stories about the past into a text about what was "really" going on in days of old – *wie es eigentlich gewesen*.

When the reactions to the new directions within the study of the history of Israel have been as violent as has been the case it is because of the realization

---

[10] Cf. Noth, 1930. I opposed Noth's hypothesis as early as 1972 (Lemche, 1972). This settlement with Noth's theory was – like all other similar opposition of the time – totally based on the premises of classic historical-critical research. From a historical point of view nothing supports Noth's hypothesis. The ironic fact is that it is possible to revitalize it as an ideological expression of Jewish nationality as found in the Old Testament.

that basic European ideas about history and the nation came under fire. This has little to do with the biblical text but instead involves the person who read the text. This means that if we look for a relevant answer to these reactions to the, in many ways, painful dissolution of Israelite history as related by the Old Testament, we should begin with ourselves and try to understand who we are, meaning the circle of persons who created and perpetuated the idea of ancient Israel on the basis of a specific literary theory, i.e., European and North American scholars who grew up within the European tradition.

Postmodernism includes a new way of thinking which embraces all corners of our civilization. It is not just an obsession with the present, a strange conglomeration of confused ideas among a few scholars who are, for their part, far removed from the realities of this world. It is rather a consequence of the fact that we Europeans, over the last century – and especially after the end of the II World War – have been forced to realize that we are not the only people living on this planet. We are not the only ones to decide what is right and what wrong. On the contrary, the realization that there are other people living on this globe has led to the understanding that there are many different ideas, norms, and values. While most of the world has been forced to conform to our culture and our sets of ideas – we may call it acculturation – some among us have accepted parts of their traditions and cultural norms thereby accepting the notion that there are ways of understanding the world different from ours and that they may be both meaningful and coherent even if the logic may be different. I only need to refer to a classic study like Claude Lévi-Strauss' *The Savage Mind* (1966), which also deals with a logical way of reasoning that does not necessarily follows the principles formulated by Aristotle or Immanuel Kant.[11]

The new ways of handling biblical studies puts pressure on us because we are forced to realize that our adopted conceptions of the world of the Bible are only *our* conceptions and as such are only shared by biblical authors to the extent that their ideas have become part of our consciousness – which implies the idea of the land and the people which found its vulgar expression in the previously mentioned *Blut und Boden* ideology – and on this basis we created ancient Israel as a mirror image of our own past history as we understood it to have happened. When we now challenge this notion based on historical speculation, we are not attacking the integrity of the Bible but we are challenging the very way in which we understand ourselves, as we have been used to doing since 1800.

---

[11] The original edition is *La pensée sauvage* (Lévi-Strauss, 1962).

When Keith Whitelam, in his new book on the invention of ancient Israel,[12] argues that the invention owes its existence to pro-Jewish sentiments which led to the formation of the modern state of Israel, he is only partly right, because this conception of Israel did not originate because of political developments in the 20th century. I doubt that any leading German historian and philosopher from the formative period of the modern age nourished any particular concerns about the fate of the Jews in their own time. As already argued, these scholars created ancient Israel as a mirror image of their own world, but this world was neither identical with Israel nor with Palestine, it was another "Germany". It is, however, equally correct that the new conception of the relationship between a nation and its land (which is a central part in German tradition with dire consequences for the rest of Europe) influenced modern Judaism when the Jews of Europe assumed this ideology which, with Theodor Herzl as its spokesperson, became Zionism. From the moment when this transformation took place the study of the history of Israel as related by Old Testament historiographers assumed importance as a political programme for the future of the Jewish nation but in this case there is little to distinguish between the Jewish interpretation of history and our way of understanding the past.

Accordingly, I will end this discussion by repeating that if we intend to carry on a meaningful debate about the history of ancient Israel, we should first remember the ancient Greek adage:

Gnothi seauton – know yourself!

---

[12] Cf. footnote 3 above (p. 259).

18 Israel as an Ideological Construction

First of all, excuse me for offering (this lecture) in English. I got the commission too late to switch it to German. Although, in a gathering like the one today, I definitely prefer German as my vehicle of communication, I have to say that English has turned out to be, almost, my second native language. Sometimes I don't realize whether I am speaking Danish or English. A couple of years ago, when writing an article in Danish – it happens sometimes – I had to include a quote in English, and a few pages later discovered that I had, without realizing it, just switched to English, and had to retranslate my English into Danish – a strange experience, indeed.

This has something to do with the theme of this lecture or maybe better this introduction to a discussion as most of this discussion has, over the last twenty-five, if not forty, years, been in English. It is strange how a strong tradition of scholarship can end up as counterproductive as happened in especially the German Federal Republic. Here the spirits – perhaps we should say ghosts – of the fathers, from Julius Wellhausen to Martin Noth, continued to haunt the German academy, preventing it from becoming an integrated part in the daily conversation between, especially, Anglo-Saxon and Scandinavian scholars. We have sometimes missed the presence in the discussion of the learned classical German tradition, but while waiting for it to appear, our German has become more and more rusty. I am sorry to say that our students do not read it any longer if they are not forced to do so.

I am certain that a lot of the, from a scholarly point of view, often rather naïve discourse among North American scholars would have been improved immensely if it had been up to the standards of the traditional continental European scholarly discussion. We might even, a long time ago, have gotten rid of the very emotional part of the discussion, a scholarly style that seems to borrow more from the habits of political demagogues than from a proper scientific argument.

Now, having just published a piece on "virtual history" – the so-called "what if"-history (Lemche, 1999b), I could of course add that if Bern Jørg Diebner had published in English, and if he had behaved more like an academic scholar instead of like a man screaming out his gospel in the gutters of Heidelberg, German scholarship might have been far ahead of everything else in contemporary Old Testament scholarship. It is hardly wrong to say that the message – the gospel – of Diebner's *Dielheimer Blätter,* if handled properly, would have had an early and lasting impact on the contemporary discussion. Now all he can hope for is a footnote in the history of scholarship. And not even that is certain if the example of Maurice Vernes has a lesson to teach to posterity.[1]

This has to do with the theme, as it shows how important Israel is as an ideological construct among people of the modern world. This is the ironic part. Because of its place in the literature of the Old Testament, the Israel of the Bible has had an unparalleled impact on the Western mind. Every person has formed an image of this Israel in his or her own mind, based on the narrative in the Bible. This ideological image has not only produced ideologically motivated political repercussions in the history of our civilization, it has certainly also prevented any chance of an objective interest in the subject as such. This special quality of biblical studies was never so evident as in that part of our intellectual history that was characterized as centred on positivistic, i.e. objective analytical research.

I have sometimes phrased it thusly: if you look into the inside of even the most critical biblical scholar, you will find a fundamentalist. Even the most articulate scholar who claims no interest in theology but wants to study the Bible in an unbiased way – like my old friend in Sheffield, Philip R. Davies – will have produced scholarship that is clearly theological not only in outline but in essence. If in doubt, you may consult Philip Davies' book from 1995, *Whose Bible Is It Anyway?* Personally, I may have myself entertained the same ideas of religiously independent scholarship as Philip Davies. Years ago Fred Cryer shot that idea to pieces when he, after having returned from Germany, made the prediction that I would be the first Scandinavian scholar of our time to write a theology of the Old Testament. I haven't done so yet. I do not know if I will write such a book, but I do not any more deem it impossible that I might end up doing so.[2]

---

[1] As this present volume is being prepared, we are trying to set things right by publishing a volume of his articles in the Copenhagen International Seminar Series: Diebner, 2024. Maurice Vernes (1845-1923) was a French biblical scholar who dated the books of the Old Testament very late, and for that reason was relegated to oblivion, at least by German and Scandinavian scholars, which did not prevent him from having a rather important career, including years as vice-chancellor at the École pratique des hautes etudes. His most important published work: Perhaps *Précis d'histoire juive dépuis les origines jusqu'à l'époque persane* (Vernes, 1889).

[2] See, however, also Lemche, 2008c, 255-392.

Precisely because of modern human beings' ideological obsession with the Bible we have been prevented from seeing the images of the Bible as ideological constructs themselves. Brought up within the Christian tradition of reading the Bible, we have remained within this tradition without being able to liberate ourselves from it. As John Strange said to his class when I was a student, "we have all been brainwashed by the Deuteronomists", implying that we have never been able to get rid of the ideological framework produced by the Deuteronomists. Even today we as scholars, for the most part, share the ideology of the Deuteronomistic – and biblical literature in general. It is still basically the framework within which we operate.

The present "minimalist-maximalist" controversy has a lot to do with this. I know that this distinction is not only partially misleading, politically intended (in the States, "minimal" is a negative word, "maximal" its positive counterpart), it also obscures the real issues of the discussion. However, the way the "minimalists" – more or less neutrally called "the Copenhagen School" – have been attacked shows that the matter is ideological and political more than directed against their actual scholarship.[3]

A couple of years ago, William G. Dever, in a public lecture, attacked us as not only as being anti-Bible (anti-Jewish was implied) but a danger to Western civilization. Some among our number became very upset by this characterization but in some way Dever is right. We can certainly be seen as endangering *his* Western civilization, which is the world of positivistic scholarship that was characteristic of the modern world.[4]

I have discussed this extensively in one of my recent books, *The Israelites in History and Tradition*, which is of course a kind of continuation of my *The Canaanites and Their Land: The Tradition of the Canaanites*, just republished in its second edition. One of the theses of *The Israelites in History and Tradition* is that it was not the Old Testament that changed, it was the reading of the Old Testament that changed in a radical way during the period of the Enlightenment and in the Romantic – i.e., modern – era. Nowhere do I find a better example of what happened than when we compare Luther's and Karl David Ilgen's readings of Num 24:24. In the wording of the Revised English Bible:

---

[3] Now, finally about twenty years after this lecture was put together, I got the opportunity during the lock-down caused by the Covid-19 epidemic to return to a project which I discussed with Philip Davies in Copenhagen in 2003: *Back to Reason: Minimalism in Biblical Studies* (Lemche, 2022).

[4] Further on this "debate": *Back to Reason*, 15–40, a paragraph with the header "Let the War Begin!".

Invaders from the region of Kittim?
They will lay waste Ashur; they will lay Eber waste:
he too will perish utterly.

In a marginal note of his *Die gantze Heilige Schrifft Deudsch* (1545), Luther writes:

> (Chittim) sind die aus Europa / Als der grosse Alexander und Römer / welche auch zu letzt untergehen. Vnd zeigt hie die Weissagung / das alle Königsreiche auff Erden eins nach dem andern vntergehen müssen / neben dem volck Jsrael / welchs ewig bleibet / vmb Christus willen.

In Ilgen's version it becomes:

> Man könnte mit einiger Wahrscheinlichkeit annehmen, daß der Pentateuch seine gegenwärtige Gestalt nicht vor der Zeit der Makkabäer erhalten habe, denn es sind Spuren eines solch späten Zeitalters darinnen. Die auffällendsten Stellen sind Deut. 28,68, wo von der Verpflanzung nach Egypten geredet wird; und Numer. 24,24, wo von den Macedoniern geredet wird, daß sie das Assyrische Reich zerstören würden, sie aber würden auch selbst unterkommen.

Luther sees the prophecy of Balaam to be exactly what it pretends to be, a prophecy; and he has no problem accepting the text as it is written. Ilgen, living at the very beginning of modern scholarship, simply accepts Luther's reading and uses it for his own dating of the Pentateuch: Post Alexander the Great. The modern reading of the Old Testament changed the interpretation of it but remained loyal to the tradition. Luther speaks about a prophecy, Ilgen about a *vaticinium ex eventu*.[5]

Somehow this "reduction" has been characteristic of the modern tradition of interpreting the Bible and has resulted in what I have several times, and in many places, characterized as a "rationalistic paraphrase" of the Old Testament narrative. By "rationalistic paraphrase" I mean the kind of reading that removes the supernatural from the narrative and solves problems in the narrative by connecting it to historical events, making the historical referent of the narrative the most important object of the study of the Old Testament narrative.

---

[5] Cf. Seidel, 1993, 173.

As a consequence, history became the primary subject of study. This is very obvious when we examine the development of biblical scholarship between, say 1800 and 1970. In the very centre of this scholarship we find interest in ancient Israel – simply the historical referent of the historical narrative in the Old Testament. The tendency was just so bold when it came to religion, and we may see much of the scholarship of the *Religionsgeschichtliche Schule* reflecting this, including especially the interpretation of Psalms as expressions of Israel's religion in Sigmund Mowinckel's work.[6]

Because the period in general was obsessed by the idea of producing objective scholarly results – something inherited from natural sciences in the tradition of Isaac Newton – the referent of the narrative, i.e. ancient Israel, was considered a historical fact that could be studied on the basis of narratives referring to this ancient Israel. A distinction could be made between false and true conclusions concerning this ancient Israel. Some of the theses were correct, some false.

However, all of this represented a transformation of textual evidence into the factual universe of the so-called real world. Although it would be wrong to say that there was no interest in the ideology of the narrative, it was an interest that was, in large part, limited to an interest in how the original written report (*wie es eigentlich gewesen*, as Leopold von Ranke put it), was corrupted by later interpretation.

All of this was made possible by an increasingly, should we say conservative, attitude when it came to the dating of the oldest part of the Old Testament. Because the opinion was that the narrative reflected real historical events, the origin of the narrative must be the historical event itself. If some of these events were old – even very old – the nucleus of the narrative relating this event must in principle be just as old. We could say, the older the text, the better.[7]

Although scholars, at least since the days of de Wette, that is since the beginning of the 19th century, had realized the problem of establishing such a

---

[6] Beginning with Mowinckel, 1916. The most important study belonging to his interests in the Psalms was undoubtedly his *Psalmenstudien I–VI* (reprint Mowinckel, 1966) and the more popular Mowinckel, 1951.

[7] This attitude becomes very clear when we read studies of the formation of the sources of the Pentateuch from the heyday of historical-critical studies where the value of the sources were calculated according to their dating: The principal source was undoubtedly the Yahwist, the greatest *and* oldest part, followed by the Elohist, which hardly reaches the intellectual level of the Yahwist. Not much interest was invested in the last source, the Priestly source dated to post-exilic times. It has been indicated that there definitely was a certain amount of anti-Judaism hiding here – if not worse.

close tie between a narrative and its historical referent, most scholars continued without much reflection "to go" for the historical nucleus. De Wette had, in his *Beiträge zur Einleitung in das Alte Testament* (1806–07), already renounced the idea that the patriarchs should be considered historical figures belonging to Israel's past.[8] Wellhausen continued this line of thinking by stating that we cannot write a nation's history before we have a nation,[9] and this attitude was subsequently inherited by many scholars, including Martin Noth, who placed the traditions of the patriarchs among the ideological content of his amphictyony.[10] In spite of the obvious, scholars both inside and outside of Germany – to a German-speaking audience I need only mention Horst Seebass, who has, to this very day, not given up the idea of a historical Abraham – continued to maintain the historicity of the patriarchs.[11] They continued to do so to such a degree that it was considered a revolution when both Thomas Thompson and John Van Seters, in the middle of the 1970s, reached the conclusion that there was no historical patriarchal age.[12] The narratives about the patriarchs reflect ideological sentiments belonging to a much later date. In Van Seters' version the Abraham tradition simply represents invented history. It is literature written with a purpose, and was never intended to report the past "as it was".

Well, sometimes the old duke – "il gattopardo" in Lampedusa's novel of the same name – is absolutely right: We need a revolution so that everything shall return to what it used to be! From a certain continental perspective it might seem that Thompson and Van Seters had invented gunpowder a second time. Still, it was considered a revolution and an attack on the integrity of the Old Testament.

The modern age had changed the Old Testament into a book about the remote past. Because it was still the Bible – or part of it – it must be true, and because truth in the modern age became the reality it really was, truth meant the historical truth. By challenging this truth, Old Testament scholars were disputing the truth of the Old Testament, thereby endangering the survival of this part of the Bible in the Christian tradition. Among Jewish circles matters were similar, yet at the same time also different because the Old Testament/ Hebrew Bible was used as a textbook for a political programme.

---

[8] Wette, 1971.
[9] Wellhausen, 1884, 10: "Die Geschichte eines Volkes last sich nicht über das Volk selber hinausführen, in eine Zeit, wo dasselbe noch gar nicht vorhanden war".
[10] Noth, 1966.
[11] H. Seebass, 1934–2015. Cf. Seebass, 1966.
[12] Thompson, 1974, Van Seters, 1975.

William G. Dever is therefore right: By challenging the historical truth of the Old Testament, modern Old Testament scholarship represents a danger to the Western world of the modern age. The question is, however, whether his modern Western world does still exist unbothered? In this connection this means: can we still believe that the epistemology of the modern age is valid when studying a subject like the Old Testament originating in a period that pre-dated the appearance of the modern worldview?

Although we may talk about a revolution in Old Testament studies, it is a revolution that originated firmly within the parameters of traditional historical-critical scholarship. I have already once in this lecture mentioned Bernd Jørg Diebner, who never understood that in order to make your message heard, you have to phrase it in such a way that people will want to listen to it. In his academic serenity he has neglected this and has therefore ended up in obscurity. Many other persons with a revolutionary message have neglected to play "according to the rules" and have suffered because of this. Although we apply the strategic approach of the greatest military thinker of the 20th century, Basil Liddell Hart,[13] that it is "the indirect attack" – in biblical studies this means that we should discuss the reason why a certain type of scholarship appears, and should not get involved in a detailed argument about single issues – we still have to at least pretend that we are following the rules of traditional scholarly discourse.

According to many scholars of the old generation, the ideology of ancient Israel as a nation and society that could be separated from its environment went back to the earliest time of Israel's presence in Canaan. In the German-speaking world Albrecht Alt and Martin Noth created the necessary conditions for such an early date of the ideological concept "Israel", in their amphictyony of the twelve tribes. In and among the circle of members of this organization, the tradition of Israel crystallized. In his Überlieferungsgeschichte *des Pentateuch*, Noth spoke about a series of themes that belonged to the *Grundbestand* of the early Israelite tradition.[14] These themes or traditions originated in Israel before the introduction of the Hebrew monarchy. They were expanded upon and united in a major historical discourse during the early period of the monarchy. Although rewritten, edited, and augmented as time went by, the essence of the message of the traditions remained the same. Although Noth may not have phrased it exactly in this way, we can say that the ideological content of the tradition about early Israel was that Israel

---

[13] Basil H. Liddell Hart (1895–1970), Cf. Hart, 1941.
[14] Cf. footnote 11 above (p. 273).

was, from its very beginning, the people of Yahweh, and Yahweh its God. The amphictyony was mostly but not exclusively a religious organization.

Now, as it happens, some theories become so popular that they have to break down some day. This, of course, also happened to the all-important idea about a sacral Israelite league of twelve times reaching back into the period of the Judges. A number of scholars – including this presenter – played their role in bringing down the amphichtyony.[15] It all happened on a traditional historical-critical stage and the methodology applied to the destruction of the amphictyony was exclusively historical-critical. Therefore, it was almost immediately accepted (apart from a few voices that still maintained the reality of the concept) that there never was an amphictyony.

It would have been a natural consequence of the demise of the amphictyony if scholars had joined in and claimed that it also meant the end of talk about Israel as an ideological concept reaching back before the introduction of the Hebrew monarchy. How might the scattered and unstructured Israelite society of the pre-monarchical period have been able to establish an identity without an organization claiming all twelve tribes constituting one *ethnos*?

I shall skip the part that has to do with the following restructuring of Israelite history – nowadays scholars belonging to my circle would probably prefer to call it Palestine's history. For the question today, the ideology of Israel as a construct this part of the historical investigation is very important. However, the question of the united Davidic-Solomonic monarchy has, in this connection, been of decisive importance.

It is obvious from the scholarship of the 1970s that there was no Israelite unity before the monarchy and accordingly no common Israelite ideology claiming Israel to be a nation of its own, easy to separate from other nations of the ancient world.

Even the Old Testament itself claims that the unity of the Israelite tribes ended with the ascension of Rehoboam and the division of the Israelite tribes into two independent states, Israel and Judah. Although some sort of "unity" was established after the Assyrian conquest of Samaria, it was a unity only obtained because one of the parts of ancient Israel had ceased to exist.

The final possibility for maintaining an ancient date for the Israelite ideology of the chosen people of the twelve tribes expounded by the historical narratives of the Old Testament must accordingly be the time of David and Solomon.

As is well known, the notion of a unified Israelite monarchy has recently become the centre of a heated discussion that has certainly not been limited

---

[15] Cf. further in Lemche, 2022, 62–83.

to the scholarly world but sometimes gets to the front page even of major daily newspapers. It is obvious that the issue of preserving the biblical image of this period is most important to scholars who want to support an early date of the notion of Israel in ancient times. It is equally obvious that this interest is more than ever mixed with religious and political ideologies. On one side it has been linked to the ideology of the Messiah – both the Christian or the Jewish – and on the other it is part of the quest for legitimacy of the modern polity of the state of Israel. Part of the official ideology of the modern state of Israel has been directly linked to the notion that there really was a major kingdom of David. A fine expression of this ideology is the huge tapestry in the Knesset in Jerusalem by Marc Chagall depicting scenes from the life of David.

As is becoming increasingly clear it is, from a strictly historical point of view, impossible to maintain the biblical impression of the 10th century BCE as the time of the great Jewish kingdom in Palestine. Studies of a very different orientation like the one by David Jamieson-Drake or by Michael Niemann as well as by the various members of the Tel Aviv School of Archaeology have effectively removed any chance of such an early Israelite empire.[16] We cannot prove that there never was a David in Jerusalem because we cannot prove nor disprove what we do not know. Often the cliché "an absence of evidence is not evidence of absence" is heard in this connection, as if it was an excuse for bringing forth a baseless argument. It is, however, certain that this David – if he ever lived – had little in common with the great king of "united Israel".

In my view, this effectively leaves out of consideration the ideology of Israel as found in the Old Testament such that it originated in ancient Palestine in the 10th century BCE. As a matter of fact, it makes it a rather hopeless affair to defend the idea that this Israel should reflect an existing historical reality. The ideology of the people of the twelve tribes belongs in a different context, and that context is not a historical one as far as it does not reflect the existence of a historical entity called Israel.

Although Israel was, in the Iron Age, a Palestinian state of some extent, it was short-lived – it existed, roughly, between 900 and 700 BCE and was in its time better known as "the House of Omri" (*Bit Ḫumriya*) or "Samarina".[17]

---

[16] Cf. further Niemann,1993, Jamieson-Drake, 1991.

[17] For a review of the evidence cf. Finkelstein, 2013. In recent times it has become quite acceptable to trace the northern kingdom back to affairs such as those reflected in the agenda of Labaya from Shechem in the Amarna Age. Contrary to Finkelstein I do not believe that the transfer of the tradition of this northern kingdom to Judah and Jerusalem after 722 BCE when the Assyrians eliminated the state of Israel but did not extinguish its population and probably not its traditions. As a matter of fact, it never happened, as the survival of the Samaritans and their traditions illustrate. The traditions of the Samarians

It never included all of Palestine, that is, the parts of Palestine reckoned to be "Israelite" by the authors of the historical narrative in the Old Testament. Furthermore, we do not know if this Israel ever included the territory of the state of Judah, a different political entity that probably only arose as a state and kingdom after 800 BCE. It can be imagined that there was some sort of Judaean dependency on Israel in the 9th century; Judah when it appears in contemporary sources only emerges in connection with the demise of the state of Israel, as if the Assyrians only reckoned that there was one more Palestinian state when they had settled matters with Israel. It is not likely that Judah was part of this Israel, as it or its territory did not share the fate of Israel. It survived for a few years as a quasi-independent fairly unimportant local polity and was almost wiped out two decades after the fall of Samaria when it tried to play an independent role in local Palestinian politics. After 700 BCE Judah was little more than an Assyrian puppet state.

The prerequisite for the emergence of the ideology of the Israelite nation of the twelve tribes is that there was no historical Israel. No historical Israel we know of ever resembled the Israel of the Old Testament, although of course Old Testament authors reckoned its territory to be part of their Israel. It is more likely that the ideology so far removed from any historical reality only arose when there was no Israel at all, when the only thing that remained was the tradition of Israel.

In simple terms, this means that as an ideological construct Israel cannot pre-date the exile. The story of ancient Israel as related in the Old Testament historiographers is in itself a reflection of the ideological construct created by the intellectual environment to which these writers belonged. We can discuss whether this environment can be identified with the community of the exiled people from Jerusalem during the exile in Babylon in the narrow meaning of the word, or it originated outside of Palestine and was later transferred to Palestine itself in the Persian period. We may also think of a development that predominantly belonged to the Hellenistic period. This leaves us – the scholars – with plenty of options for a continuous interesting discussion that will probably never end because we have few if any historical "anchors" that may support any fixed dating.

The content of the ideological construct is, however, rather obvious. I have written extensively about it in *The Israelites in History and Tradition*, and need not repeat my argument in this place. Basic to this construction is a classical, almost Greek understanding of what constitutes an *ethnos*; a common blood,

---

were more likely simply annexes to the Judean tradition as part of the settling of scores between Jerusalem and Samaria in Hellenistic times.

a common religion (the Greek meant "culture"), and a common language. The version found in the Old Testament is a common blood ("we are all sons of Abraham, Isaac and Jacob"), a common religion – needs no further comment – and a common land. Language is not an issue in the Old Testament as it was among the Greeks, probably because the people who shared the ideology of Israel spoke many languages. On the other hand, "land" became a major issue, probably because the question of possessing your own land dominated the outlook shared by the members of the circle that created the ideology of Israel, most likely because they did not possess a land of their own.

No nation can exist without a national myth. Recent times have witnessed several such national myths emerge, some of them with disastrous consequences. The biblical myth is told twice. Both versions are more or less identical: We were in the land but our fathers left the land for a foreign place. We had to free ourselves from foreign influence and move to the land of our fathers, to live there as a nation belonging to God. The first version is the exodus myth, the second the myth of the Babylonian exile, emptying the land of people, bringing them to a foreign place from which they were to repeat the conquest of the land of their fathers.

In this way the ideological construct of Israel involves a nation of "sons" in comparison to their "fathers", the former inhabitants of the Promised Land. The relationship between a "father" and his "son" shows that continuity exists between the Israel of the twelve tribes that existed once upon a time in the land of Canaan and the new society that shall re-enter and conquer the land of the fathers. The sons have, because they are sons of their fathers, every right to the land – a gift from their god – but they are freed from the accusations of having forsaken their god as their fathers did. Because of their criminal behaviour, the fathers brought upon themselves the anger of their god and were punished accordingly. Now the time of punishment is over, the fathers have died in exile, and the sons are ready to return to the country of their fathers a re-establish Israel as the kingdom of God.

For many years the myth of the exodus has, in the third world, constituted the ideological foundation of "liberation theology". It certainly had this quality when it was first formulated. I would say that it was invented – probably as an inversion of the traditional Egyptian tale about the expulsion of the Hyksos – exactly with the purpose of becoming a liberation myth. Paired with the myth of the exile, and of the empty land, it became a strong ideology that was invoked in connection with the emergence of the Jewish society and its religion most likely outside of Palestine sometime in the second half of the 1st millennium BCE.

Now, back to William G. Dever and his maximalist friends. In his eyes we, the "minimalists", constitute a threat to Western civilization. However, a proper appraisal of the scholarship of the so-called "minimalists" shows them to be "maximalists" in the sense that they try to read the narrative of the Old Testament without distinguishing between what is history and what invented story. We could just as well say that the "maximalists" are "minimalists", as they stay with the tiny fraction of the Old Testament that is indisputably historical and considers this fraction to form the most important part of biblical literature.

They have lost their case – although they do not yet know it – because they, as Gorbachov said to Honegger, were late to history. They stuck with an ideological construct called "positivistic scholarship" and they have not realized that the world moved on, that the intellectual climate changed from being modern to becoming "post-modern".

Postmodernism is a hydra with many heads. It is too often painted in only one colour – e.g. as the expression of a Derrida-like deconstruction of narrative. Postmodernism is the brainchild of the behavioural sciences, sociology, linguistics, psychology, and their demonstration of the importance of the human factor as an incalculable and ever-changing variable. In this way postmodernism represent a revival of an ancient philosophical discussion that reality is only perceived through human agents. Any perception of ancient Israel is a subjective perception. It is impossible to paint such a thing as an objective image of this Israel. If they want to discuss the historicity of ancient Israel, they will have to accept the consequences of the postmodern intellectual change that has again placed the human being in the centre and the perceived world on the periphery. If they do not follow this lead, their scholarship is methodologically obsolete.

By positing classical ideas about history, ethnicity, national identity, you name it, the "maximalists" – if we should continue to call them this, are representatives of a world that does not exist any longer and might not have been in existence for the last generation or two. We have endangered the Western world, i.e. William G. Dever's and his friends' modern world. But here we are only following a general trend in the intellectual development of humankind.

19 The Relevance of Social-critical Exegesis for Old Testament Theology

Before I start this lecture, I should like to thank Professor Snyman for his kind invitation to lecture here in this beautiful country, and to all my colleagues and especially my old friend (from the time when both of us were prettier, younger and brighter) Professor Hannes Olivier of Stellenbosch, who, alas, could not be here today. The visit to South Africa has been an overwhelming experience and I can only give you all my best wishes for a glorious future.

Now, what has sociology to do with Old Testament theology? In fact, what has sociology to do with the Old Testament? One of my colleagues once protested against the modern interest in sociology and especially in scientifically controlled sociology, at the same time arguing that as human beings we all know about society and are all able to make sociological statements thus understood. And here Old Testament scholars have neither been worse nor better than other people. Why therefore this special interest in sociology? Isn't there something perverse about such a phenomenon that suddenly seems to be on everybody's lips?

First of all, it should be recognized that sociology is at one and the same time many things, and that a certain uncertainty as to the content of this concept is surely felt in many circles. Sociology in *stricto sensu* as it is understood in my environment means the study of behavioural patterns in contemporary – mostly Western societies. The method applied would be based on field research including primarily interviews, and the collecting and reworking of such information which the interviews may have provided into a scientific hypothesis of behaviour.

However, in other traditions sociology has another or a broader definition, meaning largely the same as social anthropology (sometimes referred to as only "anthropology", which by the way in a theological environment is a dangerous term as we also use this word in a totally different way as the title of the study of human beings in a world ruled by God: Hans Walter Wolff's *Anthropologie des Alten Testaments* (Wolff, 1973) has, for example, nothing to do with social anthropology (he would probably not have understood the last-mentioned subject at all – and especially, he would hardly ever have been interested in knowing anything about it)) which also includes the study of so-called "primitive" – that is, in the wording of contemporary social anthropology, "traditional" – societies, often but not exclusively of the non-Western type. This kind of social anthropology will, as far as its methods are concerned, proceed along the same lines as plain sociology, in that the social anthropologist will also have to use interviews – now of persons belonging to a traditional society – in order to obtain the relevant information for his scientific analysis.

Then, again in the Northern European – partly German – tradition, social anthropology was in general not used as a term for such studies. We more often talk about "ethnography" or "ethnology", meaning very much the same thing as social anthropology, however, with a broader content than plain social anthropology because it, in contrast to much British and American social anthropology, also often contains information about material culture. You only have to compare a major study of nomads such as the one on the Tuaregs by the late Danish social anthropologist Johannes Nicolaisen (Nicolaisen, 1963) – one of the most comprehensive I know of – with British or American parallel studies of nomadic societies such as the British R.L. Tapper on the Shahsevan Nomads of Azerbaijan (Tapper, 1979), or the American W. Irons on Yomut Turkmen (Irons, 1968), to perceive the difference, because Nicolaisen's study contains large stretches devoted exclusively to tents, camel-breeding or the like, whereas such matters are conspicuous by their almost total absence from the other studies mentioned. Here, the interest is almost exclusively concentrated on social structure, and relations between the nomads and the outside world, that is, political affairs, and a fixed part of this tradition is to include a chapter called "Change" – not of camel-breeding methods, but of family systems or the like.

In recent times, the Anglo-Saxon way of doing social anthropology seems to have taken over in our universities, relegating the study of the material side of culture to the field of "cultural anthropology", thus severing the ties between a certain people's material and spiritual culture, and thereby perpetuating a fundamental misunderstanding that lies behind much anthropology: that these subjects can and should be divided, and that material culture may not be very interesting after all – we still very much speak of "primitive cultures"!

However, the diversification of social anthropology does not end here, for sociology and social anthropology is a huge field of study with an enormous diversification of methods and strategies. There are, in this way, enormous differences between the American cultural evolutionism propagated by scholars like Elman Service and Morton Fried, which in biblical studies have found support especially in the works of Norman Gottwald, and the British structural anthropology of, say, E.E. Evans-Pritchard and Meyer Fortes, in that the first-mentioned concentrate on broadly outlined explanations of cultural change and heuristic methodology (that is, the result is presented before the hypothesis as a kind of working hypothesis) while the second concentrates almost exclusively on single societies trying to combine various sectors of this society into a coherent structural unit that tends to be rather static. On top of this – just to mention a third variety – the so-called "processual anthropology", the top character of which may be the famous Norwegian social anthropologist Fredrik Barth, does not concentrate on either aspect, or rather seems more interested in either combining the other approaches or keeping them apart. Here the aim is to study a society as a dynamic entity, and life in a society as always developing into something different. These three kinds of social anthropology are only mentioned as examples. French structural anthropology of the sort of Claude Lévi-Strauss would make an equally interesting fourth way of doing sociology, either for its own sake or in combination with the British school, as is evident in the work of Edmund Leach.

So what? What help can Old Testament studies obtain from the huge and diverse field of social anthropology, and what kind of sociology should we speak about in this connection? The answer can only be very personal as it will depend not primarily – or so it seems, it may not be true – on decisions made in the field of Old Testament studies but rather in social anthropology.

To mention the last point first, if you belong to the school of cultural evolutionism, you will probably tend to make sweeping statements about culture and society, and thereby also about religion and theology. No doubt the contributions from such a general evolutionary theory could be of enormous importance to our field, maybe producing theological and historical works of the kind of William Foxwell Albright's famous *From the Stone Age to Christianity* (Albright, 1940), – which is certainly a macro-sociological critical interpretation of history as a theological project, and still worth reading not so much because of the learning contained in the book as in the general approach applied. Being right or wrong, Albright at least tried to *understand* culture and history as a subject of theology.

If you, however, rather tend to believe in the British more atomizing variety of anthropology, you will probably end up being more interested in establishing connections between belief and life in ancient Israel, thereby showing yourself to belong to some modern form of the old "Myth-and-Ritual School" – by the way hardly coincidentally a British tradition in biblical studies. That the theological results of such an approach could or should be important (although it is notoriously well-known that the members of the old Myth-and-Ritual School never produced anything that could be said to constitute an even remotely interesting theology of the Old Testament) is almost self-evident. They should have produced some kind of systematic theology based precisely on the combination of the myth, i.e. the beliefs, and the ritual, i.e. the social situation of the myth in the cult of a living society.

The third-mentioned variety, the processual school, should, in a modern so-called dynamic society, carry the day, as a dynamic understanding of ancient culture would also seem to recommend itself to our understanding of civilization. How it could be done along these lines has been shown in Rainer Albertz's recent magnificent opus on Israelite Religion (Albertz, 1992). In his "history" Albertz tries to trace the sociological situation of Israelite religion from the beginning of its existence to the Persian and Hellenistic Periods, thereby providing what you would call a sociological-critical commentary of Israel's religious life over a period of, say, 1,000 years – by no means an insignificant contribution, or so I would say – and by Albertz himself considered the new theology of the Old Testament – to replace the old idealistic ones of Von Rad and Eichrodt, just to mention two famous examples of the species.[1]

I have, on the other hand, recently raised severe objections to Albertz's use, not of sociology, but of history. It is obvious that his sociology is based on historical premises that would change his results in a fatal way should they show themselves to be false – which in my opinion is the case. Here, in this place, I will have to abstain from further addressing this problem. Some of you may already have heard my general lecture on "Introducing Old Testament Historiography", where my basic view on the history of Israel and on how to do a history of Israel was explained. The only thing I have time to include here (as we should also have time for some examples of what can be achieved by applying sociological methods) is simply that we, in my view, cannot reckon to possess in the Old Testament a source of Israelite history over a period of more than 1,000 years; the Old Testament being a very late blending of tradition and invention, probably belonging to the late Persian or even the Hellenistic period.[2]

According to this view, any sociological reconstruction of Israel's history and religion is about as valid as any contemporary more traditional analysis of the history of ancient Israel, which is hardly satisfying any more from a methodological *and* logical point of view.

---

[1] Von Rad, 1957–60, Eichrodt, 1933–35.
[2] On this preliminary: 1) the conclusions to Lemche, 1991a, and 2) my article Lemche, 1993a.

However, in spite of these remarks, I would consider a sociological-critical approach to be both valuable and necessary – although I am not sure that I have seen this stress of social-critical as opposed to historical-critical (?) analysis before. I shall devote the remaining part of this lecture to present you with some examples from our field where interesting results have been achieved – not always as foreseen by the author, but in practice.

Let me introduce the next section with a most interesting social-critical observation made by Albertz in the aforementioned book. In his description of pre-monarchic Israelite religion, Albertz stresses the understanding of God as a God of the family – that is, of the patriarchal religion. In the Old Testament this has been removed from its original social context – the family – and has been turned into some original form of religion. However, Albertz here sees a rather individualistic form of personal religion, representing the lower layer of the populace – but how it should represent pre-monarchical family religion fails to convince me – because that is a kind of historicism I find rather irrelevant. When Albertz continues he turns to the higher societal level, "the religion of the liberated larger group", that is the Exodus religion, or the religion of the Exodus group as he puts it. It is easily seen that his idea of liberation theology comes from Norman K. Gottwald (Gottwald, 1979). Albertz's analysis is, however, much clearer than Gottwald's and on top of this well in line with the classical German tradition of Albrecht Alt, Martin Noth, and Gerhard von Rad. His treatment of this subject is therefore superior to Gottwald's, but he makes the same basic historical mistakes, which is basing his reading of the Exodus narrative on a historically oriented and rationalistic paraphrase of the Hebrew text, which his sociological training should have warned him against. But this part of his analysis is shipwrecked because of his neglect of the issue of the social production of texts, which cannot disregard proper historical analysis in a more traditional sense, and which has shown this early part of Israel's history not to be history, but rather – fairy tales.

To me it seems as if Albertz is relying on a course of history that has been presented by the Old Testament writers, which are, however, so far removed from the historical realities of the ancient Palestinian world that it is hardly worth continuing this quest for an Exodus group via liberation theology. His historical reconstructions will have to be dismissed exactly as happened to Gottwald's when confronted by a less enthusiastic, however much sounder sociological and historical methodology, as I believe was the case in my dissertation on *Early Israel* (Lemche, 1985b), and in Thomas Thompson's *Early History of the Israelite People From the Written & Archaeological Sources* (Thompson, 1992).

Albertz's analysis of pre-state religion in ancient Israel ends not with this part – though we should let it rest here – except for one casual remark of his: this religion shows traces of being a sectarian religion. By this he means that just as the original bearers of the Old Testament tradition – i.e. in his view the Exodus religion – was a sectarian group in the Palestinian world and their religion reflected their socio-political role in Canaanite society. Be this as it may, since I am convinced that either the early Israelites themselves were Canaanites (which was my original interpretation) or that the concept of Canaan and Canaanites is an ideological concept which was introduced to create a difference between Jews and Palestinians in the Persian and Hellenistic period (which is the view I hold now) – there is no room for this notion of an Israelite pariah nation in Palestine in the Iron Age; this notion is an intrusion into this society of an ideology belonging to a far later stage of the history of the Jews.

Albertz's observation is, on the other hand, important, since seen as a solely sociological evaluation of the texts involved, Albertz's conclusion may be correct, i.e., that the Old Testament's idea of early Israelite religion may well reflect the religious expectations of a sectarian group. Then we have to address the question: When was Israel represented by a sectarian group? Before the days of the Hebrew kings? Hardly: nothing in the contemporary – mostly archaeological material remains – indicates that the villages in the highlands of Palestine (which Israel Finkelstein in a rather premature way dubbed "Israelite") (Finkelstein, 1988)[3] belonged to a sectarian society. In fact, remains relating to religion – burials, cult figurines etc. – generally indicate this society in the mountains to be a Palestinian society which developed out of the Palestinian tradition of the Bronze Age, as was to be expected, and there are no traces of an Exodus group here, this group is still only an unfounded postulate made by Old Testament historians and modern scholars naively believing what they are told.

The first probable date of anything which could be compared to a sectarian group in the history of the Jewish people would be the exilic community of Babylonia – and it cannot be denied that over the past decade a fair number of scholars have opted for seeing the exile as the point of crystallization of the Old Testament tradition.

In many respects the exile as traditionally understood will provide an excellent background for what Albertz may reckon to form a sectarian group – if it was not the Exodus tradition. The Exodus tradition is the constitutive

---

[3] See, however, Finkelstein's later remorse on this in his "New Orleans" statement in Finkelstein, 1991.

event in the narrative construction of Israel's history as told by the Old Testament historians. This Exodus was supposed to have created the Israelite nation – no more, no less! However, it is a tradition about an event that was supposed to have taken place in a past that already belonged to history. So here you are left with a problem: Would this tradition about an Exodus seem a natural starting point for a society still hoping for *its* own Exodus to come, or in a society which had already experienced an Exodus of its own? In my eyes the latter option seems to be the more natural one, which will force upon us a dating of this tradition in the post-exilic world. Here the more exact dating of the community of Jewish sectarians, about which Albertz speaks, will be dependent on a number of other decisions which have to be made by the historian. I cannot address them in detail here, but can only say that if you take the tradition in the Old Testament of the return from Babylonia and of Ezra and Nehemiah at face value, then a date in the Persian period would not be out of the way. If you are more reluctant to see the description of the Exilic Period as more than another historical reconstruction of the past – which is a view formulated by some scholars of today – then it may be advisable to turn to the formative period of the Jewish nation, which according to the view of history I am propagating only occurred in the 3rd and 2nd century BCE.

Here at last we possess a social situation that fits the idea of an Exodus that has already taken place, and which will also in the future have to take place (because of the presence of the Jewish Diaspora in Egypt, Mesopotamia, and elsewhere – in fact more Jews may have left Palestine at that time than immigrated to Palestine as the growth of the Diaspora in those days seems to indicate – the Exodus tradition can in fact be interpreted as a counter-tradition against the migrants who left, just like Jacob and his sons, to obtain a better living in foreign countries). But it was also in this period when the Hellenization of the Orient went on at full speed that people grow increasingly aware of their own separate traditions, thereby using the concepts of nationality, migrations, destructions of whole cultures to present themselves as distinct from their neighbours – especially the Greeks (in the Old Testament probably thinly disguised as the Philistines). Here such historical interpretations were a logical reaction to the Hellenistic destruction of individuality – just as is the case in present times in the Middle East where people are grasping after a native tradition that may provide them with protection against Western civilization – thereby overlooking that they are already in this behaviour continuing our tradition, not theirs, of fundamentalist interpretation of Holy Writ.

So, the best social location of Albertz's Jewish sect will, of course, be in a period in which such a Jewish sect was present, which is probably best understood to be Hellenistic Palestine – or for that matter and to a much larger extent the Jewish Diaspora, when the Jews understood themselves to be a small nation in a far bigger environment, either in Palestine in comparison to and in opposition to a more and more dominant Greek tradition that was utterly foreign to the area, or abroad where the Jews by necessity had to create minority groups (although sometimes very large ones) in an ocean of foreign nations.

The social-critical remarks of Rainer Albertz have, in this way, brought us from an unlikely placing of the tradition in "early Israel", whatever this was, to a much more likely place in a much later Jewish society. The reason why it has to be so is, however, not based on sociology and sociological readings of texts, but on historical research. This will at least be a consolation to many colleagues who are convinced that sociological readings will hardly bring anything of value with them. Without a historical analysis of Palestinian society in the Iron Age, we will hardly ever be able to figure out the difference between the picture of this society in the Old Testament and the impression we get of Palestinian society *without* the Old Testament that is from contemporary sources.

I, however, have to leave this question here to present another and very different case of a sociological reading of texts as this should not be a lecture dealing with the Exodus exclusively, but it is my aim to show how sociological interpretation can also provide us with an enormous advantage in comparison with earlier generations of biblical scholars. Here the final word on the Exodus issue shall only be: has this anything to do with *theology*? And the answer is yes; maybe not in an absolute Christian sense of the word, but as the Exodus is often considered to be the single most important act of God in history, not least by Jewish theologians, the issue is by all means a very theological one, and a description of the social setting of this Exodus that also provides for a place of this tradition in history cannot be anything except a very important contribution to our understanding of the formation of what is normally called "Old Testament theology".

My second example of social reading will be very different from the first, as it provides no clue to the dating of a tradition. It is, on the other hand, related to the Exodus tradition in that it has to do with the idea of covenant as expressed in the Sinai traditions which in the Old Testament follow the Exodus tradition closely. Here also some earlier studies and contributions can be referred to – in this instance by this speaker. I have here during my stay in South Africa contributed with a lecture on the concept of patronage, "Power and Social Organization: Some Misunderstanding and Some Proposals: Or Is It all a Question of Patrons and Clients?" (Lemche, 2013c, 158–168), thereby continuing a series of studies which I started in Uppsala several years ago and which has been continued in my lecture at the SBL International Meeting in Münster, Germany in 1993: "Kings and Clients: On Loyalty Between the Ruler and the Ruled in Ancient Israel" (Lemche, 1995b). In fact, I believe that my first article on the Hebrew slave, published way back in the 1970s (Lemche, 1975), should be considered the first draft of this sociological interpretation, although my sociological training was, in those days, almost non-existent.

However, as exposed in my lecture on "Power and Social Organization", I imagine Near Eastern society in antiquity to have mostly been structured according to what some social anthropologists call the "Mediterranean societal system", a system more or less peculiar to this part of the world (I definitely cannot agree with this evaluation – I believe the system to be of a much more general character, with well described examples from many places, from Southeastern Asia, from Western Europe before the French Revolution, from Japan (the *daimio* system under the Shogunate) and other places – as a matter of fact, in the Scandinavian welfare states of this century you might well say that the whole population have become the clients of the state). The basic issue is that poor people need rich and powerful men to protect them, thereby becoming the social clients of the rich and wealthy.

This social system seems to be common in societies that have left the tribal stage and have developed a basic bureaucratic organization, i.e. to relatively complex societies such as the ones found in Western Asia in antiquity. It is different on one side from tribal society because of the reduction of the importance of the family-oriented society and on the other from fully developed states in that it has not developed means of protecting its citizens, for example by providing a police force which can guarantee the right of the poor and destitute.

The existence of such societies has, however, mostly been ignored – I believe because of a romantic idea of the noble savage and his bonfire in the night, around which the young assemble to listen to the experiences of old people whom they revere and acknowledge as their leaders. Social anthropologists have thus clearly only partially taken this system into account. Typical is the American anthropologist John Gulick, who, in his study of the social life of a Lebanese village (Gulick, 1955), describes the power structures of his village as if it followed the family structure. However, at the end of his study he has to admit that it seems that there is, in his village, another and more important power system at hand reflected by the settlement pattern which does not follow the family system, although he is unable to acquire the necessary information to describe this alternative system in a sufficient way. I suppose that he has traced the existence of a patronage system in his village, but he cannot describe it because this system belongs in the realm of secret societies, and part of its importance rests in the fact that it shall not be disclosed to outsiders – some may here recognize the infamous *omertà* ideology of the mafia: You must not talk! It is a deadly sin to talk!

Since I have already, in other places, described the basic functions of this kind of society, we can skip the social-anthropological description of patronage here and turn directly to an area of theological interest where this system becomes conspicuous. So let us introduce the God of the Old Testament or rather the Old Testament notion of God.

It has long been recognized that the God of the Old Testament is a difficult God, hard to please although magnificent in his benevolence towards his loyal few. He demands obedience, but can on the other hand, without interference, decide to change his attitude towards men. Thus we have the famous instance of Saul who is disobedient to the Lord, although he should have been pardoned because of the delay of the man of God, Samuel, which forced him to sin against the Lord to keep an army from deserting (1 Sam 13:7–15). Because of this mishap, which seems to be caused by Yahweh himself, Saul is destroyed by his God and is offered no chance of repentance or any argument against his hard fate.

In many respects, Yahweh behaves according to his own will in a way which, in the eyes of human beings, could easily be seen to be treacherous, wilful, selfish, dominant, or simply *tyrannical*. His rule is, on the other hand, also marked by benevolence and grace. He offers his chosen people a land of its own, and he protects them against the rightful owners of this land as long as they are obedient – the poor Canaanites for their part have to die or fly: they receive, so to speak, an offer they cannot refuse.

As images of God are more often than not reflections of the society which entertains this picture of the divine, we may safely say that biblical Israel was a society dominated by ideas of patronage and clientelism, as the description of this dangerous God of the Israelites has much in common with what has been said about patrons in their relationships with clients. Thus a sociological interpretation of the image of God in the Old Testament can safely be said to have found a social context for this notion of the deity, who acts as a mafia Godfather in his own right, and whose acts are in themselves not necessarily more correct that the ones enacted by such a mafia Godfather.

Of course, since we are reckoned to be the people of God, we may be indifferent to the atrocities committed by our God; we pay our God our duty and expect his rewards in exchange for worshipping him as he wishes. So the Canaanites will have to go, and we can take over their possessions without remorse – after all, they never worshipped *our* Godfather!

We can continue along this line to the, perhaps, most important expression of the relations between God and human beings to be found in the Old Testament, i.e. the idea of a divine covenant through which Yahweh binds his chosen people to himself just as any vassal king would try to bind the hands of his vassals by forbidding them to worship other gods, and to remain obedient and loyal to himself. This does not, however, prevent *our* gracious God from behaving treacherously, as happens to the poor Job, whom Yahweh crushed in order to win a bet with Satan. And when Job approaches Yahweh to get an explanation, he is simply sent away with the message: "Shut up!" you are unimportant and have nothing to say. Finally, Job accepts his fate and is immediately rewarded.

The God of the Old Testament demands blind obedience, he also demands to be the exclusive lord of Israel. Any change of this situation will be understood as rebellion against the Lord, and will be punished. This is another important aspect of this divine patronage system. You cannot break your loyalty to God, you are not even allowed to say: enough of this! I don't like you! I want another God! The patronage system has never in history allowed the vassal or the client freedom to choose another lord, should the first one be too harsh, too cruel or too wilful. The client's only hope is to find another lord who is stronger than his previous lord and who can protect him against his former lord, should he, in spite of personal danger, decide to fly in order to improve his fate.

Here the Old Testament God is about as remorseless as any king of those days, as for example Nebuchadnezzar, who removed the Egyptian vassal, Jeconiah, without hurting him, but who destroyed his unfaithful vassal, Zedekiah in the harshest possible way. Nebuchadnezzar could not blame Jeconiah for being unfaithful to him as the Judean king owed him nothing – he was the vassal of the King of Egypt, whereas Zedekiah was enthroned by Nebuchadnezzar himself.

In the same way, Israel's hard fate is stressed from the beginning of its acquaintance with Yahweh. It will be severely punished by God if it deserts its God; however, the warning of impending doom only follows Israel's own decision to make a contract with God. We thus remember the warnings of Joshua 24 that these laws and rules contained in the covenant with the divine are hard and difficult to follow, and maybe Israel will be too weak to comply with them. However, Israel decides to follow Joshua and to worship Yahweh as it Godfather alone, thereby sealing its own fate and destruction, which belong to the future.

These examples may be enough in this place to show the enormous potential of seeing a patronage system reflected in the images of God in the Old

Testament. No doubt such a socio-political system was well known in ancient Palestine and was reflected in the theology of the Old Testament. Only a social-anthropological approach to the Old Testament will, however, be able to uncover the many facets of this system and its influence on the notion of God. To be sure: it could very well be the case that only a proper sociological analysis will be able to contribute this, thereby demonstrating that we here not only speak of the *relevance of social-critical analysis for Old Testament Theology* but of its necessity for Old Testament theology, as this kind of reading provides a context for the relationship between God and Israelite which no other approach would be able to provide.

Interestingly enough, it can be argued that the late Hellenistic image of God to be found in the New Testament and in early Christianity departed from the old system, especially as Christ's redeeming act, by creating a universal approach to God that (almost) excluded the notion of patronage: God sided with the poor and suffered their fate on the cross, thereby redeeming the human race. It is on the other hand notorious that this NT notion did not last for long, and that the patronage element of the notion of God was especially stressed in the highly personalized interpretation of the connection between the divine and human beings which is peculiar to Protestant communities: that God will only accept the ones who believe in him, and – especially in the Lutheran tradition – that it is God's decision alone whether he is interested in acknowledging us as his faithful clients; we can contribute nothing to improve our hopes – except believing in God.

APPENDIX

20 272 BCE – A *terminus a quo*

Everybody knows what a pyrrhic victory is, but nobody knows Pyrrhus.

Pyrrhus, king of Epirus (319–272 BCE), was a famous Greek general the generation after Alexander the Great, who was later mostly remembered for the costly victories over the Romans in 280 and 279 BCE. He evidently was a highly regarded general in antiquity who almost sixty years before Hannibal brought the war to the gates of Rome. He lost his life in street fighting in Argos in 272 BCE.

The main source regarding his life we are in possession of today is his biography in Plutarch's *Parallel Lives,* opposing the highly regarded Roman general Marius. However, Plutarch (46–119 CE) did have older sources. Besides, Pyrrhus is well attested from coins carrying his portrait.

Today Pyrrhus is forgotten, or so it seems. In antiquity he never was, as Livy informs us in a famous anecdote about a meeting between Hannibal and Scipio Africanus some years after the Battle of Zama: Scipio asks Hannibal about the greatest generals. Hannibal's answer; first Alexander, then Pyrrhus, and finally myself. Scipio then asks Hannibal: What if you beat me? and Hannibal answers: Then I am the greatest![1]

Of course, this is a typical tale as they loved to narrate them in classical sources, but it was told again and again, by Plutarch,[2] and by Appian (95–165 CE).[3]

However, why should Pyrrhus be of interest in a biblical context? Maybe we shall better understand the reason when we read the report of his death in Plutarch's *Life of Pyrrhus*:

---

[1] Livy *Ab Urbe Condita* XXXV 14. The conversation between Scipio and Hannibal is said to have taken place in Ephesus in 197 BCE.
[2] In his *Parallel Lives*: Flaminius 21 1.
[3] *Syriaca* 1.4.

The Death of Pyrrhus according to Plutarch's *Parallel Lives*

34 1 But Pyrrhus, seeing the stormy sea that surged about him, took off the coronal with which his helmet was distinguished, and gave it to one of his companions; then, relying on his horse, he plunged in among the enemy who were pursuing him.

Here he was wounded by a spear which pierced his breastplate — not a mortal, nor even a severe wound — and turned upon the man who had struck him, who was an Argive, not of illustrious birth, but the son of a poor old woman. 2 His mother, like the rest of the women, was at this moment watching the battle from the house-top, and when she saw that her son was engaged in conflict with Pyrrhus, she was filled with distress in view of the danger to him, and lifting up a tile with both her hands threw it at Pyrrhus. It fell upon his head below his helmet and crushed the vertebrae at the base of his neck, so that his sight was blurred and his hands dropped the reins. Then he sank down from his horse and fell near the tomb of Licymnius, unrecognised by most who saw him. 3 But a certain Zopyrus, who was serving under Antigonus, and two or three others, ran up to him, saw who he was, and dragged him into a door-way just as he was beginning to recover from the blow. And when Zopyrus drew an Illyrian short-sword with which to cut off his head, Pyrrhus gave him a terrible look, so that Zopyrus was frightened; his hands trembled, and yet he essayed the deed; but being full of alarm and confusion his blow did not fall true, but along the mouth and chin, so that it was only slowly and with difficulty that he severed the head. 4 Presently what had happened was known to many, and Alcyoneus, running to the spot, asked for the head as if he would see whose it was. But when he had got it he rode away to his father, and cast it down before him as he sat among his friends. Antigonus, however, when he saw and recognised the head, drove his son away, smiting him with his staff and calling him impious and barbarous; then, covering his face with his cloak he burst into tears, calling to mind Antigonus his grandfather and Demetrius his father, who were examples in his own family of a reversal of fortune. 5 The head and body of Pyrrhus, then, Antigonus caused to be adorned for burial and burned; and when Alcyoneus found Helenus in an abject state and wearing a paltry cloak, and spoke to him kindly and brought him into the presence of his father, Antigonus was pleased with his conduct, and said: "This is better, my son, than what thou didst before; but not even now hast thou done well in allowing this clothing to remain, which is a disgrace the rather to us who are held to be the victors." 6 Then, after showing kindness to Helenus and adorning his person, he sent him back to Epeirus, and he dealt mildly with the friends of Pyrrhus when he became master of their camp and of their whole force.

> (Plutarch. Delphi Complete Works of Plutarch (Illustrated) (Delphi Ancient Classics Book 13). Delphi Classics. Kindle Edition)

As we know from the Book of Judges 9, Pyrrhus was evidently not the only general who lost his life under such circumstances. In Judges, the unlucky hero is Abimelech:

50 Then went Abimelech to Thebez, and encamped against Thebez, and took it.

51 But there was a strong tower within the city, and thither fled all the men and women, and all they of the city, and shut it to them, and gat them up to the top of the tower.

52 And Abimelech came unto the tower, and fought against it, and went hard unto the door of the tower to burn it with fire.

53 And a certain woman cast a piece of a millstone upon Abimelech's head, and all to brake his skull.

54 Then he called hastily unto the young man his armourbearer, and said unto him, Draw thy sword, and slay me, that men say not of me, A woman slew him. And his young man thrust him through, and he died.

55 And when the men of Israel saw that Abimelech was dead, they departed every man unto his place.

Evidently it is the same narrative, with several deviations as far as the details are concerned. But is it also the same act? If we assume that the biblical account of Abimelech's death has been inspired by the story of Pyrrhus' death, we have the first absolute *terminus a quo* for the composition of at least the literature to which the Book of Judges belongs, i.e. 272 BCE. However, before we jump to that conclusion, we have to discuss whether there is any escape from such a conclusion. After all, street fighting was a common part of ancient warfare, and Pyrrhus and Abimelech were most likely not the only warriors to die in this way.

Standing alone, there is perhaps no special reason to argue that the story of Abimelech's death echoes the death of Pyrrhus. Two warriors killed in the same fashion would not be a problem. However, the story of Abimelech does not stand alone. After Abimelech follows Jephthah, with the story in Judges 11 about Jephthah's daughter whom Jephthah is forced to sacrifice because of a vow he had made to Yahweh.

Now, it is common among commentators to look for similarities between this legend and the Greek legend of Agamemnon who had to sacrifice his daughter Iphigenia at Aulis to soothe the goddess Artemis whom he had offended. Otherwise, the goddess would have prevented him from sailing to Troy with the Greek army. The similarity is obvious insofar as it is about the sacrifice of a young woman.[4] However, the motif of the sacrifice of the girl is very different from the biblical one. A much closer parallel is the Greek story preserved by Apollodoros (c. 180–120 BCE)[5] of the son of the king of Crete Idomeneus who had vowed to sacrifice the first living being he would encounter if Poseidon allowed him to return from Troy to his homeland. This first living being happened to be his son.[6]

Again, taken in isolation there might be no literary or even traditional connection between the stories of the sacrifices of, respectively, Jephthah's daughter, and Iphigenia the daughter of King Agamemnon, and certainly both a historical one if someone will insist on the historicity of either event. Abimelech's death and Iphigeneia's sacrifice – if they stood isolated – would only provide a possibility, but not a fact. However, since these stories appear almost side by side in the Book of Judges, we can safely exclude the possibility that it is only due to coincidence that they appear together. As Lady Bracknell expresses it in Oscar Wilde's *The Importance of Being Earnest*:

---

[4] The motif of child sacrifice goes further back. In later Greek tradition (at least in Euripides *Iphigenia in Aulis*, c. 408 BCE), Iphigenia was spared by Artemis and installed as ruler at Tauris (Crimea), a version which has been related by Euripides in his tragedy *Iphigenia in Tauris* (c. 412 BCE). If we look for a similar motif in biblical literature, two further examples come into focus, Abraham's sacrifice of his son Isaac, an act thwarted by God, and the note about King Mesha who sacrifices his son of the wall of his city in the eyes of the Israelites. On "Iphigeneia" and Judges 11, cf. also Gnuse, 2021, Ch.19 "The Sacrificed Maiden Iphigenia and Jephthah's Daughter" (pp. 151–64).
[5] Apollodoros' works are only preserved in fragments in the writings of other authors.
[6] In the opera by Mozart, *Idomeneo re di Creta* (1781) the son has a name: Idamante.

> To lose one parent may be regarded as a misfortune; to lose both looks like carelessness.

To claim that either case is a coincidence is out of the question because they both point in the same direction, depending on loans from the Greek world. We might go even further and say that the whole character of Abimelech is modelled on Pyrrhus, who began his military career at a very early age, and continued fighting until his death. The girl Iphigenia is of course a mythological figure; a spin-off from the arsenal of tales about the war against Troy and an example of how literature was created and elaborated founded on the basis of the central story of the war against Troy.

However, if readers are still not satisfied then we move on to the next section of the Book of Judges: The stories about the superhero Samson. Again, we are dealing with a mythological figure and do not need to worry about historical details because there are none. Samson's first proof of his strength is his bravery when he tears a lion apart with his own hand (Judg 14:5–6). However, in spite of his bravery and strength, he ends up being the victim of a treacherous woman when Delilah delivers him powerless to the Philistines. Samson ends his life with an act of bravado when he kills himself smashing the temple of Dagon in Gaza and crushing all the Philistines inside the temple (Judg 16:25–30).

Again, the similarity of the figure of Samson to the Greek superhero Heracles is so obvious that few will doubt a relation between them, which includes as its major elements the tearing of the lion and the contribution of a woman to the downfall of the hero.[7]

Finally, to underscore the importance of the Hellenistic context, we also have a Hebrew version of another classical reference, The abduction of the Sabinian women, in Judges 21 presented as the young women participating in the yearly dancing are abducted by the surviving Benjaminites. The story as we know it can be found in Livy's *Ab Urbe Condita* I.13 and placed soon after the foundation of ancient Rome allegedly in 653 BCE. Classical tradition, however, has many references to the event.[8]

All of this indicates that in the Book of Judges – probably in its entirety – we are safely within the sphere of Hellenistic tradition. The biblical stories represent rewritten Hellenistic tradition and the narrators have felt absolutely free to present their versions in a form that suited the authors' purposes. But there can be no doubt about the origin of these stories.

---

[7] Cf. also Gnuse, 2021, Ch. 9 "Samson and Heracles Visited" (pp. 131–50).
[8] Cf. also on this story and its classical background, Gnuse, 2021, 47–60.

Since one of these parallel figures is a historical person, Abimelech alias Pyrrhus, we have a *terminus a quo* for the composition of probably not only the Book of Judges but of the composition of so-called historical literature in the Old Testament. Philippe Wajdenbaum's project is thus vindicated.[9] The biblical historical literature does not go back to some unknown past. It belongs to the third and maybe even the second centuries BCE.

Russell Gmirkin has, in his works on the Hellenistic tradition in the Bible, argued in favour of a *terminus a quo* for the composition of the Pentateuch around or even shortly before 270 BCE.[10] He is right. The *terminus ante quem* will be later than 270 BCE and, as I argued back in my article from 1993 on the Old Testament as a Hellenistic book, the *terminus ad quem* is the appearance of most biblical books in some form or the other among the Dead Sea Scrolls.[11] In the case of Exodus, the tragedy by Ezekiel the Tragedian from c. 200 may serve as an earlier *terminus ante quem*.[12]

The year 272 BCE will place the emergence of the historical literature in the Old Testament within exactly the same period, and serves as another argument in favour of an original *Enneateuch,* including all the books from Genesis to Second Kings as one continuous work.[13]

In this way, if we look at these *termini* we still have about one hundred and fifty years to play with. It should be enough of a span of time to produce the literature of the – rather limited in size – Old Testament's historical books.

---

[9] Wajdenbaum, 2011.
[10] Cf. Gmirkin, 2006, 240–56. The argument is extended in his *Plato and the Creation of the Hebrew Bible* (2017, 250–99), and followed up in the third part of his trilogy *Plato's Timaeus and the Biblical Creation Accounts* (2022). Gmirkin mostly speaks about the Pentateuch and especially the primary history and the law collections.
[11] Lemche, 1993a.
[12] Only fragments have survived, in Eusebius *Praeparatio Evangelica*.
[13] And hereby this author signs up with those who are supporting Kratz (2000), arguing for the existence of an Enneateuch. The future study of the process that led to biblical literature will have to use 272 BCE as its starting point.

Bibliography

Ahlström, G.W. 1993. *The History of Ancient Palestine from the Palaeolithic Period to Alexander's Conquest with a contribution by Gary O. Rollefson.* Journal for the Study of the Old Testament Supplement Series, 146. Sheffield: Academic Press.

Albertz, R. 1992. *Religionsgeschichte Israels in alttestamentlicher Zeit,* 1-2. Göttingen: Vandenhoeck & Ruprecht, 1992.

―――― 1994. *A History of Israelite Religion in the Old Testament Period,* I-II. London: SCM.

―――― 1995. "Religionsgeschichte Israels statt Theologie des Alten Testaments! Plädoyer für eine forschungsgeschichtliche Umorientierung", in Janowski, B. and Lohfink, N. (eds.). 1995. *Religionsgeschichte Israels oder Theologie des Alten Testaments?* Jahrbuch für Biblische Theologie 10,3-24.

Albright, W.F. 1940. *From the Stone Age to Christianity.* Baltimore: The Johns Hopkins Press. Repr. New York, Doubleday, 1957.

Alt, A. 1953. "Die Heimat des Deuteronomiums", *Kleine Schriften zur Geschichte des Volkes Israel,* II. München: Beck, 250-75.

Andersen, K.T. 1989. "Noch einmal: Die Chronologie der Könige von Israel und Juda". *Scandinavian Journal of the Old Testament* 3/1: 1-45.

Assmann, J. 1992. *Das kulturelle Gedächtnis: Schrift, Erinnerung und politische Identität in frühen Hochkulturen.* München: Verlag C.H. Beck.

―――― *Cultural Memory and Early Civilization: Writing, Remembrance and Political Imagination.* Cambridge: University Press, 2011.

Assmann, A. 2011. *Cultural memory and Western Civilization: Functions, Media, Archives* Cambridge: University Press.

Attridge, H.W. and R.A. Oden. 1981. *Philo of Byblos: The Phoenician History: Introduction, Critical Text, Translation, Notes.* Washington: The Catholic Biblical Association.

Bächli. O. 1977. *Amphiktyonie im Alten Testament. Forschungsgeschichtliche Studie zur Hypothese von Martin Noth.* ThZ Sonderband, 6. Basel, Friedrich Reinhardt.

Barstad, H.M. 1997. *The Babylonian Captivity of the Book of Isaiah: "Exilic "Judah and the Provenance of Isaiah 40-55.* Oslo: Novus forlag.

Barth, F. 1969. "Introduction" in F. Barth (ed.), *Ethnic Groups and Boundaries.* Oslo: Universitetsforlaget, 9-37.

Beckman, G. 1996. *Hittite Diplomatic Texts.* Edited by Harry A. Hoffner. Society of Biblical Literature Writings from the Ancient World Series, 7. Atlanta, Georgia: Scholars Press.

Binger. 1997. *Asherah. Goddesses in Ugarit, Israel and the Old Testament.* Journal for the Study of the Old Testament Supplement Series 232/Copenhagen International Seminar 2. Sheffield: Academic Press.

Biran, A. and J. Naveh. 1993. "An Aramaic Stele Fragment from Tel Dan", *IEJ* 43, pp. 81–98

——— 1995. "The Tel Dan Inscription: A New Fragment", *IEJ* 45, pp. 1–18.

Blenkinsopp, J. 2000. *Isaiah 1-39: A New Translation with Introduction and Commentary.* Anchor Bible 19. New York: Doubleday.

Bloch-Smith, E. 1992, *Judahite Burial Practices and beliefs about the Dead.* JSOTSup, 123. Sheffield: Academic Press.

Bright, J. 1960. *A History of Israel.* London: SCM Press.

Brownlee, W.H. 1971. "Psalms 1-2 as a Coronation Liturgy", *Biblica* 52, pp. 321–336.

Brunius, Teddy. 1963. "'Wie es eigentlich gewesen': Leopold von Ranke och hans slagord", *Scandia* 29, 392–400 (www.scandia.hist.lu.se).

Buccellati, G. 1962. "La 'carriera' di David e quella di Idrimi, re di Alalac", *Bibbia e Oriente* 4, 95–9.

Budde, K. 1897. *Das Buch der Richter.* Kurzer Handkommentar zum Alten Testament, VII. Freiburg i.B.: Verlag von J.C.B. Mohr (Paul Siebeck).

Buhl, F. 1885. *Den gammeltestamentlige Skriftoverlevering.* København: Gyldendalske Boghandel, 1885.

Bultmann, R. 1921. *Die Geschichte der synoptischen Tradition.* Forschungen zur Religion und Literatur des Alten und Neuen Testaments, 29. Göttingen: Vandenhoeck & Ruprecht. 2nd rev. ed. 1931.

Burke, A.A. 2021. *The Amorites and the Bronze Age Near East.* Cambridge: University Press.

Burstein, S.M. 1978. *The Babyloniaca of Berossus.* Sources and monographs sources from the ancient near east vol. 1, fasc. 5 Malibu: Undena Publications.

Cahill, J.M. 2003. "Jerusalem at the Time of the United Monarchy: The Archaeological Evidence", in A.G. Vaughn and A.E. Killebrew (eds.), *Jerusalem in Bible and Archaeology: The First Temple Period.* Atlanta: Society of Biblical Literature, 13–80.

Carroll, R.P. 1998. "'Exile! What Exile': Deportation and Discourse of Diaspora", In Lester L. Grabbe (ed.), *Leading Captivity Captive. The "Exile" as History and Ideology.* European Seminar in Historical Methodology, 2. Sheffield: Academic Press.

—— 2001. "Exile, Restoration, and Colony: Judah in the Persian Empire". In L.G. Perdue (ed.), *The Blackwell Companion to the Hebrew Bible*. Blackwell Companions to Religion. Oxford: Blackwell Publishers.

Carstens, P., Trine Bjørnung Hasselbalch and Niels Peter Lemche (eds.). 2012. *Cultural Memory in Biblical Exegesis*. Piscataway, NJ: Gorgias Press.

Chadwick, H.M. 1912. *Heroic Age*. Cambridge: University Press.

Civil, M. 1969. "The Sumerian Flood Story', in W.G. Lambert and A.R. Millard, *Atra-Ḫasīs: The Babylonian Story of the Flood*. Oxford: At the Clarendon Press, 138–45.

Cogan, M. 1974. *Imperialism and Religion: Assyria, Judah and Israel in the Eight and Seventh Centuries B.C.E.* Society of Biblical Literature Monograph Series 19. Missoula, MT: Scholars.

Conzelmann, H. 1954. *Die Mitte der Zeit. Studien zur Theologie des Lukas*. Beiträge zur historischen Theologie 17. Tübingen: Mohr [Siebeck].

Cowley, A.E. 1923. *Aramaic Papyri of the Fifth Century B.C.* Oxford: The Clarendon Press; reprinted Eugene: Wipf & Stock, 2005.

Cryer, F.H. 1994. *Divination in Ancient Israel and its Near eastern Environment*. JSOTSup, 142. Sheffield: Academic Press.

Cubitt, G. 2007. *History and Memory*. Manchester: University Press, 2007.

Da Gud skabte: Første Mosebog 1 til Anden Mosebog 15: Det Gamle Testamente i ny oversættelse. 1985. København: Det Danske Bibelselskab.

Dalley, S. 1989. *Myths from Mesopotamia: Creation, the Flood, Gilgamesh and Others. A New Translation*. Oxford: University Press.

—— 2013. "First Millennium BC Variations in *Gilgameh*, *Atrahasis*, the Flood Story and *the Epic of Creation*: What Was Available to Berossos?", in Haubold etc. *The World of Berossus*, 165–75.

Davies, P.R. 1992. *In Search of "Ancient Israel"*. Journal for the Study of the Old Testament Supplement Series 148. Sheffield: Sheffield Academic Press.

—— 1995. *Whose Bible is it Anyway?* JSOTSup 204. Sheffield: Academic Press.

Dearman, A. (ed.). 1989. *Studies in the Mesha Inscription and Moab*. Atlanta, GA: Scholars.

Dever, W.G. 1995. "'Will the Real Israel Please Stand Up?' Archaeology and Israelite Historiography Part I", *Bulletin of the American Schools of Oriental Research* 297, 61–80.

—— 1996. "Revisionist Israel Revisited: A Rejoinder to Niels Peter Lemche", *Currents in Research: Biblical Studies* 4, 35–50.

—— 2001. *What Did the Biblical Writers Know and When Did They Know it? What Archaeology Can Tell Us about the Reality of Ancient Israel*. Grand Rapids: William B. Eerdmans Publishing Company.

Dibelius, M. 1906. *Die Lade Jahves: Eine religionsgeschichtliche Untersuchung.* Inaugural-Dissertation der Universität zu Tübingen. Göttingen: Druck der Univ.-Buchdruckerei von E.A. Huth.

——— 1919. *Die Formgeschichte des Evangeliums.* Tübingen: J.C. Mohr.

Diebner, B.J. 1984. "Es läßt sich nicht beweisen, Tatsache aber ist…Sprachfigur statt Methode in der kritischen Erforschung des AT", *Dielheimer Blätter zum Alten Testament* 18, 138-46.

——— *Failed Methods and Ideology in Canonical Interpretation of Biblical Texts.* Translators: Ingrid Hjelm, Niels Peter Lemche, and Jim West. Changing Perspectives, 9. London: Routledge, 2023.

Dietrich, W. and O. Keel. 1994. *Jahwe unter den Göttern und Göttinen des alten Orients.* 13. Kolloquium der Schweizerischen Akademie der Geistes- und Sozialwissenschaften 1993. Freiburg: Universitätsverlag.

Donner, H. and W. Röllig, 1964. *Kanaanäische und aramäische Inschriften (KAI).* Wiesbaden: Otto Harrassowitz.

——— 1984-86. *Geschichte des Volkes Israel und seiner Nachbarn in Grundzügen* I-II. Göttingen. Vandenhoeck & Ruprecht.

Dozeman, T.B. and K. Schmid (eds.). 2006. *A Farewell to the Yahwist? The Composition of the Pentateuch in Recent European Interpretation.* Atlanta: Society of Biblical Literature.

Duhm, B. 1892. *Das Buch Jesaja übersetzt und erklärt.* Göttingen: Vandenhoek & Ruprecht.

Edel, E. 1949. "KBo I 15 + 19. Brief Ramses. II nit einer Schilderung der Kadschschlacht". *Zeitschrift der Assyriologie* 48, 195-212.

Eichrodt, W. 1933-9. *Theologie des Alten Testaments* I-III. Leipzig: J.C. Hinrichs, 1933-9.

——— 1962-4. *Theologie des Alten Testament,* I-III. 7. Reviewed edn. Stuttgart: Ehrenfried Klotz Verlag.

Engel, H. 1979. *Die Vorfahren Israels in Ägypten.* Frankfurter Theologische Studien, 27. Frankfurt a/M: Josef Knecht.

Engnell, I. 1943. *Studies in Divine Kingship in the Ancient Near East.* Uppsala: Almqvist & Wiksell.

Eriksen, T.H. and Marek Jakoubek (eds.), *Ethnic Groups and Boundaries Today: A Legacy of Fifty Years.* Research in Migration and Ethnic Boundaries Series. London: Routledge, 2019.

Erslev, K. 1968. *Historisk Teknik. Den historiske Undersøgelse fremstillet i sine Grundlinier* (1911). 2nd edn. 7. Optryk. København: Gyldendal.

Evans, P.S. 2009. *The Invasion of Sennacherib in the Book of Kings: A Source-Critical and Rhetorical Study of 2 Kings 18-19.* Vetus Testamentum Supplements, 125. Leiden: E.J. Brill.

Falkenstjerne, V. and E.B. Jensen. 1942. *Håndbog i dansk litteratur*, I. København: G.E.C. Gad.

Finkelstein, I. 1988. *The Archaeology of the Israelite Settlement*. Jerusalem: Israel Exploration Society.

―――― 1991. "The Emergence of Israel in Canaan: Consensus, Mainstream and Dispute", *Scandinavian Journal of Old Testament* 1991:2, pp. 47–59.

―――― 1996. "The Archaeology of the United Monarchy: An Alternative View", *Levant* 28, 177–186

―――― 1999. "State Formation in Israel and Judah. A Contrast in Context. A Contrast in Trajectory", *Near Eastern Archaeology* 62:1, 35–52.

―――― 2001 "The Rise of Jerusalem and Judah: The Missing Link", *Levant* 33, 105–15.

―――― 2012. "Persian Period Jerusalem and Yehud Rejoinders", in Jon Berquist and Alice Hunt, *Focusing Biblical Studies: The Crucial Nature of the Persian and Hellenistic Periods. Essays in Honor of Douglas A. Knight*, LHBOTS 544. London: T & T Clark, 49–62.

―――― 2013. *The Forgotten Kingdom: The Archaeology and History of Northern Israel*. Ancient Near East Monographs, 5. Atlanta: Society of Biblical Literature, 2013

Finkelstein, I. and N.A. Silberman, 2001. *The Bible Unearthed: Archaeology's New Vision of Ancient Israel and the Origin of Its Sacred Texts*. New York: The Free Press.

―――― 2006. *David and Solomon: In Search of the Bible's Sacred Kings and the Roots of the Western Tradition*. New York: The Free Press.

Foster, B.J. 1993. *Before the Muses. An Anthology of Akkadian Literature* I–II. Bethesda, Maryland.

Frankfort, H. 1948. *Kingship and the Gods*. Chicago: University Press.

Frerichs, E.S. and L.H. Lesko (eds.). 1997. *Exodus. The Egyptian Evidence*. Winona Lake: Eisenbrauns.

Friedrichs, J. 1926–30. *Staatsverträge des Hatti-Reiches in hethitischer Sprache I–II*. Leipzig: J.C. Hinrichs.

Friis, H. 1975. "Eksilet og den israelitiske historieopfattelse', *Dansk Teologisk Tidsskrift* 38", 1–16.

―――― 1986. *Die Bedingungen für die Errichtung des davidischen Reichs in Israel und seiner Umwelt*. Dielheimet Blätter zum Alten Testament und seiner Rezeption in der Alten Kirche, 8. Heidelberg: Dielheimer Blätter.

Fritz, V. and Davies, P.R. (eds.). 1996. *The Origins of the Israelite States*. Journal for the Study of the Old Testament Supplement Series 228. Sheffield: Sheffield Academic Press.

Fussell, P. 1975. *The Great War and Modern Memory*. Oxford: University Press.

Gabler, J.Ph. 1787. "De justo discrimine theologiae biblicae et dogmaticae regundisue recte utriusque finibus", ET:

—— 2004. "An Oration on the Proper Distinction between Biblical and Dogmatic Theology and the Specific Objectives of Each", in Ben C. Ollenburger (ed.), *Old Testament Theology: Flowering and Future*. 2nd. Edition. Sources for Biblical and Theological Studies, 1. Winona Lake, Indiana: Eisenbrauns, 2004, 497–506,

Garbini, G. 1988. *History & Ideology in Ancient Israel*. London: SCM Press.

Gardiner, A. 1960. *The Ḳadesh Inscriptions of Ramesses II*. Oxford: Printed for the Griffith Institute at the University Press by Vivian Ridler.

Gellner, E. and J. Waterbury (eds.). 1977. *Patrons and Clients in Mediterranean Societies* London: Duckworth.

Gerstenberger, E. 1988. *Psalms 1. With an Introduction to Cultic Poetry*. The Forms of Old Testament Literature, XIV. Grand Rapids, MI: William B. Eerdmanns Publishing Company 1988.

Gesenius, W. 1910. *Hebrew Grammar* (ed E. Kautzsch), English ed. by A.E. Cowley. Oxford: University Press, 1910.

Glebe-Møller, J. 1989. *Jesus and Tradition: Critique of a Tradition*. Minneapolis, MN: Fortress.

Gmirkin, R.E. 2006. *Berossus and Genesis, Manetho and Exodus: Hellenistic Histories and the Date of the Pentateuch*. Copenhagen International Series, 15. Library of the Hebrew Bible Old Testament Studies, 433. New York and London: t & t Clark.

—— 2017. *Plato and the Creation of the Hebrew Bible*. Copenhagen International Seminar. London: Routledge.

—— 2022. *Plato's* Timaeus *and the Biblical Creation Accounts: Cosmic Monotheism and Terrestrial Polytheism in the Primordial History*. Copenhagen International Seminar. London: Routledge.

Gnuse, R. 2021. *Hellenism and the Primary History: The Imprint of Greek Sources in Genesis – 2 Kings*. Copenhagen International Seminar. London: Routledge.

Goody, J. 2010. Myth, *Ritual and the Oral*. Cambridge: University Press.

Gottlieb, H. 1969. "Ligklagen over Krt, II K I-II", *DTT* 32, pp. 88–105.

Gottwald, N.K. 1979. *The Tribes of Yahweh: A Sociology of the Religion of Liberated Israel, 1250–1050 B.C.E.* New York: Orbis Books.

—— 1985. *The Hebrew Bible – A Socio-Literary Introduction*. Philadelphia: Fortress.

—— 1986. *Social Scientific Criticism of the Hebrew Bible and Its Social World: The Israelite Monarchy*. Semeia 37. Decatur: Scholars.

—— 1993. *The Hebrew Bible in Its Social World and in Ours*. SBL Semeia Studies. Atlanta, GA: Scholars.

Grabbe, L.L. (ed.). 2003. *Like a Bird in a Cage: The Invasion of Sennacherib in 701 B.C.E.* Journal for the Study of the Old Testament Supplement Series 363. Sheffield: Academic Press.

Grayson, A.K. 2000. *Assyrian and Babylonian Chronicles.* 2. ed. Winona Lake: Eisenbrauns.

Grønbech, V. 1942-5. *Hellas: Kultur og Religion* I-V. 2nd. ed. København: Gyldendal, 1961.

—— 1931. *Vor Folkeæt i Oldtiden.* Copenhagen: Gyldendal.

—— 1932. *The Culture of the Teutons.* Oxford: University Press.

Guillaume, A. 1938. *Prophecy and Divination Among the Hebrews and Other Semites.* London: Hodder & Stoughton.

Gulick, J. 1955. *Social Structure and Cultural Change in a Lebanese Village.* Wenner-Gren Foundation for Anthropological Research; Paper edition. New York.

Gunkel, H. 1901. *Genesis, übersetzt und erklärt.* Göttingen: Vandenhoeck & Ruprecht, 1901.

—— 1929. *Die Psalmen.* 5th ed. Göttingen: Vandenhoeck & Ruprecht, 1968.

—— 1987. *The Folktale in the Old Testament.* Sheffield: Almond. German original *Das Märchen im Alten Testament*, Tübingen, 1917.

Gurney, O.R. 1955. "The Cuthaean legend of Naram-Sin", *Anatolian Studies* 5, 93-113

Güterbock, H.G. 1938. "Die historische Tradition in ihre literarischen Gestaltung bei Babyloniern und Hethitern bis 1200", *Zeitschrift für Assyriologie* 10, 49-59.

Halbwachs, M. 1992. *On Collective Memory*, edited, translated, and with an introduction by Lewis A. Coser. Chicago: University Press.

—— 1994. *Les cadres sociaux de la mémoire* (1925). Revised edition by Gérard Namer. Paris: Albin Michel.

—— 1997. *La mémoire collective* (1950). Critical edition by Gérard Namer. Paris: Albin Michel.

Hallbäck, G. 2012. *Hvad jeg skrev: Udvalgte artikler om Det Nye Testamente og andre ting.* København: Anis.

Hallo, W.W. (ed.). 1997. *The Context of Scripture. I: The Canonical Compositions from the Biblical World.* Leiden: E.J. Brill.

Hammershaimb, E. 1984. *Femten gammeltestamentlige salmer.* København: G.E.C. Gad.

Handy, L.K. (ed.). 1997. *The Age of Solomon. Scholarship at the Turn of the Millennium.* Studies in the History and Culture of the Ancient Near East 11. Leiden: E.J. Brill.

Harnack, A. von. 1921. *Marcion: das Evangelium vom fremden Gott; eine Monographie zur Geschichte der Grundlegung der katholischen Kirche.* Reprint of the 2nd ed. of 1924. Darmstadt: Wissenschaftliche Buchgesellschaft 1996.

Hart, B.H.L. 1941. *The strategy of indirect approach.* London: Faber & Faber.

Hasel, G.F. 1992. "Sabbath", in *Anchor Bible Dictionary* V. New York, 849-56.

Haubold, J., G.B. Lanfranchi, R. Rollinger, J. Steele (eds.). 2013. *The World of Berossos: Proceedings of the 4t International Colloquium on "The Ancient Near East between Classical and Ancient Oriental Traditions", Hartfield College, Durham 7th – 9th July 2010.* Classica et Orientalia, 5. Wiesbaden: Harrassowitz Verlag.

Herbener, J-A.P. and P. Provançal. 2001. *Ny Bibeloversættelse – på videnskabeligt Grundlag: Annoteret prøveoversættelse: Da Gud begyndte kap. 1–12: Jesjajahu kap. 1–12.* København: C.A. Reitzel Det Kongelige Bibliotek.

Herrmann, A. 1938. *Die ägyptische Königsnovelle.* Glückstadt: J.J. Augustin.

Herrmann, S. 1953-4. "Die Königsnovelle in Ägypten und Israel", *Wissenschaftliche Zeitschrift der Karl-Marx-Universität Leipzig. 3. Gesellschafts- und sprachwissenschaft-liche Reihe* 1, 51–62.

Hillers, D.R. 1964. *Treaty-Curses and the Old Testament Prophets.* Biblica et Orientalia, 16. Rome: Pontifical Biblical Institute.

Hoftizser, J. and K. Jongeling. 1995. *Dictionary of the North-West Semitic Inscriptions*, I–II. Handbuch der Orientalistik, 21. Leiden: E.J. Brill.

Høgenhaven, J. 1993. "Kristus i Det Gamle Testamente", in Mogens Müller and John Strange (eds.), *Det gamle Testamente i jødedom og kristendom.* Forum for Bibelsk Eksegese, 4. København: Museum Tusculanums Forlag, 37–56.

—— 1996. "Det gamle Testamente og teologien – efter 'Københavnerskolen'", *Fønix* 20,156–69.

Høgenhaven, J. and Mogens Müller (eds.), *Bibelske Genskrivninger* (Forum for Bibelsk Eksegese, 17. Copenhagen, Museum Tusculanum, 2012).

Holm-Nielsen, S. 1962. *Det gamle Testamente og det israelitisk-jødiske folks historie.* 8th rev. ed. København: G.E.C. Gads Forlag, 1975.

Hölscher, G. 1914. *Die Propheten: Untersuchungen zur Religionsgeschichte Israels.* Leipzig: J.C. Hinrichs'she Buchhandlung.

Huffmon, H.B. 1966. "The Treaty background of Hebrew YDA", *BASOR* 181, pp. 31–7.

Irons, W.L. 1968. *The Yomut Turkmen: A Study of Social Organization of Among Central Asian Turkic-Speaking Population.* Ann Arbor: The University of Michigan Press.

Jacobsen, T. 1939. *The Sumerian King List.* Assyriological Studies, 11. Chicago: Oriental Institute.

Jamieson-Drake, D.W. 1991. *Scribes and Schools in Monarchic Judah. A Socio-Archeological Approach.* The Social World of Biblical Antiquities Series, 9. Sheffield.

Jensen, H.J.L. 2000. *Den fortærende ild: Strukturelle analyser af narrative og rituelle tekster i Det Gamle Testamente.* Aarhus: Aarhus Universitetsforlag.

Jensen, H.J.L. 1998. "Josefhistorien" in *Gads Bibelleksikon A-K.* København: Gads Forlag), 390.

Jensen, M.S. 1968. *Hovedlinier i de sidste Aartiers Homerforskning.* Studier fra Sprog- og Oldtidsforskning nr. 267. København: G.E.C. Gad.

––––– 1980. *The Homeric Question and the Oral-Formulaic Theory.* Opuscula Graecolatina Vol. 20. København: Museum Tusculanum.

––––– 1992. *Homer og hans tilhørere.* København: Gyldendal.

––––– 1997. *Homer gennem tiden. Historie eller fiktion?* Studier fra Sprog- og Oldtidsforkning 330. København: Museum Tusculanum.

Jeppesen, K. 1987. *Græder ikke saa saare: Studier i Mikabogens sigte.* I-II. Aarhus: Aarhus Universitetsforlag.

Jonge, M. de. 1992. "Messiah", *The Anchor Bible Dictionary* 4. New York: Doubleday, pp. 777–88.

Jørgensen, J. 1941. *Psykologi på biologisk Grundlag.* København: Ejnar Munkgaard.

Kaiser, O. 1963. *Der Prophet Jesaja Kapitel 1–12 übersetzt und erklärt.* 3. Improved ed. Das Alte Testament Deutsch, 17. Göttingen: Vandenhoeck & Ruprecht.

––––– 1983. *Der Prophet Jesaja Kapitel 13–39.* Altes Testament Deutsch, 18; 3rd ed. Göttingen: Vandenhoeck & Ruprecht.

––––– 1984. *Einleitung in das Alte Testament. Eine Einfühung in ihre Ergebnisse und Probleme.* 5th ed. Gütersloh.

Kapelrud, A.S. 1961. "Levde Deuterojesaja in Judea? "*Norsk Teologisk Tidsskrift* 61: 23–27.

Kirkpatrick, P.G. 1986. *The Old Testament and Folklore Study.* JSOTSup, 62. Sheffield: JSOT Press.

Kittel, R. 1909–12. *Geschichte des Volkes Israel* I-II. 2. ed. Gotha: Gotha: Friedrich Andreas Perthes A.-G.

Kletter, R. 2004. "Chronology and United Monarchy: A Methodological Review", *ZDPV* 120, 13–54.

Kramer, S.N. 1956. *History Begins at Sumer: Thirty-Nine Firsts in Recorded History.* Philadelphia: Pennsylvania University Press.

––––– 1958. *Historien begynder med sumererne.* København: Det Schønbergske Forlag.

Krarup, P. 1964. *Homer. Blade af den nyere Forsknings Historie*: 2nd ed. 1954. Reprinted Gyldendals Uglebøger. København: Gyldendal.

Kratz, R.G. 2000. *Die Komposition der erzählende Bücher des Alten Testaments: Grundwissen der Bibelkritik*. Göttingen: Vandenhoeck & Ruprecht.

Kraus, H.-J. 1977. *Psalmen 1*, 3rd ed. Neukirchen-Vluyn: Erziehungsverein.

Kraus, F.R. 1958. *Ein Edikt des Königs Ammi-Ṣaduqa von Babylon*. Studia et Documenta, 5. Leiden: E.J. Brill.

—— 1984. *Königliche Verfügungen in altbabylonischer Zeit*. Studia et Documenta Ad Iura orientis Pertinentia 11. Leiden.

Krebs, C.B. 2011. *A Most Dangerous Book: Tacitus' Germania from the Roman Empire to the Third Reich*. London: W.W. Norton & Co.

Kreuzer, S. 1898. *Die Frühgeschichte Israels in Bekenntnis und Verkündigung des Alten Testaments*. Beiheft Zeitschrift für die alttestamentliche Wissenschaft, 178. Berlin: Walter de Gruyter.

Kuhn, T.S. 1962. *The Structure of Scientific Revolutions*. Chicago: University Press.

Kuhnen, H.-P. "Israel unmittelbar vor und nach Alexander dem Großen: Geschichtlicher Wandel und archäologtischer Befund". In S. Alkier and M. Witte (eds.), *Die Griechen und das antike Israel: Interdisziplinäre Studien zur Religions- und Kulturgeschichte des Heiligen Landes*. OBO, 201. Freiburg: Presse universitaire, 2004.

Kutsch, E. 1963. *Salbung als Rechtakt im Alten Testament und im alten Orient*. Berlin: De Gruyter.

Lambert, W.G. and Millard, A.R. 1969. *Atra-Ḫasīs: The Babylonian Story of the Flood*. Oxford: At the Clarendon Press.

Lemche, Niels Peter. 1972. *Israel i Dommertiden. En oversigt over diskussionen om Martin Noths "Das System der zwölf Stämme Israels"*. Tekst og Tolkning: Monografier udgivet af Institut for Bibelsk Eksegese, 4. Copenhagen, C.E.G. Gad, 1972.

—— 1975. "'The Hebrew Slave'. Comments on the Slave Law Ex xxi 2–11", *Vetus Testamentum* 25, 129–44. Reprint *Biblical Studies and the Failure of History*: 3: Changing Perspectives. Copenhagen International Seminar, London, Equinox, 2013, 11–25.

—— 1980. "The Chronology in the Story of the Flood", *Journal for the Study of the Old Testament* 18, 52–62.

—— 1982. "Det revolutionære Israel. En præsentation af en moderne forskningsretning", *Dansk Teologisk Tidsskrift* 45, pp. 16–39.

—— 1984. *Det Gamle Israel: Det israelitiske samfund fra sammenbruddet af bronzealderkulturen til hellenistisk tid*. Aarhus: Anis.

—— 1985a. "Fædrenes Gud", in Sigfred Pedersen (ed.), *Gudsbegrebet*. København: G.E.C. Gad, 46–59.

—— 1985b. *Early Israel. Anthropological and Historical Studies on the Israelite Society Before the Monarchy*. Vetus Testamentum Supplementum, 37. Leiden: E.J. Brill.

—— 1988. *Ancient Israel. A New History of Israelite Society*. The Biblical Seminar, 5. Sheffield: JSOTS, 1988.

—— 1989a. "Geschichte und Heilsgeschichte. Mehrere Aspekte der biblischen Theologie", *Scandinavian Journal of the Old Testament* 3/2, pp. 114-35.

—— 1989b. "On the Use of 'System Theory', 'Macro Theories' and Evolutionistic Thinking in Modern OT Research and Biblical Archaeology", *Scandinavian Journal of the Old Testament* 1990/2, 73-88, reprinted in Charles E. Carter and Caroll L. Meyers (eds.), *Community, Identity, and Ideology. Social Sciences Approaches to the Hebrew Bible*. Sources for Biblical and Theological Studies, 6. Winona Lake, IN: Eisenbrauns, 1996, pp. 273-86.

—— 1991a. *The Canaanites and Their Land: The Tradition of the Canaanites*. JSOTSup 110. Sheffield: JSOT. Reprinted with a postscript, Sheffield: Academic Press, 1999.

—— 1991b. "Our Most Gracious Sovereign: On the Relationship Between Royal Mythology and Economic Oppression in the Ancient Near East", in Morris Silver, *Ancient Economy in Mythology: East and West*. New York: Rowman & Littlefield, pp. 109-34.

—— 1992a. "Det gamle Testamente som en hellenistisk bog", *Dansk Teologisk Tidsskrift* 55, 81-101.

—— 1992b. "The God of Hosea", in Eugen Ulrich and John Wright (eds.): *Priests, Prophets, and Scribes. Essays on the Formation and Heritage of Second Temple Judaism in Honor of Joseph Blenkinsopp*. Journal for the Study of the Old Testament Supplement Series, 149. Sheffield: University Press, pp. 241-57.

—— 1993a. "The Old Testament – A Hellenistic Book?" *Scandinavian Journal of the Old Testament* 7, pp. 163-93.

—— 1993b. "Salme 2 – midt mellem fortid og fremtid", in Mogens Müller and John Strange, *Det gamle Testamente i jødedom og kristendom*. Forum for Bibelsk Eksegese, 4. København 1993), pp. 57-78.

—— 1994. "Hvad er det vi har lavet, og hvor går vi hen? Nogle personlige betragtninger omkring et paradigmeskift" in N.P. Lemche and M. Müller (eds.), *Fra dybet. Festskrift til John Strange i anledning af 60s års fødselsdagen den 20. juli 1994*. Forum for Bibelsk Eksegese 5. København: Museum Tusculanum, 130-43.

—— 1995a. "Warum die Theologie des Alten Testament einen Irrweg darstellt", *Jahrbuch für Biblische Theologie* 10, 79-92.

—— 1995b. "Kings and Clients: On Loyalty Between the Ruler and the Ruled in Ancient Israel", *Semeia* 66, 119-32.

―― 1995c. "Justice in Western Asia in Antiquity, Or: Why No Laws Were Needed", *The Kent Law Review* 70, 1695–716.

―― 1996a. "Samfundsopfattelsen i GT og i Dødehavsteksterne", in N. Hyldahl and T.L. Thompson (eds.), *Dødehavsteksterne og Det Gamle Testamente*. Forum for Bibelsk Eksegese, 8. København: Museum Tusculanum, pp. 64–78.

―― 1996b. "Clio is also among the Muses. Keith W. Whitelam and the History of Palestine: A Review and a Commentary", *Scandinavian Journal of the Old Testament* 10, 88–114).

―― 1996c. "From Patronage Society to Patronage Society", in Fritz and Davies (eds.), *The Origins of the Israelite States*, pp. 106–20.

―― 1996d. *Die Vorgeschichte Israels. Von den Anfängen bis zum Ausgang des 13. Jahrhunderts v. Chr.* Biblische Enzyklopädie 1. Stuttgart: W. Kohlhammer.

―― 1997. "Københavnerskolen "– eller: Det Gamle Testamente efter syndfloden, *Fønix* 21, 22–29.

―― 1998a. "Israel og det land", in Lemche, N.P. and Tronier, H. (eds.). *Etnicitet i Bibelen*. Forum for Bibelsk Eksegese 9, 11–22.

―― 1998b. *Prelude to Israel's Past. Background and beginnings of Israelite History and Identity* Peabody, MA: Hendrickson, 1998.

―― 1998c. "Om historie, sociologi og teologi – gammeltestamentlige perspektiver", in Theodor Jørgensen and Peter K. Westergaard (eds.), *Teologien i samfundet: Festskrift til Jens Glebe-Møller*. København: Anis, 1998, 269–88.

―― 1998d. *The Israelites in History and Tradition*. Library of Ancient Israel. Louisville, KY/London: Westminster-John Knox/SPCK.

―― 1998e. "The Understanding of Community in the OT and in the DSS", in F.H. Cryer and T.L. Thompson (eds.), *Qumran between the Old and New Testament*. Journal for the study of the Old Testament Supplement Series 290/The Copenhagen International Seminar, 6, Sheffield, 181–93.

―― 1999a. "Om historisk erindring i Det Gamle Testamentes historiefortællinger", in Geert Hallbäck and John Strange (eds.), *Bibel og historieskrivning (Forum for Bibelsk Eksegese* 10. København 1999), 11–28.

―― 1999b, "What if Zedekiah Had Remained Loyal to His Master?" In J. Cyril Exum (ed.), *Virtual History and the Bible*, Leiden, 1999, pp. 115–28 (= *Biblical Interpretation* 8 [2000]).

―― 2000. "Ideology and the History of Ancient Israel", *Scandinavian Journal of the Old Testament* 14, 165–93.

―― 2001a. "How does One Date an Expression of Mental History? The Old Testament and Hellenism", in L.L. Grabbe (ed.), *Did Moses Speak Attic? Jewish Historiography and Scripture in the Hellenistic period*. JSOTSS, 317. Sheffield 2001, 200–24.

――― 2001b. "Prægnant tid i Det Gamle Testamente", in Geert Hallbäck and Niels Peter Lemche (eds.), *"Tiden" i bibelsk belysning*. Forum for Bibelsk Eksegese, 11. København: Museum Tusculanum, 2001, 29-47.

――― 2008a. *Gammeltestamentlig og bibelsk teologi: Ti forelæsninger*. København: Anis.

――― 2008b. *Det Gamle Testamente mellem teologi og historie*. København: Anis.

――― 2008c. *The Old Testament between Theology and History*. Louisville: Westminster John Knox.

――― 2010. "The Deuteronomistic History – Historical Reconsiderations", in in K.L. Noll and Brooks Schramm (eds.), *"Raising Up a Faithful Exegete": Essays in Honor of Richard D. Nelson"*. Winona Lake, Eisenbrauns, 41–50.

――― 2012a. "The Greek Israelites and Gerizim", in *Plogbillar & svärd: En festskrift till Stig Norin*, ed. Tal Davidivich. Uppsala: Molin & Sorgenfrei, 147-54.

――― 2012b. "Da studenterrådet blev voksen", *Hvad er imod Studentens Kaar: Festskrift til Det Teologiske Fagråds Hundredårsjubilæum 1912-2012*, red. Emil Bjørn Saggau. København: Det Teologiske Fakultet, 33-36.

――― 2012c. "Gammeltestamentlige tekster som genskrevet litteratur", in Jesper Høgenhaven and Mogens Müller (ed.), *Bibelske Genskrivninger*. Forum for Bibelsk Eksegese, 17. København: Museum Tusculanum, 2012", 51-73.

――― 2013a. *Biblical Studies and the Failure of History*. Changing Perspectives, 3. Copenhagen International Seminar. London: Equinox.

――― 2013b. "Power and Social Organization: Some Misunderstandings and Some Proposals: Or Is It All a Question of Patron and Clients?", published in Niels Peter Lemche, *Biblical Studies and the Failure of History*. Changing Perspectives, 3. Copenhagen International Seminar. London: Equinox, pp. 158-68.

――― 2013c. "When the Past Becomes the Present", *Scandinavian Journal of the Old Testament 27"*, 99-109.

――― 2013d. *Biblical Studies and the Failure of History*. Copenhagen International Seminar. Changing Perspectives 3. London: Equinox.

――― 2015. *Ancient Israel: A New History of the Israelite Society*. Second edition: London: T&T Clark.

――― 2016. "Is the Old Testament Still a Hellenistic Book?", in Ingrid Hjelm and Thomas L. Thompson, *Biblical Interpretation Beyond Historicity. Changing Perspectives*, 7. Copenhagen International Seminar, London: Routledge, 61-75.

――― 2022. *Back to Reason: Minimalism in Biblical Studies*. Discourses in Ancient Near Eastern and Biblical Studies. London: Equinox, 2022.

———— 2023. "A Social Anthropology of Biblical Memory", in Emanuel Pfoh (ed.), *T & T Clark Handbook of Anthropology and the Hebrew Bible*. London: Bloomsbury, 373-93.

Lemche, N.P. and Müller, M. (eds.). 1994. *Fra Dybet. Festskrift til John Strange i anledning af 60 års fødselsdagen den 20. Juli 1994*. Forum for Bibelsk Eksegese 5. København: Museum Tusculanum.

Lemche, N.P. and Tronier, H. (eds.). 1998. *Etnicitet i Bibelen*. Forum for Bibelsk Eksegese 9. København: Museum Tusculanum.

Lévi-Strauss, C. 1962. *La pensée sauvage*. Paris: Pocket.

———— 1966. *The Savage Mind*, Chicago: University Press.

Lewis, I. 1971. *Ecstatic Religion: An Anthropological Study of Spirit Possession and Shamanism*. Pelican anthropology library. Harmondsworth: Penguin Books.

Liddell, H.G. & R. Scott. 1940. *A Greek-English Lexicon*. A New Edition revised and augmented by Henry S. Jones. 9. Ed.. Oxford: Clarendon Press.

Lindblom, J. 1934. *Profetismen i Israel. Profetismen i Israel*, Stockholm: Svenska kyrkans diakonistyrelses bokförlag.

———— 1962. *Prophecy in Ancient Israel*. Oxford: Blackwell's.

Lipschits, Oded. 2005. *The Fall and Rise of Jerusalem: Judah under Babylonian Rule*. Winona Lake, Indiana: Eisenbrauns.

———— 2011. "Shedding New Light on the Dark Years of the 'Exilic Period': New Studies, Further Elucidation, and Some Questions Regarding the Archaeology of Judah as an 'Empty Land'", i Brad Kelle, Frank Ritchel Ames, and Jacob L. Wright (eds.), *Interpreting Exile*. Atlanta: Society of Biblical Literature, 57-90.

Lipschits, Oded, and Joseph Blenkinsopp (eds.). 2003. *Judah and the Judeans in the Neo-Babylonian Period*. Winona Lake, Indiana: Eisenbrauns.

Liverani, M. 1966. "Problemi e indirizzi degli studi storici sul Vicino Oriente antica", *Cultura e Scuola* 20, pp. 72-9.

———— 1967. "Contrasti e confluenze di concezioni politiche nell'età di El-Amarna", *Revue d'assyriologie et d'archéologie* 61, pp. 1-18.

———— 1971. "Συδυκ and Μισώρ." *Studi in onore di Edoardi Volterra*, VII. Pubblicazioni della Facultà di Giurisprudenxa dell Università di Roma. Milano, pp. 55-74.

———— 1972. "Partire sul carro, per il deserto", *Annali dell'Istituto Universitario Orientale di Napoli* NS 22, 403-15.

———— 1977. "Storiografia politica hittita II: Telipinu, ovvero: della Solidarietà", *OA* 16, pp. 105-31; transl. in: Mario Liverani, *Myth and Politics in Ancient Near Eastern Historiography*. London: Equinox, 2004, pp. 27-52.

———— 1983. "Political Lexicon and Political Ideologies in the Amarna Letters", *Berytus* 31, pp. 41-56.

―― 1988. *Antico Oriente. Storia società economia*. Bari: Editori Laterza.

―― 1990. *Prestige and Interest. International Relations in the Near East ca. 1600-1100 B.C.* Padova: Sargon.

―― 2003: *Oltre la Bibbia: Storia antica di Israële*. Roma-Bari: Editori Laterza.

―― 2004. "Leaving by Chariot for the Desert", in Mario Liverani, *Myths and Politics in Ancient Near Eastern* Historiography. Studies in Egyptology and the Ancient Near East. London: Equinox, 85-96.

―― 2005. *Israel's History and the History of Israel*. London: Equinox.

―― 2021. "Ḫattušili Dealing with Ramesside Propaganda". In *Historiography, Ideology and Politics in the Ancient Near East and Israel*. Eds. N.P. Lemche and E. Pfoh. Changing Perspectives, 5. London: Routledge, 123-34.

Lord, A.B. 1960, *The Singer of Tales*. Cambridge, Mass.: Harvard University Press.

Luckenbill, D.D. 1924. *The Annals of Sennacherib*. Chicago: Oriental Institute; reprinted Eugene, Oregon: Wipf & Stock, 2005.

―― 1926. *Ancient Records of Assyria and Babylonia*, I. Chicago: Oriental Institute.

Luther, M. 1545. *Die gantze Heilige Schrifft Deudsch* (Wittenberg 1545; reprinted Darmstadt: Wissenschaftliche Buchgesellschaft, 1972).

Magen, Y. 2007. "The Dating of the First Phase of the Samaritan Temple at Mount Gerizim in Light of Archaeological Evidence" in O. Lipschits, G.N. Knoppers, and R. Albertz, *Judah and the Judeans in the Fourth Century B.C.E.* Winona Lake: Eisenbrauns, 157-211.

Malamat, A. 1982. "A Political Look on at the Kingdom of David and Solomon and Its Relations with Egypt", in T. Ishida (ed.), *Studies in the Period of David and Solomon*. Winona Lake: Eisenbrauns, pp. 189-204.

Martínez, F.G. and E.J.C. Tigchelaar. 1997. *The Dead Scrolls: Study Edition*, I. Leiden: E.J. Brill.

Mendels, D. 1987. *The Land of Israel as a Political Concept in Hasmonean Literature*. Tübingen: Mohr.

―― 1992. *The Rise and Fall of Jewish Nationalism*. The Anchor Bible Reference Library. New York: Doubleday.

Mendenhall, G.E. 1954. "Covenant Forms in Israelite Tradition", *BA* 17, pp. 50-76.

―― 1962. "The Hebrew Conquest of Palestine", *The Biblical Archaeologist* 25, pp. 102-25.

Mettinger, T.N.D. 1976. *King and Messiah*. Lund: Gleerup.

Meyer, E. 1905. *Die Israeliten und ihre Nachbarstämme*. Halle: Niemeyer (reprint Darmstadt: Wissenschaftliche Buchgesellschaft, 1967).

Miller, J.M. and J. Hayes. 1986. *A History of Ancient Israel and Judah.* Philadelphia: Westminster.

Miller II, R.D. 2011. *Oral Tradition in Ancient Israel.* Eugene, Or.: Cascade Books.

Morante, W. 1974. *La Storia* (Torino: Giulio Einaudi editore).

Mowinckel, S. 1916. *Kongesalmerne i Det Gamle Testamente.* Kristiania: Forlagt av H. Aschehough & Co (W. Nygaard).

———. 1966. *Psalmenstudien I-VI.* Reprinted In two volumes. Amsterdam: Verlag P. Schippers N.V.

——— 1922/1966. *Der Thronbesteigungsfest Jahwäs und der Ursprung der Eschatologie.* Psalmenstudien II. Oslo: 1922. Reprint Amsterdam: Verlag P. Schippers N.V., 1966.

——— 1951a. *Offersang og sangoffer.* Oslo: Ashehoug.

——— 1951b. *Han som kommer. Messiasforventningen i Det gamle Testamente og på Jesus tid.* København: Ashehoug.

——— 1956. *He that Cometh: The Messiah Concept in the Old Testament and Later Judaism.* Nashville: Abingdon, 1956; reprint: Grand Rapids: Eerdmans, 2005.

——— 1962. *The Psalms in Israel's Worship.* Oxford: Blackwells, 1962, reprint Grand Rapids: Eerdmans, 2004.

Namer, G. 2000. *Halbwachs et la mémoire sociale.* Paris: L'Harmattan.

Narroll, R. 1964. "On Ethnic Unit Classification", *Current Anthropology 5"*, 283–291.

Nicolaisen, J. 1963. *Ecology and Culture of the Pastoral Tuareg.* Copenhagen: Nationalmuseet.

Nicoll, A. and J. Nicoll (eds.). 1965. *Holinshed's Chronicle as used in Shakespeare's Plays.* London: Dent, Everyman's Library.

Nielsen, E. 1955. *Shechem: A Traditio-Historical Investigation.* Copenhagen: G.E.C. Gad.

——— 1960. *Grundrids af Israels historie.* 2. ed. København: G.E.C. Gads Forlag.

——— 1990. *31 udvalgte salmer fra Det gamle Testamente.* Frederiksberg: Anis.

——— 1992. "En hellenistisk bog?" *Dansk Teologisk Tidsskrift* 55, pp. 161–74.

Nielsen, F.A.J. 1997. *The Tragedy in History. Herodotus and the Deuteronomistic History.* The Copenhagen International Seminar, 4/Journal for the Study of the Old Testament Supplement Series, 251. Sheffield: Sheffield Academic Press.

Nielsen, K. 1978. *Yahweh as Prosecutor and Judge.* Journal for the Study of the Old Testament Supplement Series, 9. Sheffield: JSOT Press.

Niemann, H.M. 1993. *Herschaft, Königtum und Staat. Skizzen zur soziokulturellen Entwicklung im monarchischen Israel.* Forschungen zum Alten Testament 6. Tübingen.

Nissinen, M. 1998. *References to Prophecy in Neo-ASSYRIAN Sources.* State Archives of Assyria, VII. Helsinki: University Press.

—— 2003. *Prophets and Prophecy in the Ancient Near East.* With a contribution by C.L. Snow and Robert K. Ritter. Edited by Peter Machinist. Society of Biblical Literature Writings from the Ancient World Series, 12. Atlanta, Georgia: Society of Biblical Literature.

Noth, M. 1948. *Überlieferungsgeschichte des Pentateuch Überlieferungsgeschichte des Pentateuch.* Reprint: Darmstadt: Wissenschaftliche Buchgesellschaft, 1966.

—— 1950. *Geschichte Israels.* Göttingen: Vandenhoeck & Ruprecht.

Olmo Lete, G. 2004. *A Dictionary of the Ugaritic Language in the Alphabetic Tradition.* Handbuch der Orientalistik, 67. Leiden: E.J. Brill.

Ong, W.J. 2012. *Orality and Literacy: The Technologies of the Word*, 13th edition. London: Routledge.

Ørsted, P. 1978. *Romersk historieskrivning: En analyse af en række generelle træk i antikkens opfattelse af historiens væsen og formål.* København: Gyldendal.

Otzen, B. 1977. *Israelitterne i Palæstina.* København, C.E.G. Gad. 2. ed. 1982.

Otzen, B. 1984. *Den antike jødedom.* København: G.E.C. Gad.

Pallis, S.A. 1926. *The Babylonian Akîtu Festival.* Copenhagen: Høst.

Parker, S.B. (ed.). 1997. *Ugaritic Narrative Poetry.* SBLWAW, 9. Atlanta, GA: Scholars.

Parpola, S. 1997. *Assyrian Prophecies.* State Archives of Assyria, IX. Helsinki: University Press.

—— 1988. *Neo-Assyrian Treaties and Loyalty Oaths.* Helsinki: University Press.

Pedersen. J. 1926. *Israel, Its Life and Culture, I–II.* Oxford: University Press.

Pedersen, J. 1960. *Israel, III–IV: Hellighed og Gudommelighed.* 2. Ed. København: Branner og Korch.

Perlitt. 1965. *Vatke und Wellhausen. Geschichtsphilosophische Voraussetzungen und historiographische Motive für die Darstellung der Religion und Geschichte Israels durch Wilhelm Vatke und Julius Wellhausen.* BZAW, 94. Berlin: De Gruyter.

—— 1969. *Bundestheologie im Alten Testament.* WMANT, 36. Neukirchen: Neukirchener Verlag.

Petersen, A.R. 1998. *The Royal God. Enthronement Festivals in Ancient Israel and Ugarit.* JSOTSup, 259/CIS, 5. Sheffield: Academic Press.

Pfoh, Emanuel. 2016. *Syria-Palestine in the Late Bronze Age: An Anthropology of Politics and Power.* Copenhagen International Seminar. London: Routledge.

―――― 2022. (ed.), *Patronage in Ancient Palestine and in the Hebrew Bible: A Reader.* The Social World of Biblical Antiquity, Second Series, 12. Sheffield: Sheffield Phoenix Press.

Pinson, P. *"The Voices of Jerusalem"*, MA Thesis, Polis Institute of Jerusalem 2019/20.

Pritchard, J.B. (ed.). 1955. *Ancient Near Eastern Texts Relating to the Old Testament.* 2nd ed. Princeton NJ: Princeton University Press.

Raby, F.J.E. 1927. *A History of Christian-Latin Poetry from the Beginnings to the Close of the Middle Age.* Oxford: At the Clarendon Press.

Rad, G. Von. 1938. *Das formgeschichtliche Problem des Hexateuch.* Beiträge zur Wissenschaft des Alten und Neuen Testament, IV.26. Stuttgart: Kohlhammer), reprinted in his *Gesammelte Studien zum Alten Testament* (München: Chr. Kaiser, 1958)", 9-86.

―――― 1944. "Der Anfang der Geschichtsschreibung im alten Israel", reprinted in Gerhard von Rad, *Gesammelte Studien zum Alten Testament.* Theologische Bücherei, 8. München: Chr. Kaiser, 1965, 148-88.

―――― 1957-60. *Theologie des Alten Testaments* I-II. München: Chr. Kaiser.

Ranke, L. von. 1824. *Geschichten der romanischen und germanischen Völker von 1494 bis 1535.* Leipzig u. Berlin: G. Reimer.

Ravn, O.E. 1939. *Herodots Beskrivelse af Babylon.* København: Nyt Nordisk Forlag Arnold Busk 1939.

―――― *Herodotus' Description of Babylon*, Copenhagen: Nyt Nordisk Forlag Arnold Musk, 1942.

Redford, D.B. 1970. *A Study of the Biblical Story of Joseph.* Vetus Testamentum Supplements, 20. Leiden: E.J. Brill.

―――― 1992. *Egypt, Canaan, and Israel in Ancient Times.* Princeton: University Press.

Renz, J. 1995. *Die althebräischen Inschriften Teil 1. Text und Kommentar.* Darmstadt: Wissenschaftliche Buchgesellschaft.

Ringgren, H. 1987. *Psaltaren 1-41.* Uppsala: EFS förlag.

Römer, T. 2005. *The So-Called Deuteronomistic History: A Sociological, Historical and Literary Introduction* London: T & T Clark.

―――― 2006. "The Elusive Yahwist: A Short History of Research", in Thomas B. Dozeman and Konrad Schmid (eds.), *A Farewell to the Yahwist?* 9-28

Rost, L. 1965. "Das kleine geschichtliches Credo", in *Das kleine Credo und andere Studien zum Alten Testament.* Heidelberg: Quelle & Meyer, 1965", 11-24.

Roth, M.T. 1997. *Law Collections from Mesopotamia and Asia Minor.* 2. Ed., SBL Writings from the Ancient World Series, 6. Atlanta: Scholars Press.

Sandars, J.A. 1992. "Canon", *The Anchor Bible Dictionary* I. New York: Doubleday, 1992.

Schmid, H.H. 1968. *Gerechtigkeit als Weltordnung: Hintergrund und Geschichte des altorientalischen Gerechtigkeitsbegriffes*. Beiträge zur historischen Theologie, 40. Tübingen: J.C.B. Mohr.

Schmid, K. 2006. "The So-Called Yahwist and the Literary Gap between Genesis and Exodus", in Thomas B. Dozeman and Konrad Schmid (eds.), *A Farewell to the Yahwist? The Composition of the Pentateuch in Recent European Interpretation*. Atlanta: Society of Biblical Literature, 29–50.

Schmidt, Hans. 1934. *Die Psalmen*. HAT XV/1: 15. Tübingen.

Seebass, H. 1934–2015. *Der Erzvater Israel und die Einfuhrung der Jahwe-Verehrung in Kanaan*. BZAW, 98. Berlin: De Gruyter, 1966

Seidel, B. 1993. *Karl David Ilgen und die Pentateuchforschung im Umkreis der sogenannten Älteren Urkundenhypothese*. Beihefte Zeitschrift für die alttestamentliche Wissenschaft, 213. Berlin: De Gruyter.

Shanks, H. 1997. "Face to Face: Biblical Minimalists meet their Challengers", *Biblical Archaeology Review* 23/4, 26–42, 66.

Skydsgaard, J.E. 1978. *Pompejus vender tilbage*. Studier i romersk politik år 62–59 f. Kr. Studier fra Sprog- og Oldtidsforkning 293. København: G.E.C. Gad.

Soggin, J.A. 1967. "Zum ersten Psalm", *TZ* 23, pp. 81–96

――― 1984. *A History of Israel from the Beginnings to the Bar Kochba Revolt, AD 135*. London: SCM.

――― 1991. *Einführung in die Geschichte Israels und Judas*. Darmstadt: Wissenschaftliche Buchgesellschaft.

――― 1993. *An Introduction to the History of Israel and Judah*. London: SCM.

Spieckermann, H. 1982. *Juda und Assyrien in der Sargonidenzeit*. Forschungen zur Religion und Literatur des Alten und Neuen Testament, 129. Göttingen: Vandenhoeck & Ruprecht.

Steiner, M.L. 2001. *Excavations by Kathleen M. Kenyon in Jerusalem 1861–1867, Volume III: The Settlement in the Bronze and Iron Ages*. Copenhagen International Series, 9. London: Sheffield Academic Press.

Strange, J. 1985. "Frelseshistorie og historie. Et synspunkt på bibelsk teologi", *Dansk Teologisk Tidsskrift* 45, pp. 225–37

――― 1989a. "Replik an Niels Peter Lemche", *Scandinavian Journal of the Old Testament* 3/2, 136–9.

――― 1989b. "Heilsgeschichte und Geschichte. Ein Aspekt der biblischen Theologie", *Scandinavian Journal of the Old Testament* 3/2, pp. 100–13.

――― 1993. "The Book of Joshua. A Hasmonaean Manifesto?" In Lemaire, A. and Otzen, B. (eds.), *History and Traditions of Early Israel. Studies Presented to Eduard Nielsen May 8th 1993*. Supplements to Vetus Testamentum, 50. Leiden. E.J. Brill, 136–41.

―――― 1998. *Bibelatlas*. 3. Rev. ed. København: Det Danske Bibelselskab.

Tapper, R.L. 1979. *Pasture and Politics. Economics, Conflict and Ritual among the Shahsevan Nomads of Azerbaijan*. London: Academic Press.

Theissen, G. 1977. *Soziologie der Jesusbewegung. Ein Beitrag zur Entstehungsgeschichte des Urchristentums*. München: Kaiser.

Thompson, T.L. 1974. *The Historicity of the Patriarchal Narratives: The Quest for the Historical Abraham*. Beiheft zur Zeitschrift für die alttestamentliche Wissenschaft, 133. Berlin: W. de Gruyter.

―――― 1992. *Early History of the Israelite People. From the Written and Archaeological Sources*. Studies in the History of the Ancient Near East IV. Leiden: E.J. Brill.

―――― 1999. *The Bible in History: How Writers Create a Past*. London: Jonathan Cape.

―――― 2005. *The Messiah Myth: The Near Eastern Roots of Jesus and David*. New York: Basic Books.

Tigay, J.H. 1986. *You Shall Have no Other Gods*. HSS, 31. Atlanta, GA: Scholars.

Torrey, C.C. 1896. *The Composition and Historical Value of Ezra-Nehemia*. Reprint: Leopold Classic Library. South Yarra, Victoria, 2015.

―――― 1910. *Ezra Studies*. republished Wolcott, NY: Scholar's Choice, 2015.

Treves, M. 1988. *The Dates of the Psalms. History and Poetry in Ancient Israel*. Pisa: Giardini editori e stampatori.

Trolle Larsen, M. 1997. *Gudens skygge. Det assyriske imperiums historie*. København: Gyldendal.

Ussishkin, D. 1982. *The Conquest of Lachish by Sennacherib*. Tel Aviv: Tel Aviv University The Institute of Archaeology.

Vanderkam, J.C. 1995. *Dødehavsrullerne - teorier og kendsgerninger*. Frederiksberg: Anis.

Van Seters, J. 1975. *Abraham in History and Tradition*. New Haven: Yale University Press.

―――― 1983. *In Search of History. Historiography in the Ancient World and the Origins of Biblical History*. New Haven, CT: Yale University Press.

―――― 1988. "The Primeval Histories of Greece and Israel Compared", *Zeitschrift für die alttestamentliche Wissenschaft* 100, 1–22, reprinted in Van Seters 2011. 335–58.

―――― 2006a. *The Edited Bible: The Curious History of the 'Editor' in Biblical Criticism*. Winona Lake, Indiana: Eisenbrauns, 2006.

―――― 2006b. "The Report of the Yahwist's Demise Has Been Greatly Exaggerated!" in Thomas B. Dozeman and Konrad Schmid (eds.), *A Farewell to the Yahwist?* 143–58.

—— 2011. *Changing Perspectives I: Studies in the History, Literature and Religion of Biblical Israel* (London: Equinox 2011),

—— 2013. *The Yahwist: A Historian of Israelite Origins*. Winona Lake: Eisenbrauns.

Vaux, R. De. 1939. "Titres et fonctionnaires égyptiens à la court de David et de Salomon", *Revue Biblique* 48, pp. 394–405, reprinted in his *Bible et Orient*. Paris: Éditions du Cerf, 1967, pp. 189–201.

Vernes, Maurice. 1889. *Précis d'histoire juive dépuis les origins jusqu'à l'époque persane*. Paris: Librairie Hachette.

Wajdenbaum, P. 2011. *Argonauts of the Desert: Structural Analysis of the Hebrew Bible*. Copenhagen International Seminar: London: Equinox.

Weidner. E.F. 1923. *Politische Dokumente aus Kleinasien*. Leipzig: J.C. Hinrichs.

Wellhausen, J. 1878. *Prolegomena zur Geschichte Israels*. Leipzig: Hinrichs.

—— 1884. *Israelitische und jüdische Geschichte*. 9th ed. Berlin: Walter de Gruyter & Co. 1958.

—— 1994. *Prolegomena to the History of Ancient Israel*, with and introduction by W. Robertson Smith and a preface by Douglas A. Knight. Atlanta: Scholars.

Welten, P. 1973. *Geschichte und Geschichtsdarstellung in den Chronikbüchern*. Neukirchen-Vluyn: Verlag des Erziehungsvereins.

Wessels, A. 1972. *A Modern Arabic Biography of Muḥammad: A Critical Study of Muḥammad Ḥusayn Haykal's Ḥayāt Muḥammad*. Published by Brill Archive.

Westenholz, U. and A. 1997. *Gilgamesh of Enuma Elish: Guder og mennesker i oldtidens Babylon*. Verdensreligionernes Hovedværker. København: Spektrum.

Westermann, C. 1974 *Genesis*. Biblischer Kommentar Altes Testament Neukirchen: Neukirchener Verlag.

Wette, Wilhelm Martin Leberecht De. 1971. *Beiträge zur Einleitung in das Alte Testament. I-II*. Darmstadt: Wissenschaftliche Buchgesellschaft, 1971.

Whitelam, K.W. 1996 *The Invention of Ancient Israel. The Silencing of Palestinian History*. London: Routledge.

Wiggins, S.A. 1993. *A Reassessment of "Asherah"*. AOAT, 235: Neukirchen: Neukirchener Verlag.

Wildberger, H. 1972. *Jesaja*. Biblischer Kommentar Altes Testament. 1. Teilband Jesaja 1–12. Neukirchen-Vluyn: Neukirchener Verlag des Erziehungsvereins.

—— 1978. *Jesaja*. 2. Teilband. Jesaja 13–27. Biblische Kommentar zum Alten Testament X/2. Neukirchen: Neukirchener Verlag.

Williamson, H.G. 1977. "The Historical Value of Josephus' *Jewish Antiquities* xi. 297–301", *JTS N.S.* 28, 1977, 49–66.

—— "The Governors of Judah under the Persians", *Tyndale Bulletin* 39, 1988, 59–82.

Winnett, F. 1965. "Reexamining the Foundations", *Journal of Biblical Literature* 84, 1–19.

Wolff, H.W. 1973. *Anthropologie des Alten Testaments.* Gütersloh: Gütersloher Verlagshaus.

Wyatt, N. 1998. *Religious Texts from Ugarit: The Words of Ilimilku and His Colleagues.* The Biblical Seminar, 53. Sheffield: Academic Press.

Zimmern, H. 1905, 1918. *Zum babylonischen Neujahrsfest I–II.* Leipzig: B.G. Teubner.

Index of Scripture References

Genesis

Genesis 1	44, 45, 139, 230, 231
Gen 1:1	41
Gen 1:10	43
Gen 1:28	45
Genesis 1–2	230
Genesis 1–3	230, 231
Genesis 1–11	83, 139
Genesis 2	44, 45, 230, 231
Gen 2:1-3	33, 34
Gen 2:1–4a	231
Genesis 3	44
Gen 5:24	87
Gen 6:1–4	74
Gen 6:5–7	84
Gen 6:7	82
Gen 6:9	85
Gen 6:11–14	84
Genesis 6–8	30, 75, 82, 87, 89
Gen 7:4	31
Gen 7:6	31
Gen 7:7	31
Gen 7:11	31
Gen 7:12.17	86
Gen 7:18	85
Gen 7:21.22	85
Gen 7:24	31
Gen 8:4	31
Gen 8:5	31
Gen 8:6	86
Gen 8:7	87
Gen 8:8	85
Gen 8:10	31
Gen 8:12	31
Gen 8:13	31, 32
Gen 8:14	31, 32, 83
Gen 9:29	87
Genesis 10	254
Genesis 11	84, 260
Genesis 11–12	254
Genesis 12	254
Genesis 12:1–9	260
Genesis 12; 20; 26	69
Gen 16:11	57
Genesis 18	230
Genesis 18–19	89
Gen 19:24	88
Genesis 20	69
Genesis 24:3	262
Genesis 26	69
Gen 26:34	262
Gen 27:46	262
Gen 29:15–39	30
Gen 39	75
Genesis 41	30
Gen 50:1–3	30

Exodus

Exod 3:8	66
Exodus 16	30
Exod 17:8–16	227
Exod 20:8	34
Exod 20:9–10	36
Exod 20:11	34
Exodus 21–23	36
Exod 21:2	26

Index of Scripture References

Exodus 23	262	1 Samuel 8 and 12	27
Exod 23:10–11	36	1 Sam 13:7–15	289
Exod 23:12	36	1 Samuel 24 and 26	70
Exod 23:20–33	156		
Exod 23:32	157	**2 Samuel**	
Exod 23:10-11	157	2 Sam 5:4-5	27
		2 Samuel 7	71
Leviticus		2 Sam 7:1	150
Leviticus 19	69	2 Samuel 8–2 Kings 2	227
Leviticus 23	142		
Leviticus 25	36	**1 Kings**	
		1 Kings 2:11	27
Numbers		1 Kings 3:1	95
Num 14:27-35	37	1 Kings 6–8	28
Numbers 24:24	56	1 Kings 7	71
Num 25:10	40	1 Kings 9:16	96
		1 Kings 11:42	27
Deuteronomy		1 Kings 12	143
Deuteronomy 1–3	70	1 Kings 14:21	27
Dtn 4	153	1 Kings 14:25–26	98
Deut 5:12	34	1 Kings 15:2	27
Deut 5:13–14	36	1 Kings 15:10	27
Deut 6:20–5	143	1 Kings 15:12-15	28
Deuteronomy 15	36, 37, 39	1 Kings 16:15	29
		1 Kings 21:42	28
Joshua		1 Kings 22	120
Joshua 6	160, 161		
Joshua 6:3–5	26	**2 Kings**	
Josh 10:12	227	2 Kings 2:23–4	123
Joshua 24	143, 153, 185, 290	2 Kings 3	174, 175
		2 Kings 8.17	28
Judges		2 Kings 8:26	28
Judg 1:8	2	2 Kings 10:15–16	66
Judges 9	296	2 Kings 11	26
Judg 10:1-5; 12:8-15	25	2 Kings 11:3	28
Judges 11	297	2 Kings 12	28
Judg 12:7	27	2 Kings 12:2	28
Judg 14:5–6	298	2 Kings 15	167
Judg 16:25–30	298	15:1-2	24
Judg 16:31	26	15:17.22	25
17:6; 21:25	27	2 Kings 15:19–20	167
Judg 18:1	27	2 Kings 15:29–30	167
Judg 19:1	27	15:32-33	24
Judges 21	298	2 Kings 16	168
		2 Kings 16:2–4	168
1 Samuel		2 Kings 16:7	58
1 Sam 4:18	27	2 Kings 16:7–10	167
1 Samuel 8	186	2 Kings 18–19	167

2 Kings 18–20	61, 214, 216, 217
2 Kgs 18:1–8	105
2 Kings 18:13–16	75, 216
2 Kings 18:17–37	169
2 Kings 18:26	260
2 Kings 18–19	75, 171, 172, 173, 175
2 Kings 19:1–7	169
2 Kings 19:9	172
2 Kings 19:35	75
2 Kings 22–23	105
2 Kings 23	72, 242, 243
2 Kings 23:22	72
2 Kgs 23:28–30	105
2 Kings 23	72
2 Kings 23:22	72
2 Kings 25	45
2 Kings 25:1	28
25:27–30	71
2 Kings 25:27–30	71

1 Chronicles

1 Chronicles 6:40	181
1 Chronicles 28	71
1 Chron 29:27	181

2 Chronicles

2 Chronicles 3	72
2 Chron 16	71
2 Chron 18	71
2 Chron 29–31	105
2 Chronicles 31	72
2 Chron 34–35	105
2 Chron 34:29–33	72
2 Chronicles 35	72
2 Chron 35:20–27	72
2 Chron 35:26	72
2 Chron 36:21	25
2 Chron 36:22–23	71

Ezra

Ezra 2	178
Ezra 3:8	182
Ezra 3:12–13	140
Ezra 7:1	182
Ezra 8:1	181
Ezra 10	262
Ezra 10:18	182

Nehemiah

Neh 1:1	178
Neh 2:1	178
Neh 6:15	178
Nehemiah 7	178
Nehemiah 8	178
Nehemiah 9	178, 185, 186
Nehemiah 10	178
Nehemiah 11	178
Nehemiah 12	178
Nehemiah 13	178

Job

Job 19:25–26	54

Psalms

Ps 1	111, 112, 113, 114, 116
Ps 2	92, 93, 110, 111, 112, 113, 114, 115, 116
Ps 2:1–2	112
Ps 2:2	116
Ps 2:4–6	114
Ps 2:7	111, 116
Ps 2:7a	99
Ps 2:7b	90, 91, 94, 99, 100
Ps 2:7c	100
Ps 2:9	
2:10–12	115
Ps 2:12c	114
Psalm 2;10–12b	115
Ps 3	115, 116
Ps 9:9	49
Ps 10:7	116
Ps 18:51	116
Ps 23	113
Ps 28:8	116
Ps 36	113
58:2	49
Psalm 72	92, 93, 94, 179
Ps 84:10	116
Psalm 89	92, 93
89:39.52	116
Ps 98:9	49
Ps 99:4	48
Ps 104	186
104–106	185, 186
105	186

105:15	116	11:1–10 (16)	103
110	92, 93	Isa 11:9	61, 65
132	92, 93	Isaiah 13–23	61
132:10.17	116	Isaiah 24–27	60, 61, 214
Ps 137	3, 6, 16	Isaiah 28–35	61
137:2	16	Isa 35:5–6	53
151	110	Isaiah 36–39	61, 214
		Isaiah 40	52
Proverbs		Isaiah 40–55	60
Prov 1:3	49	Isa 40:1–2a.3	52
2:9	49	Isa 40:4	52
Proverbs 8	51	Isa 40:5	52
		Isa 40:11	53
Isaiah		Isaiah 42	61
Isaiah 1	63, 126, 127	42:1–4 (7)	214
Isaiah 1–12	60, 61, 62, 67	44:28	61
1–39	60, 66	45:1	61
Isa 4	150	Isa 45:7	47
1–6	258	45:19	49
Isa 4:3	63	Isa 44:28	61
5:1 – 7	62	45:1	61
Isa 6	64, 150	49:1–6	214
Isaiah 6–10	60	Isa 49:6	67
Isaiah 7	60, 64	50:4–9	214
Isa 7:11–17	64	52:13–53:12	214
Isa 7:14	52, 55, 56, 57, 58, 60, 61	Isaiah 53	53, 54, 55
Isa 7:15	66	Isa 53:3–6	54
Isa 7:17	64	Isa 53:8	54
7:17–22	66	Isa 55:3	67
Isa 7:20	64	56–66	60
Isa 7:21–22	66	Isa 65:25	67
Isaiah 8	65		
Isa 8:1–4	65	**Jeremiah**	
Isa 8:23–9:6	106	Jeremiah 25:11-12	25
Isa 8:21	65	Jer 1:4–5	51
8:23–9:6	103	29:10	25
Isaiah 9	53, 59	Jeremiah 35	66
Isa 9:1–6	65		
Isa 9:5	59	**Ezekiel**	
Isa 9:5–6	58	Ezekiel 23	71
Isa 9:6	53	Hezekiel 28	74
Isa 10	172	Ezekiel 40–48	8
Isa 10:28–32	63		
Isaiah 11	54, 65, 67	**Hosea**	
Isa 11:1	149	Hos 9:10	66
11:1–4	49	Hos 12:10	66
Isa 11:4; 19	49		

Matthew

Matthew 1	91
Matt 1:1–17	148
Matt 3:13–17	90, 110

Mark

Mark 1:9–11	90

Luke

Luk 2	53
Luke 3:21–22	90

John

1 :1	51

Acts

Acts 13:33	111

Galatians

Gal 4:4	196

2 Peter

2 Peter 1:17	91

Hebrews

Hebrews 1:5	91
5:5	91

Revelation

21	8

Index of Modern Authors

Ahlström, G.W. 198
Albertz, R. 152, 153, 163, 245, 246, 283, 284, 284, 286, 287
Albright, W.F. 196, 207, 245, 282
Alt, A. 3, 148, 189, 207, 274, 284
Andersen, K.T. 174
Arndt, E.M. 7, 13
Assmann, J. 220, 221, 230
Assmann, A. 220
Attridge, H.W. 49
Bächli, O. 191,
Barth, F. 263, 282
Barthes, R. 215
Bright, J. 207
Barstad, H. 56
Beckman, G. 136
Ben Zvi, E. 222
Binger, T. 194, 218, 238, 242
Biran, A. 235
Bjerg, S. 206
Blenkinsopp, J. 61, 125, 214
Bloch-Smith, E. 198
Blunden, E. 249
Brownlee, W.H. 112
Brunius, T. 132
Buccellati, G. 138
Budde, K. 27
Buhl, F. 92
Bultmann, R. 213
Cahill, J. 3
Carroll, R.C. 61
Carstens, P. 220
Chadwick, H. 138

Civil, M. 77
Conzelmann, H. 213
Coser, L.A. 221
Cowley, A.E. 140
Cryer, F.H. 198, 269
Cubitt, G. 222
Dalley, S. 68, 76, 78
Davies, P.R. 117, 145, 146, 147, 149, 155, 162, 165, 193, 194, 197, 204, 223, 234, 257, 269, 270
Dearman, A. 174, 235
Dever, W.G. 164, 219, 257, 270, 274, 279
Dibelius, M. 213
Diebner, B.J. viii, 99, 206, 212, 268, 269, 274
Dietrich, W. 194
Donner, H. 95, 160
Dozemann, T.B. 214,
Droysen, G. 7, 160, 161
Duhm, B. 214
Dumezil, G. 233
Edel, E. 250
Edelman, D. 198
Eichrodt, W. 147, 154, 283
Engel, H. 228
Engnell, I. 101, 102
Eriksen, T.H. 263
Erslev, K. 159, 160, 163, 173
Evans, P.S. 217, 282
Evans-Pritchard, E.E. 282
Falkenstjerne, V. 248
Ferdinand, K. 209

Fevre, L. 234
Finkelstein, I. 3, 12, 29, 137, 138, 140, 276, 285,
Fish, S. 215
Fortes, M. 282
Foster, B.J. 262
Frankfort, H. 93
Frerichs, E.S. 148
Fried, M. 282
Friedrichs, J. 93
Friis, H. 190, 191, 192, 212,
Fritz, V. 149, 165
Fussell, P. 249
Gabler, J.Ph. 202
Garbini, G. 98, 179, 187
Gardiner, A. 136
Gerstenberger, E.S. 99, 100, 112, 114
Gesenius, W. 103
Gmirkin, R.E. 68, 299
Gnuse, R. 297, 298
Goody, J. 213
Gottlieb, H. 102
Gottwald, N.K. 145, 192, 209, 282, 284,
Grabbe, L. 217
Graves, R. 249
Grayson, A.K. 136, 137
Greimas, A.J. 215
Grønbech, V. 231, 232
Grundtvig, N.F.S. 55
Gulick, J. 288
Gunkel, H. 99, 103, 112, 201, 213
Gurney, O.R. 262
Güterbock, H.G. 262
Halbwachs, M. 220, 221
Hallbäck, G. 215
Hallo, W.W. 68, 74, 139
Hammershaimb, E. 98, 99
Handy, L.K. 149, 165
Harnack, A. von 206
Hart, B.L. 274
Hasel, G.F. 34
Hasselbalch, T.B. 220
Haubold, J. 68
Hayes, J. viii, 95, 96
Herbener, J.-A. 41
Herrmann, A. 100

Herrmann, S. 100
Hermansen, B.D. 220
Herlz, T. 267
Hillers, D.R. 154
Høgenhaven, J. 213, 257
Hoftizser, J. 47
Holm-Nielsen, S. 95, 205, 210
Huffmon, H.B. 154
Ibsen, H. 233
Ilgen, K.D. 271
Imber, N.H. 13
Irons, W. 281
Jacobsen, T. 46
Jakoubek, M. 263
Jamieson-Drake, D.W. 29, 97, 104, 276, 308
Jensen, H.J.L. 74, 215
Jensen, M.S. 159
Jeppesen, K. 59
Jørgensen, J. 208
Jørgensen, T. 208
Jonge, de, M. 102
Jongeling, K. 47
Jünger, E. 249
Kaiser, O. 27, 57, 214
Kapelrud, A.S. 56
Keel, O. 194
Kirkpatrick, P.G. 201
Kittel, R. 160
Kjærgaard, M.S. 218
Kletter, R. 3
Klopstock, F.G. 248
Kramer, S.N. 77
Krarup, P. 158, 159
Kratz, R.G. 299
Kraus, F.R. 40, 47
Kraus, H.-J. 99, 112, 115
Krebs, C.B. 253
Kreuzer, S. 186
Kuhn, T. 206
Kuhnen, H.-P. 142
Kutsch, E. 101
Lambert, W.G. 34, 77, 78, 81
Lanfranchi, R. 68
Larsen, M.T. 167, 171, 172, 208
Leach, E. 282
Lesko, L.H. 148

Lévy-Strauss, C. 215, 233, 266, 282
Lewis, C.S. 122
Lewis, I. 128
Lindblom, J. 119, 120, 128, 198
Lindhardt, J. 206
Lipschits, O. 3, 61, 138
Liverani, M. 50, 59, 93, 96, 100, 138, 146, 207, 208, 228, 229, 250
Løgstrup, K.E. 206
Lord, A.B. 69
Luckenbill, D.D. 75, 137, 167, 170, 217
McCarter, K. 164
Magen, Y. 138
Malamat, A. 95
Martínez, F.G. 68
Mendels, D. 165, 187
Mendenhall, G.E. 153, 154, 190, 192
Mettinger, T.N.D. 101
Meyer, E. 228, 229
Millard, A.R. 34, 77, 78, 81
Miller, J.M. viii, 95, 96
Miller, R.D. 213
Møller, J.G. 145, 146
Morante, E. 152
Mowinckel, S. 56, 91, 93, 109, 116, 198, 240, 241, 272
Müller, M. 68, 223
Muilenburg, J. 215
Namer, G. 220, 221
Naveh, J. 235
Neale, J. M. 9
Nicolaisen, J. 281
Nicoll, A. and J. Nicoll 127
Niebuhr, B. 7
Nielsen, E. 29, 91, 95, 98, 99, 114, 143, 191, 210
Nielsen, F.A.J. 150, 161
Nielsen, K. 63
Nielsen, Kj. 190
Niemann, M. 29, 276
Nissinen, M. 121, 123
Nora, P. 253
Noth, M. 95, 96, 147, 189, 191, 207, 265, 268, 273, 274, 284
Oden, R.A. 49
Ørsted, P. 135, 159

Olivier, H. 280
Olmo Lete, G. 47
Ong, W.J. 213
Otzen, B. 95, 105, 107, 191
Oz, A. 3, 16
Pallis, S.A. 240
Pardee, D. 241
Parker, S.B. 241
Parpola, S. 93, 123
Pedersen, J. 143, 231, 232
Perlitt, L. 154, 155
Perlt, M. 220
Perrin, B. 151
Petersen, A.R. 240
Pfoh, E. 156
Popper, K. 207
Provançal, Ph. 41
Rad, G. von 43, 99, 128, 141, 147, 165, 166, 185, 212, 283, 284
Ranke, L. von 7, 132, 162, 265, 272
Ravn, O.E. 135
Redford, R.B. 74, 95, 96, 98, 139
Renz, J. 237, 240, 242
Ringgren, H. 99
Römer, T. 214, 271
Rollinger, R. 68
Rost, L. 186
Roth, M. 46
Sandars, J.A. 92
Schmid, H.H. 51
Schmid, K. 214
Schmidt, H. 112
Seebass, H. 272
Seidel, B. 187, 271
Service, E. 282
Shanks, H. 164
Shemer, N. 14, 16
Silberman, N.A. 3, 137
Simonsen, H. 2
Soggin, J.A. viii, 95, 96, 112, 198
Steele, J. 68
Steiner, M.L. 3, 59
Strange, J. 152, 153, 163, 165, 170, 189, 190, 195, 196, 205, 209, 211, 212, 214, 270
Tapper, R.L. 281
Theissen, G. 145

Thompson, T.L. viii, 137, 145, 150, 162, 164, 193, 204, 273, 284
Tigchelaar, E.J.C. 68
Torrey, C.C. 179
Treves, M. 108
Ussishkin, D. 171, 217
Vanderkam, J.C. 111
Van Seters, J. vii, 124, 125, 140, 150, 161, 212, 213, 214, 273
Vaux, R. de 94
Vernes, M. 191, 269
Wajdenbaum, Ph. 73, 74, 140, 222, 299
Weidner, E.F. 93
Wellhausen, J. 126, 148, 154, 268, 273
Welten, P. 105
Wessels, A. 12
Westenholz, Aa. & U. 76
Westermann, C. 43, 76, 77, 79, 84, 85, 86
Wette, W.L.M. de 272, 273
Whitelam, K. 163, 204, 257, 267
Wiggins, S.A. 194
Wildberger, H. 57, 58, 153, 154, 214
Williamson, H.G. 180
Wilson, J.A. 100
Wittgenstein, L. 207
Wolff, H.W. 128, 280
Wyatt, N. 35, 102, 241
Zimmern, H. 240

Index of Subjects

A

Abiathar 227
Abdi-Ḥeba 2
Abimelech 25, 296, 297, 298, 299
Abraham 69, 70, 88, 95, 184, 186, 194, 204, 230, 235, 254, 255, 260, 262, 273, 278
Acculturation 266
Aelia Capitolina 3
Aeneid 138, 141, 200
Agamemnon 297
Ai 254
Ahab 174
Achaz 57
Akhnaten 245
Akitu festival 240
Allenby, E. 12
Al-Quds 3, 17, 18
Amalekites 227
Amarna Age 59, 276
Amarna letters 2, 93
Amenophis IV 245
Ammiṣaduqa 47, 78
Amorite(s) 47, 178, 227
Amphichtyony 189, 190, 191, 265, 273, 274, 275, 282,
Argumenta ex silention 206
Armchair-sociology 36, 209
Anat 243

Ancient Israel viii, 54, 94, 108, 117, 119, 128, 138, 146, 147, 150, 151, 152, 153, 155, 160, 162, 164, 175, 191, 192, 193, 197, 198, 199, 204, 207, 209, 210, 211, 219, 222, 226, 230, 232, 234, 236, 239, 241, 244, 245, 265, 266, 267, 272, 275, 277, 279, 282, 283, 285, 288
Anthropology 128, 129, 209, 280, 281, 282
Antiquitates 68, 72
Andurarum 40
Anubis and Bata 74
Apollodoros 297
Apollonius of Rhodes 222
Appian 294
Argumentum ex silentio 240
Ariosto 11
Aristotle 266
Ark 28, 31, 32, 33, 82, 83, 84, 85, 87
Asa 27, 28, 38
Asarhaddon 123
Ashera 194, 218, 242, 243
Ashurbanipal 123
Assyria 50, 56, 62, 64, 65, 123, 167, 168, 169, 170, 171, 172, 216,
Athaliah 26, 28
Athena viii, 249, 252
Atraḫasis 77, 78, 79, 81, 84, 86
Azitawadda 50, 51

B

Barbarian 259, 260
Babylon 3, 4, 5, 6, 46, 47, 56, 61, 134, 135, 194, 238, 240, 241, 277
Babylonia 177, 178, 181, 190, 193, 194, 285, 286
Babylonian exile 25, 38, 61, 104, 106, 162, 192, 210, 212, 278
Babylonian tradition 39, 77, 86, 87, 250
Baptism of Jesus 90, 110, 111
Battle at Qadesh 136, 250
Bernhard of Cluny 9
Berossus 68, 78, 86
Bethel 254, 255
Biblical Israel 137, 142, 147, 152, 153, 193, 194, 196, 197, 198, 234, 235, 236, 237, 238, 239, 240, 243, 244, 245, 246, 256, 289
Biblical Israelites 193, 243, 244
Bismarck, O. von 265
Bīt Ḫumriya 276
Blut und Boden ideology 13, 264, 266
Book of the Covenant 36

C

Caesar 252, 253
Canaan 37, 66, 153, 161, 162, 194, 210, 254, 255, 262, 274, 278, 285
Canaanites 178, 185, 186, 192, 193, 211, 244, 245, 259, 262, 270, 285, 289
Canaanite society 210, 285
Canon 73, 92, 110, 195, 199, 200
Canonical literature 68
Canonical tradition 6, 72
Christian fundamentalism 219
Christian interpretation 67
Christological interpretation 54, 55
Chronicles, Books of 70, 71, 72, 105, 106, 151, 171, 181
Circular argumentation 67, 187, 206
Clermont-Ferrand 1095 8
Codex Leningradiensis 112
Codex Hammurabi 46, 48, 98
Collective memory 132, 133, 220, 221, 223

Conquest of Canaan 153, 161, 162, 210, 262
Copenhagen School vii, 61, 145, 162, 164, 165, 204, 208, 210, 219, 223, 226, 257, 270
Co-regencies 28
Cosmos 44, 45, 102
Covenant 36, 67, 92, 94, 143, 153, 154, 155, 156, 157, 235, 242, 243, 287, 290
Covenant theology 154, 155
Creation 33, 34, 41, 42, 43, 44, 45, 51, 100, 139, 186, 195, 197, 230, 231, 237, 299
Creation stories 230
Croesus 134
Cultural evolutionism 281, 282
Cultural memory 6, 7, 9, 12, 13, 16, 18, 19, 132, 133, 139, 140, 141, 143, 144, 220, 221, 222, 223, 256,
Cyrus 61, 67, 71, 177, 178, 181, 182
Cyrus' decree 71, 177, 194
Cultural memory 6, 7, 9, 12, 13, 16, 18, 19, 132, 133, 139, 140, 141, 143, 144, 220, 221, 222, 223, 256

D

Daimio system 288
Dante 42
David 2, 3, 10, 27, 28, 38, 58, 59, 63, 65, 67, 70, 71, 72, 91, 92, 94, 95, 96, 97, 98, 104, 105, 110, 112, 113, 115, 116, 137, 138, 141, 148, 149, 150, 162, 165, 186, 194, 204, 210, 227, 270, 275, 276
David redivivus 149
Davidic empire 59, 92, 94, 95, 97, 98, 149
Davidic kingdom 92, 97
Dead Sea Scrolls 8, 43, 68, 111, 118, 258, 261, 299
Delilah 298
Delos 141
Deutero-Isaiah 56, 59, 60, 61, 67, 214
deuteronomistic authors 105, 124

Deuteronomistic History 2, 105, 106, 124, 127, 150, 173, 183, 185, 192, 212, 214
Deuteronomy 143, 212
Diaspora 194, 219, 286, 287
Diaspora-literature 219
Divine king, divine kingship 94, 101, 103, 105, 106, 107, 108
Droysen, G. 7, 160, 161, 162, 173

E

Egyptian Execration Texts 2
Egyptian influence 59, 99
Egyptian royal ideology 93, 94, 96, 98, 99, 100, 101, 104, 106
Egyptian tradition 74
Elephantine 107, 140, 180
Empire of David 95, 96, 149
Ekron 169, 170, 171, 217
Enoch 87, 184,
Enthronement festival 239, 241, 242
Epic tradition 159
Eternal father 58, 59
Ethnicity 261, 262, 263, 264, 279
Ethnic cleansing 264
Ethnic group 193, 260, 261
Ethnos 259, 275, 277
Euripides 138, 297
Exile 4, 5, 6, 18, 25, 38, 56, 60, 61, 63, 64, 65, 104, 106, 124, 137, 162, 182, 186, 190, 192, 193, 194, 210, 212, 235, 239, 242, 243, 244, 250, 277, 278, 285
Exilic Period 60, 137, 154, 162, 184, 186, 192, 193, 210, 211, 230, 286
Exodus from Egypt 148
Exodus myth 278
Ezra 71, 140, 177, 178, 179, 180, 181, 182, 183, 184, 187, 188, 262, 286,
Ezekiel 256
Ezekiel the Tragedian 299

F

Fairuz 3, 17
Fairy tale(s) 161, 201, 284
Festivals 142, 143

Flood 30, 31, 32, 33, 39, 65, 68, 73, 75, 76, 77, 78, 79, 81, 82, 83, 84, 85, 86, 87, 88, 89, 139, 204, 223
Folk literature 201
Form criticism 213
Fundamentals, The 219

G

Garden architecture 247
Gaza 169, 171, 298
genealogy manipulation 182
Genesis Apocryphon 68, 84
Geography 247, 248, 250, 251, 252, 253, 254, 255, 256
German Empire 264, 265
Gesta Danorum 160
Gezer 96
Gezer calendar 240
Gilgamesh 250
Gilgamesh epic 68, 69, 73, 75, 76, 77, 78, 79, 81, 84, 85, 86, 87, 139
God of the Old Testament 152, 289, 290
Gouraud, H. 12
Greeks 133, 134, 151, 219, 232, 250, 259, 278, 286
Greek historiography 150
Greek history writing 135, 161

H

Hammurabi 39, 46, 48, 98
Hadrian 3
Handel, G.F. 52, 53, 54, 56, 67
Harran 254, 255
Hashepsut 253
Hasmoneans 142, 165
Hatikva 13
Hattusilis III 250
Hebrew slave 26, 288
Hebron 27, 218, 254
Heilsgeschichte 147, 153
Hellenism 73, 140, 211, 213
Hellenistic Jewry 91, 118
Hellenistic literature 126

Hellenistic Period viii, 59, 60, 68, 73, 107, 108, 110, 111, 114, 116, 125, 140, 161, 165, 183, 187, 194, 212, 213, 219, 221, 222, 223, 235, 243, 244, 246, 252, 258, 277, 283, 285
Hellenistic tradition 74, 298, 299
Hellenization 3, 142, 286
Herodotus of Halicarnassus 126, 133, 134, 135, 150, 218, 259, 260, 261
Heroic age 138
Herzl, T. 267
Hesiod 221
Heuristic methodology 282
Hexapla 42, 43
Hezekiah 58, 71, 72, 75, 104, 105, 106, 168, 169, 170, 171, 172, 173, 175, 216, 217
Hiram 98
Historical-critical scholarship viii, 56, 58, 60, 146, 147, 148, 153, 155, 206, 219, 227, 240, 274
Historical determinism 196
Historical Israel 147, 193, 194, 196, 197, 198, 210, 234, 235, 236, 237, 238, 239, 240, 243, 245, 246, 265, 277
Historical method 162, 208, 210, 219, 223, 284
Historicity 95, 96, 104, 105, 148, 150, 153, 183, 204, 273, 279, 297
Historiography of the Old Testament 136, 158
History of Israel 24, 29, 126, 162, 185, 191, 195, 197, 198, 209, 210, 211, 226, 234, 245, 246, 257, 265, 267, 283
Hittite historiography 135, 228
Hittites 136, 178, 250, 262
Holinshed 127
Homer 158, 159, 242, 260
Homeric scholarship 159
Hyksos 148, 278

I

Ideas of geography 247, 248
Idea of history 163, 192, 196, 218, 222

Immanuel 53, 56, 57, 58, 60, 61, 62, 64, 65, 66
Iphigenia 297, 298
Isaac 70, 194, 235, 255, 262, 278, 297
Isaiah 56, 57, 58, 60, 62, 64, 65, 127, 169, 171
Isaiah, Book of 52, 53, 54, 55, 56, 57, 59, 60, 61, 63, 64, 66, 67, 72, 126, 149, 214, 244
Israel, modern 13
Israel-centric 204
Israel in Egypt 189, 255
Israel's religion 154, 197, 210, 212, 226, 237, 239, 244, 245, 246, 283, 284, 285
Israelite society 119, 128, 192, 194, 259, 275
Israelite Empire 92, 94, 97, 149, 235, 276
Israelite nation 192, 197, 277, 286

J

Jacob 30, 49, 185, 194, 235, 255, 262, 278, 286
Jebel Mousa 255
Jeconiah 290
Jehonadab Ben Rechab 66
Jehoram 28, 174
Jehu 66
Jephthah 26, 27, 297
Jephtah's daughter 297
Jeremiah, prophet 51, 121
Jeremiah, Book of 25, 66, 127
Jericho 14, 15, 26, 160, 161
Jesus ben Hananiah 122, 124, 183
Jesus Sirach 183, 184, 185
Jewish Diaspora 194, 219, 286, 287
Jewish monotheism 210, 211
Jewish nation 181
Jewish society 108, 141, 178, 182, 219, 221, 243, 246, 278, 287
Jews 6, 13, 17, 19, 61, 107, 140, 177, 178, 181, 182, 187, 193, 194, 200, 211, 219, 238, 239, 243, 244, 267, 285, 286, 287

Job 41, 54, 290
John Hyrcanus 142
Joseph and the wife of Potiphar 73, 74
Joshua 38, 153, 160, 290
Joshua, Book of 155, 161, 164, 165, 186, 199, 262
Joshua, the son of Jozadak 177, 181, 184
Jubilees, Book of 74, 111
Judges 25, 26, 27, 29, 72, 138, 162, 186, 210, 227, 265, 275
Judges, book 2, 25, 26, 27, 29, 37, 49, 186, 199, 296, 297, 298, 299
Jerusalem vii, 2, 3, 4, 5, 6, 7, 8, 9, 10, 11, 12, 13, 14, 15, 16, 17, 18, 19, 24, 27, 28, 29, 37, 38, 52, 56, 58, 59, 60, 61, 62, 63, 64, 65, 71, 72, 73, 75, 94, 97, 98, 105, 106, 107, 108, 110, 117, 121, 122, 137, 138, 140, 141, 142, 143, 150, 168, 169, 170, 171, 172, 177, 178, 180, 181, 183, 184, 187, 192, 193, 194, 211, 216, 217, 235, 242, 243, 255, 256, 258, 260, 276, 277
Jerusalem Muslim conquest 8
Jerusalem, Golden 9, 14, 16, 19
Jotham 24, 167
Judah 2, 25, 28, 29, 37, 56, 59, 60, 65, 71, 95, 97, 104, 105, 106, 111, 117, 138, 140, 143, 149, 166, 168, 169, 170, 171, 173, 174, 177, 178, 211, 216, 235, 242, 243, 275, 276, 277
Joseph story 30, 73, 74, 75, 139, 254
Josephus 68, 72, 122, 148
Josiah 71, 72, 104, 105, 106, 142, 242
Jubilee 36, 37, 40
Justice vii, 41, 45, 46, 47, 48, 49, 50, 51, 65, 66, 89

K

Kadesh Barnea 255
Kant, I. 266
Khalif Umar 8
Khirbet el-Qom 218
King of Assyria 50, 62, 64, 65, 167, 169, 171, 172, 216

Kingdom of God 54, 61, 62, 63, 66, 67, 102, 278
Kingdom of Israel 29, 71, 167, 168, 175
kingdom in Judah 97
Kirta 35, 36, 101, 161
Kittum 47, 48, 50, 51
Königsnovelle 100
Kuntillet Ajrud 218, 242

L

Labaya 276
Lachish 3, 169, 171, 172, 217, 251
Landscape 149, 211, 248, 251, 254, 255
Law 12, 26, 36, 40, 49, 64, 112, 113, 114, 115, 116, 117, 126, 143, 153, 154, 155, 177, 178, 180, 181, 184, 187, 299
Leah 30
Liberation theology 278, 284
Lieux de mémoire 251, 253
Limmu 216
Linguistics 146, 208, 215, 279
Literary studies 198, 214
Literati 222
Little apocalypse 60, 214
Livy 66, 141, 294, 298
Luther, M. 42, 55, 56, 271

M

Maccabees, Maccabean 6, 104, 108
Mafia Godfather 289
Magic societies 198
Maḫḫu priest 120
Manasseh 106
Manetho 148
Manual of Discipline 258
Marcion 206
Mari 121
Masoretes 43
Massah and Meriba 255
Maximalists 270, 279, 198
Mediterranean societal system 155, 263, 288
Mehmed II 12
Menahem 25, 167

Merenpthah 100
Meriones 158
Mesha 173, 174, 175, 297
Mesha Inscription 97, 174, 235
Mesopotamia 4, 47, 48, 58, 88, 99, 101, 107, 120, 121, 135, 136, 178, 182, 183, 194, 211, 250, 254, 286
Messiah vii, 52, 53, 54, 55, 56, 62, 64, 65, 66, 67, 91, 98, 101, 102, 103, 104, 107, 108, 110, 116, 117, 118, 148, 149, 150, 204, 276
Messiah, The 52
Micah 59, 60
Micah, Book of 59
Michaiah ben Imla 120
Middle East viii, 12, 17, 142, 156, 209, 211, 248, 255, 286
Midian 255
Minimalists 199, 270, 279
Minor judges 25, 26
Mišarum 48
Moralistic history 151
Moses 54, 72, 126, 153, 154, 155, 177, 178, 180, 181, 184, 232, 245, 255, 261
Moses Montefiore 13
Mycenaean world 158, 159
Myth-and-Ritual School 282, 283

N

Naram-Sin 261, 262
Narnia 23, 24, 122
Narmar plate 250
Nation, nationality 6, 63, 124, 141, 143, 148, 157, 181, 184, 190, 192, 193, 197, 244, 246, 259, 263, 264, 266, 267, 273, 274, 275, 277, 278, 285, 286, 287
Nationalism 7, 187, 265
National myth 278
Nebuchadnezzar 71, 137, 179, 290
Nehemiah 71, 178, 180, 182, 183, 184, 188, 286
Next year in Jerusalem 7, 13, 16, 19
Ninive 170

Noah 31, 32, 33, 77, 78, 82, 83, 84, 85, 86, 87, 184

O

Odysseus 158, 249
Odyssey 249
Old Testament Theology 152, 280, 287, 291
Omri 174, 175
Omride Dynasty 97
Omri's House 235, 276
Orally transmitted poetry 69
Oral tradition 173, 175, 205, 213
Origin 43
Ovid 249

P

Palestine 3, 4, 12, 17, 59, 90, 94, 96, 98, 104, 105, 107, 117, 137, 140, 142, 144, 146, 148, 149, 155, 160, 163, 166, 167, 168, 170, 173, 177, 189, 190, 195, 197, 198, 199, 210, 211, 212, 217, 219, 222, 234, 235, 236, 238, 242, 244, 245, 250, 255, 256, 265, 267, 276, 277, 278, 285, 286, 287
Palestine Exploration Fund 12
Pan-Babylonism 73, 140
Pan-Hellenism 73, 140
Paradigm 33, 146, 162, 189, 190, 191, 192, 194, 195, 196, 197, 198, 199, 206, 207, 212, 232
Passover 72, 105, 142
Patriarchal Age 273
Patriarchal history 186
Patriarchal narratives 201, 204
Patriarchal religion 284
Patriarch (2) 69, 185
Patronage 156, 157, 263, 264, 287, 288, 289, 290, 291
Pausanias (geographer) 251, 252
Pekah 24, 167
Pentateuch 2, 30, 68, 125, 126, 127, 165, 177, 179, 180, 184, 185, 186, 187, 212, 222, 229, 232, 254, 271, 272, 274, 299

Per Gynt 233
Period of the judges 29, 138, 162, 210, 265, 275
Persian Period 60, 104, 107, 117, 138, 165, 182, 193, 277, 286
Personal names 237, 238, 242
Philistines 26, 254, 286, 298
Philo of Byblos 49
Plato 299
Pliny the Elder 251, 261
Plutarch 151, 294, 295, 296
Postmodernism 266, 279
Priestly document 82, 239
Priestly writer 84
Primeval History 83, 184, 186, 221, 222
Processual anthropology 282, 283
Prophets 2, 118, 119, 120, 121, 122, 123, 124, 126, 127, 128, 152, 154, 155, 186, 214
Propaganda 6, 47, 138, 142, 143, 165, 172, 200, 250, 251
Prophetical literature 119, 120, 127
Psalm Scroll 111, 118
Psalms of David 92, 110, 113
Ptolemeans 235
Pyrrhus 294, 295, 296, 297, 298, 299

Q

'Q' -fever 70
Qumran 84, 92, 111, 118, 187
Qumran cave 11 111, 118
Quantitative time 24

R

Rachel 30
Racism 264
Ramesses II 136, 250
Ramesses IV 100
Rationalistic paraphrase viii, 146, 162, 193, 206, 227, 229, 271, 284
Reader response 145, 215,
Rebecca 70, 262
redaction-history 230, 231
Rehoboam 27, 98, 275
Religious-historical school 205

Residue 159, 160, 161, 162, 163, 164, 166, 173
Rewriting viii, 68, 69, 70, 72, 73, 74, 75, 83, 84, 86, 87, 139
Robert the Monk 8, 9
Roman history writing 141
Royal decrees 47, 48
Royal ideology 58, 92, 93, 94, 95, 98, 99, 100, 101, 104, 105, 106, 107, 108
Ruth 262

S

Sabbath 30, 33, 34, 35, 36, 37, 39, 40, 67, 231
Sacrificium intellectum 152, 163, 196
Saladin 11, 12, 19
Salvation history 147, 152, 163, 195, 196,
Saul 70, 71, 227, 289
Samaria 3, 25, 58, 61, 66, 71, 138, 168, 180, 218, 235, 236, 237, 238, 275, 277
Samarians 277
Samaritan temple 140, 142
Samaritans 140, 142, 276
Samson 26, 298
Samuel 27, 289
Samuel, Books of 27, 70, 116, 117, 118, 150, 227
Sarah 57, 69, 70, 254
Saxo 160, 162
Sect 117, 286
Sectarian 117, 152, 246, 258, 259, 285
Sectarian group 246, 285
Sectarian religion 285
Seleucid period 107
Seleucids 107, 235
Semiology 215
Sennacherib 75, 137, 168, 169, 170, 171, 172, 173, 216, 217
Septuagint 42, 57, 74, 103, 110, 111, 179, 183
Shakespeare 127
Shechem 138, 142, 143, 153, 254, 276
Shishak 98
Shogunate 288

Sinai 82, 153, 185, 186, 218, 242, 244, 255, 287
Sinai covenant 153
Sinuhe 250
Sirach 183, 184, 185
social anthropology 128, 129, 209, 280, 281, 282
social classes 156
Sociologic History 208
Sociology 119, 124, 128, 129, 145, 146, 155, 157, 208, 209, 279, 280, 281, 282, 283, 287
Sola scriptura 73
Solomon 27, 28, 59, 71, 72, 94, 95, 96, 97, 137, 141, 149, 162, 165, 179, 186, 210, 212, 235, 275
Solon 250
Sophronios 7, 8
Spinoza 54
Strabo 251, 252,
Succession Narrative 227
Sumerian kinglist 46
Sumerian flood story 77
Sumerians 68, 77, 99
Synchronisms 24
Syria 12, 47, 75, 95, 101, 149, 167, 174, 197, 198, 235, 245, 250
Systematic theology 145, 208, 218, 283

T

Tacitus 151, 234, 253
Tasso, T. 11, 19
Tel Dan inscription 235
Temple 2, 8, 11, 12, 14, 15, 28, 38, 62, 63, 71, 72, 92, 94, 107, 108, 117, 120, 121, 124, 137, 138, 140, 141, 142, 143, 168, 169, 171, 172, 177, 178, 181, 182, 183, 184, 187, 192, 194, 216, 240, 242, 252, 253, 298
Terentius Mauro 204
Thales of Miletus 140
Theodicé 196
Theology vii, viii, 145, 146, 147, 148, 149, 152, 153, 154, 155, 188, 191, 200, 205, 206, 208, 210, 211, 218, 239, 269, 278, 280, 282, 283, 284, 287, 291,
Theology of the Old Testament 283
Thucydides 135, 151
Tiglath-Pileser I 251
Tiglath-Pileser III 167
Tirhaka 171
Torah 62, 63, 64, 68, 113, 126, 154, 155, 187
Trito-Isaiah 56, 60, 214
Turkish attack on Europa 12
Twelve tribe league 274

U

Ugarit 57, 58, 81, 194, 241, 242
Ugaritic poems 241, 242
Ugaritic poetic circle about Ba'al 241
Unified Israelite monarchy 275
Ur in Chaldea 254
Urban II 8
Utnapishtim 78, 79, 80, 85, 86

V

Vassal treaties 93, 153
Vaticinium ex eventu 56, 271
Verdi, G. 5, 247
Vergil 125, 138, 200
Virtual history 268

W

Wagner, R. 191
Wenamun 120
Wie es eigentlich gewesen 137, 162, 265, 272
Wild thinking 233

Y

Yahweh 4, 28, 37, 58, 61, 62, 63, 64, 65, 66, 67, 72, 90, 92, 94, 106, 113, 114, 115, 116, 123, 124, 125, 127, 140, 143, 145, 154, 156, 157, 172, 174, 175, 186, 194, 217, 218, 226, 227, 235, 237, 238, 239, 240, 241, 242, 243, 244, 245, 254, 275, 289, 290, 297

Yahwist 30, 32, 33, 82, 83, 85, 86, 87, 165, 212, 213, 214, 229, 272

Yahwistic monotheism 197

Yam Suph 253
Yehimilk-inscription 50
Yerushalaim shel zahav 14, 17

Z

Zedekiah 2, 28, 290
Zion 3, 4, 9, 13, 14, 62, 63, 64, 65, 66, 90, 92, 94, 98, 100, 102, 104, 107, 115, 116, 150, 258
Zionism 267
Ziusudra 78
Zerubbabel 107, 182, 184

www.ingramcontent.com/pod-product-compliance
Lightning Source LLC
Chambersburg PA
CBHW050836230426
43667CB00012B/2016